T0304096

Inside Blockchain, Bitcoin, and Cryptocurrencies

Inside Blockchain, Bitcoin, and Cryptocurrencies

By

Niaz Chowdhury

CRC Press
Taylor & Francis Group
Boca Raton   London   New York

CRC Press is an imprint of the
Taylor & Francis Group, an **informa** business

AN AUERBACH BOOK

CRC Press
Taylor & Francis Group
6000 Broken Sound Parkway NW, Suite 300
Boca Raton, FL 33487-2742

Visit the Taylor & Francis Web site at
http://www.taylorandfrancis.com

and the CRC Press Web site at
http://www.crcpress.com

To my mother
Parveen Chowdhury

Contents

SECTION II SMART CONTRACTS

5 Ethereum and Smart Contracts...93

SECTION IV ADVANCED LEDGERS AND APPLICATIONS

SECTION VI   SOCIO-ECONOMIC LANDSCAPE

List of Figures

List of Tables

About the Author

Dr Niaz Chowdhury is a postdoctoral researcher working with blockchain technology in the European Union-funded project QualiChain. His research experience spans over a decade across England, Scotland and Ireland. He presently holds a Research Associate position in the Open Blockchain group of Knowledge Media Institute, a small but renowned and well-regarded research lab within the Open University in England. He also completed two more postdocs before joining this position, one in the Department of Computing and Communication in the same university, working for the Big Data and Smart City project MK:Smart, and another at his current lab in the Data Science group.

Dr Chowdhury earned his PhD from the School of Computing Science at the University of Glasgow in Scotland, as a recipient of the prestigious Scottish ORS Scholarship. He was also a research scholar at the School of Computer Science in Trinity College Dublin where he received the Government of Ireland IRCSET Embark Initiative Scholarship. His earlier academic achievements include a bachelor's degree and a master's degree with gold medal distinction in computer science and engineering from East West University, Bangladesh. Dr Chowdhury has published numerous journal articles, conference papers and book chapters on blockchain technology, the Internet of Things, wireless networks and data science.

About the Author

BLOCKCHAIN
AND BITCOIN

I

BLOCKCHAIN AND BITCOIN

Chapter 1

Introduction to Blockchain

Blockchain was first introduced to facilitate the virtual currency Bitcoin. The development of this disruptive technology, however, did not stop there. Researchers and developers around the world have been continuously exploring new areas where blockchain can be used to expedite innovative applications beyond Bitcoin. It is now considered one of the most influential inventions of the 21st century capable of reshaping the face of many existing industries. While this book presents an elaborate commentary on this technology as to how it aids the development of exciting new applications and improves current use-cases, this chapter provides a general overview to start. The subsequent chapters will be arranged on this foundation to expand the discussion and understand blockchain technology without limiting its capacity as the Bitcoin facilitator.

1.1 The Birth of Bitcoin

Unless someone lives in a stranded island or on a remote mountaintop, it is highly unlikely that he or she has not heard the name *Bitcoin*. When this virtual currency reached a price as high as approximately $20,000 in December 2017, the internet was flooded by news, views and rumours related to Bitcoin and other cryptocurrencies. TV channels, newspapers and web portals all tried to cover news circling this price hike. Many people called it the biggest bubble of the century, prominent figures in the tech and financial industries expressed their scepticism against it, and many openly declared their faith in this new technology. If the entry of this technology sounds grand, its making was no less appealing either. It all started in 2008.

1.1.1 A Mysterious Scientist

The year 2008 saw the world adapting many new technologies. The mobile phone model that revolutionised the use of smartphones, the iPhone 3G, hit the market in July followed by the first commercial Android device launch in September. The social networking site Facebook reached the 100-million-users milestone, while Twitter experienced a massive 250 times growth in its tweets-per-quarter metric compared to that of the previous year. Camera giant Nikkon launched the first video-enabled SLR camera, pocket cameras became HD, notebook laptops began to show up in the stores and USB 3.0 was released. GPS, an old technology that almost stayed out of sight of the public for many years, suddenly popped up everywhere triggered by the rise of the smartphone and notebook computers. The launch of Apple's App Store took place the same year [Ganapati, 2008].

Amid the arrival of these thriving technologies, most people were oblivious to a discovery that a mysterious scientist stated. Nobody knew him. Nobody ever heard of him. Google searches for his name returned no relevant information. He fancied staying behind the curtain, disregarding the conventional norms of scientific discoveries. Generally, scientists submit their works in peer-reviewed journals that follows a long and stressful journey of getting scrutinised by the experts and gaining recognition through discussions and constructive criticisms. This mysterious scientist, instead of picking up a journal, published his work on the cryptographic mailing list metzdowd.com. Initially, he failed to gain much attention from the core scientific community, but within a couple of years, researchers around the world realised the potential of his invention. His work that was supposed to be a digital currency transaction protocol turned out to be a whole new branch of technology centred on the fundamental concept known as *blockchain*.

The name of the mysterious scientist that appeared on the publication is Satoshi Nakamoto, and the currency transaction protocol that made him famous is Bitcoin. It is now widely anticipated that this name is a pseudonym. It could refer to an individual or a group of individuals whose identity remained undisclosed and untraceable. It means there is no one to publicly take the credit for one of the most famous inventions of the 21st century.

1.1.2 What is Bitcoin?

Bitcoin (BTC) is a virtual currency or more particularly a currency transaction protocol. It transfers money over a digital medium [Nakamoto, 2008]. This invention does not sound groundbreaking; rather pretty ordinary as we frequently use digital transactions in the form of bank-to-bank money transfers, credit card transactions, PayPal payments and so forth. Why would we call Bitcoin special in the presence of so many alternatives? The answer lies in how it functions. There is a big difference between a bank transaction and a Bitcoin transaction. Transactions offered by banks and financial institutions as a service do not move the money physically, instead the providers need to facilitate the actual transfer between them afterwards. What they offer is a centralised infrastructure that users can rely upon and trust.

For example, if Bob* sends $100 to Alice using his mobile banking app, Alice's account could be debited instantly by her bank based on the trust that Bob's bank will settle this payment later. What makes Bitcoin a groundbreaking invention is its ability to virtually move the money over a digital medium and settle the payment almost immediately without the need for a central body. If Bob sends 100 BTC to Alice, she receives the amount in her wallet straightway. There will be no institutional involvement and no need for a further settlement process (Figure 1.1).

1.1.3 Double-Spending Problem

One might think, what would go wrong if we send digital money as if sending an image or an email. The short answer is sending money like an image or an email

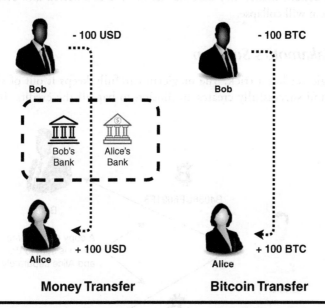

Figure 1.1   Centralised and decentralised currency transfer.

---

* *Alice* and *Bob* are fictional characters commonly used as placeholder names in cryptology. Ron Rivest and his fellow co-authors Adi Shamir and Leonard Adleman created these characters for their 1978 paper "A method for obtaining digital signatures and public-key cryptosystems". The primary motivation of creating Alice and Bob is to describe the cryptosystem conveniently to the readers. Subsequently, these characters have become common archetypes in many scientific and engineering fields including quantum cryptography, game theory and physics. As the use of Alice and Bob became more popular, additional characters were added, each with a particular meaning. In this book, *Carol* is used as an honest third participant and *Chuck* as a third participant of malicious intent.

is *technically* and *technologically* possible. In fact, Bitcoin transfers money using a similar method, if not the same. The problem, however, is not in how to send the money but rather how many times the same money is sent; hence it introduces a puzzle – the *double-spending problem* [Antonopoulos, 2010].

This problem states a flaw in the system allowing a person to spend the same money more than once. In an ideal world, the same money can be spent only once. To facilitate this requirement, there exists some mechanisms that prevent the bearer from copying or recreating money again and again. Banknotes and metal coins carry some special features to validate the authenticity and are made such a way that those features cannot be counterfeited to reproduce the same token.

It is difficult to adapt the same concept in the digital world as files, or more specifically bits can be easily copied. For example, as shown in Figure 1.2, Chuck has 100 BTC that he is to send to Alice. Before executing the transaction, he makes copies and sends the same tokens to Bob. Since Alice and Bob are unaware of the other transactions made, they become victims of a counterfeit and eventually the whole system will collapse.

1.1.4 Nakamoto's Solution

Every magic act has a trick. The magician carefully keeps it out of sight of the audience and successfully creates an illusion to bag all the credits. If Bitcoin is

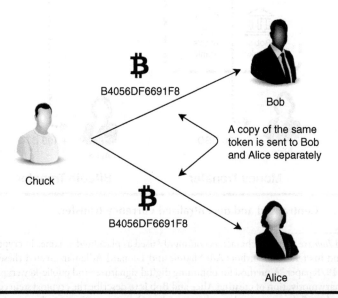

Figure 1.2 Double-spending in digital currency is the act of using the same token more than once. Here, Chuck sends the same token to Alice and Bob creating double-spending of the token B4056DF6691F8 (an imaginary serial number).

a magic trick, Nakamoto's magic trick must be the underlying blockchain. It endows Bitcoin with the ability to transfer money over a digital network and settle the transaction in real time that no bank or financial institution could ever demonstrate.

The blockchain is like an accounting ledger that sits over a distributed network and keeps records of all previous transactions. From the data-structure viewpoint, it is a continuously growing list of records linked one after another. Each of these records is called a block, which contains transactions. Blocks are linked to each other using cryptographic principles in such a way that if a single block is edited out of order, the whole chain collapses; thus making blockchain immutable where transactions cannot be rewritten or altered. This arrangement prevents Chuck from sending the same 100 BTC to Bob, as the blockchain would already hold a transaction against the token that had been sent to Alice. If Chuck makes copies of the token and tries to send them to Bob, the blockchain reveals that Chuck no longer retains the token and, therefore, that transaction will be rejected. Nakamoto solved the double-spending problem using the blockchain and successfully started transferring money over a digital medium without the presence of a central entity; hence, Bitcoin, the world's first cryptocurrency, was born.

1.2 Blockchain

Despite multiple proposals in the literature to solve the double-spending problem for digital currencies using a decentralised approach that predate Bitcoin, Nakamoto's method remains the first successfully implemented solution to this problem. Although blockchain was first introduced to facilitate Bitcoin transactions, the potential of this technology extends well beyond the concept of virtual currencies. This new technology looks so powerful that it is already considered a game changer by the experts who anticipate this will change the face of many existing industries that operate differently at the moment. Let us now look inside the blockchain to understand more of its technical details.

1.2.1 Motivation

The concepts that led to the birth of Bitcoin and blockchain are not inventions of Nakamoto. His role, in this case, is merely a collaborator. The notion of blockchain sits on three ideas, namely *distributed ledger*, *decentralisation* and *incentivisation*, which all existed before the arrival of Bitcoin.

The idea of a cryptocurrency was not even new; in 1998, Nick Szabo and Wei Dai independently proposed two conceptualised versions of such currency in *Bit gold* and *B-money* respectively. None of them, however, implemented their ideas. Of those, Dai discussed his proposal as a possible application of another algorithm: *Hashcash*. Hashcash arrived just a year before B-money when British cryptographer Adam Back described this algorithm to fend off the spamming attacks in emails.

What makes Nakamoto's invention unique is the blend of Bit gold, B-money, Hashcash and other related concepts. Throughout Part I of this book (Chapters 1–4), readers will experience the amalgamation of many pre-existing concepts in one solution that conclusively delivered the blockchain.

1.2.2 Definition of Blockchain

A blockchain is an immutable public ledger for recording transactions. Its transactions are called 'immutable' because once inserted, they become permanent and cannot be modified retroactively, not even by the authors, without the alteration of all subsequent transactions. A formal definition of blockchain can be given as:

> *A blockchain is an immutable distributed ledger secured by cryptographic techniques and managed by a decentralised community over a peer-to-peer network through incentivisation.*

1.2.3 Distributed Ledger

The blockchain is often called a distributed ledger because of its operating as a distributed system and impersonating the general ledger book used in accounting as shown in Figure 1.3. As a matter of fact, the name blockchain was first given to the distributed ledger of Bitcoin. The terms blockchain and distributed ledger are often used interchangeably, although they have different meanings.

A distributed ledger is a consensus of replicated, shared and synchronised digital data geographically spread across multiple sites, countries or institutions without any central administrator or centralised data storage [Scardovi, 2016]. This definition is also partially valid for blockchain, which creates the confusion. A close look at this definition reveals that it states the working principles rather the actual structure of the ledger. In practice, the model of distributed ledger can vary, and despite having the same working principles, depending on their data structure, distributed ledgers can be of different types. For example, *Tangle* is a distributed ledger that solves the double-spending problem decentrally using consensus, but unlike blockchain that uses linked list, its data structure is very different due to using a directed acyclic graph (DAC). So the bottom line is all blockchains can be considered distributed ledgers, but not all distributed ledgers are blockchains.

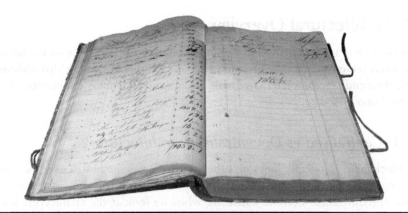

Figure 1.3   A general ledger from the 19th century. The blockchain impersonates this book digitally and operates distributedly over a peer-to-peer network providing incentives to the participants. (Image created by RaphaelQS.)

1.2.4 Key Properties

The blockchain has some typical properties that can be considered its hallmarks.

- A blockchain is open, verifiable and permanent by nature. Data of a blockchain is shared across the network where each node has a copy of it.
- A decentralised consensus needs to be achieved with a blockchain to create each block.
- Its transactions are immutable. When a set of transactions is validated, a new block is created based on a consensus making the data of those transactions permanent. It is not possible to alter a single transaction in that block without the support of the majority of the participating nodes.
- As opposed to a centralised client–server architecture, it is managed by decentralised networks for internode communication and validating new blocks; thus, it embodies a distributed computing system with high Byzantine fault tolerance.
- Because any transaction of a blockchain is verifiable, it establishes digital trust. The 'openness' of a blockchain also makes it permissionless, meaning there will be no need to have access control and passwords (considering the blockchain is of public type).
- The blockchain is often called secure-by-design. As an open system, blockchain does not require safeguarding the data from the attackers. The data is already open, and there is no point for the attackers to manipulate it as any such change will soon be disregarded.

The remainder of this chapter, along with Chapters 2 and 3, explains the blockchain and the jargon used to describe the aforementioned properties. Chapter 4 then shows how this technology actually works using the example of Bitcoin.

1.3 Architectural Overview

A blockchain is a mesh network of computers, commonly known as nodes, having no central server; rather they are linked to one another. Nodes in this architecture define and agree upon a shared state of data and adhere to certain constraints imposed upon the data.

1.3.1 Centralised vs Decentralised Architecture

The blockchain apparently looks no different than a website hosted over the internet, apps running on a smartphone or computers connected to a local area network. The differences become noticeable when we look at the architecture level. A website, an app or a local area network all have one thing in common – they are all part of a centralised structure managed by a supreme authority. This structure is commonly known as the client–server architecture as shown in Figure 1.4.

When a user visits a website, she or he becomes the client of a central server that provides with all the services and data. A smartphone app also operates in the same fashion. In a local area network, there is a server doing the job of assigning participating devices with the IP addresses and handling their joining and leaving activities, as well as giving them access to the internet. Under the client–server hood, the

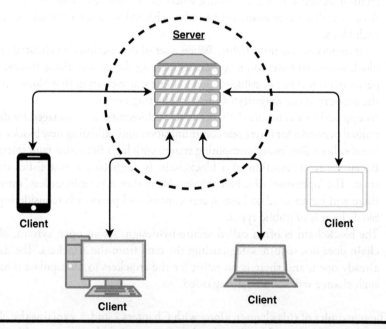

Figure 1.4 A centralised client–server architecture where the server retains the absolute power of providing or denying any service and data.

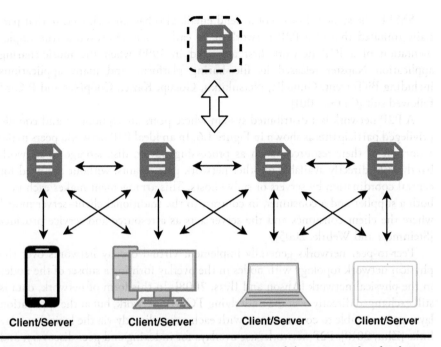

Figure 1.5 **A blockchain over a peer-to-peer network is an example of a decentralised architecture where every participating node simultaneously acts as a server and a client.**

central authority retains the supreme power of denying the users of services and data, and amends rules without prior notices.

However, when we look at the blockchain in Figure 1.5, a different architecture can be seen. This architecture is very distinct from that of a client–server architecture. Every participating node in this architecture acts as a client as well as a server, removing the need for a central authority. This type of network is called a *peer-to-peer* network, or simply P2P network. Blockchain adapts this network as its underlying communicating and operating framework to achieve a number of goals fundamental to this new technology.

1.3.2 Peer-to-Peer Network

The idea of a P2P network predates even the invention of the internet. The basic concept of such computing was envisioned in earlier software systems and networking discussions, reaching back to principles stated in the first Request for Comments (RFC) [Crocker, 1969]. Tim Berners-Lee's vision for the World Wide Web was close to a P2P network that assumed each user of the web would be an active editor and contributor, creating and linking content to form an interconnected "web" of links [Berners-Lee, 1996]. As time passed, the internet became an ideal example of the client–server paradigm.

SMTP, the standard protocol to send email, also had an architecture that partially imitated that of a P2P network at its early stage. However, a true implementation of a P2P network first appeared in 1999 when the music-sharing application Napster released its file-sharing platform, and many applications including BitTorrent, Gnutella, Netsukuku, Gossip, Kazaa, CoopNet and P-Gird followed suit [Oram, 2001].

A P2P network is a distributed system where peers are equipotent and equally privileged participants as shown in Figure 1.6. In an ideal P2P network, peers make a portion of their resources, such as processing power, disk storage or network bandwidth, directly available to other network participants, without the need for central coordination by servers or stable hosts. This arrangement makes each peer both a supplier and a consumer, in contrast to the traditional client–server model where the client consumes and the server acts as a resource and service provider [Steinmetz and Wehrle, 2005].

Peer-to-peer networks generally implement virtual overlay networks over the physical network topology with nodes in the overlay forming a subset of the nodes in the physical network [Ahson and Ilyas, 2008]. In this form of network, data is still exchanged directly over the underlying TCP/IP network, but at the application layer peers are able to communicate with each other directly via the logical overlay links [Zhu, 2010]. P2P networks use overlays for indexing and peer discovery, and

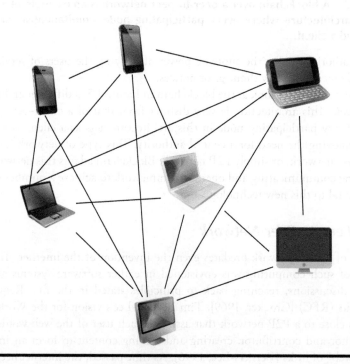

Figure 1.6   A peer-to-peer network.

making the system independent from the physical network topology. Based on how the nodes are linked within the overlay network, and how resources are indexed and located, P2P networks are divided into two categories: unstructured or structured. Unstructured P2P networks do not impose a particular structure on the overlay network by design; rather they are formed by nodes that randomly establish connections to each other. In structured P2P networks, on the other hand, the overlay is organised into a specific topology, and the protocol ensures that any node can efficiently search the network for files or resources, even if the resource is extremely rare [Jin and Chan, 2010; Filali, 2011].

1.3.3 Characteristics

Blockchain, operating over P2P networks, exhibits many characteristics inherited from the network architecture. Being distributed is arguably the most noticeable trait that anyone having moderate knowledge of computer networks can quickly identify looking at the architectural overview presented in Figure 1.7. What may not be very clear to many, however, is that the architecture also indicates blockchain is decentralised. What is the difference between being distributed and being decentralised, and how are both of these characteristics applied to a blockchain.

The notion of being distributed implies the resources are shared over the participating nodes, while decentralised means there is no central node to dictate the operations [Raval, 2016]. As a distributed system, a blockchain sits on hundreds of

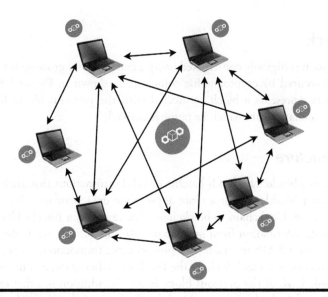

Figure 1.7 **A blockchain over a P2P network is an example of a decentralised architecture where every participating node simultaneously acts as a server and a client by keeping a copy of the blockchain.**

thousands of nodes and shares their resources as it keeps operating. It also demonstrates attributes fundamental to distributed systems such as the need for a consensus in making key decisions, fault tolerance and so on.

Blockchain, as a decentralised system, demonstrates no node instructing any other node what to do. Such an operational principle seems chaotic, particularly if not all nodes wish to play by rule, but in reality that never happens. There will always be nodes that try to bend the rules in their favour. However, the distributed nature of blockchain prevents such nodes from taking unwanted benefits by enforcing consensus through proof of work or similar method.

Blockchain stores data across its P2P network, eliminating a number of risks that comes with data being held centrally. There is no dependency on a single server; hence blockchain does not have a central point of failure. Its decentralised architecture makes every participating node keep a copy of the blockchain, making data quality maintained by massive database replication and computational trust [Raval, 2016]. There is no centralised official copy of data, and no user is 'trusted' more than any other in this architecture. With a blockchain, transactions are broadcast to the network and messages are delivered on a best-effort basis. On arrival of new transactions, validator nodes, known as miners, validate and add them to the block they are building, and then broadcast the completed block to other nodes. This operation continues to run until the end of the blockchain's life cycle in exchange for small rewards or incentives for the nodes that take part in the validation process, commonly known as block mining.

1.4 Block

The blockchain is digitally constructed using a continuously growing list of records linked and secured by cryptographic principles as shown in Figure 1.8. Each of these records represents a block connected with the previous block; hence they jointly form a chain, from which its name is derived.

1.4.1 Structure

Each block in a blockchain holds batches of valid transactions that are hashed and encoded into a Merkle tree or a more appropriate data structure. The size of the block varies from blockchain to blockchain. For example, a Bitcoin block size is 1 MB and holds information from more than 500 transactions, while the block size of Bitcoin Cash is 8 MB to enable it to process more transactions every second.

The elements of a block include the block identifier, data, a timestamp and a cryptographic hash of the previous block header in addition to other extra fields. The insertion of the hash of the last block header in the following makes the blockchain resistant to modification of the data, and any attempt to alter a single block results in the collapse of the whole chain. Because of this characteristic of the

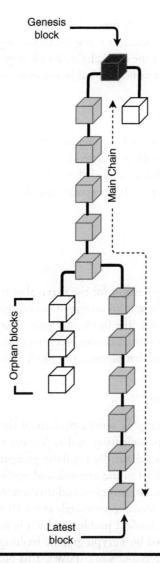

Figure 1.8 A blockchain where the main chain consists of the longest series of blocks from the genesis block (in black) to the latest block. Orphan blocks (in white) created by forks exist outside of the main chain.

blockchain, despite being decentralised, it remains immutable without the cooperation of the network majority.

1.4.2 Block Identifier and Height

The block identifier is the cryptographic hash of its header. Different blockchains may generate this hash differently. For example, Bitcoin uses the double hash of its header as its identifier, which means hashing the hash of the header. There is another way to identify a block. It is using the block height. This metric represents the position of the block in the blockchain. Block height is not unique, as several blocks may compete for the same position in the event of a fork (discussed later).

1.4.3 Genesis Block

There is a particular block in each blockchain which is called the *genesis block*. It is sometimes called *block 0* or *block 1* depending on the indexing of the blocks. The genesis block is the first block of a blockchain that is almost always hardcoded into the software of the applications. It is a special case that does not have a reference to its previous block.

1.5 Mining

Block mining is a vital requirement for the survival of the blockchain. It would be misleading to think that there is an analogy between gold mining and cryptocurrency mining, such as Bitcoin. The fact is that gold miners receive rewards for producing gold, while Bitcoin miners do not receive a reward for producing Bitcoins; rather they provide a service that protects the whole system.

1.5.1 What is Mining?

Block mining is a record-keeping service performed through the use of computer processing power by the participating nodes. Miners authorise new transactions and write them on the blockchain. By regularly grouping new transactions into a block, which is then broadcast to the network and verified by recipient nodes, they keep the blockchain consistent, complete and unalterable.

In Bitcoin, a block is mined approximately every 10 minutes when miners compete to determine a mathematical problem, which is moderately difficult but the solution easy to verify, based on a cryptographic hashing algorithm. The answer to this problem is called the proof of work (PoW). This proof shows that a miner did spend a significant amount of time to solve the problem and is not an adversary with the intention to gain improper benefits from the blockchain. In this context, it must be realised that mining is not about creating new Bitcoins; rather mining allows the blockchain to continue operating in the absence of a central authority without letting any adversary jeopardise its principles and security.

1.5.2 Consensus

The process of building a block involves a particular consensus mechanism for each blockchain. The PoW is one of the earliest mechanisms that many blockchains including Bitcoin use. PoW received heavy criticism due to its inefficient energy usage approach leading to the wastage of a large amount of electricity every year. More recent blockchains, however, use energy-efficient consensus mechanisms such as proof of stake, proof of space, proof of authority and so on that shifted the focus from the energy usage to something else such as allocating a significant amount of memory in proof of space. We learn more about various consensus mechanisms later in this chapter.

The consensus mechanism, alongside the chaining of blocks using cryptographic principles, makes modifications of the blockchain extremely hard, as an attacker must modify all subsequent blocks in order for the modifications of one block to be accepted. As new blocks are mined all the time, the difficulty of modifying a block increases as time passes and the number of subsequent blocks increases.

1.5.3 Incentivisation

Block mining utilises the concept of incentivisation. Because the miners act as record-keepers by verifying the transactions, each time a block is built, the quickest miner who solves the puzzle first receives a reward in exchange for his or her service, usually in the form of some native currency, fees or both.

1.6 Forks

The decentralised nature of public blockchains means that participating nodes must agree on the shared state of the ledger. A consensus amongst the participants results in a block that everyone deems as correct. A fork is an unusual situation when a blockchain diverges into two potential paths forward following a consensus.

1.6.1 When Does a Fork Occur?

As a distributed system, forks may occur when two miners find a block almost at the same time. The ambiguity is resolved when subsequent blocks are added to one chain, making it the longer chain, and the other block gets orphaned or abandoned by the network. In Figure 1.8, the grey blocks represent the main chain, while the white blocks are orphaned. They were built at the same time, but eventually one chain got established and the other became orphaned.

Forks can be willingly introduced to the network by the developers when they seek to bring in a change. It is a technical event where diverse participants need to agree on common rules. This kind of fork may occur because of many reasons such as the protocol needs a change or a new rule is required in deciding what makes a transaction valid. As a result, those who use the blockchain have to show support for one choice over the other.

1.6.2 Types of Forks

Forks can be of three types: *temporary fork, hard fork* and *soft fork.* A temporary fork occurs when miners discover a block at the same time as explained earlier. The other two types of forks are not incidental but rather enforced by the community. A hard fork is a software upgrade requiring a new rule that is not compatible with the previous version. For example, changing a blockchain from 1 MB to 2 MB will require a hard fork.

A soft fork introduces changes which are backwards compatible. For example, instead of a 1 MB block, a new rule may enforce a block size of 500 KB. This does not require a hard fork as non-upgraded nodes will still see the new transactions as valid.

A classical example of hard fork is the creation of Bitcoin Cash, forked at block 478558 on 1 August 2017, where for each Bitcoin an owner got 1 Bitcoin Cash. Amongst the soft forks, Bitcoin's change of address formatting is worthy of mention.

1.7 Consensus Mechanisms

A fundamental problem in distributed systems is achieving overall system reliability in the presence of some faulty nodes. A solution to this problem can be nodes agreeing on some data value during computation making the system achieve agreement. This process is called *consensus* within the scope of distributed systems and computing. Blockchain being a distributed system requires its nodes to reach a consensus while running the system and keeping its data secure.

1.7.1 Proof of Work (PoW)

The PoW is a system requiring an amount of effort that is not significant yet feasible enough to deter malicious actors in a distributed system. These actors generally attempt to send spam emails and launch denial-of-service (DoS) attacks. Cynthia Dwork and Moni Naor developed the concept, and later Adam Beck independently improved and used it in his anti-spam system Hashcash. Nakamoto adapted a Hashcash-like PoW system in Bitcoin that also forms the basis of many other cryptocurrencies that followed the footsteps of this pioneering virtual currency.

Within the context of the blockchain, PoW ensures coordination of the network and security of the data. It requires participating nodes or miners to compete for a position to determine who gets the chance to build the next block. In doing so, they use computational power to find a specific hash value. There exists no known shortcut or optimised approach to discover the hash other than going one by one incrementally. This approach requires huge energy and time for a miner to find the targeted hash, but the verification process is simple enough for others to quickly check if the claim is justified.

The PoW system in a blockchain acts as a consensus mechanism for the miners to decide who will build the next block. Blockchain is a distributed system operates decentrally, meaning there is no leader to lead the block-building process. As such, PoW helps miners to get selected as the lucky winner to fill the position of the one-off leader in the expense of energy and time. Chapters 3 and 4 of this book present thorough descriptions as to how this system works in the real world using Bitcoin as an example.

Because of this system needing energy and time, it becomes expensive for the attackers to launch spamming attacks in the network. The same constraint working with cryptographic principles also shields the blockchain from being altered. Attackers want to change the entries face, a nearly impossible task of redoing old blocks due to the need of enormous computing power.

1.7.2 Alternative Consensus Algorithms

The biggest drawback of the PoW system is the misuse of enormous energy. Critics of Bitcoin often criticise this virtual currency for not being sustainable and energy efficient because of its consensus mechanism [O'Dwyer and Malone, 2014]. Although PoW effectively deters potential attackers, the concerns surrounding energy issues drove researchers to look for alternative approaches [Vranken, 2017].

The proof of stake (PoS) is arguably the most used alternative to the PoW system. Instead of making operation expensive by consuming electricity, this system requires miners to deposit a wealth that bad actors will lose if try to bend the rules. PoS uses several randomised approaches to select the miner who is going to build the next block. For instance, two blockchains, *Nxt* and *BlackCoin*, use the "randomised block selection" strategy, while *Peercoin* incorporates "coin age", a numerical value derived from the product of the number of coins multiplied by the number of days the coins have been held, in selecting the miner. The delegated proof of stake (DPoS) is another method that utilises a limited number of nodes, known as the delegate, to verify transactions and build blocks for the blockchain. The native token holders generally retain the right to vote in the election to select delegates. *EOS* is amongst the most notable blockchains that use DPoS as its consensus mechanism.

The proof of burn (PoB) is another distributed consensus mechanism and an alternative to PoW and PoS. It can also be used for bootstrapping one cryptocurrency off another. The idea is that the miners show the proof of burning some tokens by sending them to a verifiably unspendable address. This is expensive from their individual point of view, just like PoW, but consumes no resources other than the burned underlying asset. PoB is often criticised due to its reliance on PoW-mined tokens. Critics identify the fact that if miners only burn PoW-mined tokens while practising the PoB mechanism, the ultimate source of scarcity remains the same and unnecessary energy consumption seems to become inevitable. However, that may not always be the case. For example, on average, it takes 48,800 kWh to mine 1 Bitcoin. By burning 10 Bitcoins or consuming 488,000 kWh and releasing 488,000 Tincoin tokens, each of the new coins would be considered the equivalent result of 1 kWh of work done, which is significantly lower than Bitcoin and less energy consuming. In addition to Tincoin, *Slimcoin* and *XCP* are amongst the many that have used PoB as their consensus mechanism [Prahalad, 2018].

Proof of space (PoSpace), also called proof of capacity (PoC), is a means of showing that one has a legitimate interest in a particular service by allocating a non-trivial amount of memory or disk space to solve a challenge presented by the service provider. PoSpace is very similar to PoW, except that instead of computation, storage is used. The concept was formulated by Dziembowski et al. in 2015 [Dziembowski et al., 2015]. Proof of authority (PoA) is another consensus mechanism based on identity as a stake where approved accounts, known as validators, validate transactions and blocks. It has many similarities with the DPoS method described earlier [Naumoff, 2017].

1.7.3 Comparison

Amongst the aforementioned consensus mechanisms, there is no one clear favourite. Protocols prefer one over another depending on the type of service and necessary security they seek. Some blockchain protocols also modify the generic algorithm to further enhance its security. To compare the mechanisms and obtain an idea of their nature, three parameters, namely sustainability, usability and security, are used in Table 1.1. Amongst the methods described here, PoW is not sustainable at all, while PoB is partially sustainable as it could use PoW-based coins that in turn misuse energy. Because of the other three methods not using energy as a means of proving genuine interest, those mechanisms can be deemed sustainable.

From the usability perspective, PoW, PoB and PoSpace are more user-friendly. These methods generally do not require further arrangements such as organising election or monitoring behaviours. However, PoS and PoA require participating nodes to go through a number of extra steps.

While participating in a consensus process using the PoS method, nodes need to create an impression to win the election, followed by forming a team of

Table 1.1   Consensus Mechanism Comparison

Consensus Mechanism	Sustainability	Usability	Security
Proof of work	Not sustainable	High	High
Proof of stake	Sustainable	Low	Medium
Proof of burn	Partially sustainable	High	High
Proof of space	Sustainable	High	Medium
Proof of authority	Sustainable	Low	Low

delegates, and in event of failure to wait for the right moment to get elected. The PoA process requires monitoring the nodes to screen out potential malicious actors. Security-wise, PoW and PoB are considered the most secure methods due to these methods needing to sacrifice real assets. While PoS and PoSpace are also secure, PoA may pose threats as reputation is used as the asset in this method. Nodes willing to perform a one-off foul play could potentially target blockchains using the PoA consensus mechanism.

1.8 Types of Blockchains

There are several types of blockchains available [Bashir, 2017]. Some are permissionless, while some require permission or access approval; some are controlled by a predefined set of entities, whereas some demonstrate a mix of multiple types. The following presents a discussion covering possible blockchains; their compositions; and a comparison based on security, services and suitability for specific domains.

1.8.1 Public and Private Blockchains

There are primarily two different types of blockchains available, namely the public blockchain and private blockchain. All other blockchains are either public or private blockchain with a variety of setups, structures and controls.

A *public blockchain* has absolutely no access restrictions. Anyone with an internet connection can act as a participating node, send transactions and become a validator. For such a network to keep operating and motivating miners to continue mining, the blockchain provides some form of economic incentive or reward. Often it comes in the form of giving away some native currency, but sometimes it can be fees too.

A *private blockchain*, on the other hand, requires permission, as nodes' participation and validator access in such blockchains are restricted. One cannot join a private blockchain unless invited by the network administrators. This type of blockchain can be considered middle ground for companies that are interested in the blockchain technology in general but are not comfortable with a level of control offered by public networks. Typically, companies seek to incorporate blockchains into their accounting and record-keeping procedures without sacrificing autonomy and running the risk of exposing sensitive data to the open internet.

1.8.2 Consortium, Shared Ledger, Sidechain

As mentioned earlier, all blockchains are either public or private, yet they can form different types. A *consortium blockchain* is one of those blockchains. It is sometimes referred to as a shared ledger or federated ledger because of multiple approved parties using this blockchain within a federated environment. These blockchains are private blockchains operated by a group or consortium. Shared ledgers are usually semi-decentralised and require permission. However, instead of a single body controlling it, various organisations might each operate a node on such a network. The administrators of a consortium blockchain may restrict users' reading rights and allow a limited set of trusted nodes to execute a consensus protocol.

A *sidechain* is another special type of blockchain. It is an emerging type that stays alongside a so-called parent blockchain or main chain. It allows tokens and other digital assets from the main chain to be securely used in it and then be moved back to the main chain if needed. Typically a sidechain remains attached to its main chain using a two-way peg. The two-way peg enables interchangeability of assets at a predetermined rate between the parent blockchain and the sidechain. Many new blockchains which are public in nature allow creating private sidechains. It is anticipated that this trend will help to build more robust applications on top of large blockchains.

1.8.3 Hybrid Blockchains

It is not rare to encounter hybrid blockchains coming from the combination of properties seen in both public and private blockchains. For example, *semi-private blockchains* and *proprietary blockchains* are the kind of blockchains that inherit properties from both private and public types. The former (semi-private) is a primarily public type having some private properties, while the latter (proprietary) is a very restricted blockchain but still demonstrates some public properties.

1.8.4 Comparison

We have seen so far a variety of blockchains that might lead to the question of why we would need so many types if one or two are good enough. The answer to this question is simple: there is no one perfect blockchain, as the nature of applications and requirements may vary. For instance, a public blockchain offers open access and governance but comes with slow performance.

A private blockchain, however, can be much faster than a typical public blockchain, but it takes away the essence of this technology which is freedom. Private blockchains are controlled by one or more central authorities bringing back the central control to blockchain technology. This in no way indicates that such blockchains are worthless, as many use-cases such as banks, hospitals and other organisations that work with sensitive data can benefit from these blockchains that public blockchains fail to offer.

The concept of the consortium blockchain brings back freedom despite being private. Because a number of organisations control a consortium blockchain, it creates the vibe of a public blockchain within the territory of a private type. A sidechain can be public or private. It depends on how the applications are designed. For example, a medical application storing patient information can have a private sidechain

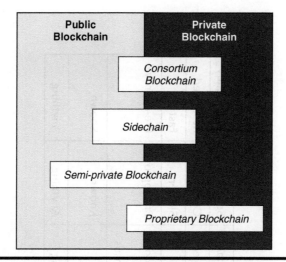

Figure 1.9   Types of major and customised blockchains.

where it stores sensitive data, while the main chain can have information that is suitable to share with third parties such as drug manufacturers, pathological labs, administrative divisions of hospitals and so on. Semi-private and proprietary block-chains also have their pros and cons that the users need to look at carefully before deciding on which type they actually require. Figure 1.9 overlays the customised blockchains over public and private counterparts to show their relative positioning as to how much each of those customised blockchain acquires from the two major types. Later Table 1.2 complements this figure by comparing their properties.

1.9 Applications

Bitcoin is the most discussed application of blockchain technology that assisted in solving the double-spending problem. The ability of this disruptive technology, however, goes beyond Bitcoin. Numerous use-cases can benefit from using this technology and many existing applications would perform better in the presence of a blockchain.

Because storing a piece of information in a blockchain remains there forever, blockchain technology helps to establish trust. In other words, it eradicates the need for trust, hence it is often referred to as trustless. On the contrary to the usual convention of trust that heavily relies on knowing the actualities, a blockchain operates over a decentralised network formed by people whom the users may or may not know; but that hardly matters. It creates a world where everybody is trust-worthy because nobody is capable of cheating.

The ability of a blockchain to establish trust in a decentralised digital environ-ment makes it an instant solution for many working use-cases. e-Governance is

Table 1.2 Blockchain Comparison

	Public	Private	Consortium	Sidechain	Semi-Private	Proprietary
Access	Open	Restricted	Controlled	Controlled	Controlled	Restricted
Speed	Slow	Fast	Fast	Slower	Slower	Fast
Security	Consensus	Pre-approval	Pre-approval and/or consensus	Pre-approval and/or consensus	Pre-approval	Pre-approval
Identity	Anonymous and/or pseudonymous	Known	Known	Known	Known	Known
Asset	Native token	Anything	Anything	Anything	Anything	Anything

an excellent example where building citizen-centric applications can appropriate blockchain technology. National identity management, voting, birth certificate generation, event recording, electronic auction and citizen welfare services are a few examples.

Blockchain has the potential to contribute to the education sector. Day-to-day management activity such as record-keeping, tuition fees payment, and badge and identity management are some of the applications that some institutions around the globe have already initiated. One of the finest use-cases for education is qualification verification. It takes a substantial amount of time to verify a candidate's diploma and degree credentials in current practice. Blockchain can make it faster and reliable. Alongside education, healthcare is another huge sector where blockchain can play a pivotal role in building a diverse range of applications. Data provenance and integrity, patients' data management, and data security for clinical trials are amongst the essential use-cases that hospitals and general practitioner authorities can adopt to ensure more secure and faster services. Drug traceability is another application that pharmaceutical industries are considering implementing.

Financial services is amongst the most discussed sectors that blockchain is capable of changing from the core. Industries such as asset management and insurance are likely to adopt this technology within a few years. Cross-border payments, remittance, interbank money transfers and regular payment facilities are some areas where blockchain can help build useful applications. Smart property or smart agreement is a futuristic concept that can be developed using blockchain technology. It has the potential to revolutionise the traditional lending system. Mortgage, car loan, industrial loan, purchase of land and so on can be tied up with blockchain to remove traditional credit rating systems making the process simple and less bureaucratic.

Production and supply chain is an area where traceability is the most important and challenging subject. It is difficult to establish and maintain trust, particularly when products move over international borders. Blockchain, having immutability property at its core, is an ideal technology to develop tracking applications for areas like this.

Online marketplaces and gaming, bidding and betting industries can significantly improve the quality of their services and introduce a high degree of accountability and transparency by using blockchain-based decentralised applications. Physical and cybersecurity of workplaces like sensitive laboratories, drug manufacturing industries and nuclear power plants can be ensured using blockchain technology.

Last but not least, the Internet of Things (IoT) and artificial intelligence (AI) are two thriving technologies heavily used in building contemporary applications. If blockchain joins them in developing applications such as smart cities, smart homes, smart transportations and smart grids, then the quality and the ability of the finished product would be far better than what they can achieve without blockchain.

1.10 Revisiting the Double-Spending Problem

Earlier this chapter we discussed the double-spending problem and how Nakamoto solved it. The description of Nakamoto's solution was consciously kept simple to avoid delivering lots of jargon at the beginning of the book.

Now that at the end of Chapter 1 when we have sufficient knowledge about blockchain technology, let us revisit the problem.

So far we have learned that Nakamoto solved the double-spending problem employing an immutable ledger book called blockchain where every transaction gets recorded. This ledger reveals any attempt of sending the same token multiple times. Validators encountering such mischief reject the transactions and prevent the system from double-spending.

There remain two issues that the chapter did not resolve. First, there were several mentions in the cryptographic principles that would make the entry of the blockchain permanent and irreversible. In a digital world where bits are easy to copy and modify, how cryptography institutes such a challenging job of making blockchain immutable is yet to be seen. Second, we know that because of the P2P network being distributed and decentralised, blockchain does not sit in a central server; rather each participating entity of the system keeps a copy of this ledger. For the sake of argument if we accept that cryptographic principles make transactions immutable, how can blockchain stop someone from recreating everything from scratch when the participating nodes remotely hold the copies? Without resolving these two issues, Nakamoto's solution cannot be considered complete.

The solution Nakamoto presented had these two situations for which he used the application of cryptographic hash functions and a consensus mechanism called the proof of work to establish trust in a decentralised trustless environment. Next, we cover these two topics and learn the complete solution. Chapter 2 of this book tells us how Nakamoto made blockchain immutable, and Chapter 3 describes the method of preventing individual nodes from recreating and distributing counterfeit blockchains.

1.11 Summary

This chapter introduced blockchain and explained how it came into being. It stated the double-spending problem leading to the development of the blockchain distributed system by Satoshi Nakamoto that is open, immutable and decentralised. The architecture, network, data structure, fundamental characteristics, consensus mechanisms and types of blockchains are amongst the topics discussed in this chapter. However, the chapter left out two important topics of blockchain: cryptographic principles that make blockchain immutable and how a consensus is agreed upon to keep the blockchain updated. These two topics will be addressed in Chapters 2 and 3 respectively before concluding the first part of this book in Chapter 4 describing the Bitcoin protocol.

Chapter 2

Immutability of Blockchain

The blockchain is immutable – once a transaction is written, it cannot be changed, modified or deleted, even by the author of the transaction. This property of blockchain is fundamentally vital as Nakamoto used it in Bitcoin to solve the double-spending problem. Bitcoin, however, is just the beginning and many other applications can benefit from using this property where trust plays a central role. Two branches of computer science namely cryptography and distributed systems laid the foundation of blockchain where cryptography offers the underlying principles required to make blockchain data immutable. This chapter presents the necessary theory to realise how blockchain introduces the immutability property and prevents its data from being altered.

2.1 Cryptography

If blockchain is the magic trick behind Bitcoin, then cryptography is the trick behind blockchain. Several essential components of blockchain technology including the immutability property are built using cryptographic principles. It is, therefore, necessary to present a brief discussion on cryptography before we proceed further. Nevertheless, cryptography is a vast area, and a part of a chapter can hardly do justice to such a rich and broad discipline; hence it will not be attempted to encompass everything related to cryptography in this brief review. The objective of having this discussion is to present a summary of the necessary principles to help readers understand the subsequent topics of this book.

2.1.1 What Are Cryptography and Cryptanalysis?

Cryptography is the practice and study of methods to secure communications in the presence of potential third-party adversaries [Rivest, 1990]. More formally it can be defined as the protocols to prevent third parties and the public from reading private messages [Bellare and Rogaway, 2015]. Numerous features of information security such as authentication, data confidentiality, data integrity and non-repudiation are central to modern cryptography [Menezes et al., 2005]. Its existence can be recognised in the disciplines of mathematics, computer science, electrical engineering, communication science and physics where applications include electronic commerce, chip-based payment cards, computer passwords, military communications and, of course, cryptocurrencies.

Cryptanalysis is the opposite of cryptography. It is the method of breaching cryptographic security systems and gaining access to the contents of encrypted messages, even if the cryptographic key is unknown. It is the branch of study of the information system to understand the hidden aspect of an encrypted message.

2.1.2 Background

Cryptography predates the invention of the modern computer by thousands of years. The period before the computer was made available for applying the cryptographic algorithm is known as the classical era. Methods and techniques to secure messages during the classical era are called classical cryptography.

Classical cryptography perhaps traces its roots to carved ciphertext on stones in Egypt around 1900 BCE. The scholarly consensus on this, however, rules it out as cryptographic work and identifies it as a drawing created out of amusement of literate observers that had nothing to do with concealing information. If we accept this verdict, the Greek transposition tool *scytale* and the Hebrew monoalphabetic substitution cipher *Atbash* would be the earliest form of cryptographic tools. The mention of a scytale by the Greek poet Archilochus, who lived in the 7th century BC, is the oldest documented evidence of any cryptographic tool, although its operation was unknown until around the 2nd century AD when Greek biographer Plutarch described it in his book *Plutarch's Lives* [Perrin, 1916].

Sometimes Biblical commentators such as the medieval French rabbi Shlomo Yitzchaki and Rabbi David Kimhi claimed that there are verses in the Hebrew Bible that concealed the original names of several places and instead replaced those with Atbash words. One famous example in favour of this claim is the 26th verse from the 25th chapter of the book of Jeremiah. This verse states: "The king of Sheshach shall drink after them." In this verse, "Sheshach" is claimed to be a cipher word that can be reverted to "Babylon" in Atbash. There appears to have been the mention of two different ciphers in the 2000-year-old Kamasutra of Vatsyayana in India. The ciphers are called *Kautiliyam* and *Mulavediya* where the substitutions are made based on phonetic relations. In the Kautiliyam, vowels become consonants, while the cipher alphabet in the Mulavediya is comprised of pairs of letters [Kahn, 1967].

The oldest cryptographic system with a practical purpose is generally credited to the Caesar cipher. It is due to the fact that this system had been in place with real applications and a documented history since the beginning of the systematic use of cryptography. The association of Julius Caesar's name may have created a false impression that Caesar is the inventor of this technique, which may not be true. It is anticipated that the Greeks might have known this technique before the Romans; however, Caesar made it famous by adapting its use in his communications [Singh, 2002]. Roman historian Suetonius mentioned this method in the *Life of Julius Caesar* stating that Caesar was in use of this encryption technique shifting three alphabets to the right to communicate with his generals. Although there exists evidence that Caesar used even more complicated systems, Caesar cipher had been the most common and iconic secret communication method during that period, which his nephew and the first Roman Emperor Augustus also adapted with a minor alteration [Graves, 1957].

A more complex system involving the use of a series of interwoven Caesar ciphers, commonly known as Vigenere cipher, had been in use since the 15th century, but it was centuries later that German military officer and cryptographer Friedrich Kasiski first published a general method of deciphering Vigenere ciphers [Martin, 2012]. In recent time but still predating the modern computer, the Enigma machine, invented by the German engineer Arthur Scherbius at the end of World War I, was one of the most advanced and arguably the most popular encryption device to protect military, commercial and diplomatic communications. A superior version of the Enigma machine was used by Nazi Germany in World War II and subsequently the breaking of its code by British scientist Alan Turing and his team at Bletchley Park in England has been a celebrated event for the West [Singh, 2002].

The invention of the computer marked the beginning of the modern cryptography era. Although sometimes the Enigma machines and similar mechanical devices are considered to be the beginning of the modern cryptography, they were more like a bridge between the classical and modern periods, and the first work of modern cryptography is credited to Claude Shannon and his paper titled "A Mathematical Theory of Cryptography" written in 1945 at Bell Laboratory in the United States and published in 1948 [Shannon, 1948].

2.1.3 Basic Concepts

The goal of cryptography is to transform any data from its original form, called the *plaintext*, into an obscure form known as the *ciphertext*. This process is called *encryption*. The reverse process of recovering the plaintext from the ciphertext is called *decryption*. It is essential to understand that the plaintext does not have to be a textual message. It can be a computer file representing binary or other types of data, an image, a database and so on. A particular cryptosystem works depending on specific encryption and decryption algorithms. An algorithm is a computational procedure that follows some set of rules. The process of encrypting plaintext using a particular algorithm depends on a code, commonly known as the *secret key*. A secret key is nothing but a large number.

There exists a fundamental principle of modern cryptography, known as Kerckhoffs's principle. Dutch linguist and cryptographer Auguste Kerckhoffs in the 19th century stated that an algorithm defining a cryptosystem should be publicly known, but the key must remain secret [Shannon, 1949]. Modern cryptography follows this principle where a publicly known cryptographic algorithm using a secret key jumbles up the plaintext to make it incomprehensible. The process is performed such a way that although the ciphertext looks like a meaningless piece of information, by employing the secret key it can be reversed.

Cryptographic algorithms use several methods. Most classical algorithms either use a substitution or transposition approach. A substitution approach is a method of encrypting by which units of plaintext are replaced with ciphertext where the units may be single letters, pairs of letters, triplets of letters, mixtures of these and so forth. The receiver deciphers the text by performing the inverse substitution. A transposition approach is a method of encryption by which the positions held by units of plaintext are shifted according to a regular system so that the ciphertext constitutes a permutation of the plaintext; hence the orders of the units change. Mathematically a bijective function is used on the characters' positions to encrypt and an inverse function to decrypt [Reinke, 1992].

In the modern era, cryptographic algorithms deal with digital bits instead of plain letters and the operations are performed using exclusive-OR. There are two main approaches used in regular symmetric-key encryption, namely stream cipher and block cipher. In a stream cipher, each plaintext bit is encrypted one at a time with the corresponding bit of a stream of random characters commonly known as the keystream and each bit of the ciphertext stream is generated. A block cipher, in contrast, is a deterministic algorithm operating on fixed-length groups of bits, called a block, with an unvarying transformation that is specified by a symmetric key [Paar and Pelzl, 2009].

2.2 Modern Cryptography

Modern cryptography is the cornerstone of computer and network security. Its foundation is laid on various concepts of mathematics such as probability theory, number theory and computational complexity theory. There are two principal branches of modern cryptography, namely *symmetric-key cryptography* and *public-key cryptography*.

2.2.1 *Symmetric-Key Cryptography*

An encryption system where both the sender and receiver of a message share a single, common key to encrypt and decrypt the message is called symmetric-key cryptography. Symmetric-key systems are simpler and faster, but they come with a big drawback. The two parties involved in the process must exchange the key to successfully decrypt the ciphertext. This exchange process is potentially vulnerable, as it could reveal the key to a third party.

For example, Bob wants to exchange a message with Alice as seen in Figure 2.1. Using a secret key, Bob encrypts the message "Hello Alice" and sends it to Alice. Bob also exchanges the secret key with Alice. This exchange of the secret key may or may not take place online, as Bob can give Alice the key in a pen drive. Having received the message, Alice, who we assume that in possession of the secret key, decrypts the message using the key. Although a cryptographic algorithm secures the transfer of the message described in this example, the key is not. An adversary gaining possession of the key would be easily able to reveal the secret message. This process necessitates the two parties to securely exchange the key to make symmetric-cryptography work.

Amongst the popular symmetric-cryptography algorithms, the Data Encryption Standard (DES) had been in use for many years and was highly influential in the

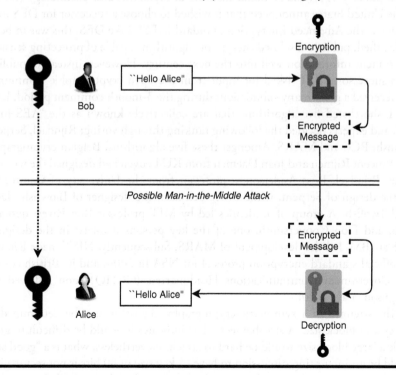

Figure 2.1   Steps of a symmetric-key encryption.

advancement of modern cryptography. This block cipher was developed in 1975 at IBM based on an earlier design of the German-born cryptographer Horst Feistel and standardised in 1977. The National Bureau of Standards (NBS) and National Security Agency (NSA) of the United States led this project to protect sensitive and unclassified electronic government data.

As the computational power increased over time, DES and similar algorithms became vulnerable to brute-force attack. The International Data Encryption Algorithm (IDEA) was developed by James Massey and Xuejia Lai to replace DES in 1991. Blowfish, a more sophisticated algorithm developed by Harvard University professor Bruce Schneier, came into existence in 1993. The following year the Russian government declassified the GOST algorithm that was developed by the KGB in 1989 to protect the sensitive information of the Soviet and Russian government. The same year academics David Wheeler and Roger Needham from the University of Cambridge presented the Tiny Encryption Algorithm (TEA) in an academic workshop held at KU Leuven in Belgium. The implementation of TEA typically needs a few lines of code, and the algorithm is not subject to any patents. In 1998, a variant of the DES algorithm that applies encryption three times on each block was released in a bid to strengthen the original algorithm. It is commonly known as Triple DES.

In January 1997, the National Institute of Standards and Technology (NIST) of the United States announced that it wished to choose a successor for DES to be known as the Advanced Encryption Standard (AES). Like DES, this was to be an unclassified, publicly disclosed encryption algorithm capable of protecting sensitive government information well into the next century. However, instead of publishing a successor, NIST asked for input from the open cryptographic community and received a great many submissions during the 3-month comment period. Later NIST shortlisted five algorithms that are collectively known as the "AES finalists", and experts decided the following ranking through voting: Rijndael, Serpent, Twofish, RC6 and MARS. Amongst these five algorithms, Belgian cryptographer duo Vincent Rijmen and Joan Daemen from KU Leuven had designed the winning cipher Rijndael. Ross Anderson, a professor from the University of Cambridge, led the design of Serpent, while Bruce Schneier, the designer of Blowfish, developed Twofish. A group of academics led by MIT professor Ron Rivest designed RC6, and Don Coppersmith, one of the key persons involved in the design of DES at IBM, led the development of MARS. Subsequently, NIST made Rijndael the official standard encryption protocol for NSA in 2000, and its British equivalent Government Communications Headquarters (GCHQ) soon followed suit [Ferguson et al., 2010].

The strength of a symmetric-cryptography algorithm can be determined by its key and block size. A sizeable secret key indicates it would be difficult to guess while a large block size would be hard to attack. Nevertheless, what is a "good size" would be an interesting discussion to have. A key size of 80 bits is not secure given today's computational power, but extending it to 128 bits dramatically increases the amount of effort required to guess the key. To put it in context, if there was a computer capable of searching a billion keys per second, and we employed a billion such computers, it would still require 10,783 billion years to explore all possible 128-bit keys. Scientists anticipate that within the next 4 billion years our sun will become a red giant and destroy the Earth and humanity, meaning a 128-bit encryption key should be adequate for most cryptographic uses, considering that there are no other weaknesses in the method used [Garfinkel et al., 1991]. Table 2.1 presents known and renowned symmetric-key algorithms and their keys and block sizes to promptly comprehend the strength of each of those ciphers.

2.2.2 Public-Key Cryptography

Public-key cryptography, or asymmetric cryptography, is the cryptographic system that uses pairs of keys: a public key which may be disseminated widely and a private key which is known to the owner only. This process accomplishes two purposes: *authentication*, where the public key verifies that a holder of the paired private key sent the message, and *encryption*, where only the paired private key holder can decrypt the message encrypted with the public key. Figure 2.2 shows the following:

(a) Bob encrypts the message "Hello Alice" using his private key which is known to him only. Once Bob sends this message to Alice, she decrypts it using the public key of Bob. The decryption yielding a positive outcome authenticates

Table 2.1   Renowned Symmetric-Key Algorithms

Year	Name	Key Size	Block Size
1975	DES	56 bits (+ 8 parity bits)	64 bits
1989	GOST	256 bits	64 bits
1991	IDEA	128 bits	64 bits
1993	Blowfish	32–448 bits	64 bits
1994	TEA	128 bits	64 bits
1998	Triple DES	168, 112 or 56 bits	64 bits
1998	MARS	128, 192 or 256 bits	128 bits
1998	RC6	128, 192 or 256 bits	128 bits
1998	Twofish	128, 192 or 256 bits	128 bits
1998	Serpent	128, 192 or 256 bits	128 bits
1998	AES (Rijndael)	128, 192 or 256 bits	128 bits

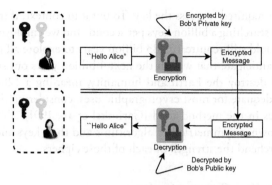

A: Authentication

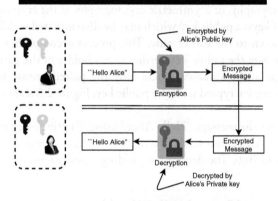

B: Encryption

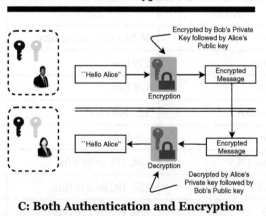

C: Both Authentication and Encryption

Figure 2.2   Steps of a public-key encryption.

that the message is sent by Bob. Although this communication ensures authenticity, it does not provides the encryption and is subject to a potential man-in-the-middle attack where anyone with Bob's public key, which is known to the world by convention, can read the message.

(b) Bob encrypts the message "Hello Alice" using the public key of Alice. Once Bob sends this message to Alice, she decrypts it using her private key. This communication is safe from the man-in-the-middle attack as it offers encryption confirming that nobody can decrypt it without the private key of Alice which is known to her only. This, however, does not confirm the authenticity of the message as anyone can send it by using Alice's public key.

(c) Bob encrypts the message "Hello Alice" using his private key, followed by Alice's public key. Having received the message, Alice decrypts the message using her private key followed by Bob's public key. Unlike part (a), this communication is safe from the man-in-the-middle attack. Nobody can read the message without Alice's private key; hence it provides encryption. If the decryption yields a positive result, this also confirms the authenticity of the message.

Public-key cryptography systems often rely on cryptographic algorithms based on mathematical problems that currently admit no efficient solution, particularly those inherent in certain integer factorisation, discrete logarithm and elliptic curve relationships. Because of the computational complexity of asymmetric encryption, it is usually used only for small blocks of data, typically in the transfer of a symmetric encryption key. This symmetric key is then used to encrypt the rest of the potentially long message sequence.

Merkle's puzzle is considered one of the earliest forms of public-key encryption. Computer scientist Ralph Merkle, as an undergraduate student at the University of California, Berkeley in 1974, attended a course taught by Lance Hoffman, another celebrated computer scientist. In this course, Merkle submitted a term paper titled "Secure Communications over Insecure Channels" where he proposed a method allowing two parties to agree on a shared secret by exchanging messages, even if they have no secrets in common beforehand. Merkle failed to make Hoffman understand his proposal and eventually dropped the course. Later when he published this work 4 years later, it became Merkle's puzzle [Schneier, 1996].

Arguably the first person to develop a public-key cryptosystem was British cryptographer and mathematician Clifford Cocks, who, while working at GCHQ in 1973, implemented an idea previously conceptualised by his colleague James H. Ellis [Cocks, 2001]. The discovery remained classified until 1997, and the RSA became the first known public-key cryptosystem that Ron Rivest, Adi Shamir and Leonard Adleman developed and published in 1978. The asymmetry in RSA is obtained based on the practical difficulty of the factorisation of the product of two large prime numbers, commonly known as the "factoring problem" [Rivest et al., 1978].

Since the 1970s, a large number and variety of encryptions, digital signatures, key agreements, and other techniques have been developed in the field of public-key cryptography. This includes the Rabin cryptosystem published by Turing Award–winning Israeli computer scientist Michael O. Rabin; ElGamal encryption based on Diffie–Hellman key exchange (DH), originally conceptualised by Ralph Merkle; the Digital Signature Algorithm (DSA) developed at NIST; and elliptic curve cryptography (ECC) first proposed in 1985 by Neal Koblitz from the University of Washington and Victor Miller at IBM. The ECC is particularly important in the context of this book, as Bitcoin utilises this algorithm to execute transactions. We learn more about this scheme later in this chapter.

2.3 Cryptographic Applications

Cryptographic algorithms and theories have a wide range of use in securing information, files, filesystem, databases, communication channels and so forth. Many applications have been developed using one or more algorithms combined into a system that provides a specific service. Amongst those, the following presents three popular applications.

2.3.1 TLS and SSL

Transport Layer Security (TLS) and its predecessor Secure Sockets Layer (SSL) are cryptographic protocols designed to provide security over a computer network [Dierks and Rescorla, 2008]. A website can use TLS to secure all communications between the servers and the browsers. This protocol can also be found in applications providing email, instant messaging and Voice over Internet Protocol (VoIP) services.

The TLS protocol aims primarily to provide privacy and data integrity between two or more communicating computer applications. When secured by TLS, connections between a client and a server are considered secure because symmetric cryptography is used to encrypt the data transmitted. The keys for this symmetric encryption are generated uniquely for each connection and are based on a shared secret negotiated at the start of the session commonly known as TLS handshake. The server and client negotiate the details of which encryption algorithm and cryptographic keys to use before the first byte of data is transmitted. The negotiation of a shared secret is both secure, because the negotiated secret is unavailable to eavesdroppers and cannot be obtained, even by attackers who place themselves in the middle of the connection, and reliable, due to attackers' inability to modify the communications during the negotiation without being detected.

The identity of the communicating parties can be authenticated using public-key cryptography. This authentication can be made optional, but generally requires at least one of the parties. The connection remains reliable because each transmitted

Figure 2.3   Bitcoin.org, the original domain that Nakamoto registered for Bitcoin, using "https" protocol. The HTTPS is referred to as "HTTP over SSL" (now TLS).

message includes an integrity check using a message authentication code to prevent undetected loss or alteration of the data during transmission.

The use of TLS can be found in secure website connections. When we try to log into Facebook, Gmail or similar sites, the "http" protocol becomes "https" indicating the secured nature of the communication as shown in Figure 2.3. HTTPS uses TLS underneath to make the end-to-end connection secured. The messenger service WhatsApp and Telegram also use TLS-like public-key cryptography to provide secure communications.

2.3.2 Cryptographic Hash Function

A cryptographic hash function is a mathematical algorithm that maps data of arbitrary size to a bit string of a fixed size, called hash, and is designed to be a one-way function which is infeasible to invert. The only way to recreate the input data from the output of an ideal cryptographic hash function is to attempt a brute-force search of possible inputs to see if they produce a match.

Figure 2.4 shows an excerpt from the book *The Memoirs of Sherlock Holmes* written by Scottish author Sir Arthur Conan Doyle. The excerpt presents a famous conversation between Sherlock Holmes and his friend John Watson. The SHA256 hash of the conversation and the title of the book yielded the same length hash values. Despite the title being much smaller than the conversation text, the length of the generated hashes remains equal. If it were not the conversation rather the whole works of Doyle, the length would still have been the same. The point is, regardless of the size of the input, the hash function results in a fixed size output.

The ideal cryptographic hash function has five main properties: (1) it is deterministic, so the same message always results in the same hash, (2) computing the hash value for any given message is quick, (3) it is infeasible to generate a message from its hash value except by trying all possible combinations, (4) a small change to a message should change the hash value so extensively that the new hash value appears uncorrelated with the old hash value, and (5) finding two different messages with the same hash value is infeasible.

The Merkle–Damgard construction, a scheme independently developed by Ralph Merkle who described it in his PhD thesis at Stanford University in 1979 and Danish cryptographer Ivan Damgard who published it in 1989, is credited to be the first cryptographic hash function that many popular algorithms use today [Merkle, 1979; Damgard, 1989]. Ron Rivest, one of the authors of RSA, developed the MD2 algorithm in 1989 [Kaliski, 1992]. Although MD2 is not secure

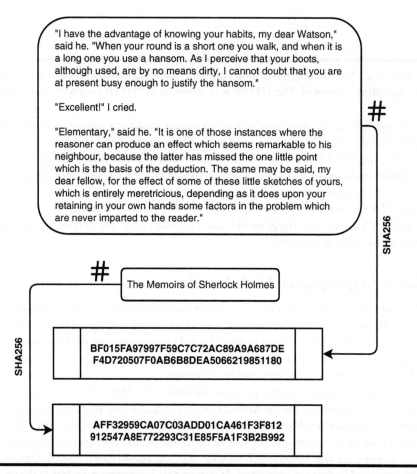

Figure 2.4 **The SHA256 hash generation of an excerpt from a Sherlock Holmes book and its title. It is notable that regardless of the size of the input, hash function results in a fixed size output.**

anymore, it remains in use in public-key infrastructures as part of certificates generated with MD2 and RSA.

Several algorithms can be used to build a hash function, including MD5, SHA-1, SHA-2 (all use Merkle–Damgard construction), SHA-3, Whirlpool and BLAKE. The cryptographic hash function is particularly important in the context of blockchain, as its immutability is established using the SHA256 algorithm from the SHA-2 family that we discuss later in this chapter.

2.3.3 Digital Signature

A digital signature is a cryptographic analogue of a handwritten signature to validate the authenticity integrity and non-repudiation of a message or documents transferred over a digital medium. A valid digital signature provides a recipient with the basis of believing that a known sender created the message; hence it ensures authenticity, that the sender cannot deny sending the message indicating non-repudiation and that the message was not altered in transit confirming the integrity.

A digital signature scheme is generally used by a signer who generates a pair of private and public keys followed by publicising his or her public key so that we can assume the verifier will have it or can obtain it at the time of verification. Once the public key of a signer is established, the digital signature scheme allows the signer to *sign* or certify the message in such a way that any other party knowing the signer's public key and the corresponding algorithm can verify that it is originated from the signer and nobody modified it in the middle [Katz, 2010].

Whitfield Diffie and Martin Hellman first described the possibility of such a concept in 1976 before the invention of public-key cryptography [Diffie and Hellman, 1976]. Later when RSA became available, it paved the path for the digital signature to become a reality. The following example shows the steps of a simple RSA and hash-based digital signature scheme.

Let suppose Bob wants to send a message to Alice using an RSA-based digital signature as shown in Figure 2.5. He needs to go through the following steps:

1. Bob generates a hash value of the message.
2. Bob encrypts the hash value using his private key. The encrypted hash value can only be decrypted by his public key; hence it acts as his signature.
3. Bob attaches his signature at the bottom of the original message and sends it to Alice using a digital communication medium.
4. Having received the message, Alice performs two tasks: first, she decrypts Bob's signature using his public key to obtain the hash value, and, second, she creates a hash value for the original message sent.
5. By comparing two hash values, Alice can confirm the authenticity of the message. It is because if someone in the middle changes the message, the new hash value will be different than that of stored in Bob's signature. Due to this signature being encrypted, the man in the middle would not be able to change it, or any modification attempt would result in a damaged signature that cannot be decrypted using the public of key of Bob anymore revealing the alteration.

The digital signature is another essential cryptographic principle used in the making of cryptocurrency and blockchain technology. There are several digital signature algorithms available, of which Bitcoin uses the Elliptic Curve Digital Signature Algorithm (ECDSA). The foundation of ECDSA is based on elliptic curve cryptography. A brief introduction to this cryptosystem is presented next. Various chapters of this book will later refer to that discussion.

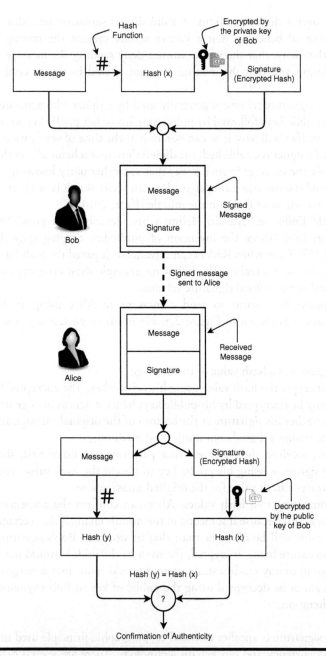

Figure 2.5   Steps of a typical digital signature.

2.4 Elliptic Curve Cryptography (ECC)

ECC is a process of encrypting data using publicly known information so that only a specific person or a group of people having certain secrets in hand can decrypt it; hence it forms a public-key cryptosystem. There are many such cryptographic techniques in use, notably RSA and Diffie–Hellman (DH). Unlike RSA and DH, ECC is much complicated and more secure. Due to the complex nature of ECC, it is beyond the scope of this book to explain detailed procedures as to how this system works, therefore, it provides a brief overview of ECC. Interested readers, however, may consider reading the book *Guide to Elliptic Curve Cryptography* published by Springer to obtain a broad knowledge on this topic [Hankerson et al., 2004].

2.4.1 Basic Concept

The foundation of all public-key cryptosystems is the same. There must be a process commonly known as "trapdoor" to obtain a piece of information using some publicly available knowledge that cannot be reversed. For instance, if $A + X$ easily gives us B, to form a public-key cryptosystem, obtaining A using $B + X$ must not be feasible. The following would shed more light on this.

If this is feasible:
"This is a simple message" + Public Key = "s80s1q8sadjds9s"

Then this must not be feasible:
"s80s1q8sadjds9s" + Public Key = "This is a simple message"

The RSA is designed utilising the difficulty of very large prime factorisation. This algorithm uses two large prime numbers (let us suppose p and q) in its trapdoor function to obtain r such that $p \times q$. If we have p and q, we can quickly determine r, but if we have r, it is infeasible to obtain p and q, at least within a practical timeframe.

ECC utilises the difficulty of solving number problems instead of prime factorisation. It employs curves given by equations of the form

$$y^2 = x^3 + ax + b \qquad (2.1)$$

where a and b are constants.

The elliptic curve, shown in Figure 2.6, has two interesting properties that help to develop the cryptosystem: (1) drawing an intersecting line will cut at three points maximum, and (2) the curve is symmetric over the x-axis. It is possible to the two properties in elliptic curve point multiplication operations to successively add a point along an elliptic curve to itself repeatedly. This method in ECC ultimately leads to producing the one-way trapdoor function. Because it is a scalar multiplication, the

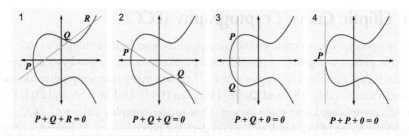

Figure 2.6 Examples of elliptic curves. (Image created by Chas zzz brown and released under Creative Commons [CC BY-SA 3.0].)

most common name for it in literature is *elliptic curve scalar multiplication*. It is also called the "double-and-add" algorithm [Hankerson et al., 2004].

Due to a cryptographic elliptic curve being a very large succession of points, an arbitrary point on the curve can be reached quickly from a predecessor if the number of steps is known. The elliptic curve protocol begins from a given known point called the generator. A public key is a point in the curve, and a private key is the number of steps from the generator that must be traversed to arrive at the public key point.

The process of obtaining the public key is swift if we have the private key. It is calculated using the double-and-add algorithm. However, the reverse, given the public key finding out the private key, is very difficult. This is known as the discrete logarithm problem. The brute-force algorithm to solve the discrete logarithm problem would traverse the points in the elliptic curve one at a time commencing from the generator until it arrives at the desired point. This algorithm is computationally infeasible, taking many years to complete with classical computers [Franco, 2015].

2.4.2 Public and Private Keys

The ECC is designed based on the generalised discrete logarithm problem on elliptic curves. The curve in Figure 2.6 is on a two-dimensional plane whose points verify Equation 2.1. Our interest in this curve is not the real numbers but rather the integers. We set a maximum value – a prime order p that defines the boundary. All operations are performed modulo this p in the calculation. Therefore, the new equation will look like

$$y^2 = x^3 + a{\cdot}x + b \bmod p \tag{2.2}$$

All the points $P_i = (x_i, y_i)$ that satisfy this condition are said to belong to the elliptic curve. A group operation, often called *addition*, is defined over this set of points as follows:

$$P3 = P1 + P2 \tag{2.3}$$

If the two points are the same, then the tangent to the elliptic curve at this point is drawn. The result of the operation is then the reflection over the x-axis of the intersection of this line with the elliptic curve. This operation is sometimes called point doubling.

$$P' = P + P \tag{2.4}$$

This leads to *point multiplication* – given a point on the elliptic curve A and an integer d, point multiplication is defined as the point T in the elliptic curve, which is the result of adding A to itself d times:

$$T = d \cdot A = A + A + \dots + A \tag{2.5}$$

The discrete logarithm operation is the inverse of point multiplication. Given a starting point A, it is computationally fast to advance d positions in the sequence of points using point multiplication to reach T.

$$T = d \cdot A \tag{2.6}$$

However, given a point T in the group it is difficult to know how it has been reached or, in other words, the number of elements in the sequence from the generator to this point. In order to achieving this, we must visit points in the curve one by one to discover the number of steps taken to reach the destination point. This operation requires an exponential number of steps making the discrete logarithm problem hard [Franco, 2015].

Having gone through the preceding calculation, we obtain two elements, T and d, that give us the required key pairs. T is the public key, which is a point on the elliptic curve. It is made of two components: x and y coordinates where both are large integer numbers. The private key, on the other hand, is represented by d, which is the number of steps taken to reach T; hence a large single integer.

2.4.3 How Does ECC Compare to RSA?

The biggest differentiator between ECC and RSA is the key size compared to cryptographic strength. As Table 2.2 shows, ECC can provide the same cryptographic strength as an RSA-based system with much smaller key sizes. For example, a 256-bit ECC key is equivalent to RSA 3072-bit keys, which are 50% longer than the 2048-bit keys commonly used today. Earlier in Table 2.1, we saw that the latest and the most secure symmetric algorithm currently in use is AES. This algorithm uses at least 128-bit keys demonstrating that the asymmetric keys provide ECC's level of security [Olenski, 2015].

Table 2.2   NIST Recommended Key Size

Symmetric (bits)	RSA and DH (bits)	ECC (bits)
80	1024	160
112	2048	224
128	3072	256
192	7680	384
256	15360	521

2.5 Making Blockchain Immutable

The immutability of blockchain is confirmed using cryptographic principles and applications. The idea of using a distributed ledger is to prevent double-spending by keeping records of previous transactions. In doing so, distributed computing played a vital role, but for the time being, if we ignore the contribution of that discipline, what we have is all cryptography. Nakamoto used linked timestamping, Merkle tree and cryptographic hash functions to make transactions of the blocks irreversible even for the authors. The following sections first discuss the components and then seek to explore how those components are used to make blockchain immutable.

2.5.1 Block and Block Header

Each block of a blockchain is made of at least two parts: a block header and a data structure. The block header contains some meta information, and the data structure holds the actual data. The type of data structure depends on the data itself. Because Nakamoto's design of blockchain administers virtual currency transfers, it holds transactions. Seemingly a simple list or a vector would have been sufficient to store the data, but auditing transactions from a large pool of data would be an expensive operation. In dealing with this problem, blockchain uses Merkel tree as its data structure.

A block header contains a variety of information, amongst which three fields are particularly important for ensuring immutability. These are a time variable indicating the block generation time, a link to the data structure and a link to the previous block. Blockchain uses the Unix timestamp to designate the block-building time, while Merkle tree provides the Merkle root that establishes a connection with the data structure, and the hash value of the previous block header is used to connect the blocks.

2.5.2 Timestamp

A timestamp is a representative of a specific time. A Unix time timestamp is the number of seconds that have passed since 00:00:00 (UTC), Thursday, 1 January

1970, minus leap seconds. In this timestamping, every day is considered to have precisely 86,400 seconds to subtract the leap seconds since the epoch. In addition to working as a source of variation for the block hash, the timestamps also make it more challenging for an adversary to manipulate the blockchain. Bitcoin protocol considers a timestamp valid if it is greater than the median timestamp of the previous 11 blocks, and less than the network-adjusted time plus 2 hours. The "network-adjusted time" means the median of the timestamps returned by all nodes connected to a participating node.

2.5.3 Merkle Tree

A Merkle tree is a binary tree data structure designed by Ralph Merkle. Unlike a regular tree, it is constructed by recursively hashing pairs of nodes. Every leaf node of a Merkle tree contains the cryptographic hash of a data, whereas every non-leaf node stores the hash of concatenated hashes of its child nodes. If there remains an odd number of child nodes, the last hash gets duplicated.

Merkle tree is used to summarise and verify the integrity of a large dataset. Figure 2.7 shows a Merkle tree with eight transactions (T1 to T8). If we are to ascertain the integrity of T5, we would require H6, H78, H1234 and the Merkle root, and must compute and compare the following:

$$MerkleRoot \rightarrow Hash(Hash(Hash(Hash(T5) + H6) + H78) + H1234) \quad (2.7)$$

If the above equation satisfies, this proves that T5 belongs to the tree. It is because if the integrity of T5 gets compromised, H56 will be affected that subsequently returns a different Merkle root for the tree. The use of the Merkle tree in blockchain enables miners with the ability to verify the transactions efficiently and securely from a large pool of data. When N data elements are hashed and summarised in a Merkle tree, a miner can ascertain if a particular transaction is already in the tree with at most $2\log_2(N)$ number of calculations.

2.5.4 Building the Chain

Having acquired the required knowledge, now we explore how blocks are chained in a blockchain using a visual description presented by Figure 2.8. In a blockchain, the genesis block, which is also the first block of the chain, is a special case that does not have a reference to its previous block; every other block is chained using cryptographic principles. The genesis block is almost always hardcoded into the software of the applications that utilise the blockchain.

The blockchain uses two components to chain the blocks. The first is the Merkle root that represents all the transactions of a block in a hashed format. Any attempt of changing a single transaction in the tree leaf would result in a new Merkle root revealing the change. The second component is the hash of the previous block's

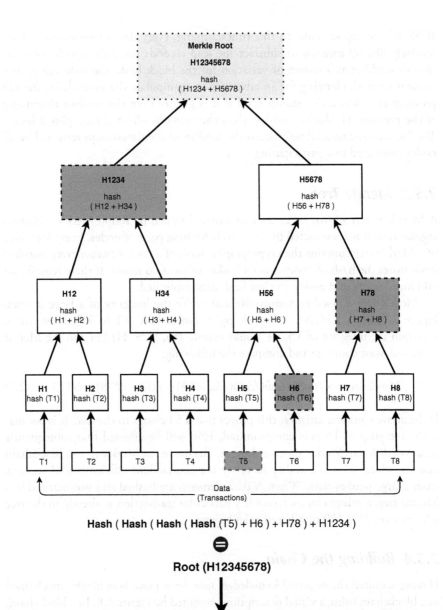

Figure 2.7   A typical Merkle tree.

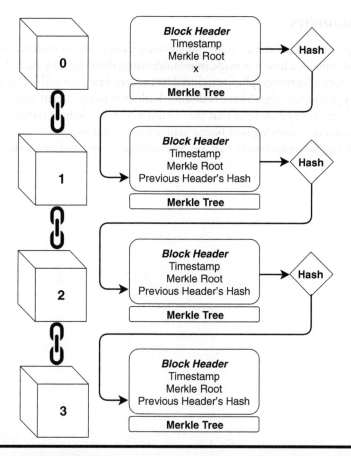

Figure 2.8 **Each block in a blockchain is chained to one another using crypto-graphic hashes. Putting the hash of the previous block's header in the header of the following block, that also contains the Merkle root, creates the ultimate bond to develop the whole chain.**

header. Because the Merkle root is part of this header, its hash effectively ties up the transactions in the chaining mechanism. Finally, the hash of the previous block's header is placed in the header of the following block to complete chaining of two consecutive blocks. Every time miners build a block, they put it at the end of this chain; hence the chain keeps growing.

Only chaining the blocks with each other, however, does not make blockchain immutable. Its immutability also depends on the block-building process. If the task of building a block becomes too easy, anyone willing to alter a transaction can rebuild the whole chain from scratch. Thus, if half of the credit of making block-chain goes to the cryptography disciple, the other half is due to the principles of distributed systems that we learn in the next chapter.

2.6 Summary

This chapter presented the cryptographic principles required to understand blockchain and explained how it is made immutable using those techniques. It described a brief history of cryptography, introduced its modern branches and stated the necessary cryptographic algorithms including hash functions, digital signature and the elliptic curve cryptography that play a vital role in blockchain technology. The chapter concluded showing how blockchain utilises a combination of some of those algorithms to construct blocks that are impossible to erase, alter or rewrite.

Chapter 3

Consensus Mechanisms of Blockchain

Two branches of computer science, cryptography and distributed systems, act as the enabling technology of blockchain. We learned about cryptography in the previous chapter that discussed how the principles of this branch make blockchain immutable. Although it is no overstatement that cryptographic principles make blockchain data immutable, cryptography can achieve this success only when all nodes agree upon a constructed block to be included in the blockchain. This agreement requires a mechanism to coordinate thousands of participating nodes in the network to reach a consensus, and this chapter takes the opportunity to explain how that is accomplished.

3.1 Distributed Systems and Consensus

Blockchain is a decentralised system without the existence of a central authority that leads and coordinates. While this removes the possibility of corruptions from a single entity, the decentralised approach creates some significant concerns such as who is going to take the decisions and how the executions of the process are performed. If we think of a centralised system, it is easy to figure out a boss who makes all the decisions. This is not possible in a blockchain because a blockchain has no "leader". For the blockchain to make decisions, all participating nodes must reach a consensus on the best choice for the system.

Reaching a consensus is a fundamental element of a distributed system. Being a distributed ledger, the blockchain is a distributed system at its core. It uses one of the finest examples of the distributed system, a peer-to-peer network, to keep the data stable, permanent and immutable where nodes agree upon the decision of building new blocks through consensus. It is, therefore, necessary to briefly introduce distributed systems to readers and explain how participating nodes, or more appropriately miners, reach an agreement remotely about the data integrity of the blockchain.

3.1.1 Distributed Systems

A distributed system is a computing paradigm where two or more components (also referred to as nodes, processes and actors) work with each other in a coordinated fashion intending to achieving a common goal. Although the system remains distributed at its execution, it is modelled in such a way that the end users recognise it as a single logical platform. The components or nodes of a distributed system stay apportioned amongst multiple machines to improve efficiency and performance; hence computer networking is used to communicate and coordinate the actions of the components by passing messages to one another. A distributed system demonstrates three vital characteristics – concurrency of components, lack of a global clock and independent failure of components – that govern its execution and performance [Andrews, 2000; Coulouris et al., 2011].

Distributed computing uses distributed systems to solve computational problems. The problems are divided into numerous tasks, each of which is solved by one or more nodes spread across the network via message passing. A computer program that runs within a distributed system is called a distributed application (DApp). Examples of distributed systems can be as small as an office where employees share resources like printers and file storages via the Local Area Network (LAN) to big cloud platforms such as Dropbox and Google Drive to massive peer-to-peer platforms like BitTorrent.

Typical properties of a distributed system include the following [Ghosh, 2007; Lynch, 1996]:

- The system must tolerate failures in the individual node.
- The structure of the system including network topology, network latency and the number of nodes is not known in advance.
- The system may consist of different kinds of computers and network links, and may change during the execution of a distributed program.
- Each node has only a limited, incomplete view of the system.
- Each node may know only one part of the input.

3.1.2 Coordination and Agreement

Distributed nodes often require coordination of their activities, particularly when they share a collection of resource, to prevent interference and ensure consistency of accessing the resources. Coordination in a synchronised system with no failures is relatively easy, but if a system is asynchronous where failures may occur or messages may be delayed, an indefinite amount of time, coordination and agreement become much more challenging.

A node in a distributed system is said to be correct if it exhibits no failures at any point in the execution under consideration. If a node fails, it can fail in one of two ways: a crash failure or a Byzantine failure. A crash failure means a node stops working and does not respond to any messages. A Byzantine failure implies that a node exhibits arbitrary behaviour. For example, it may continue to function but send incorrect values.

3.1.3 Consensus

A fundamental problem in distributed computing is achieving overall system reliability in the presence of some faulty nodes. This often requires nodes to agree on some data value that is needed during computation. The method that makes a distributed system achieve this agreement is called *consensus*. In simpler terms, a consensus is a dynamic way of reaching agreement in a group. While a general voting system rectifies the majority rule without caring for the well-being of the minority, a consensus, on the other hand, ensures an agreement is reached which could benefit the entire group as a whole. The method by which a consensus is achieved is called the *consensus mechanism*. Examples of distributed executions where a consensus mechanism is required by design include committing a transaction to a database, state machine replication, atomic broadcasts, agreeing on the identity of a leader and so on.

There are some properties a consensus mechanism typically has:

- Agreement seeking: A consensus mechanism should bring about as much agreement from the group as possible.
- Collaborative: The participating nodes should aim for working together to achieve a result that benefits the best interest of the group.
- Cooperative: The participating nodes should not put their own interests first, but rather work as a team than a collection of individuals.
- Inclusive: As many people as possible should be involved in the consensus process.
- Participatory: The consensus mechanism should be such that everyone actively participates in the process.
- Impartial: A group trying to achieve consensus should be as fair as possible. It essentially means that each vote has equal weighting where one vote cannot be more significant than another.

The consensus mechanism requires agreement between a number of nodes for a single data value. Some of the nodes may fail or be unreliable in other ways, so consensus protocols must be fault tolerant or resilient. The nodes must somehow put forth their candidate values, communicate with one another and agree on a single consensus value. One approach to generating consensus is for all nodes to agree on a majority value. In this context, a majority requires at least one more than half of the available votes, where each node is considered to have one vote. However, one or more faulty nodes may skew the resultant outcome such that consensus may not be reached or reached incorrectly.

Before Bitcoin, many failed attempts saw scientists and developers trying to establish decentralised peer-to-peer currency, but they were unable to answer the most significant problem when it came to reaching a consensus. This problem is called the Byzantine Generals Problem.

3.2 Byzantine Generals Problem

The *Byzantine Generals Problem* is derived from another problem commonly known as the *Two Generals Paradox*. It is an analogy of computer communication. It was first proposed by Akkoyunlu et al. in their paper "Some Constraints and Trade-Offs in the Design of Network Communications" in 1975 [Akkoyunlu et al., 1975]. The paper described the problem in the context of communication between two groups of gangsters, but later Turing Award–winning computer scientist Jim Gray named it the Two Generals Paradox. Roughly six years later, the Byzantine Generals Problem came as a modified version of this paradox that another Turing Award–winning computer scientist Leslie Lamport and his co-researchers Robert Shostak and Marshall Pease published in 1982 [Lamport et al., 1982]. This problem is now widely used to explain the fault tolerance of the distributed systems.

3.2.1 Two Generals Paradox

Let suppose two generals (A and B as seen in Figure 3.1) planning an attack on a common enemy struggle to decide on an attacking strategy due to the location of the enemy city. The city is securely placed in a valley and has a solid defence that can easily fight off a single army. The only chance of winning against this enemy is to attack from two sides of the city at the same time. This constraint requires the generals to communicate with each other to plan a synchronised attack. As the enemy's city separates two attacking armies, the generals must communicate with each other by sending a messenger across the territory. If the enemy captures the messenger of General A, the message will go lost, and General B would not know when to attack and vice versa.

Now, consider a scenario where General A, who is the leader amongst them, sends a message to General B – "Attack at dawn tomorrow". General B receives the message and acknowledges sending another message, "Message received, attacking at dawn tomorrow". A receives B's confirmation and starts preparing for the attack. But, is this enough to reach a consensus between the generals? Sadly, not. General A knows B received the message, but B still does not know if A received his

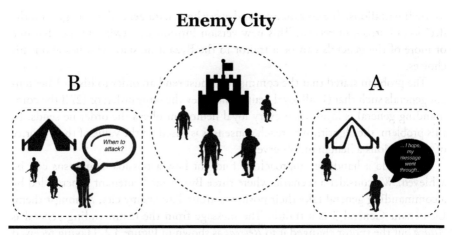

Figure 3.1   Two generals planning an attack on a common enemy.

acknowledgement and will be ready for the attack. If General A sends a confirmation of receiving B's response, that makes B relieved, but then A starts to worry. This way they end up in an infinite exchange of confirmations.

In another scenario, let us assume that General A posts a message to General B. As time passes, General A starts to wonder what might happen to his message because of General B not sending an acknowledgement yet. There might be two possibilities. Either General A's messenger got captured and failed to deliver the message, or B's soldier carrying the message ended up in the enemy's hand. In both situations, the two generals cannot come to a consensus again. A is not sure if his message or B's confirmation was lost, and B is doubtful if A received his response.

The preceding scenarios show no matter how many different combinations we try and how many messages we send, it is not possible to guarantee that a consensus is reached and the generals cannot be certain that their ally will attack at the same time. This is an unsolved problem to date.

Many people tried to solve this paradox and came up with a few useful approaches. Although there exists mathematical proof that this problem is unsolvable, accepting the uncertainty of the communication channel is a potential solution that can improve the likelihood of a synchronised attack. The Transmission Control Protocol (TCP), the backbone of the modern World Wide Web (WWW), establishes the connection between a client computer and the server using a mechanism called three-way handshake that mimics the attempted agreement between the generals described in this paradox.

3.2.2 Byzantine Generals Problem

The Byzantine Generals Problem is a modified version of the Two Generals Paradox. In this setup, the leader is called the *commanding general* or the *commander* who leads the Byzantine army consisting of $n-1$ number of *lieutenant generals* responsible for their battalions. The commander and every lieutenant general must agree on the decision of attack or retreat. This new version introduces a twist stating that one or more of the generals can be a traitor to the Byzantine state who lies about his choices.

The problem stated that the commander must send an order to his $n-1$ lieutenant generals such that (1) all loyal lieutenants obey the same order; or (2) if the commanding general is loyal, then every loyal lieutenant obeys the order he sends. In this problem, the algorithm to reach consensus is based on the value of the majority of the decisions a lieutenant observes.

Let us do a hands-on approach to find out how a possible consensus can be achieved. We consider a scenario where three Byzantine lieutenant generals led by a commanding general take their positions around an enemy city. Amongst them, Lieutenant General 3 is a traitor. The message from the commanding general is *Attack* but the traitor changed it to *Retreat* as shown in Figure 3.2. Having received the message from the commander, each lieutenant forwards it to other lieutenants. Despite having a traitor, the general consensus, in this case, is Attack, which was the original message sent by the commander.

In the same scenario, what if the commander himself is the traitor rather than a lieutenant? Let us draw the same diagram again but with commander as the traitor who sends three different kinds of messages – *Attack*, *Wait* and *Retreat* – to his lieutenants as shown in Figure 3.3. Despite the commander being the traitor, the

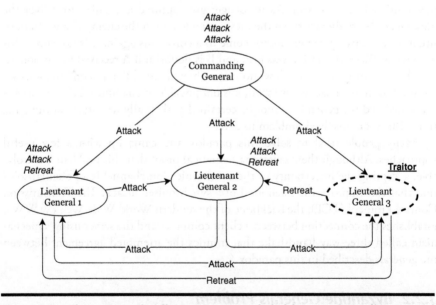

Figure 3.2   Three Byzantine lieutenant generals led by a commanding general planning to attack an enemy city. The message from the commanding general is *Attack*, but the traitor (Lieutenant 3) changed it to *Retreat*. Despite that, the consensus is Attack, which was the original message sent by the commander.

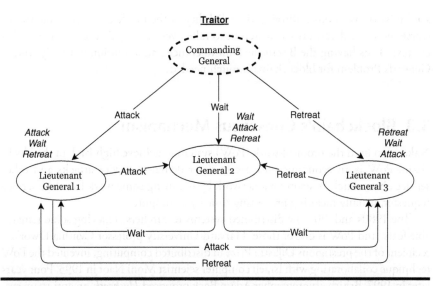

Figure 3.3   Three Byzantine lieutenant generals led by a commanding general, who is the traitor in this scenario, planning to attack an enemy city. The message from the commanding general is *Attack, Wait* and *Retreat*. Despite that, the consensus is "Retreat" is the default option.

generals still reach a consensus. To understand the outcome of this consensus we must realise that because each lieutenant receives three different kinds of messages from multiple sources, they cannot decide on attacking the city and act on the default option, which is Retreat.

The original paper by Lamport et al. provided a theorem stating that for any m, the algorithm reaches consensus if there are more than $3m$ generals and at most m traitors. This implies that the algorithm can reach consensus as long as 2/3 of the generals are honest. If the traitors are more than 1/3, consensus is not reached, the armies do not coordinate their attack and the enemy wins.

3.2.3 Byzantine Fault Tolerance

The fault tolerance is the property that enables a system to continue operating properly in the event of the failure of some of its components. The Byzantine fault tolerance (BFT) is a special class of fault tolerance that is very challenging to achieve. In a "Byzantine failure", a component such as a server can inconsistently appear both failed and functioning to failure-detection systems, presenting different symptoms to different observers. BFT is the characteristic defining a system that tolerates the Byzantine failure.

Blockchains are decentralised ledgers by definition that are not managed by a central authority. This gives bad nodes the motivation to try to cause faults to achieve unfair economic benefits. In the absence of BFT, a node will be able to send false transactions nullifying the reliability of the blockchain. To make things worse, no central authority can step in to take over and repair the damage in this context. Thus having the Byzantine fault tolerance and a solution to the Byzantine Generals Problem for blockchains is much needed.

3.3 Blockchain's Consensus Mechanism

Nakamoto used the proof-of-work (PoW) system to achieve high BFT in the block-chain. PoW is an economic measure to deter denial-of-service attacks and other service abuses such as spam on a network by requiring some work from the service requester, usually meaning processing time by a computer.

The 1980s and '90s saw distributed systems researchers achieving some remarkable feats, and PoW is one of those. Harvard University professor Cynthia Dwork, a recipient of the prestigious Dijkstra Prize in distributed computing, invented the PoW technique collaborating with Israeli computer scientist Moni Naor in 1993. Four years later in 1997, British cryptographer Adam Back proposed *Hashcash*, an anti-spam system, and customised the PoW system to work with his application. Nakamoto almost identically used the Hashcash PoW algorithm in his Bitcoin protocol.

3.3.1 Hashcash Proof of Work

Back developed Hashcash to limit email spamming. The Hashcash PoW algorithm requires a selectable amount of work to compute, but the proof can be efficiently verified. For email, a textual encoding of a Hashcash stamp is added to the header of an email to prove the sender has expended a modest amount of CPU time calculating the stamp prior to sending the email. In other words, as the sender has taken a certain amount of time to generate the stamp and send the email, it is unlikely that he or she is a spammer. The receiver can, at negligible computational cost, verify that the stamp is valid.

However, the only known way to find a header with the necessary properties is brute force, trying random values until the answer is found; though testing an individual string is easy, if satisfactory answers are rare enough it will require a substantial number of tries to find the answer. The hypothesis is that spammers, whose business model relies on their ability to send large numbers of emails with very little cost per message, will cease to be profitable if there is even a small cost for each spam they send. Receivers can verify whether a sender made such an investment and use the results to help filter email.

Let us examine an example to understand how the PoW is used to send emails. There is a sample Hashcash version 1 header line shown in Figure 3.4.

X-Hashcash: 1:20:1303030600:adam@cypherspace.org::McMybZIhxKXu57jd:ckvi

Figure 3.4   A sample Hashcash version 1 header.

In this header, "ckvi" represents a counter in base64 that the sender must randomly generate and append at the back of all other required fields. Once all set, the sender computes the 160-bit SHA-1 hash of the header including the counter. If the first 20 bits, which is the 5 most significant hex digits, of the hash are all zeros, this is an acceptable header. If not, then the sender increments the counter and tries the hash again. Out of 2^{160} possible hash values, there are 2^{140} hash values that satisfy this criterion. Thus the chance of randomly selecting a header that will have 20 decimal or 5 hex zeros as the beginning of the hash is 1 in 2^{20}.

The number of times that the sender needs to try to get a valid hash value is modelled by geometric distribution. Hence the sender will on average have to try 2^{20} values to find a valid header. Given reasonable estimates of the time needed to compute the hash, this would take about one second to find. A normal user on a desktop PC would not be significantly inconvenienced by the processing time required to generate the Hashcash string, but spammers would suffer significantly due to a large number of spam messages sent by them.

3.3.2 Proof of Work in Blockchain

We know that blockchain is a decentralised system with no central authority. As such, it is necessary that someone plays the role of a leader for a brief period to choose the next block to be added to the blockchain. Participating nodes, called miners hereafter, in a blockchain elect this leader using the PoW algorithm that engages them to find the hash fulfilling the criterion. The node discovering the hash first gets elected to choose the next block.

Like the Hashcash where the header of the email is used as the base string, blockchain uses the block header. The header of a blockchain contains a counter – in Bitcoin it is called *nonce* – that the miners need to increase gradually. There are two more elements in blockchain PoW: *target* and *difficulty*. A target is a large number, and the hash of the block header must be lower than or equal to this number to be accepted. The difficulty is a measure of how difficult it is to find a hash below a given target. The protocol generally monitors the block-building process and adjusts the difficulty to keep the block generation rate the same.

This mining process is used in blockchain to coordinate the block-building process by electing a miner out of thousands of them who want to build the next block. All miners get the chance to construct a block by picking up transactions of their choices. However, only one of those blocks becomes the next block in the blockchain. Once individual blocks are created, miners attempt to find the required hash which must be smaller than or equal to the given target at that moment. The miner who finds the appropriate hash first becomes the leader to build the next block and receives the reward. All other miners destroy their blocks and start over from the beginning to compete in the next round of the block-building process; hence the operation continues to run and despite being decentralised, blockchain operates in a coordinated and organised manner. Section 4.7 of Chapter 4 further describes this process as it happens in Bitcoin.

3.3.3 BFT in Blockchain

It is important to realise that PoW helps blockchain achieve high Byzantine Fault Tolerance. In order for a miner to insert false information in a block, it must have at least 51% of the computational power of the whole network. How difficult it is to achieve such power is explained in Figure 3.5.

Let suppose miners have been working to build block 40 where Chuck is one of the miners in the process. Instead of building block 40, he wants to alter a transaction in block 23. If Chuck does that, the link of the blockchain will be broken, and the community will reject the copy of the blockchain presented to them later. So he must redo blocks 23 to 39, which is 17 blocks before all other miners finish building block 40. This is the only way Chuck can cheat the network and alter one or more transactions in the blockchain.

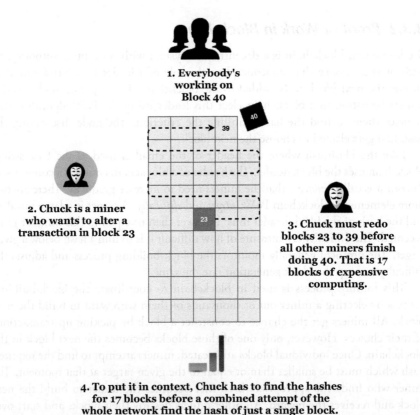

1. Everybody's working on Block 40

2. Chuck is a miner who wants to alter a transaction in block 23

3. Chuck must redo blocks 23 to 39 before all other miners finish doing 40. That is 17 blocks of expensive computing.

4. To put it in context, Chuck has to find the hashes for 17 blocks before a combined attempt of the whole network find the hash of just a single block.

Figure 3.5   Byzantine fault tolerance in blockchain.

However, doing this is not an easy task. Changing a transaction will effectively give a new Merkle root leading to a new block header. When the block header is different, Chuck must find a new hash for that block fulfilling the condition; otherwise, the community will find the cheat and reject Chuck's copy of the blockchain. Therefore, he must find 17 new hashes to connect the blocks, and he must do it before a combined attempt of the whole network finds the hash for a single block.

The preceding example tells us that the success of Chuck's attempt depends on computational power. If Chuck could gain a computational power greater than the whole network, he can achieve this exploit. This can be accomplished either by building a powerful computer having the computational power greater than the power of the network combined or by convincing the majority of the miners to join him in the cheat; hence, the 51% Byzantine fault tolerance.

3.4 Solving the Double-Spending Problem

In Chapter 1, we left the explanation of the double-spending problem incomplete due to the lack of sufficient knowledge required to comprehend the answer. As we have now covered the fundamental theories and mechanisms to understand how blockchain works, it is time to complete that explanation.

There is a blockchain for Bitcoin that keeps the record of all transactions. This blockchain hypothetically floats over a peer-to-peer network managed by remote nodes commonly known as miners. Figure 3.6 shows a heat map of Bitcoin miners from around the globe. Between 9000 and 12,0000 miners generally take part in the mining process, where every miner has a copy of the blockchain that it stores in its local computer. However, miners do not have the ability to change the block entries or add new blocks, as the network will reject any such attempt. Miners

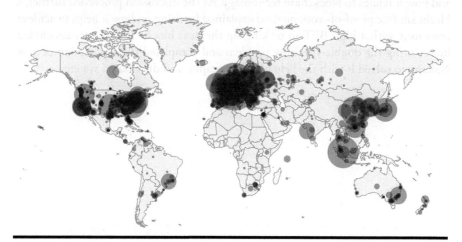

Figure 3.6   Heat map showing Bitcoin miners from around the globe.

manage the blockchain in a decentralised and distributed manner where editing an entry of the blockchain is restricted by the cryptographic principles, and adding new blocks or attempting to rebuild old blocks are prevented by distributed consensus.

As such, Bob wants to send 100 Bitcoins (BTC) to Alice. What he does next is to initiate a transaction stating the amount he intends to send to Alice. However, the money does not go to Alice instantly; rather goes through a verification process. Bob's request for transferring the Bitcoin stays in a request pool that miners regularly monitor. Some miners pick up Bob's transaction from the pool and look up at the blockchain entries to verify that he retains sufficient Bitcoin for sending the requested amount to Alice, and therefore not attempting to double spend. Once confirmed, those miners place the transaction in the Merkle tree of their blocks. The transfer of the money remains pending until the blocks go through the consensus and a miner discovers the hash smaller than or equal to the target. The block-building process comes to an end when a consensus is achieved, and the winner block becomes the new addition in the blockchain.

If Bob is lucky enough to have his transaction in this block, Alice becomes the rightful owner of the 100 BTC sent from Bob. Otherwise, Bob needs to wait until his transaction gets included in a winning block and transferred to Alice. There will be no need for an arrangement to move the money physically or involve a central authority having superior power.

3.5 Summary

This chapter presented distributed systems and explained the need for a consensus to make such systems operational. It described the Byzantine fault tolerance (BFT) and how it relates to blockchain technology. As the discussion proceeded further, a Hashcash-like proof-of-work method explained focusing on how it helps to achieve consensus with a high BFT in picking up the next block. The chapter concluded by revisiting the double-spending problem and completed the explanation of how Nakamoto solved it with the help of cryptography and distributed systems.

Chapter 4

Bitcoin: World's First Cryptocurrency

Bitcoin is the first application of blockchain technology. Although it is a currency transaction protocol, the application is useful to understand blockchain as a whole. The opening three chapters of this book introduced blockchain and described how principles of cryptography and distributed systems contributed to its development. In this chapter, readers will mostly find the same topics but from a practical point of view. The chapter arranges the discussion in such a way that readers can relate the theories with a working example (e.g. Bitcoin) to comprehend the operation of blockchain technology in the real world.

4.1 What is Bitcoin?

Bitcoin is a virtual currency constructed using cryptographic principles and conceived by the blockchain and proof-of-work mechanism in a distributed and decentralised environment; hence it is also called cryptocurrency. Although there had been proposals in the literature for developing similar currency employing cryptographic techniques, it remains the world's first implemented cryptocurrency. In solving the double-spending problem using a distributed ledger, Nakamoto delivered the process of moving money virtually that was previously impossible. This ability of Bitcoin made it one of a kind and introduced a new branch of technology.

This virtual currency, however, has more mystery to it. Bitcoin is called a virtual currency because it does not have an existence in reality. We cannot touch it or feel it despite it having a tangible value. Chapter 1 of this book discussed an example in Section 1.1.3 where Chuck copies Bitcoin to send to Alice and Bob as if copying a digital file. That example described Bitcoin at a very high level. In reality, Bitcoin is even more virtual than a digital file. It is so virtual that it does not have an existence even in the digital world. There exists no such digital file on our computer or on a server that we can call Bitcoin.

Nakamoto visualised Bitcoin from a very different perspective. His protocol examines the transactions to discover the amount of Bitcoin someone holds. From the creation of each Bitcoin, its life story resides on the pages of a ledger famously known as *blockchain*. Blockchain keeps records of every transaction revealing whether someone claiming to have a particular unit of Bitcoin is true.

Bitcoin is created by mining. Once miners validate the transactions and build a block, through a puzzle one miner gets selected to have a specific number of Bitcoin as an incentive; hence new Bitcoin comes into existence. From that moment on, every time these newly created tokens change hands, miners write transactions in the blockchain.

An example would perhaps make it clearer. Let suppose Bob gets 10 Bitcoins (BTC) as a reward for his mining work. If he wishes to send Alice 5 BTC, he must declare it to the network so that miners can check existing transactions in the blockchain and validate that Bob indeed holds sufficient units of Bitcoins to send 5 BTC to Alice, and therefore, they write a new transaction in the block showing 5 BTC going to Alice from Bob. At this point, Bob loses his claim on the tokens and Alice becomes the rightful owner of those Bitcoins until she sends those to someone else.

If Bob gets 10 BTC from Carol in the meanwhile and wants to send 15 BTC to Alice, that request will be considered valid because he already holds 5 BTC from the mining reward and received another 10 BTC from Carol. By combining two transactions, miners will be able to reach an affirmative decision on Bob's request. However, if he wants to send 20 BTC, miners will identify that Bob does not have the required amount and his request will be discarded. There will be no transaction entry for that request in the blockchain and Alice will not get any Bitcoins.

Therefore, it is not the token but rather the transactions Bitcoin protocol keeps track of. The tracking is implemented pseudonymously using a pair of cryptographic public and private keys telling the network of the right of an individual on that transaction. Instead of using the public key directly, the protocol uses the hash of the public key as an address. When Bob announced his interest in sending Alice 5 BTC, without revealing his identity Bob unlocked some of the unspent tokens that he received in the past. While unlocking this fund, Bob used a digital signature telling the protocol of his wish. Bitcoin protocol, having identified the presence of Bob's private key in the relevant tokens' address, made those available for him. This signature cannot be generated without the private key, ensuring miners that he is indeed the person holding the tokens; hence he is not attempting to double spend.

Bitcoin has a dark history for its use in criminal activities since its inception. Its transactions can store information on the blockchain in obscure style and establish contracts between multiple parties. The pseudonymous nature of these transactions also gives users the ability to hide their identities while trading. These features of Bitcoin make criminals, drug cartels and firearms dealers interested in this virtual currency.

It is no exaggeration that Nakamoto's Bitcoin took the world by storm. The protocol itself has a lot to offer in it, but it also hugely motivated other researchers to come up with new ideas using blockchain technology. As we progress through this book, it will unfold how the concept behind Bitcoin evolved into many other protocols and platforms capable of offering diverse applications far beyond the scope of currency transactions.

4.2 Brief History of Bitcoin

Bitcoin is the world's first cryptocurrency, which Satoshi Nakamoto proposed and developed between mid-2008 and early 2009. The invention of Bitcoin, however, did not happen overnight; rather this virtual currency traces its origin nearly three decades ago. The following sections present the history of Bitcoin in brief and introduce key persons and their contributions behind this invention.

4.2.1 Before Bitcoin

The first attempt at developing a currency based on cryptographic principles took place in 1982 when American computer scientist and cryptographer David Chaum proposed *Ecash*. In his seminal paper in 1982, Chaum described the architecture of an untraceable payment system that he developed using blind signatures. He again outlined a method for ensuring security without identification in a bid to bypass Big Brother. This research took place in 1984 coinciding with the name of the famous novel by George Orwell. Chaum published his work a year later in one of the most reputed computer science journals [Chaum, 1985]. He again wrote a refined version of Ecash in 1990 for offline transactions. His research primarily explored the possibility of making transactions that cannot be traced. Ecash, however, never got implemented, and a significant difference between this scheme and Bitcoin is the former was intended to be anonymous while the latter is pseudonymous, i.e. transactions are made in disguise.

The 1980s and '90s were a golden period for distributed systems research. Harvard University professor Cynthia Dwork, a recipient of the prestigious Dijkstra Prize in distributed computing, developed the proof-of-work technique collaborating with Israeli computer scientist Moni Naor in 1993 [Dwork and Naor, 1993]. Four years later, British cryptographer Adam Back proposed *Hashcash*, an anti-spam system, similar to the proof-of-work concept in 1997 [Back, 1997]. Later Back mentioned on his website that he was not aware of the works of Dwork and Naor, but he did praise their version of proof of work and listed it amongst the collection of Bitcoin-related prior works.

The most notable works that influenced Nakamoto in developing Bitcoin are perhaps *Bit gold* and *B-money*, two independently invented distributed digital money schemes published in 1998. Computer scientist and cryptographer Nick Szabo proposed the former, while Wei Dai described the latter scheme. Neither of these schemes requires a central server; they instead utilise a distributed database for storage. Like Ecash, these schemes also never got implemented.

4.2.2 Bitcoin Era

Nakamoto might have started developing the Bitcoin protocol a decade later since the arrival of Hashcash, Bit gold and B-money, but he was well informed of these works and cited two of these three schemes in the description of Bitcoin. On 18 August 2008, Nakamoto registered the domain name bitcoin.org, and later on 31 October published his famous paper "Bitcoin: A Peer-to-Peer Electronic Cash System" to the cryptography mailing list *metzdowd.com*. On 3 January 2009, the Bitcoin network became live when Nakamoto mined the genesis block of Bitcoin, for which he had a reward of 50 Bitcoins. He released the first open-source Bitcoin client at *SourceForge* 6 days later on 9 January.

One of the early supporters of and contributors to Bitcoin was programmer Hal Finney who was the recipient of the first Bitcoin transaction. Finney downloaded the Bitcoin software the day it was released and received 10 Bitcoins from Nakamoto in the world's first Bitcoin transaction on 12 January 2009. Bit gold creator Nick Szabo and B-money inventor Wei Dai also praised Nakamoto's work and later became acquaintances. Adam Back was also amongst the first people Nakamoto contacted.

New England–based programmer Gavin Andresen and Florida-based programmer Laszlo Hanyecz are two of the earliest supporters of Bitcoin. Hanyecz conducted the first real-world Bitcoin transaction when he indirectly purchased two pizzas delivered from Papa John's paying 10,000 Bitcoins. David Forster, a Massachusetts-based farmer, was the first to accept Bitcoin as payment.

Nakamoto continued to collaborate on the Bitcoin software with other developers until 2010 when he handed over the authority of the source code repository and network alert key to Andresen and transferred related domains to several notable members of the Bitcoin community. As of 12 December 2010, Nakamoto stopped his involvement in the project.

4.3 Token: BTC

Bitcoin, or BTC, is the native token for the Bitcoin protocol. This protocol is designed to orderly generate Bitcoin token until the year 2140. There will be no new Bitcoin in the network afterwards, but the protocol will continue to operate normally.

4.3.1 Bitcoin Mining and Supply

Bitcoin is a mined coin, which means its token must be created out of the mining process. The mining of Bitcoin is different from the mining of gold because in the Bitcoin process miners act as verifiers of the transaction rather than mining the coin like gold. In doing so, miners attempt to solve a puzzle to complete building a block. The successful miner who gets to solve the puzzle first receives a reward as the incentive for his or her service; hence new Bitcoin comes to existence.

As of December 2018, the reward amount for each block added to the blockchain is 12.5 newly created Bitcoins. The Bitcoin protocol specifies that the reward for adding a block will be halved every 210,000 blocks, which occurs approximately every 4 years. As this process continues, the reward will reduce to zero ensuring that there will be a maximum of 21 million tokens available throughout its lifetime. As the token generation gets decreased, by 2140, the network will have the targeted amount of tokens, and there will be no more new coin creation. The record-keeping will then be rewarded solely by transaction fees.

Each block in its transaction list has a unique transaction called the *coinbase*. Unlike other transactions that show the source of the funds, this transaction does not have a reference to its origin. It is because the coin in a coinbase transaction is created from scratch as soon as the block is built.

The price of a Bitcoin token has been very volatile throughout its lifetime. It has become the centre of attention since its sharp rise in 2016. On 18 December 2016, the average price of each Bitcoin in the exchanges was $791. A year later, on the same day, 18 December 2017, Bitcoin hit $19,758 – its all-time high price that saw an incredible yearly gain of 2397.85%. A year later on the same day in 2018, Bitcoin's price fell below $3190. Figure 4.1 shows the bumpy ride of Bitcoin in the exchanges in US dollars (USD).

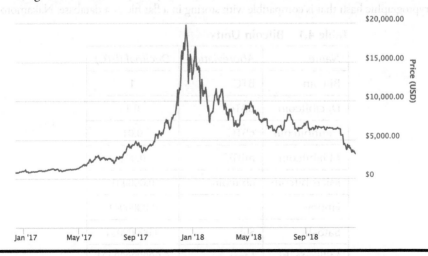

Figure 4.1   Bitcoin price from 18 December 2016 to 18 December 2018.

4.3.2 Units of Bitcoin

There are provisions for Bitcoin to be divided into smaller pieces. The smallest possible unit of Bitcoin that can be recorded on the blockchain is called a *satoshi*. It is one hundred millionth of a single Bitcoin (0.00000001 BTC). The unit has been named in collective homage to the creator of Bitcoin, Satoshi Nakamoto.

The practice in Bitcoin protocol is that all amounts are denominated in satoshi before being converted for display. The source code also uses satoshi when specifying an amount of Bitcoin. When displaying an extremely fine fraction of a Bitcoin, such as calculating fee per byte or a faucet reward, satoshi is used to display the amount. Although the satoshi is the smallest amount to be recorded in the blockchain, payment channels may need to make very granular payments and so are sometimes denominated in millisatoshi, which are one hundred billionths of a single Bitcoin.

The BTC unit was chosen to represent a value of 10^8 to give subunit precision rather than large whole numbers. Mirroring the SI unit system, this allows for divisions of 1/10 (decibitcoins, dBTC), 1/100 (centibitcoins, cBTC), 1/1000 (millibitcoins, mBTC), and 1/1000000 (microbitcoins, μBTC). The microbitcoin is also called bits. Between bits and satoshi, there exists another unit, *finney*, representing 1/10000000 of a Bitcoin. It is named after computer programmer Hal Finney, the recipient of the first Bitcoin transaction. Table 4.1 demonstrates how the BTC unit gets divided into smaller units.

4.4 Bitcoin's Blockchain

The Blockchain data structure in the Bitcoin protocol represents a linear list linked by the cryptographic hash that is compatible with storing in a flat file or a database. Nakamoto

Table 4.1 Bitcoin Units

Name	Abbreviation	Decimal (BTC)
Bitcoin	BTC	1
Decibitcoin	dBTC	0.1
Centibitcoin	cBTC	0.01
Millibitcoin	mBTC	0.001
Microbitcoin	μbitcoin	0.000001
Finney	—	0.0000001
Satoshi	Sat	0.00000001
Millisatoshi	Msat	0.00000000001

blends the ideas of linked timestamping and Hashcash-like proof of work in creating this distributed ledger, the main innovation introduced by Bitcoin. The first three chapters of this book offered a review of this ledger but did not provide a real example explaining its functions. This chapter presents the nitty-gritty details of Bitcoin's blockchain and how this ledger helps the protocol to transfer money over a digital medium.

4.4.1 Block Header

In the blockchain, each block contains a block header and a Merkle tree to store the transactions. The block header is comprised of seven fields, as shown in Table 4.2. Amongst those, two 32 byte hashes (the hash of the previous block's header and the Merkle root of the native block) and two unsigned integers (timestamp and nonce) are the most notable fields. The SHA256 cryptographic hash algorithm generates the hash values in the header of the respective block. By saving the hash of the previous block's header in the header of the current block, blockchain establishes the link that is nearly impossible to break.

4.4.2 Timestamp

Each block contains a Unix time timestamp. This timestamp is the number of seconds that have passed since 00:00:00 (UTC), Thursday, 1 January 1970, minus leap seconds. In this timestamping, every day is considered to have precisely 86,400 seconds to subtract the leap seconds since the epoch.

In addition to working as a source of variation for the block hash, the timestamps also make it more challenging for an adversary to manipulate the blockchain. Bitcoin protocol considers a timestamp valid if it is greater than the median timestamp of the previous 11 blocks, and less than the network-adjusted time plus 2 hours. The "network-adjusted time" means the median of the timestamps returned by all nodes connected to a participating node.

Bitcoin uses an unsigned integer for the timestamp rather than a signed integer to avoid the Year 2038 problem, at least by some years. The maximum value that can be stored in a signed integer is 2,147,483,647. It means, after 03:14:07 UTC on 19 January 2038, the timestamp will overflow causing potential disruption in the communication and computing systems. Because Bitcoin uses an unsigned timestamp, it can store values up to 4,294,967,295 delaying the overflow by another 68 years.

4.4.3 Merkle Tree

Bitcoin employs the Merkle tree data structure to store transactions. We have already seen in Section 2.5.3 in Chapter 2 that a Merkle tree is constructed by recursively hashing pairs of nodes until the root hash is left. In this tree, every leaf node contains the hash of a transaction as its label, whereas every non-leaf node stores the cryptographic hash of the labels of its child nodes as shown in Figure 2.7

Table 4.2 Bitcoin Header Fields

Size	Description	Data type
4 bytes	Version	Signed integer
32 bytes	Previous block hash	Characters
32 bytes	Merkle root	Characters
4 bytes	Timestamp	Unsigned integer
4 bytes	Difficulty bits	Unsigned integer
4 bytes	Nonce	Unsigned integer
1 byte	Transactions count	Variable length integer

(Chapter 2). Because a Merkle tree is a binary tree, if there remains an odd number of transactions to summarise, the last transaction hash will be duplicated.

Bitcoin applies the double hash of the SHA256 algorithm in its Merkle tree as it does for referencing blocks in the blockchain. The use of the Merkle tree in Bitcoin enables miners to verify the transactions efficiently and securely from a large pool of data. When N data elements are hashed and summarised in a Merkle tree, a miner can ascertain if a particular transaction is already in the tree with at most $2\log_2(N)$ number of calculations.

4.4.4 Hash Generation

A distinctive feature of Bitcoin is that when a hash is computed, it is computed twice. An example of double-SHA256 hashing is shown next:

hello

2cf24dba5fb0a30e26e83b2ac5b9e29e1b161e5c1fa7425e73043362938b9824

first round of SHA256

9595c9df90075148eb06860365df33584b75bff782a510c6cd4883a419833d50

second round of SHA256

In this example, the original text is passed through the first round's hash function, while the second round's hash function takes the hash generated in the first round as input. The construction of the Merkle tree leading to obtaining the Merkle root and the generation of the block header's hash in the Bitcoin protocol follow this procedure.

4.4.5 Genesis Block

The first block of the blockchain is called the *genesis block*. Bitcoin protocol numbers the genesis block as *block 0*, although very early versions of this protocol counted their blocks from 1. The convention in Bitcoin and all other protocols that followed suit is to hardcode the genesis block into the software of the applications that utilise the blockchain. It is a special case in that it does not reference a previous block, and for Bitcoin and almost all of its derivatives, it produces an unspendable subsidy. The hash of the genesis block of Bitcoin is

000000000019d6689c085ae165831e934ff763ae46a2a6c172b3f1b60a8ce26f

There is a special parameter in Bitcoin called the *coinbase* (a later part of this chapter explains this parameter in detail) that may contain plain text. Nakamoto inserted the following text in the coinbase of the genesis block of Bitcoin (Figure 4.3).

The Times 03/Jan/2009 Chancellor on brink of second bailout for banks

This refers to the headline of the British newspaper *The Times* published on 3 January 2009 as shown in Figure 4.2. The headline mentioning the chancellor (the British equivalent to the role of finance minister in other nations) stated the turmoil Britain had undergone during the global financial crisis in 2009. It is anticipated that Nakamoto used this reference as proof that the block was created on or after 3 January 2009, as well as a comment on the instability caused by traditional banking. It also suggests that Nakamoto might have lived in the United Kingdom [Davis, 2011].

Although the average time between Bitcoin blocks is 10 minutes, the timestamp of the next block indicates a gap of 6 full days between the genesis block and the second block in the blockchain. There exist multiple interpretations for this oddity, with one suggesting that Nakamoto might have been working on the protocol when the front page of the *Times* prompted him to release using a backdate. He then mined the genesis block with a timestamp in the past and matched the headline. Another interpretation suggests that since it was the very early days and the difficulty of the hash was high, he could have spent 6 days mining the block before proceeding to the next.

Bitcoin protocol rewarded the first 50 BTC for mining the genesis block to the following address:

A1zP1eP5QGefi2DMPTfTL5SLmv7DivfNa

The source code of the protocol exhibits a twist in the way that the genesis block reward cannot be spent. Nakamoto might have intentionally designed his protocol this way or it was accidental. There is also doubt whether Nakamoto had a private key for this specific address.

4.5 Bitcoin Address

The phrase "Bitcoin address" is somewhat misleading, as Bitcoins cannot be individually identified. The blockchain only keeps the record of the amount of Bitcoin

Figure 4.2 The headline of the British newspaper *The Times* published on 3 January 2009. This headline is used as the coinbase text in the genesis block of Bitcoin.

```
00000000   01 00 00 00 00 00 00 00   00 00 00 00 00 00 00 00   ................
00000010   00 00 00 00 00 00 00 00   00 00 00 00 00 00 00 00   ................
00000020   00 00 00 00 3B A3 ED FD   7A 7B 12 B2 7A C7 2C 3E   ....;£íýz{.²zÇ,>
00000030   67 76 8F 61 7F C8 1B C3   88 8A 51 32 3A 9F B8 AA   gv.a.È.Ã^šQ2:Ÿ.ª
00000040   4B 1E 5E 4A 29 AB 5F 49   FF FF 00 1D 1D AC 2B 7C   K.^J)«_Iÿÿ...¬+|
00000050   01 01 00 00 00 01 00 00   00 00 00 00 00 00 00 00   ................
00000060   00 00 00 00 00 00 00 00   00 00 00 00 00 00 00 00   ................
00000070   00 00 00 00 00 00 FF FF   FF FF 4D 04 FF FF 00 1D   ......ÿÿÿÿM.ÿÿ..
00000080   01 04 45 54 68 65 20 54   69 6D 65 73 20 30 33 2F   ..EThe Times 03/
00000090   4A 61 6E 2F 32 30 30 39   20 43 68 61 6E 63 65 6C   Jan/2009 Chancel
000000A0   6C 6F 72 20 6F 6E 20 62   72 69 6E 6B 20 6F 66 20   lor on brink of
000000B0   73 65 63 6F 6E 64 20 62   61 69 6C 6F 75 74 20 66   second bailout f
000000C0   6F 72 20 62 61 6E 6B 73   FF FF FF FF 01 00 F2 05   or banksÿÿÿÿ..ò.
000000D0   2A 01 00 00 00 43 41 04   67 8A FD B0 FE 55 48 27   *....CA.gŠý°þUH'
000000E0   19 67 F1 A6 71 30 B7 10   5C D6 A8 28 E0 39 09 A6   .gñ¦q0·.\Ö¨(à9.¦
000000F0   79 62 E0 EA 1F 61 DE B6   49 F6 BC 3F 4C EF 38 C4   ybàê.aÞ¶Iö¼?Lï8Ä
00000100   F3 55 04 E5 1E C1 12 DE   5C 38 4D F7 BA 0B 8D 57   óU.å.Á.Þ\8M÷º..W
00000110   8A 4C 70 2B 6B F1 1D 5F   AC 00 00 00 00            ŠLp+kñ._¬....
```

Figure 4.3 The hexadecimal version of the Genesis block of Bitcoin. Headline of *The Times* published on 3 January 2009 can be read amongst the texts.

moving from one hand to another. The address, instead of pointing the token, points its bearer. As such, a Bitcoin address is an identifier that represents a possible destination for a Bitcoin payment. For example, if Bob wants to send 10 BTC to Alice, she must provide him with an address to where Bob directs the transaction. Bitcoin protocol, using the blockchain, moves the authority of the tokens stated in the transaction from Bob to the person the address belongs to – in this case, Alice.

4.5.1 Formats

The Bitcoin address is made of 26–35 alphanumeric characters. Addresses can be generated at no cost by any user of Bitcoin using the client software, an account at an exchange or an online wallet service. It is, however, not a requirement to stay connected with the Bitcoin protocol while generating the address. It can also be created while staying entirely offline.

There are several address formats available in Bitcoin, but most transactions experience three major types. The first format is known as *Pay-to-PubkeyHash (P2PKH)*. It always begins with the numeric character of 1. The second format is known as *Pay-to-Script-Hash (P2SH)*, and starts with a 3 instead of a 1. The third format is called *Bech32* and begins with the alphanumeric characters bc1. As of December 2017, this address format is not recommended for use until more software supports the format. Examples of these three formats are shown next.

Pay-to-PubkeyHash

1BvBMSEYstWetqTFn5Au4m4GFg7xJaNVN2.

The first character is 1.

Pay-to-Script-Hash
3J98t1WpEZ73CNmQviecrnyiWrnqRhWNLy
The first character is 3.

Bech32
bc1qar0srrr7xfkvy5l643lydnw9re59gtzzwf5mdq
It begins with the alphanumeric characters bc1.

4.5.2 Hash Generation

The Bitcoin address is an identifier used for each transaction. Generally, recipients generate a brand new address each time they send an invoice or payment request. The address is the hash representation of a public key corresponding to a private key known to the rightful owner of the Bitcoin token.

While Bitcoin protocol uses a double-SHA256 hash generator algorithm to create the Merkle root or block header's hash, a shorter hash function RIPEMD-160 is applied on the first round result obtained by the SHA256 hash function. In that case, the hash of "hello" would result in the followings:

hello
2cf24dba5fb0a30e26e83b2ac5b9e29e1b161e5c1fa7425e73043362938b9824
first round hash using SHA256
b6a9c8c230722b7c748331a8b450f05566dc7d0f
second round using ripemd-160

4.5.3 Address Structure

A Bitcoin address is comprised of a hash of the ECC public key obtained from the double hashing described in the earlier section, a checksum and an address prefix to distinguish different types of addresses. The process of generating an address is illustrated in Figure 4.4. Bitcoin utilises the OpenSSL, an open-source cryptography library that implements the SSL and TLS protocols, to execute the elliptic curve cryptography. It denotes the points in an elliptic curve using a 65-byte data frame. The first byte of the frame is used to store the type of point in the elliptic curve, while the remaining 64 bytes are contributed by the x and y components of the ECC public key as described in Section 2.4 (Chapter 2).

Once the hash becomes available, a checksum of 4 bytes is added to the end of it. This checksum holds the first 4 bytes of the double-SHA256 hash of the public key. A single byte is also appended at the front containing an address prefix for each of the addresses. This value for P2PKH is 0 and for P2SH is 5, which create a leading symbol of 1 and 3 respectively.

A Bitcoin address is meant to be a single-use identifier for each transaction, although the same address can be used multiple times. The design evolved this way to safeguard users from theft and other cyberattacks. Using the identical address

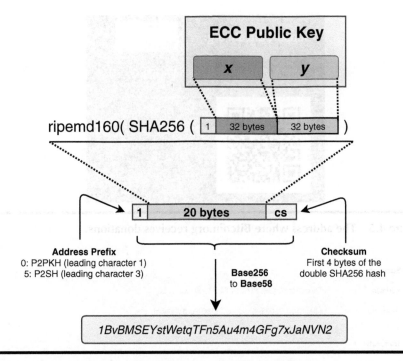

Figure 4.4 Steps showing the address generation of Bitcoin.

to accept multiple payments increases the risk of seizing the attention of hackers. Keeping many tokens under a single address also means if somehow the address gets hacked, the owner will lose everything. That said, it is not atypical finding such an address. Visiting Bitcoin.org, the original website that Nakamoto registered in 2008, shows an address where anyone can donate to support the Bitcoin ecosystem. Figure 4.5 shows the address in written form next to a QR code that can also be scanned to obtain it. Donations from around the world move to this address (Figure 4.6).

4.6 Transactions

We already learned that Bitcoin does not reside on our computer. It even does not dwell on the blockchain. Despite having no virtual presence of the token, what still makes Bitcoin real is the transactions. A transaction is a process of transferring a token that is broadcast to the network and collected into blocks. Each transaction typically references previous transaction outputs as new transaction inputs and assigns all input tokens to new outputs. Table 4.3 presents the format of a typical transaction.

Because transactions are not encrypted, it is possible to browse and view every transaction ever recorded into a block. Once transactions are buried under enough

Figure 4.5   The address where Bitcoin.org receives donations.

Summary		
Address	3FkenCiXpSLqD8L79intRNXUgjRoH9sjXa	
Hash 160	9a41c65d0622032eb35dda93d92122c3180090af	
Transactions		
No. Transactions	364	
Total Received	17.60476121 BTC	
Final Balance	14.50663051 BTC	

Figure 4.6   As of 15 December 2018, the donation address of Bitcoin.org was involved in 364 transactions receiving 17.60 BTC. Because some of the tokens were spent, the current balance of this address is 14.50 BTC.

confirmations, they can be considered irreversible. All transactions are openly visible in the blockchain and can be explored using a blockchain browser which is a site for viewing blockchain data in human-readable form. This is useful for examining the technical details of transactions in action and for verifying payments. In this book, real examples related to Bitcoin and other cryptocurrency transactions are presented using a wide range of explorers including *Blockchain.com*, *Blockcypher. com* and *Blockexplorer.com*.

4.6.1 Input and Output

A transaction is comprised of two lists, namely *TxIn* and *TxOut*, with the former being the list of inputs and the latter holds outputs of a transaction. TxIn contains the sources of the token to be used for a particular transaction and the TxOut indicates the rightful owner of the tokens after the successful execution of the

Table 4.3 Transaction Format

Size (byte)	Name	Description
4	Version	Currently 1
2	Flag	If present, always 0001, and indicates the presence of witness data.
1–9	In-counter	Positive integer
List	List of inputs	—
1–9	Out-counter	Positive integer
List	List of outputs	—
Variable	Witness	A list of witnesses, 1 for each input; omitted if flag above is missing.
4	Lock time	If non-zero and sequence numbers are less than 0xFFFFFFFF block height or timestamp when transaction is final.

transaction. The output list can have multiple addresses designating the recipient of the tokens from a transaction (Figure 4.7).

The purpose of a transaction is to access and distribute the fund from one or more old TxOuts through the TxIns of the current transaction to the new TxOut. Figure 4.7 shows a Bitcoin transaction. Let suppose, Bob sends 7 BTC to Alice in this transaction. In order for Bob to execute this transaction, he must unlock his one or more old TxOuts having the required fund. In this example, Bob utilises two old TxOuts to access 10 BTC; of those, he sent 7 BTC to Alice and 1 BTC as the transaction fee. The remaining 2 BTC return to him as change.

In this example, Bob redeemed two TxOuts to access 10 BTC. Although he was supposed to send only 7 BTC to Alice, he had to initially utilise both TxOuts followed by returning the change in the form of a payment, but this time to himself. The design of the Bitcoin protocol does not allow spending the funds of a TxOut partially; hence this approach is used. It is called "unspent transaction output" or simply *UTXO*.

Most Bitcoin transactions generally have two outputs: one is spent, and the other unspent or change to the original owner of the token. Figure 4. 8 shows a real transaction that took place in the Bitcoin network on 12 December 2018 in block 553694. This example, observed using a blockchain explorer, demonstrates that a person redeemed a previously received TxOut having 5.29309756 BTC for the TxIn of this transaction. The person then spent 1.13899376 BTC to send the amount to *37JJB- jZik...Vd7ezls*. The remaining 4.1537534 BTC moved to the

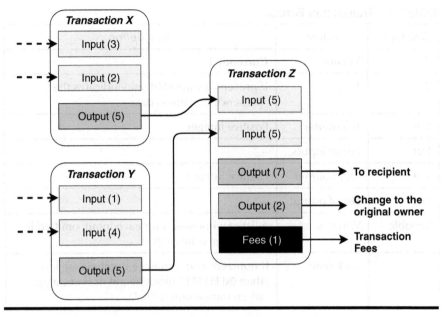

Figure 4.7   A conceptual transaction on the Bitcoin network.

original input address of *17kb7c9nd...egNkcGc,* which the person has access to. A careful look at the amount would reveal that there still remains a small portion of the token (0.0003504 BTC) that did not enter either of the TxOuts. These input tokens that had not been redeemed in an output are considered a transaction fee. The node that generates the block can claim it by inserting it into the coinbase transaction of that block. In this transaction, the transferred fund had not been redeemed until at the time of writing this chapter.

Hash	d49f085bc09ff018d43a194f91342b37e48ed20f4ac66bb03b95c0781c53f4d3
Block Height	553694 :17 (5 confirmations)
Block Date/Time	2018-12-13 22:04:50
Total Output	5.29274716 BTC
Fees	0.0003504 BTC

Inputs / Outputs   Raw Transaction

Inputs

Index	Previous output	Address	Amount
0	dbe97bbd1e56d0ea...:1 in 553693	17kb7c9ndg7ioSuzMWEHWECdEVUegNkcGc	5.29309756 BTC

Outputs

Index	Redeemed in	Address	Amount
0	Not yet redeemed	37JJBjZik2kH4j4kGUdLCkm4ZDvVd7ez1s	1.13899376 BTC
1	Not yet redeemed	17kb7c9ndg7ioSuzMWEHWECdEVUegNkcGc	4.1537534 BTC

Figure 4.8   A real transaction on the Bitcoin network.

Bitcoin Address

Summary

Address	3D2oetdNuZUqQHPJmcMDDHYoqkyNVsFk9r
Hash 160	7c6775e20e3e938d2d7e9d79ac310108ba501ddb

Transactions

No. Transactions	5589
Total Received	1,943,295.01673553 BTC
Final Balance	138,660.86136859 BTC

Figure 4.9 **The cold storage wallet of the Bitcoin exchange Bitfinex that uses a single 3-of-6 multi-signature address. As of December 2018, it contained 138,660 BTC, which will cost more than $2.5 billion if Bitcoin hits its all-time high price again.**

4.6.2 Redeeming Tokens

The transaction process we learned so far is incomplete. There remains a missing piece of a jigsaw puzzle that must be put into the right place to have the process completed. In the example mentioned earlier, Bob sent Alice 5 BTC. The transaction will only become successful if Alice can redeem those tokens. However, Bob only had Alice's Bitcoin address that he utilised in sending the tokens to her. This address contains the hash of her public key, not the key itself, making it impossible for Alice to unlock the fund using her private key. The Bitcoin address is designed this way to disguise the original identity of the recipient. However, the protocol employing a pair of scripts (scriptPubKey and scriptSig) pseudonymously identifies the rightful owner of the token.

Bitcoin uses a Forth-like stack-based scripting system that is simple, not Turing-complete and does not have loops. It is intentionally kept simple so that no attack can be launched using the native scripts. A script in this system is a list of instructions recorded with each transaction describing how the new owner can gain access to the token. Scripting also provides the flexibility of changing the parameters as to what needs to be incorporated to spend the transferred Bitcoins. For example, the scripting system can be used to enforce the necessity of two private keys, or a combination of several keys or even no keys at all. The scriptPubKey is the first half of the script that takes input from the sender, while the scriptSig is the remaining half that communicates with the recipient to unlock the funds.

Because a Bitcoin address is only a hash, Bob was not aware of the full public key of Alice and therefore could not pass it to the scriptPubKey. When redeeming the token that had been sent to Alice's address, she had to provide both the signature and the public key to scriptSig. The script first verifies that the hash of the provided public key matches with the hash in scriptPubKey, and then it checks the signature against the public key to confirm the identity of Alice. If the signature is proved to be valid, it implies the person is the owner of the private key corresponding to the public key used in the address; hence it unlocks the funds for her future transactions.

4.6.3 Multi-Signature

A multi-signature is a type of Bitcoin transaction that requires more than one key to spend the fund. It is generally used to divide up responsibility for possession of Bitcoins.

The standard transaction of Bitcoin protocol is basically a "single-signature" transaction because transfers require only one signature from the owner of the private key associated with the Bitcoin address. The protocol, however, supports more complicated transactions that require the signatures of multiple people before the funds can be transferred. These transactions are often referred to as *m-of-n* transactions. The idea is that Bitcoins become "encumbered" by providing addresses of multiple parties, thus requiring the cooperation of those parties in order to do anything with those tokens. These parties can be people, institutions or programmed scripts.

4.6.3.1 Escrow

The multi-signature endows the Bitcoin protocol with an *Escrow* service. An escrow is a contractual arrangement in which a third party receives and disburses money (or documents) for the primary transacting parties, with the disbursement dependent on conditions agreed by the transacting parties. Using multi-signature, users can create an *m-of-n* escrow in Bitcoin. For example, in a 2-of-3 escrow, Alice wants to pay Bob. She sends a transaction to a multi-signature address, which requires at least two signatures from the group of "Alice, Bob and Carol" to redeem the money. If Alice and Bob disagree on who should get the money, such as Alice wants a refund while Bob believes he fulfilled his obligations and therefore demands the payment, they can appeal to Carol. Carol then grants her signature to Alice or Bob, so one of them can redeem the funds.

4.6.3.2 Cold Storage

The multi-signature is also used to safeguard the reserved funds kept at a secured wallet. One of the most notable examples of such kind is the *cold storage* wallet. Cold storage in the context of Bitcoin refers to keeping a reserve of Bitcoins offline. This is often a necessary security precaution, especially dealing with large amounts of Bitcoins.

The following is the address of the cold storage wallet of the Bitcoin exchange Bitfinex that uses a single 3-of-6 multi-signature address:

3D2oetdNuZUqQHPJmcMDDHYoqkyNVsFk9r

As of December 2018, it contained 138,660 BTC, which will be worth more than $2.5 billion if Bitcoin hits its all-time high price again. (Figure 4.9)

4.6.4 Generation Transaction

The *generation* is the transaction that creates Bitcoin. The generation transaction is also sometimes referred to as the "coinbase transaction". It has a single input that links to no previous outputs; hence it does not contain the scriptSig. Instead, it has a unique parameter called the *coinbase*. The data in the coinbase can be anything. If we recall the genesis block of Bitcoin, the coinbase parameter of its generation transaction contains "The Times 03/Jan/2009 Chancellor on brink of second bailout for banks".

4.6.5 Storing Data

Bitcoin facilitates storing data on the blockchain in exchange for small transaction fees. It is common to find many transactions in the blockchain where output does not point to a valid address. It happens not because of an invalid address but rather the execution of these transactions is almost always intentional. Using PUSHDATA in the script, users can store 32 bytes in the blockchain. Although storage of 32 bytes capacity is too small to store anything meaningful, this can be utilised more appropriately in conjunction with cryptographic hashing. Because keeping anything on the blockchain establishes trust, a hash of a piece of data from a database can be stored in the blockchain to prove the authenticity of its generation date as well as integrity.

4.6.6 Contracts

A distributed contract is a method of using Bitcoin to form agreements with people via the blockchain. Contracts enable users to solve common problems in a way that minimises the need of trust. It makes things more convenient by allowing human judgements to be taken out of the loop, creating complete automation.

By building low-trust protocols that interact with Bitcoin, users can develop entirely new products. For example, a smart property is a type of contract-based application that can be used to automatically trade and sanction loans to customers using blockchain. Distributed markets are another example that pave the path to implement peer-to-peer bond and stock trading using blockchain technology.

It is interesting that Bitcoin was not developed to support contracts. There is no evidence that Nakamoto had this concept in his mind when he designed the protocol. It was not until the mature phase of the protocol when programmers and researchers identified this potential to extend Bitcoin's capacity beyond the currency transfer use-case. Nick Szabo was the pioneer in promoting contracts, and many of the ideas underlying Bitcoin contracts were first described by him in his seminal paper "Formalizing and Securing Relationships on Public Networks". Szabo's effort eventually led to creating the *smart contract*, a concept that encompasses the next part of this book.

4.7 Mining

The Bitcoin protocol is a decentralised protocol that operates over a distributed peer-to-peer network. This means the blockchain does not reside in a single computer, rather every node in the network keeps a copy of it. When nodes are in need of adding new blocks to the blockchain, they must cooperate to decide which block should get the chance to get included. An individual node operating in the Bitcoin network makes its own block and competes for it to be included. These nodes are also called miners and the process of building blocks is called mining. If a miner succeeds in adding a block to the blockchain, he or she receives two types of rewards: transaction fees for all transactions included in its block and the mining reward, which was 12.5 BTC at the time of this writing. Because of these incentives, many nodes join the network and become miners and help the Bitcoin protocol to keep operating through their mining service.

4.7.1 Method

There are thousands of nodes around the world regularly taking part in the mining operation of Bitcoin. These nodes are located across six continents from more than a hundred countries. Figure 4.10 demonstrates a 2018 heat map of the Bitcoin

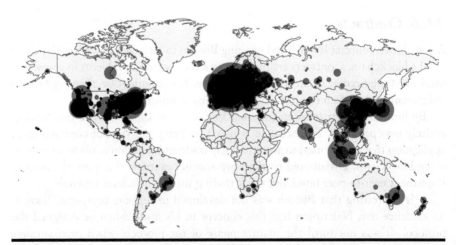

Figure 4.10   Heat map showing the presence of miners from around the globe.

Table 4.4   Percentage of Bitcoin Miners from Top 15 Countries

Rank	Country	Nodes (%)
1	United States	24.45%
1	Germany	19.26%
3	France	7.04%
4	Netherlands	4.46%
5	China	4.69%
6	Canada	3.88%
7	United Kingdom	3.50%
8	Russia	2.74%
9	Singapore	2.73%
10	Japan	2.47%
11	South Korea	1.94%
12	n/a	1.76%
13	Australia	1.65%
14	Hong Kong	1.48%
15	Switzerland	1.34%

Source: Bitnodes.

network showing nearly ten thousands of nodes mining blocks. To add more context in the discussion, Table 4.4 lists the top 15 participating nations in the mining process, while Figure 4.11 shows how the number of miners varied throughout 2018. These miners produce a block roughly every 10 minutes, but not all of them can produce one. There must be only one lucky miner whose efforts will see success and the work of the remaining miners will go in vain.

Bitcoin employs a cryptographic puzzle competition to select the lucky miner who contributes to building the immediate next block. This puzzle could be as simple as a lottery or evaluating a simple mathematical expression, but that in turn would create a problem. Amongst those thousands of nodes, there exist some dishonest nodes which might try to misuse the system by spamming or launching a distributed denial-of-service (DDoS) attack on the network. Some nodes would not even verify the transactions and build nodes with false information. So there must have been a method in place showing that any node claiming to be building a block has a genuine interest.

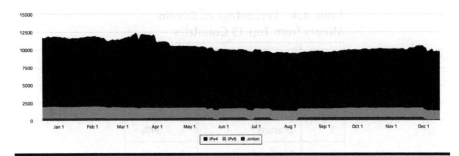

Figure 4.11   The number of miners throughout 2018.

Nakamoto utilised a Hashcash-like proof-of-work (PoW) as this puzzle. It involves producing a piece of data which is difficult (costly and time consuming) to find but easy for others to verify the required conditions. PoW in Bitcoin establishes consensus between the miners and selects the new block to add at the tail of the blockchain. In this puzzle, miners search for a target hash that fulfils a particular condition. There is no way to guess this hash, and the only option that leads to success is to go through all the hashes one after another until reaching the targeted piece. This process is both time and energy consuming, and any node that takes the effort of going through PoW demonstrates its fair participation in the process. It also prevents dishonest nodes from launching a DDoS attack on the network and exploiting the services without the support of the majority of the network.

4.7.2 Proof of Work

PoW involves miners looking for a specific hash. Table 4.2 shows the fields of a block header. Once a miner creates a new block, it gets a header of this format with real data. Because this header includes the Merkle root, its values will vary from miner to miner depending on the transactions the miners include in their blocks.

Next, each miner generates a double hash of its own header using the method described in Section 4.4.4 and verifies if it is lower than or equal to a certain hash, commonly known as the target, decided by the protocol. The target is correlated to another parameter called difficulty, which Bitcoin uses to control the difficulty of the puzzle. We learn more about this later. For now, let us consider that the required hash must be lower than or equal to the target. In the block header, there is a field called nonce that plays a vital role in this quest. Each time a miner fails to find the required hash, it increases the nonce value by one, meaning that there will be a different hash next time. This way miners continue to move forward to try to find the hash fulfilling the condition set by the protocol, i.e. lower than or equal to the target.

For example, let suppose "Hello, world!" is our base text (which in real mining operation will be the block header) and target is 2^{240}. The first three attempts result in the following:

Hello, world!0

1312af178c253f84028d480a6adc1e25e81caa44c749ec81976192e2ec934c64

$$2^{252.253458683}$$

Hello, world!1

E9afc424b79e4f6ab42d99c81156d3a17228d6e1eef4139be78e948a9332a7d8

$$2^{255.868431117}$$

Hello, world!3

ae37343a357a8297591625e7134cbea22f5928be8ca2a32aa475cf05fd4266b7

$$2^{255.444730341}$$

As none of these is smaller than the target hash of 2^{240}, the process continues by incrementing the nonce. When we reach the 4250th nonce, the result shows that it is indeed the required hash, as it is lower than the target.

Hello, world!4250

0000c3af42fc31103f1fdc0151fa747ff87349a4714df7cc52ea464e12dcd4e9

$$2^{239.61238653}$$

The miner who finds the required hash first broadcasts its block in the network for other miners to verify its proof of work. Having received the block, other miners then verify if the hash of the block header is indeed lower than or equal to the target. If that is the case, they send a confirmation to the network. Once the majority of the network confirms that the block fulfils the condition, it becomes the next block in the blockchain. All other miners disregard their work and start building a block from scratch again. They cannot keep working with their old block because of a new timestamp and possible new transactions.

If more than one miner broadcasts their blocks at the same time, all are considered the next block and added at the same height. Miners continue to build new blocks and add on to one of the blocks. This way one chain gets established, while other blocks become orphans [Jimi, 2018].

4.7.3 Target and Difficulty

The *target* in Bitcoin is a 256-bit number that miners share. It is an extremely large number. Bitcoin protocol sets the condition that the required hash must be lower than or equal to the current target for the block to be accepted by the network. The lower the target, the more difficult it is to generate a block; hence the *difficulty* is defined as a measure of how difficult it is to find a hash below a given target. The Bitcoin network has a global block difficulty that is adjusted after the generation of every 2016 blocks. It is calculated using the following formula:

$$\text{difficulty} = \text{target}_{\text{difficulty}} 1/\text{target}_{\text{current}} \tag{4.1}$$

The target$_{\text{difficulty1}}$ traditionally represents a hash where the leading 32 bits are zero and the rest are one. This is the most difficult target in the Bitcoin protocol. It is because each SHA256 hash gives a random number between 0 and the maximum value of a 256-bit number, probabilistically the lower the target, the more difficult it is to find the required hash.

Bitcoin tries to produce one block every 10 minutes to ensure the stability and low latency in transactions; hence every 2016 blocks, which should take 2 weeks, miners compare the actual time it took to generate these blocks with the 2-week goal and update the target.

4.7.4 Mining Process

We have so far learned about the blockchain, addressing, transactions and the proof-of-work system of Bitcoin. Now we combine this knowledge to understand how this protocol works as a system. Nodes willing to become Bitcoin protocol install a software called "Bitcoin Core". This software provides them with the ability to take part in the mining operations. Anyone having a Bitcoin wallet with unspent coins in it can request for a transaction.

The process starts with one single step initiated by a Bitcoin owner attempting to send Bitcoin to someone else. In doing so, an owner (let suppose Alice) signs off a transaction from her wallet application. She must have obtained the address of the person she is going to send Bitcoin to. Let's suppose it is Bob. She provides Bob's address to be inserted in the scriptPubKey script.

The wallet application broadcasts the transaction to the network. It then waits to be picked up by a miner. As long as it is not picked up, the transaction hovers in a pool of unconfirmed transactions. Miners on the network select transactions from these pools and insert them into their own blocks, which are nothing but collections of transactions with some metadata. Miners are free to select transactions of their choice. This makes multiple miners select the same transaction to include in their blocks.

We can assume that one or more miners picks up the transaction Alice sent to the network and validates if she is actually the owner of the token and not attempting to double-spend looking at the blockchain. If Alice requested a valid transaction, those miners insert it into their blocks.

Once a miner finds the required hash, the miner broadcasts the block for other miners to verify its proof of work. This verification process also verifies the transactions within making those ready to be permanently placed in the blockchain. If Alice's transaction is one of those, it becomes confirmed making Bob the new owner of the transferred token. However, if none of the miners who picked up Alice's transaction fail to find the required hash, they have to start over again and Alice must wait for at least another round of block mining.

Once the transaction becomes confirmed, Bob can check if he receives the token. If it is a simple one-to-one transaction, he will be able to redeem the fund when he initiates a transaction using his wallet. Otherwise, it remains unspent.

4.8 Split Coins and Altcoins

Bitcoin was the first application of blockchain technology and the first crypto-currency ever developed. This protocol later inspired the development of many next-generation cryptocurrencies such as Ethereum and Ripple. Between Bitcoin and these new cryptocurrencies, there exists a group of coins that are either created from a hard fork of Bitcoin, or using full or part of the source code of this pioneering cryptocurrency. The former type is known as *split coin* and the latter is called *altcoin*. A review of Bitcoin remains incomplete without mentioning split coins and altcoins, hence the remainder of the chapter briefly describes these coins before concluding the discussion on Bitcoin.

4.8.1 Split Coins

Hard forks create split coins in the Bitcoin network as a means of introducing changes in the blockchain rule and sharing a transaction history with Bitcoin up to a specific time and date. The first hard-fork splitting Bitcoin happened in August 2017 resulting in the creation of Bitcoin Cash. Later two other stable split coins, Bitcoin Gold and Bitcoin Private, were created out of hard forks that survived the initial turmoil despite suffering attacks from unknown adversaries.

4.8.1.1 Bitcoin Cash

Bitcoin Cash (BCH) is a split coin created by the fork occurring at block 478558. During mid-2017, a group of developers interested in increasing Bitcoin's block-size limit prepared a code change. Bitcoin Cash offers several new features. It has a much larger block size. Its 8 MB block is eight times bigger than a typical Bitcoin block. The new design offers replay and wipe-out protection, and a transaction signature slightly different than Bitcoin. It also adjusts the block difficulty relatively quickly compared to Bitcoin, which updates the difficulty every 2016 blocks.

The changes triggered a hard fork that took effect on 1 August 2017. As a result of these reforms, the Bitcoin ledger and the cryptocurrency split in two. At the time of the fork, anyone owning Bitcoin was also in possession of the same number of Bitcoin Cash tokens [Larson, 2017].

4.8.1.2 Bitcoin Gold

Forked at block 491407, Bitcoin Gold (BTG) was created on 24 October 2017. The stated purpose of the hard fork is to restore the mining functionality with common graphics processing units (GPUs) in place of mining with specialised ASIC-customised chipsets used for mining Bitcoin. The GPU-powered mining provides a solution to become a miner with standard off-the-shelf laptop comput-ers. As this kind of hardware is ubiquitous, anyone with minimalistic effort can

BTG Address

Summary		Transactions	
Address	GTNjvCGssb2rbLnDV1xxsHmunQdvXnY2Ft	No. Transactions	80
BTC Format	1AXpW4wvtjRZWsUvZ5JrSXS1sEr5ZsUaUc	Total Received	388,202.93071754 BTG
Final Balance	0.00 BTG	Total Send	388,202.93071754 BTG

Figure 4.12 A Bitcoin Gold address used to transfer the funds from exchanges after a successful 51% hashing attack by an unknown adversary in 2018.

join the network [Wirdum, 2017]. After the fork, owners of each BTC received a BTG token.

In 2018, the network was hit by a successful 51% hashing attack by an unknown adversary. The attackers successfully committed a double-spend attack on Bitcoin Gold and transferred millions of dollars worth of tokens from the exchanges. A Bitcoin Gold address, *GTNjvCGssb2rbLnDV1xxsHmunQdvXnY2Ft* (shown in Figure 4.12), implicated in the attack had received more than 388,200 BTG in the space of 8 days. Assuming all of those transactions were associated with the double-spend exploit, the attacker could have stolen as much as $18.6 million worth of funds from exchanges [Wilmoth, 2018a].

4.8.1.3 Bitcoin Private

Bitcoin Private (BTCP) was created out of fork at block 511346 on 28 February 2018. For each Bitcoin, an owner received 1 BTCP. Jacob Brutman, Christopher Sulmone and Rhett Creighton led the project on behalf of the Bitcoin Private Community.

The Bitcoin Private protocol gives users the choice of generating either public or private addresses, redeemable for transactions to either address type. Private addresses function using the Zero-Knowledge Succinct Non-Interactive Arguments of Knowledge (zk-SNARKs), as opposed to the older technique of ring signatures used in coins such as *Monero*. In this protocol, the evidence of ownership is given without revealing units owned by an address, allowing the owner to redeem funds without any traceable history [Brutman et al., 2018].

It was reported in October that the ethical hacker "Geocold" launched a successful 51% attack on the network to demonstrate the vulnerability of the coins having a low hash rate. It was, however, purely for educational purposes, and no significant damage was done in the network because of this attack [Teodoro, 2018].

4.8.2 Altcoins

Altcoin is a union of two words: *alt* implying "alternative" and *coin* meaning "cryptocurrency". Together these words signify a category of cryptocurrency alternative to Bitcoin. Altcoins were launched after the success of Bitcoin and generally project themselves as better substitutes to the world's first cryptocurrency. Bitcoin paved the way for many Altcoins to come into existence, but only a handful of those became successful. Altcoins typically target any perceived limitations that Bitcoin has and come up with newer versions with competitive advantages. Many altcoins are conceived using the source code of Bitcoin and often designed following the architecture Bitcoin exercised. In this section, only a handful of altcoins that successfully made a name for themselves are briefly introduced.

4.8.2.1 Namecoin

Namecoin (NMC) was the first altcoin. It was created in April 2011 intending to establish a decentralised name server. Instead of having a central authority like the Internet Corporation for Assigned Names and Numbers (ICANN) in control over the DNS, the idea was to mould this process into proof-of-work mining to release name slots with every block. Each of these slots could be used by the miner of a block to register a free .bit domain.

The problem Namecoin attempted to solve is known as Zooko's triangle. It is a trilemma stating that the names of participants in a network protocol cannot have the three following properties simultaneously: human-meaningful, secure and decentralised. This is the reason why the DNS is administered by a central authority that maps domains to IP addresses.

Despite being an excellent idea, the implementation of a decentralised, self-sufficient DNS protocol is challenging. Furthermore, registering domains and renewing them is not as simple as a regular domain name. These hurdles eventually make users less interested in using the system. A study from Princeton University found that over 120,000 domain names were registered on Namecoin in 2015. However, only 28 of those were in use, exposing the harsh reality behind the very first altcoin [Kalodner et al., 2015].

4.8.2.2 Litecoin

Litecoin (LTC), released in October 2011 soon after the release of Namecoin, is the most successful altcoin. As of December 2018, it has a market capitalisation of slightly below 3% of Bitcoin. During the early days of cryptocurrency, Litecoin was dubbed *silver* to Bitcoin's gold status.

Litecoin uses *scrypt* as its proof-of-work consensus mechanism. Scrypt is a memory-hard key derivation function proposed by Colin Percival [Percival, 2012]. It requires a fairly large volume of Random Access Memory (RAM) to be evaluated. The principle behind this technique is to limit the hash generation rate, making large-scale custom hardware attacks costly. Litecoin also aims to reduce the block generation time. With a targeted 2.5 minutes for each block, it creates blocks four times faster than that of Bitcoin. Its creators claimed that faster block generation of this coin led to faster transactions, although this may not always be true [Franco, 2015].

4.8.2.3 Peercoin

Scott Nadal and Sunny King created Peercoin (PPC) in 2012. The principal innovation that Peercoin offers is the use of a hybrid consensus mechanism using a proof-of-stake (PoS) and proof-of-work (PoW) system. In this coin, a portion of the new blocks are mined by holders of tokens in proportion to how many coins they control. Because PoS does not involve solving a partial hash inversion problem, it requires minimal electricity consumption; hence Peercoin is often regarded as the green alternative to Bitcoin.

In Peercoin there exist two types of blocks generated using PoS and PoW techniques respectively. The PoW-generated blocks follow rules similar to Bitcoin's block generation, but for PoS-generated blocks, the rules are slightly different. For these blocks, the award is distributed in a manner that is proportional to the transaction's "coin age". Coin age can be defined as follows: the product of the number of coins in the transaction output multiplied by the time since those funds were last spent [Franco, 2015]. As of December 2018, Peercoin's market capitalisation is just over 0.02% of Bitcoin.

4.8.2.4 Nxt

Nxt (NXT) was launched in 2013 by the anonymous software developer *BC-Next*. It uses the PoS system to reach consensus for transactions. The operation of Nxt requires a static money supply, but no mining process is involved in its architecture; hence 1 billion tokens were generated at the time of creation. Nxt was explicitly conceived as a flexible platform to build applications and financial services.

Nxt provides the tools to create customised tokens on the blockchain. It enables creating either assets or the more complex monetary system currencies. These tokens can be used by projects to build a bridge from the virtual world of digital currency to the real world. A token in the Nxt platform can represent anything: property, stocks/bonds, commodities, or even concepts. As of December 2018, Nxt had a market capitalisation of around 0.04% of Bitcoin.

4.8.2.5 Dash

Dash (Digital Cash) was launched in 2014 as Xcoin, but later rebranded to its current designation in 2015. It is a global payments network with a native cryptocurrency offering businesses and individuals instant payments for less than a cent per transaction. Its use-case focuses on providing users with a better way to pay and get paid.

Dash is a form of decentralised autonomous organisation (DAO) run by a subset of users known as "masternodes". Masternodes enable Dash's fast and secure payments by reaching consensus via "quorums" on the validity of transactions. The coin mining, however, still uses the PoW system using a hash function called "X11". It takes 11 rounds of hashing with an average time of 2.5 minutes to mine each coin.

Running a masternode in the Dash ecosystem requires ownership of 1000 Dash; a static IP address; and meeting the minimum requirements for CPU, RAM, disk space and network bandwidth. The distribution of the Dash token is achieved as follows: 45% of mined coins go to miners, 45% to masternodes and the remaining 10% into a fund that the DAO invests. As of December 2018, Dash has a market capitalisation of around 1% of Bitcoin.

4.9 Summary

This chapter presented Bitcoin, the world's first cryptocurrency. The discussion was limited to technical details explaining how the protocol makes use of blockchain technology and successfully establishes a decentralised currency transaction system. The chapter shed light on its history, blockchain, address, transaction, mining and altcoins. Discussions related to economic and sociopolitical topics of Bitcoin were not part of this chapter but will be covered later in the book.

SMART CONTRACTS

II

Chapter 5

Ethereum and Smart Contracts

Nakamoto developed Bitcoin as a currency transaction protocol. His design includes a Forth-like stack-based scripting system that is simple, not Turing-complete and does not have loops. It is intentionally kept simple so that no attack can be launched using the native scripts but still be able to facilitate complex transactions between multiple parties. Although there is no evidence that Nakamoto ever intended to use this feature to write contracts, developers and researchers working with Bitcoin later found it useful to extend the capacity of Bitcoin beyond a currency transaction protocol. The scripting system, however, has some significant limitations. Writing complicated contracts between multiple parties generally requires a programming language with loops and features provided by high-level languages like C, Java and Python. Because of Bitcoin's scripting system being not Turing-complete, it proves to be less effective in writing such complicated contracts. With this limitation in mind, Vitalik Buterin co-founded Ethereum, a new blockchain platform that is Turing-complete and enables users to write contracts using high-level programming languages, thus the name *smart contract*. This chapter aims to introduce smart contracts and describes how Ethereum stands out from Bitcoin and opens a new world for the development of distributed applications.

5.1 Introduction to Smart Contracts

The term contract means a legal document that binds two or more parties into a deal. In the field of distributed computing, the meaning remains almost intact with the exception that instead of a solicitor or, in the worst case, a judge to intervene and settle any dispute, this digital contract is self-sufficient to handle such situations on its own; hence the prefix *smart* arrives. More formally, a smart contract is a decentralised computer protocol that digitally facilitates, verifies and executes the agreement of a deal. Smart contracts allow the enforcement of credible transactions without third parties. The transactions of a smart contract are immutable and trackable.

5.1.1 Vending Machine Analogy

To explain the concept of a smart contract more clearly, let us reflect on an example of a vending machine as shown in Figure 5.1. If we want to buy a Coke, the process should be quite straightforward. We must insert the amount required in the device and press the desired option. The vending machine then dispenses the selected product, in this case, a bottle of Coke, and returns any change that it owes to the buyer.

In this example, despite having no formal agreement, there always remains an unspoken deal between the machine and the potential buyer. If the buyer provides the necessary money, the device will be ready to release the desired product. In the absence of a third party, the vending machine acted as the middleman and executed the deal. The role of the machine in this instance can be compared to a smart contract.

Figure 5.1   A vending machine selling cold drinks.

The problem arises when we feel the lack of trust and doubt in its operation as to what if the machine fails to deliver the product and does not release the inserted money. In case of a Coke that costs around $2, we may not care much. However, in case of buying a car using a vending machine (let suppose the machine also sells real vehicles worth of thousands of dollars), we think twice before inserting $10,000. A vending machine is operated by a third party who retains the sole control of the device. We have no reason to trust them unless they are someone well-established and reputed.

The smart contract being decentralised separates itself from all existing applications like this vending machine. Inside a decentralised and distributed smart contract with high Byzantine fault tolerance, both the data and the code are immutable and therefore it is not possible to alter the behaviour of the contract afterwards. If it is programmed to deliver a Tesla Model 3 car, it is going to deliver a Tesla Model 3 as long as it is in stock; otherwise, it returns the money. Smart contracts do not establish trust, rather they remove the need for trust from an agreement.

5.1.2 Nick Szabo and Bit Gold

Bit gold is arguably the earliest attempt at creating a decentralised digital currency, proposed by Nick Szabo in 1998. Although Szabo's scheme had never been implemented, it is regarded as the direct precursor to Bitcoin because of the many similarities between the two schemes particularly in design, transaction process and the security mechanisms.

The proof of work (PoW)–based consensus mechanism is the driving force behind both Bitcoin and Bit gold that utilises the computing power as a means of solving a cryptographic puzzle to establish the agreement between decentralised peer-to-peer participating nodes with high Byzantine fault tolerance. In the process, both create a cryptographic hash chain linking the most recent solution to its predecessor to validate transactions. Bitcoin, however, remains one step ahead of its precursor for solving the double-spending problem that Bit gold could not address at that time. Because of such close parallels between the schemes, people often speculate Nick Szabo being the anonymous Satoshi Nakamoto despite his denial. We discuss more on that in the last chapter of this book.

The main inspirations for Bit gold were the inefficiencies of the traditional financial system and the use of precious metals as currency. Traditional financial systems require parties to rely on trust in order for transactions to take place. For instance, to approve loans, the bank must trust the recipients have the ability to repay the loan, and their clients must trust that their deposits are secured and not being mishandled by banks. Dealing through trust-based systems also imports costly problems in the mix such as fraud or theft; for example, a 2009 study showed that merchants in the United States are losing approximately $190 billion a year to credit card fraud [Shaughnessy, 2011].

Too much reliance on the trust-based system and subsequent losses motivated Szabo to conceptualise a trustless system in his seminal paper "Formalizing and Securing Relationships on Public Networks" in 1997 where he described smart contracts. However, due to the lack of an implemented decentralised protocol where smart contracts can be built upon, Szabo's concept failed to come into prominence for at least a decade until Bitcoin came into being.

The scripts in Bitcoin finally paved the way for establishing contracts, although within a limited capacity. Bitcoin was never designed to support contracts, and its scripts are deliberately kept Turing-incomplete to avoid launching potential attacks from its core. This security measure in turn significantly restricts the ability to write complex and elaborate contracts using the scripting system of this protocol. After having a long debate as to whether Bitcoin needs to change its scripting system, a part of the community decided to create a new protocol, Ethereum – the world's first decentralised Turing-complete smart contract–supported protocol that successfully implemented Szabo's original concept nearly two decades later in 2015.

5.1.3 Turing-Completeness

To understand the concept of Turing-completeness, we must apprehend the *Turing machine* first. English mathematician Alan Turing designed this machine in 1936. He named it an *a-machine* where the prefix *a* stands for "automatic". The definition of a Turing machine can be the following:

> *A mathematical model of computation that defines an abstract machine, which manipulates symbols on a strip of tape according to a table of rules.*

Despite the simplicity of the model, given any computer algorithm a Turing machine is capable of simulating that algorithm's logic. Thereby it is widely regarded as the abstract model of what ultimately becomes the modern computer.

"Turing-completeness" can be interpreted as the ability for a system of instructions to simulate a Turing machine. In computability theory, a system of data manipulation rules, such as a computer's instruction set, a programming language or a cellular automaton, is said to be Turing-complete or computationally universal if it can be used to simulate any Turing machine. A programming language that is Turing-complete is theoretically capable of expressing all tasks accomplishable by computers.

5.2 What is Ethereum?

Ethereum is a protocol for building decentralised applications running on a peer-to-peer network without a central coordinator. The purpose of developing Ethereum was to create an alternative option to Bitcoin-like protocols. It emphasises the issues of rapid development time, security for small and infrequently used apps, and the capability of efficiently interacting with others. Ethereum does this by introducing an abstract foundational layer of blockchain embedded with a Turing-complete programming language. It enables users to write smart contracts and decentralised applications creating their own arbitrary rules for ownership, transaction formats and state transition functions.

Ethereum extends the concept of blockchain one step further, and instead of only validating, storing, and replicating transaction data, it also allows users to write and run computer programs. If Bitcoin is considered distributed data storage, then Ethereum is a distributed computer. The small computer programs that run on Ethereum are called smart contracts. The contracts run on the participating node's computer using the Ethereum Virtual Machine (EVM).

Ethereum is featureless or value-agnostic by nature. The developers decide what it should be used for. However, because of its decentralised nature, certain application types benefit more than others from its capabilities. Specifically, it is suited for applications that automate direct interaction between peers or facilitate coordinated group action across a network. Bitcoin could allow individuals to exchange cash without involving any middlemen like financial institutions, banks or governments. The design of Ethereum recognises that its impact can be far more than what Bitcoin achieved; for instance, asset registries, voting, governance, the Internet of Things and a wide variety of use-cases could be massively impacted by the Ethereum platform.

Ethereum was initially defined in a white paper by Vitalik Buterin in late 2013 [Buterin, 2013]. Buterin argued that Bitcoin must have a scripting language for application development, but he failed to gain an agreement, which led to him proposing the development of a new platform with general scripting language capabilities. The core Ethereum team included Buterin, Mihai Alisie, Charles Hoskinson and Anthony Di Iorio at the time of the public announcement in January 2014. The development of the Ethereum project began in early 2014 and the system went live on 30 July 2015.

5.3 Token: ETH

Ether (ETH) is the native token of Ethereum. It is used to pay fees for running smart contracts, transactions and state transitions in the protocol. As of December 2018, Ether is the third largest cryptocurrency just behind Bitcoin and Ripple, with a market capitalisation of 19.41% of the former.

5.3.1 Pre-Mining

Unlike Bitcoin, not all Ethers are created through mining. Buterin, the creator of Ethereum, is regularly criticised because of popularising pre-mining tokens and selling them through initial coin offerings (ICOs). Nakamoto's original concept was to bring Bitcoin into existence in exchange for a service, that is verifying transactions. Every Bitcoin token is created and given away as a reward to the miners. Ethereum broke this convention and created a substantial portion of its total circulation without mining. A total of 12 million tokens were pre-mined at the time of launching the blockchain, followed by creating another 60 million that were sold through an online public crowdsale in exchange for Bitcoin. As of December 2018, these pre-mined tokens account for about 70% of the total circulating supply.

5.3.2 Price

Ether is listed under the code ETH on cryptocurrency exchanges where the Greek letter xi, Ξ, denotes its currency symbol. It retained the position of the second largest cryptocurrency by market capitalisation for most of its lifetime; although recently during the latter half of 2018 it lost this position to Ripple.

Ether had been traded in the exchanges below $10 until the end of 2016, before rising to prominence in April the following year as its value continually increased, hitting an all-time high price of about $1400 on 15 January 2018. Following the crypto-market crash of the year, the price of Ether nosedived to below $100 in 12 months. Figure 5.2 shows the price of Ether in US dollars (USD) and Bitcoins (BTC) since its inception until the end of the year 2018.

5.3.3 Units

Ethereum has a metric system of denominations used as units of Ether. Each denomination has a unique name with some bearing the name of seminal figures

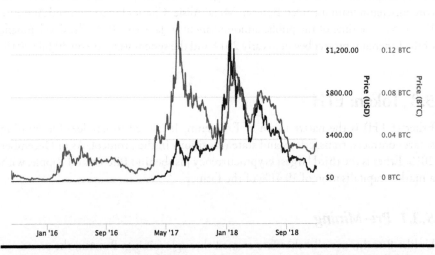

Figure 5.2   The price chart of Ether in USD (black) and BTC (grey) from August 2015 to December 2018.

Table 5.1   Ether Units

Name	Wei Value	Wei
Wei	1 wei	1
Kwei (babbage)	1e3 wei	1,000
Mwei (lovelace)	1e6 wei	1,000,000
Gwei (shannon)	1e9 wei	1,000,000,000
Microether (szabo)	1e12 wei	1,000,000,000,000
Milliether (finney)	1e15 wei	1,000,000,000,000,000
Ether	1e18 wei	1,000,000,000,000,000,000

who played a role in the evolution of computer science and crypto-economics. The base unit of Ether is called *wei* named after Wei Dai. Table 5.1 lists the named denominations and their corresponding values in wei up to Ether.

5.4 Architecture

The primary motivation of designing Ethereum was to extend the capabilities of Bitcoin, therefore, it incorporates many features and technologies that its predecessor utilised. Nevertheless, it also introduces many modifications and innovations of its own in the design. The following presents a brief introduction to the architecture of this blockchain comparing features to that of Bitcoin's.

5.4.1 Ethereum Virtual Machine (EVM)

As mentioned, Ethereum is a programmable blockchain. Unlike the Bitcoin protocol that provides users with a set of predefined operations in the form of transactions, Ethereum allows users to create operations of any complexity they want. In this sense, it serves as a platform for building decentralised applications. At its heart, Ethereum utilises a virtual machine called the Ethereum Virtual Machine or simply EVM. EVM is capable of executing code of arbitrary algorithmic complexity, or, in other words, it is Turing-complete. Developers can create applications that run on the EVM using high-level programming languages similar to JavaScript and Python.

Ethereum, like other blockchain protocols, operates over a peer-to-peer network. The Ethereum blockchain is maintained and updated by many nodes connected to the network that runs the EVM and executes the same instructions. This massive parallelisation of computing across the entire Ethereum network, however, is not arranged to make computation more efficient; rather this process slows the computation on Ethereum and making it more expensive than on a traditional computer. The advantage of such an architecture lies elsewhere: Every participating node runs the EVM in order to maintain consensus across the blockchain giving Ethereum extreme levels of fault tolerance, ensures zero downtime, and makes data stored on the blockchain forever unchangeable and censorship-resistant.

5.4.2 Account

The account is central to the design of Ethereum. It is perhaps the most notable architectural change that distinguishes Ethereum from Bitcoin. Previously we learned that transactions are the heart of Bitcoin that help track the ownership of a Bitcoin token. The Ethereum blockchain did not follow that footstep; it instead ties up all exchanges with the account to recognise the transfers of value and information. It functions with accounts and their corresponding balances in a manner called *state transition*. The state transition is a mathematical model of computation to represent the behaviour of an object, process, concept or system. It follows the states of a system through transitions and represents the changes as the system continues to function. Figure 5.3 presents a simple example explaining state transitions.

The use of state transitions in Ethereum removes the need for utilising Unspent Transaction Outputs (UTXOs) that we saw playing a vital role in Bitcoin. A state

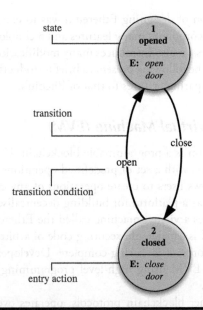

**Figure 5.3   An example of a state transition diagram showing the states of a door –
either closed or opened. Ethereum blockchain uses a similar concept in tracking
transactions.**

in Ethereum denotes the current balance of an account and relevant metadata. In order for a state to move to a new one, the network needs to reach a consensus.

Ethereum accounts can be loosely compared to Bitcoin's wallets, although they are fundamentally different. Accounts represent identities of external agents such as human personas, mining nodes and automated agents. Accounts use public-key cryptography to sign transactions so that the EVM can securely validate the identity of a transaction's sender.

There are two types of accounts in Ethereum: externally owned accounts (EOAs) and contract accounts (Contracts). EOAs are entities that trigger transactions and send tokens to another EOA. It is, in fact, the contracts that make Ethereum distinctive. If we remove contracts from Ethereum, what remains just mimics the functions of Bitcoin.

The Ethereum platform defines every account by a pair of keys: a private key and a public key, where the latter is used to generate the address of the account. The platform encodes the private key and the address pair in a keyfile of JSON format. This keyfile is human-readable, and the contents can be viewed using a text editor. Because the private key of the keyfile is sensitive, the platform encrypts it using a password provided by the user. Due to security measures, Ethereum does not allow its users to reset the account password; hence forgetting the password means losing access to the account forever.

5.4.3 Address

The Ethereum address is composed of the prefix "0x" concatenated with the rightmost 20 bytes of the Keccak-256 hash of the ECDSA public key. The following is an example of an Ethereum account which is one of the Ethereum cold storage accounts of Bitfinex that holds up nearly 2.3% of the total Ethereum circulated:

0x742d35cc6634c0532925a3b844bc454e4438f44e

A contract in Ethereum also has an address. It comes in the same format of an account address but determined by the program. A major difference between a contract address and an account address is that the former is capable of receiving both data and tokens, while the latter only receives tokens.

Any valid Keccak-256 hash in the described format is a valid address, even if it does not correspond to an account with a private key or a contract. This is unlike Bitcoin, which uses base58check to ensure the correctness of the address.

5.4.4 Mist

Unlike Bitcoin where wallet does not have a central role, Ethereum provides a native wallet called the *Mist*. It is a decentralised application that comes with a browser in addition to its wallet features. It allows users to create accounts and wallets. While creating a wallet, users have the option to create either an individual wallet or a

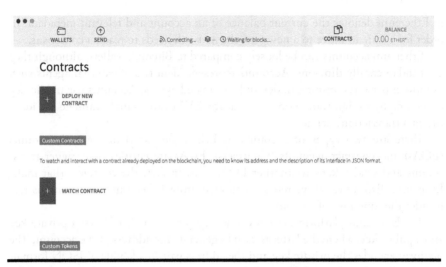

Figure 5.4   The interface of the Ethereum wallet application Mint.

multi-signature wallet. The Mist helps users to send and receive Ether, and manage contracts using a friendly interface as shown in Figure 5.4.

5.5 Mining

The Ethereum blockchain is in many ways similar to the Bitcoin blockchain, although it does have some differences. The following presents a brief introduction to transactions and the mining process of Ethereum.

5.5.1 Mining Process

Ethereum employs an incentive-driven model of security. Like Bitcoin, the consensus in this blockchain utilises choosing the block with the required hash using a PoW system where miners produce blocks and others check for validity. There has been an ongoing discussion in the Ethereum community of ditching the PoW and replacing it with proof-of-stake (PoS) model in the near future, though nothing has been finalised as of writing.

We have learned earlier that the state transitions manage transactions in Ethereum. This requires blocks to contain a copy of both the transaction list and the most recent state. The PoW algorithm used in this blockchain is called *Ethash* and involves finding a nonce input to the algorithm so that the result remains below a certain difficulty threshold. It is not drastically different from Bitcoin, but there are some features that the current blockchain incorporates. For instance, Ethash replaces SHA256 hashing with a stronger hash function called Keccak, which is the superset of SHA-3. Ethash also makes mining inconvenient for Application

Specific Integrated Circuit (ASIC) by making the process memory-hard. A desktop computer or a laptop can be more useful than ASICs in Ethereum mining. It engages a Directed Acyclic Graph (DAG)–based dataset known as the Ethash DAG that regenerates 1 GB of data every 30,000 blocks. Miners are to grab a slice from the Etash DAG to produce hashes resulting in a memory-hard job.

5.5.2 Block-Generation Rate

The protocol dynamically adjusts the difficulty of mining in such a way that on average the network produces one block every 15 seconds, a stark contrast to Bitcoin's 10-minute block-generation time. This rapid generation approach helps Ethereum achieve an excellent rate of 15 transactions per second in its blockchain.

5.5.3 Rewards

The successful miner of the winning block receives two rewards. Like the Bitcoin protocol: a reward for building the block and the fees for verifying the transactions, which in Ethereum is called *gas*. We learn more about gas in the discussion of contracts.

The block-building reward is a static 5 Ethers in addition to the cost of the gas price. An extra reward is given in Ethereum for including uncles, the orphan blocks, as part of the block at a rate of 7/8 of the regular block reward per uncle. All the gas consumed by the execution of all the transactions in the block submitted by the winning miner is paid by the senders of each transaction. The gas cost incurred is credited to the miner's account as part of the consensus protocol. Over time, it is expected that the gas cost will dwarf the static block reward.

5.6 Smart Contracts in Ethereum

A smart contract, or simply contract, is a collection of code and data that resides at a specific address on the Ethereum blockchain. Contract accounts are able to pass messages amongst themselves as well as doing practically Turing-complete computation. Contracts live on the blockchain in a binary format called EVM bytecode.

5.6.1 Transactions

A transaction refers to the signed data package that stores a message to be sent from an EOA to another on the blockchain. It contains the address of the recipient of the message in addition to a signature identifying the sender and proving their intention to send the message via the blockchain to the recipient. The value field of the transaction includes the amount of wei that the sender intends to transfer to the recipient. An optional data field is also available to send messages to the contract.

A transaction includes two special parameters representing the maximum number of computational steps its execution is allowed to take and the fee the sender is willing to pay for gas. One unit of gas corresponds to the execution of one atomic instruction, i.e. a computational step.

A contract can send messages to other contracts. These messages are virtual objects that exist only in the Ethereum execution environment. It is important to realise that a message is like a transaction but produced by a contract, not an external user.

5.6.2 Gas

Every participating node in the network runs the EVM as part of the block verification process. They go through the transaction in the blocks under verification and run the code within the EVM. Each node in the network does the same calculations and stores the same values. This practice in Ethereum is not about optimising the efficiency of computation; instead, this parallel processing is redundantly parallel. It subsists to offer an efficient way to reach a consensus on the system state without needing the presence of a trusted third party.

The redundantly replicated nature of contract executions across nodes makes them expensive; hence, it discourages users to use the blockchain for computation that can be performed off the chain. As such, decentralised applications, while interacting with the blockchain to read and modify their states, are expected to put only the business logic and states that are crucial for consensus on the blockchain.

There is a cost for every executed operation in Ethereum. It is typically expressed using *gas* units. The gas is the name of the execution fee that senders of the transaction need to pay for the operation performed on an Ethereum blockchain. The real-world analogy of fuel inspires the name gas, as this fee acts as the crypto fuel driving the motion of smart contracts.

The miners who execute the code sell gas in exchange for Ether to the users. There is a reason for keeping Ether separated from gas in this protocol. It is because the price of Ether fluctuates as a result of market forces while the miners charge a specific fee for their services. Using Ether instead of gas would have created chaos, as miners would be required to set new fees every other day. The current practice takes the conversion out of the operation, and users pay the specific fees as long as they have Ether in their account. Depending on the conversion rate of Ether for gas, their accounts get debited.

5.6.3 High-Level Languages

Ethereum supports two major high-level languages, namely *Solidity* and *Serpent*. Solidity is the most popular and the flagship language of this blockchain. It is a contract-oriented programming language for writing smart contracts on many blockchain platforms including Ethereum. A team of core contributors of Ethereum including Gavin Wood, Christian Reitwiessner and Alex Beregszaszi developed this language. Solidity is very similar to JavaScript that produces EVM bytecodes after compilation.

The other programming language, Serpent, is equivalent to Python. It combines many benefits of a low-level programming language with easy-to-use style and particular domain-specific features. Contracts written in Serpent are compiled using a low-level language called "Lisp-Like Language", or simply LLL, which is similar to assembly language. LLL is designed minimalistic and straightforward providing just a tiny wrapper over coding in EVM directly.

5.7 ERC Standards

To make smart contracts work and communicate with one another, the developers set up standards for the Ethereum platform. These standards are produced based on the feedback from the developers; hence the name "ERC" or "Ethereum Request for Comment". ERCs are application-level standards and can include token standards, name registries, and library and package formats. An ERC is written by developers in the form of a report describing the methods, behaviours, research and innovations applicable to the functioning of the Ethereum ecosystem. This report is then submitted for peer review by the network, and once approved by the developer community, the proposal becomes a standard. The following discusses some of the most popular ERC standards and their usage.

5.7.1 ERC-20

The ERC-20 is the most popular and well-known ERC standard. This is a token standard used for initial coin offerings. The advantage of this standard is that the vast majority of smart contracts and decentralised applications (DApps) is capable of interacting with ERC-20 tokens natively without the need for token details. As such, a smart contract implementing this standard can be quickly listed on an exchange platform without additional integration effort.

The ERC-20 standard contains six essential functions that must be implemented to meet the standard. The following outlines these functions:

- **totalSupply()** – Used to get the token supply of a specific ERC-20 token.
- **balanceOf()** – Keeps track of the token balance in each Ethereum wallet.
- **transfer()** – Upon token creation, this function can send all the tokens to one wallet or distribute them to ICO investors.
- **transferFrom()** – Enables token holders to exchange tokens with one another after the initial distribution occurs.
- **approve()** – Used to "approve" other accounts to withdraw a certain amount of tokens from the account calling the function.

- **allowance()** – After **approve()** is used, **allowance()** is used to see the number of tokens the approved account is allowed to withdraw from the original account.

ERC-20 tokens are easy to create and used for more than 80% of the total ICO ever took place. As of December 2018, there are more than 150,000 ERC-20 contracts deployed on the Ethereum blockchain.* Some of the most valuable ERC-20 tokens include Binance Coin (BNB), Maker (MKR) and VeChain (VEN) with market caps of $1.6 billion, $687 million and $249 million respectively.

5.7.2 ERC-223

The ERC-223 standard is a suggestion to solve some problems with the ERC-20 token. As of this writing, ERC-223 remains at the proposal stage and is not widely used. Only a few projects have decided to implement it, including MobileGo, Coss and Follow Coin.

This standard ensures avoiding accidental loss of tokens when sending to a smart contract that is not designed to work with the sent token. ERC-223 allows cancelling a transaction that would lead to such a loss of tokens before it occurs. The standard also allows reduced gas consumption during transfers compared to the ERC-20 tokens. To implement this standard, the developers have made the ERC-223 standard backwards compatible with the ERC-20 tokens. All functions of the ERC-20 tokens work with the ERC-223 tokens.

5.7.3 ERC-721

The primary motivation behind suggesting the ERC-721 standard was to create a non-fungible token (NFT) which is unique and non-divisible. ERC-20 or 223 provides a stock of fungible tokens where one unit is equivalent to another. However, ERC-721 addresses use-cases that require non-identical tokens with specific parameters and a different value.

The most famous example of the use of this standard is for the blockchain-based video game *CryptoKitties* that raised $12.5 million in investments. ERC-721 can also be used in many other areas such as software license and digital art management. Unlike ERC-20 tokens, which are present on the leading trading platforms, ERC-721 tokens can be traded in marketplaces specialising in the sale of collectables such as Rarebits, Opensea and Emoon.

---

* The total number of tokens on the Ethereum blockchain can be seen in the form of a ranking using the following URL: www.etherscan.io/tokens.

5.7.4 Other Standards

ERC-777 is a new standard that aims to mitigate the shortcomings of ERC-20 tokens. It takes motivation from another standard known as ERC-820 that ensures backwards compatibility with older standards. ERC-1400, proposed in September 2018, offers a common framework so that issuers, investors, wallets, trading platforms and developers can work under the same conditions.

5.8 Comparison to Bitcoin

Ethereum is similar to Bitcoin in many ways. It closely follows the design approach of Bitcoin and mimics many of its functionalities. There are, however, differences in terms of performances where Ethereum improved the quality of its blockchain significantly compared to that of Bitcoin. Although the chapter already described these contrasts between the blockchains, the following aims to summarise the differences:

- The block-building time of Ethereum is 14 to 15 seconds, compared with 10 minutes for Bitcoin.
- Mining of Ether generates new coins at a usually consistent rate, occasionally changing during hard forks, while for Bitcoin the rate halves every 4 years.
- For proof of work, Ethereum uses the Ethash algorithm, which reduces the advantage of specialised ASICs in mining. Bitcoin uses a regular Hashcash-like proof of work that encourages the use of specialised ASICs.
- Transaction fees (known as gas) in Ethereum differ by computational complexity, bandwidth use and storage needs, while Bitcoin transactions compete using transaction size in bytes.
- Ethereum gas units each have a price that can be specified in a transaction. This is typically measured in gwei. Bitcoin transactions usually have fees specified in satoshis per byte.
- Transaction fees are generally considerably lower for Ether than for Bitcoin. During the cryptocurrency bull run in December 2017, the median transaction fee for Ether corresponded to $0.33, while for Bitcoin it corresponded to $23.
- Ethereum uses an accounting system where values in wei are debited from accounts and credited to another, as opposed to Bitcoin's UTXO system, which is more analogous to spending cash and receiving change in return.

5.9 Summary

This chapter presented Ethereum, the world's first smart contract–supported blockchain platform. Because this new blockchain is designed following the footsteps of

Bitcoin, the discussions of this chapter frequently compared this new blockchain with its predecessor. It introduced the concept of a smart contract followed by describing the Ethereum platform, its native token, architecture, mining process and ERC standards. The chapter concluded with a comparison between Bitcoin and Ethereum blockchain to give users the necessary idssswea of how this new blockchain extended the capacity of Bitcoin.

Chapter 6

NEO

Ethereum revolutionised blockchain technology by introducing the concept of smart contracts and proves that this innovative technology is far more capable than just being a currency transaction protocol. Following the success of Ethereum, many blockchain platforms adapted its concept and made the smart contract feature available in their core – NEO is one of them. This chapter intends to provide a brief introduction to the NEO blockchain platform introduced from China. The chapter seeks to describe two native tokens of this blockchain (NEO and GAS), its network, its customised consensus mechanism commonly known as dBFT and its ability to support smart contracts with a wide range of programming languages. The focus will be given to introducing readers to the technical details of the NEO blockchain and how it works. These details also help interested buyers of the NEO token to understand the potential of this blockchain and evaluate its future.

6.1 What is NEO?

NEO is a blockchain platform and cryptocurrency designed to build a scalable network of decentralised applications [NEO, 2014]. It supports a wide range of commonly used programming languages including JavaScript, C#, Python, Java and Go. Using a customised version of Docker called NeoVM, the blockchain platform compiles the code into a secure executable environment to run applications.

NEO is often regarded as the Chinese reply to Ethereum and called "Ethereum's killer" [Khatwani, 2018]. It was originally launched in 2014 as *AntShares* to become the first open-source blockchain project in China. The founders, Da Hongfei and Erik Zhang, thought of an economy where digital and real-life assets are traded on the blockchain. AntShares was a reply to the problems caused by China's Digital Signature Act 2005, which allowed people to sign legal documents digitally.

109

Hongfei and Zhang presented an ideal solution to these identity verification problems using this blockchain.

Their intention was always to build a government-compliant blockchain so that companies can legally develop their contracts on AntShares. They continued with this name until 2017 when they rebranded it as NEO to give a more credible image to the company. All AntShares tokens subsequently became NEO tokens [Garner, 2018].

6.2 Token: NEO and GAS

This blockchain has two native tokens known as NEO and NeoGas, abbreviated as GAS. The former token manages the network, while the latter is the operational token to power the smart contract. Development of the NEO blockchain was motivated by and created as a competitor to Ethereum. It followed a number of footsteps of its predecessor including a gas token. In Ethereum, ETH is used as the gas token, but the NEO blockchain from the beginning kept bookkeeping and fuel tokens separate. A total of 100 million NEO tokens represent the right to manage the network where management rights include voting for bookkeeping and NEO network parameter changes. Unlike Bitcoin, ETH and many other tokens, the minimum unit of NEO is 1 meaning it cannot be subdivided. GAS has the maximum total limit of 100 million with a minimum unit of 0.00000001 GAS. This token can be utilised for fractional usage.

6.2.1 Token Generation

NEO is a pre-mined token; in the genesis block of the network 100 million tokens were generated. An equal amount of GAS will be generated through a decay algorithm in about 22 years time corresponding to each of its counterpart tokens. If NEO is transferred to a new address, the subsequent GAS will be credited to the new address.

GAS is generated with each new block. The initial total amount of GAS is zero. With the increasing rate of new block generation, the total limit of 100 million will be achieved in about 22 years. The interval between each block in this blockchain is about 15–20 seconds, meaning 2 million blocks are generated each year. The initial generation of GAS is 8 tokens per block with an annual reduction of 1 GAS per block per year to coincide with the passing of every 2 million blocks. The reduction will continue down to just 1 GAS per block and then the rate stays unchanged until reaching the 22-year milestone. After the generation of the 44 millionth block, the total number of GAS reaches 100 million, and from this point on there will be no further generation of tokens from the new blocks. According to this release curve, 16% of the GAS will be created in the first year, 52% in the first 4 years and 80% in the first 12 years. The GAS tokens will be distributed proportionally in accordance with the NEO holding ratio, recorded in the corresponding addresses. NEO holders can initiate a claim transaction at any time to receive these GAS tokens at their holding addresses.

6.2.2 Token Distribution

The distribution of the NEO token has been taking place in two phases. Amongst the 100 million tokens, the first 50 million tokens were distributed proportionally to supporters of NEO during crowdfunding. The remaining 50 million NEO, managed by the NEO Council to support NEO's long-term development, will never enter the exchanges. There are plans to use 20 million tokens to motivate NEO developers and members of the NEO Council, with another 15 million to be used for cross-investment in other blockchain projects.

6.3 Architecture

NEO is a distributed and decentralised peer-to-peer (P2P) network. Nodes that store the blockchain are called "full-node". They establish the network and share the blockchain amongst them using the P2P network. All nodes in the NEO network are equal. They act both as a client interface and as a server.

6.3.1 Basic Structure

The NEO blockchain platform has two full-node programs, namely *Neo-GUI* and *Neo-CLI*. The former has all the essential functions for the client including a graphical interface and is intended for NEO users, while the latter provides an external API for the required wallet functions and is intended for NEO developers. The CLI also helps other nodes achieve consensus with the network and is involved in generating new blocks.

The NEO network protocol provides a low-level API for some transaction types that are not currently supported by the CLI, such as claiming GAS or sending NEO without an open wallet. The CLI neither provides the required functionality to switch the wallet on or off remotely nor verifies the process when opening a wallet. Therefore, it becomes a requirement that the wallet must be kept open all the time to respond to the withdrawal requests of users.

The NEO blockchain supports running private networks (private chain), in particular for writing and testing DApps and smart contracts. A private network is a complete NEO blockchain for individuals, isolated from the public network where the owner can spin it up quickly, claim the initial 100 million NEO and experiment with all aspects of it.

6.3.2 Advanced Features

This blockchain has three advanced features under development. The first is *NeoX* that aims to traverse blockchains. It also aims to provide the much-required private–public blockchain linkages on the platform. The second feature is called

NeoFS. In the near future, this blockchain aims to support file and data storage facility for its contracts. The third and final feature is called *NeoQS*. Possibly it is not going to happen soon, but NEO has the plan to fight against quantum computing power to protect its blockchain using this feature once the new computers come into existence.

6.4 Consensus Mechanism: dBFT

The design of the consensus mechanism in the NEO blockchain is different from that of Bitcoin's and Ethereum's where proof of work is applied. NEO uses a custom-built algorithm called "delegated Byzantine fault tolerant" or simply dBFT. It is a BFT consensus mechanism that enables large-scale participation in consensus through proxy voting. The holder of the NEO token can pick the bookkeeper it supports by voting. Then the selected group of bookkeepers reach a consensus through the BFT algorithm and generate new blocks in this blockchain [Zhang, 2014].

6.4.1 Algorithm

In the NEO consensus algorithm, "consensus nodes" are those who participate in the consensus activity by verifying the validity of the transactions. These nodes are also referred to as *bookkeepers* and elected by NEO token holders. During a consensus activity, consensus nodes take turns assuming the following two roles: *speaker*, who is responsible for transmitting a block proposal to the system, and *delegates*, who are responsible for reaching a consensus on the transaction.

The dBFT algorithm ensures the security and usability of the NEO blockchain. Because erroneous nodes in the consensus can make maximum $\lceil (n - 1)/3 \rceil$ support, the functionality and stability of the system look guaranteed. In this algorithm, $n = |R|$ suggests the total number of nodes joined in the consensus making, while R stands for the set of consensus nodes. In $f = \lceil (n - 1)/3 \rceil$, f stands for the maximum number of erroneous nodes allowed in the system. In fact, the total ledger is maintained by bookkeeping nodes, while ordinary nodes do not participate in the consensus making.

All consensus nodes are required to maintain a state table to record the current consensus status. The dataset used for a consensus from the beginning to the end is called a *View*. If consensus cannot be reached within the current View, a *View Change* will be required. The algorithm identifies each View with a number v, starting from 0 and it may increase until achieving the consensus.

In this algorithm, each consensus node is identified with a number, starting from 0 making the last node numbered $n - 1$. For each round of consensus, a node plays speaker of the house, while other nodes play congressmen. The speaker's number p is determined by the following formula: hypothetically, if the current block height is h, then $p = (h - v)$ mod n, where p's range will be $0 \leq p < n$.

A new block will be generated with each round of consensus, with at least $n - f$ signatures from bookkeeping nodes. Upon the generation of a block, a new round of consensus begins, resetting $v = 0$.

6.4.2 Procedure

With block generation time interval t, under normal circumstances, a node broadcasts transaction data to the entire network with the sender signature attached. All bookkeeping nodes monitor the broadcasted transaction data independently and store it in memory. After time t, the speaker sends

$$\langle PrepareRequest, h, v, p, block, \langle block \rangle \, \sigma p \rangle$$

Having received the proposal, congressman i sends

$$\langle PrepareRequest, h, v, i, block, \langle block \rangle \, \sigma i \rangle$$

Any node receiving at least $n - f$ *block* σi reaches a consensus and publishes a full block. Following the arrival of a full block, other nodes delete the transaction in question from their memory and begin with the next round of the consensus.

It is required that for all the consensus nodes, at least $n - f$ nodes are in the same original state. This is to say, for all the nodes i, the block height h and View number v are the same.

6.4.3 Transaction Validation

Nodes, having monitored the broadcasting and received the proposal, must validate the transactions. They cannot write an illegal transaction in the memory once one of the reasons mentioned in the following is revealed. If the proposal contains an illegal transaction, that round of consensus will be abandoned and the View change will take place immediately.

A transaction is ruled illegal, if

- The data format of the transaction is not consistent with the system rules.
- The transaction is already in the blockchain.
- All the contract scripts of the transaction are not correctly executed.
- There is a multiple-spend in the transaction.

If the transaction has not been ruled illegal based on the preceding conditions, it will be ruled legal.

6.4.4 View Change

If, after $(2v + 1) \times t$ time interval, the nodes cannot reach a consensus or should they receive proposals that contain illegal transactions, the View Change will take place as follows (Figure 6.1):

1. Given $k = 1$, $vk = v + k$.
2. Node i sends View Change request $\langle ChangeView, h, v, i, vk \rangle$
3. Once any node receives at least $n - f$ same vk from different i, the View Change ends. Set $v = vk$ and the consensus begins.
4. If, after $(2v + 1) \times t$ time interval, the View Change does not complete, the k increases and the process returns to the step 2 (Figure 6.1).

6.4.5 Fault Tolerance and Transaction Time

The dBFT provides Byzantine fault tolerance of $\lfloor (n - 1)/3 \rfloor$ for a consensus system consisting of n consensus nodes. This fault tolerance also includes both security and availability, resistant to general and Byzantine failures, and is suitable for any network environment. dBFT has good finality, meaning that once confirmations are final, the block cannot be bifurcated, and the transaction will not be revoked or rolled back.

In the NEO dBFT consensus mechanism, taking about 15 to 20 seconds to generate a block, the transaction throughput is measured up to about 1000 TPS, which is excellent performance amongst the public chains. Through appropriate optimisation, there is potential to reach 10,000 TPS, allowing it to support large-scale commercial applications.

The dBFT combines digital identity technology, meaning the bookkeepers can be the real name of the individual or institution. Thus, it is possible to freeze, revoke, inherit, retrieve and transfer ownership due to judicial decisions on them. This facilitates the registration of compliant financial assets in the NEO network. The NEO network plans to support such operations when necessary.

6.5 Smart Contracts

The NEO blockchain implements smart contracts, which is much different from Ethereum. It currently runs its Smart Contract 2.0 that features three different types of contracts, namely validation contracts, function contracts and application contracts.

The NeoVM virtual machine is the contract execution environment in this blockchain that starts up fast and uses resources efficiently. It comes with support for arrays and complex data structures and enables developers to write their contracts in a wide range of programming languages. Unlike the native Solidity

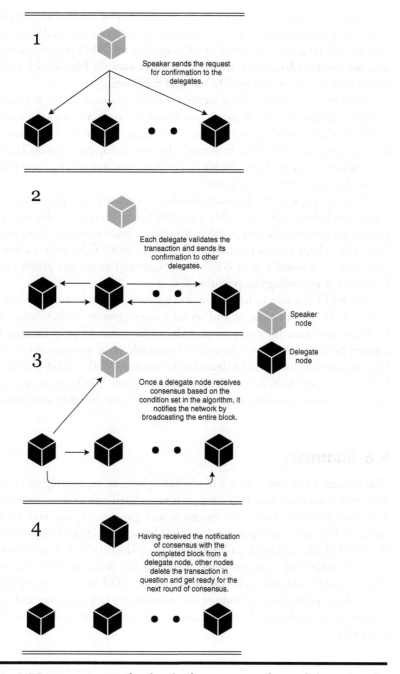

1

Speaker sends the request
for confirmation to the
delegates.

2

Each delegate validates the
transaction and sends its
confirmation to other
delegates.

Speaker
node

Delegate
node

3

Once a delegate node receives
consensus based on the
condition set in the algorithm, it
notifies the network by
broadcasting the entire block.

4

Having received the notification
of consensus with the
completed block from a
delegate node, other nodes
delete the transaction in
question and get ready for the
next round of consensus.

**Figure 6.1   NEO consensus mechanism in the presence of a no dishonest node;
hence the view change is not shown.**

language in Ethereum, the NEO smart contract can be used directly by almost any high-level programming language. The current batch of supported languages is C#, VB.Net, F#, Java, Python, JavaScript, Go and Kotlin. NEO provides compilers and plug-ins for these languages, which are used to compile high-level languages into instruction sets supported by NEO virtual machines.

NEO Smart Contract 2.0 achieves a scalable approach through a combination of high concurrency and dynamic partitioning, combined with its low-coupling design. The low-coupling contract procedure is executed in the virtual machine and communicates with the outside through the interactive service layer. Therefore, the vast majority of upgrades to the smart contract function can be done through the API of the interactive service layer.

There is a deployment fee that a developer must pay to deploy a smart contract on the blockchain. Currently, this fee is 500 GAS. There is another cost called the execution costs that the user pays for executing a smart contract. All operations in a NEO blockchain incur a fee; most defaulting to 0.001 GAS with the first 10 GAS given free. It is possible with NEO Smart Contract to achieve priority processing by manually increasing the execution fee.

The NEO blockchain has emerged as a strong contender to Ethereum in smart contracts. Its focus on assets and identity management further makes it unique for those use-cases. Its ability to provide a wide range of programming language support positions this blockchain in a favourable place amongst other smart contract–supported distributed ledgers in the market. With a solid plan for moving forward, as blockchain technology continues to grow, NEO is expected to do better and attract more consumers who will be willing to use its smart contract in future.

6.6 Summary

This chapter presented NEO, a blockchain platform supporting smart contracts. This new generation distributed ledger is considered one of the competitors to the Ethereum platform; hence the emphasis was given to explain how NEO stands out from Ethereum in the discussion. The chapter provided a brief introduction to the NEO blockchain by describing its tokens (NEO and GAS), networks, consensus mechanism and smart contract. Although the objective of the chapter was to inform readers with the technical details of the NEO blockchain and its underlying working principles, the body of the text can also help investors and investment enthusiasts to understand the potential of this blockchain and the intrinsic value of its token.

Chapter 7

EOS

The popularity of the smart contract in the blockchain industry attracted a good number of platforms to provide contract supports. We have already learned about Ethereum and NEO in the previous two chapters. This chapter takes the opportunity to present EOS, another blockchain renowned for providing smart contracts. EOS is one of the latest platforms to support some of the most cutting-edge features for deploying smart contracts and decentralised applications. The blockchain is not only famous for its technological excellence, but also as the most successful business project in terms of raising funds through a crowdsale. This chapter aims to explain EOS' technical details as well as how it generated a hefty $4.2 billion in capital for its operation through an initial coin offering (ICO).

7.1 What is EOS?

EOS is a blockchain protocol developed by the Cayman Islands–registered private company *Block.one*. The EOS ecosystem is comprised of two components: EOS.IO, the operating system, and Cryptocurrency EOS, its native token. The protocol emulates most of the attributes of a real computer, including CPU and GPU for processing, RAM and hard disk, with computing resources distributed equally amongst EOS cryptocurrency holders. EOS operates as a smart contract platform and decentralised operating system for the deployment of industrial-scale decentralised applications (DApps). The founders claimed that EOS is the first decentralised operating system providing the right environment for large-scale DApp development, although several other blockchain platforms also claimed to provide a similar environment, if not the same, including NEO described in the previous chapter.

The CTO of Block.one, Daniel Larimer, is the lead engineer of the development team and has some original contributions in the making of this blockchain. The delegated proof of stake (DPoS), a consensus algorithm invented by Larimer for two of his previously founded blockchains, is used as the consensus mechanism of EOS.

There exists no official full form for the EOS abbreviation. The founders have decided not to formally define it themselves either.

7.2 Token: EOS

The EOS does not have the notion of "mining" but introduces a new concept called "block producing". A *block producer* generates new blocks and gets rewarded by the creation of new EOS tokens for each block. A more detailed explanation as to how these blocks are produced and the rewards are distributed will be covered later while discussing the consensus mechanism and the reward distribution.

7.2.1 Initial Coin Offering

A significantly large portion of EOS tokens were pre-created, even before the launch of the platform, and sold through an ICO. The ICO was distributed as ERC-20 tokens by Block.one that created 1 billion tokens intending to generate an equal amount of US dollars (USD) from the sell. The tokens were sold for almost a year, the longest of any major blockchain project. It created a massive hype that led to generating $4.2 billion from the sell, and by the end of April 2018, each token hit $22.

As of December 2018, 20 people owned 60% of the total EOS tokens with 100 individuals retaining over 75% stakes [Wilmoth, 2018b] (Figure 7.1). This indicates that the success of the blockchain as an excellent business project is down to the

Figure 7.1   As of December 2018, 100 individuals owned over 75% of the tokens with only 20 people retaining over 60% of the total.

parent company Block.one who successfully targeted high net-worth individuals to sell tokens.

Such a concentration of ownership is not good for Bitcoin-like blockchain platforms, but in the case of EOS as a business project, this can be an advantage for the future development and growth of this platform. While funds gathered from most ICOs look scattered amongst small investors and crypto- enthusiasts, having high net-worth individuals with big stakes on the board can potentially bring stability in the operation. The block-building process, consensus mechanism and management operation of the EOS blockchain have a direct relationship to individuals having tokens (we learn about it in Section 7.4) making this platform more like a public limited company boardroom than a new start-up company.

7.2.2 Transaction Fees

EOS does not use transaction fees to pay for infrastructure but instead uses inflation. The practice is that users must deposit an amount (a stake) of tokens to use resources. This stake remains locked up until the resources are released. Upon releasing the resources, users get their full stake back. This approach, however, does not mean they get to use the blockchain for free. For validating transactions and producing blocks, a block producer receives a reward in EOS tokens that the blockchain generates out of nowhere; hence the concept of inflation arrives. Because of the presence of the newly generated tokens, existing EOS tokens lose value, which is the indirect price for using the blockchain [Floyd, 2018].

7.2.3 Inflation

The EOS system creates inflation of 5% each year, although the token holders can vote on decreasing or increasing the inflation rate. Of those, 1% is dedicated to funding the block producers responsible for running the blockchain, while the remaining 4% is paid into the Worker Proposal Fund (WPF). The WPF is intended to be a source of funding for community-driven ideas that help grow the ecosystem. The idea is anyone willing to offer a service would be able to serve the community using this fund. It is still a matter of debate whether EOS needs this option and the large volume of reserves kept for this fund [Yi, 2018].

7.3 Architecture

Two groups of nodes form the EOS network. The first is individuals having EOS tokens, who have the supreme power in the network. The EOS blockchain operates based on the selection of *delegates* who produce blocks. Token holders are the entities who retain voting power and select delegates. Token holders' strength is determined by how many tokens they hold. This means that nodes with greater tokens influence the network more than nodes having fewer tokens.

The second is the block producers who run the election in a bid to becoming a delegate. There runs a continuous approval voting system in this blockchain where anyone may choose to participate to become a block producer. Once elected, they are called delegates and given the opportunity to produce blocks. The election in EOS is an open and free process where anyone can get elected provided that they can persuade token holders to vote for their nomination.

The voting system in the EOS network works because it is able to get rid of bad nodes quickly and at the same time appreciate new valuable members. The system is reliant upon active voters (token holders) in the community, hence educating them about how the system works is essential to the well-being of the blockchain.

7.4 Consensus Mechanism: DPoS

The delegated proof of stake (DPoS) was invented by Daniel Larimer who used it for two of the blockchains he founded before EOS, namely *Bitshare* and *Steemit*. It was no secret that Bitcoin mining is too wasteful of energy and needs alternatives. Larimer also realised that Bitcoin mining would become centralised in the future, with giant mining pools taking over the control of the network. Additionally, he wanted to build a system capable of handling more than 100,000 transactions per second, which Bitcoin or Ethereum are unable to support. These disadvantages led him to invent this new DPoS consensus mechanism [Konstantopoulos, 2018].

7.4.1 Algorithm

DPoS runs by using reputation systems and utilises real-time voting to form a panel of limited trusted parties. Members of this panel, known as delegates, then have the right to create blocks that they consequently add to the blockchain. This selection process prohibits untrusted parties from participating where only the panel of trusted parties takes turns creating blocks in a randomly assigned order that changes with each iteration [Grigg, 2017].

It is important to realise that the selected panel does not have to be highly trusted, as the block creators, or more appropriately delegates, can either successfully create or fail to create blocks. In other words, they can only insert transactions to a block or fail to do so. They do not have the power of changing the details, making them nearly harmless. In the worst case, if delegates fail to create a block, the next delegate's block will be twice the size or at least include the missing transactions, and the confirmation time will be twice the regular time. Due to the malicious delegates' behaviour being publicly visible, the community can quickly vote them out. If that happens, it will result in the delegate losing their income as delegates with no potential upside; hence this discourages such an attack.

The EOS blockchain requires delegates to create blocks exactly every half a second and one delegate is allowed to create a block at any given point in time. If the delegate fails to create the block at the scheduled time, the block for that time slot is skipped. When one or more blocks are skipped, a gap of half a second or more becomes evident in the blockchain.

7.4.2 Procedure

DPoS runs in rounds of 126 where six blocks are produced each time with 21 delegates (block producers) for each block. At the beginning of each round, 21 unique delegates get selected by the token holders through voting. The scheduling of the delegates must be in an order agreed upon by 15 or more members of the delegate panel (Figure 7.2).

If delegates miss a block and it turns out that they did not create any blocks within the last 24 hours, they will be removed from further consideration until the blockchain hears from them with an intention to start creating blocks again. It ensures the network operates smoothly by identifying the delegates proven to be unreliable.

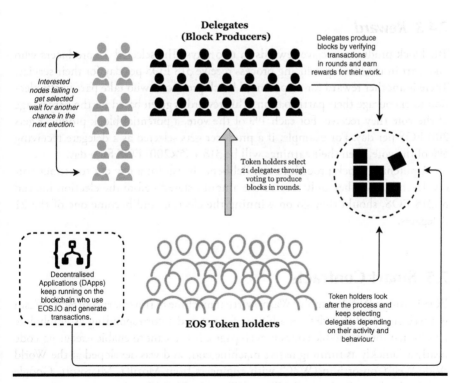

Figure 7.2   The consensus mechanism of EOS blockchain platform.

Under normal circumstances, a DPoS blockchain does not experience any forks because, rather than compete, the delegates cooperate to create blocks. In the event there is a fork, consensus will automatically switch to the longest chain. This method works because the rate at which blocks are added to a blockchain fork is correlated to the percentage of delegates that share the same consensus. In other words, a blockchain fork with more delegates will grow in length faster than one with fewer delegates because the former experiences fewer missed blocks. No delegate should be creating blocks on two forks at the same time. A delegate caught doing so is likely be voted out. Cryptographic evidence of such double-production is also used to remove abusers automatically.

The Byzantine fault tolerance (BFT) is added to DPoS by allowing all delegates in a panel to sign all blocks. It makes it impossible for delegates to sign two blocks with the same timestamp or the same block height. Once 15 delegates have signed a block, the block is deemed irreversible. Under this model, an irreversible consensus should be reachable within 1 second. A transaction can be considered confirmed with 99.9% certainty after an average of one-quarter of a second from the time of its broadcast. In addition to DPoS, EOS also adds asynchronous Byzantine fault tolerance (aBFT) for faster achievement of irreversibility. The aBFT algorithm provides 100% confirmation of irreversibility within 1 second.

7.4.3 Reward

The block producers receive rewards in two ways. The selected 21 producers who take part in the block-producing process receive 318 EOS per day for their service. There is another reward for all potential block producers who take part in the election to encourage their participation. This reward is given based on the percentage of the vote they receive. For each 1% of the vote, a potential block producer gets 200 EOS per day. For example, if a producer gets selected as a delegate receiving 5% of the vote, then their earnings will be 318 + (5×200) EOS for a day.

A potential block procedure can deliberately ask for a pay cut to attract voters. In that case, they only receive the amount stated before the election instead of 318 EOS, should they go on winning the election and become one of the 21 delegates.

7.5 Smart Contracts

EOS is using a WebAssembly (Wasm) virtual machine to run smart contracts. Wasm is a web standard that defines a binary format and a corresponding assembly-like text format for executable codes in web pages. It is meant to enable executing code nearly as quickly as running native machine code and was developed at the World Wide Web Consortium (W3C) with engineers from Mozilla, Microsoft, Google and Apple. As such, the availability of Wasm in EOS.IO means programmers are free to use any language that compiles into Wasm, although the recommended way in this blockchain's smart contract is to use the C++ library and the *eosio-cpp* tool.

In the EOS.IO smart contracts, the phrase *Action* and *Transaction* have special meaning. An Action is a call to a smart contract to give the decision as to how it should operate, while a Transaction is a collection of one or more Actions. A contract and an account communicate using two communication modes: "Inline", which is executed with the current transaction, and "Deferred", which gets scheduled later at the producer's discretion.

7.6 EOS.IO Operating System

The development of EOS.IO identifies the gap between existing platforms providing business applications and established centralised applications such as eBay, Uber, Airbnb and Facebook, and intends to mitigate that gap. As such, these centralised use-cases require handling tens of millions of active daily users, and in some instances, an application may not work unless a critical mass of users is reached. The EOS operating system aims to provide the platform that can handle vast numbers of users with low latency of transactions [EOS, 2018].

There are three broad categories of resources that applications can potentially consume. They are bandwidth and log storage (Disk); computation and computational backlog (CPU); and state storage (RAM). Bandwidth and computation have two components: instantaneous usage and long-term usage. The blockchain maintains a log of all actions that all full nodes store. With this log, it is possible to reconstruct the state of all applications.

Blockchain state storage is information that is accessible from application logic. It includes information such as order books and account balances. If an application never reads the state, then that information should not be stored.

Block producers publish their available capacity for bandwidth, computation and state. The EOS.IO allows each account to consume a percentage of the available capacity proportional to the number of tokens held in a 3-day staking contract. For example, if an account holds 1% of the total tokens, then that account has the potential to utilise 1% of the state storage capacity.

7.6.1 Schema-Defined Actions and Database

In EOS.IO, Actions sent between accounts are defined by a schema which is part of the blockchain consensus state. This schema allows seamless conversion between binary and JSON representation of the Actions. The database state is also defined using a similar schema. This ensures that all data stored by all applications is in a format that can be interpreted as human readable JSON, but stored and manipulated with the efficiency of binary. Developing smart contracts requires a defined database schema to track, store and find data. Developers commonly need the same data sorted or indexed by multiple fields to maintain consistency amongst all the indices.

7.6.2 Separation of Authentication from Applications

EOS.IO separates the authentication from the applications. The authentication is a read-only process of verifying that an Action can be applied while the applications do the actual work. Both calculations need to be performed in real time, but once a transaction is included in the blockchain, the authentication operation is no longer required.

7.6.3 Inter-Blockchain Communication

EOS.IO is designed to facilitate inter-blockchain communication, another name for cross-chain transactions, that makes transactions happen between blockchains, moving tokens from one blockchain to another. This interoperability between blockchains relies on a light client version of Merkle proofs, the technology at the heart of all blockchains invented by Ralph Merkle. There are several use-cases that could utilise EOS inter-blockchain communication and potentially make it easier for existing DApps utilising ERC-20 tokens on the Ethereum blockchain to port over to EOS.

7.7 Summary

This chapter presented EOS, one of the latest and most technologically developed blockchain platforms available. The blockchain is mainly designed to support large-scale DApps deployment with smart contract facilities; hence the chapter emphasised on the topics that are relevant to this objective of the blockchain. It described the architecture of the blockchain, its consensus mechanism, smart contracts and the EOS operation system. The technical details are presented in such a way that even investment enthusiasts who have little, or no knowledge of distributed systems can also comprehend the potential of this blockchain.

FINANCIAL
NETWORKS

FINANCIAL
NETWORKS

Chapter 8

Ripple

The book has so far discussed blockchain technology and its first applications to Bitcoin. It went on to introduce the concept of smart contract in the second part and explained how three new generation distributed ledgers, namely Ethereum, NEO and EOS, extended the ability of Bitcoin beyond a currency transaction protocol. In this third part, we learn about Ripple and Stellar, two new distributed ledgers that aim to extend the capability of Bitcoin as dynamic financial networks. These protocols stick to Bitcoin's original use-case of transferring funds but extend its nature from currency to anything valuable. This chapter presents the Ripple protocol, discusses financial aspects of its token XRP, and explains the technical details of the architecture and the consensus mechanism as well as describes the partnership of Ripple with various participating companies.

8.1 What is Ripple?

Ripple is a distributed payment protocol and a real-time gross settlement system. Unlike Ethereum that extended the capability of Bitcoin across various use-cases, Ripple sticks to the original objective of Bitcoin: decentrally transferring money over a digital medium. In doing so, Ripple stretches the concept of money from currency to anything valuable. It allows users to exchange their assets decentrally over a distributed network. For example, Bob lives in London and has British Airways frequent flyer miles that will expire soon. He wants to exchange these miles with someone for a Netflix membership. The Ripple protocol can help Bob to find Alice who lives in New York and has a Netflix membership for a year, but she is rather interested in exchanging the membership for frequent flyer miles because of the impending world tour she has planned with her friends. In this example, instead of exchanging currency of the same or different types, Bob and Alice will

127

be able to exchange their assets. A currency, for example Bitcoin, may form a part of the exchange if the value of the assets is not even.

From the preceding example, it is evident that Ripple needs intermediaries to facilitate such an exchange. At this point, it moves away from the original use-case Nakamoto created for his Bitcoin protocol, which was to transfer money without the help of any institution. Ripple, instead, enables banks and even non-bank financial service providers to allow their customers to use this protocol for instantly transferring funds or assets globally. The role of these institutions is not to act like a central authority in this case. Their role is merely as brokers to help customers use Ripple. If we look at the earlier example, Bob and Alice may deposit their assets to a facilitator who then finds a match for them and administrates the exchange.

Ripple protocol makes it possible to execute global financial transactions of any size in exchange for a minimal fee. The protocol supports a variety of tokens representing fiat currencies, cryptocurrencies, commodities and other specialised units (such as frequent flier miles, store-card points, mobile-phone minutes). Alongside supporting external tokens, the protocol comes with a native cryptocurrency that can be used in the transactions.

The US-based company Ripple Labs created the Ripple protocol in 2012. It is built atop a distributed open-source internet protocol. At its core, the network is a distributed shared public ledger and follows the consensus mechanism for confirming the validity of a transaction. Despite Ripple Lab creating the network, Ripple can operate without the presence of the company. Unlike Bitcoin whose main backers are crypto-enthusiasts, Ripple is heavily promoted by its parent company that successfully managed contracts with renowned banks such as UniCredit, UBS and Santander for using the protocol.

8.2 Token: XRP

XRP is the native currency of the Ripple protocol. It is currently divisible to six decimal places, and the smallest unit is called a drop with 1 million drops equalling 1 XRP. Users of the Ripple protocol are not required to use XRP as a store of value or a medium of exchange. Each Ripple account, however, is required to have a small reserve of 20 tokens.

8.2.1 Token Generation and Distribution

XRP tokens are all pre-mined at the genesis block. One hundred billion tokens were generated at the time of the creation of this distributed ledger. The design of this ledger does not allow coin mining; hence there will be no chance of having more than 100 billion XRP in existence unless a hard fork enforces generation of more coins. On the contrary, XRP has been decreasing every moment. The Ripple protocol charges a small transaction cost. This amount is, however, not given to anyone but is rather simply destroyed. The protocol does this to prevent the network from a DDoS or spam attack. This practice makes the number of XRP decline every moment. The transaction cost is designed to increase along with the load of the network. The current minimum cost is 0.00001 XRP for each transaction, but it may change if the network gets congested. As of 3 December 2017, there were 99.993094043 billion XRP in existence, and the remaining got destroyed over the last 5 years. Since no new XRP can be generated, this makes this token more scarce and benefits its holders by making it more valuable [Ripple, 2018].

The distribution of XRP tokens has been a topic of debate since its inception. The founders of the Ripple protocol retained 20% of the total XRP tokens for themselves and transferred the remaining 80% to Ripple Labs, which takes responsibility to distribute these tokens phase by phase to charities and companies using the protocol [Kurson, 2013]. When the concerns surrounding XRP supply mounted in May 2017, Ripple Labs placed 55 billion XRP (88% of its holdings) into a cryptographically secured escrow. The escrow allows it to use up to 1 billion on a monthly basis. Ripple Labs returns the unused sum at the end of each month to the escrow and starts over again the next month [Pilkington, 2017].

8.2.2 Bridge Currency

One of the functions of XRP is to bridge currencies in the absence of a direct exchange rate, for example when transacting between two rarely traded currency pairs where finding an exchange rate is not possible. Within the network's currency exchange, XRPs are traded freely against other currencies, and its market price obtained from those trade helps to create the bridge [Liu, 2015].

8.2.3 Market Capitalisation

XRP is the second largest cryptocurrency by market capitalisation. There has been competition between XRP and Ethereum's ETH to take over the second spot throughout 2018 when XRP emerged as one of the market giants (Figure 8.1). XRP initially took the second position surpassing ETH for a brief period at the beginning of 2018 but later surrendered the position when its price nosedived. As the crypto market continued to show volatility, ETH's price also dropped significantly pushing it to third place. As of December 2018, XRP and ETH were very close with Ripple's token retaining the position just behind Bitcoin [Bambrough, 2018].

8.3 Architecture

The Ripple protocol mimics an age-old informal value transfer system commonly known as *hawala* and connects financial and non-financial brokers globally to take part in the exchange of assets. Like other protocols built around distributed ledger

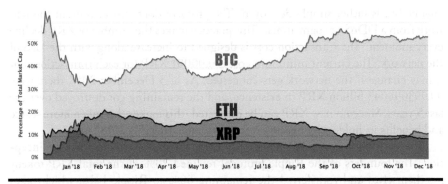

Figure 8.1   The competition between Ripple (XRP) and Ethereum (ETH) between 4 December 2017 and 4 December 2018 to become the second largest cryptocurrency by market capitalisation after Bitcoin (BTC).

technology, Ripple is also a decentralised peer-to-peer network. Its nodes are distributed around the world and decisions are made through consensus while validating transactions.

8.3.1 Hawala

Hawala originated in the Middle East but soon became popular amongst people living in and around the Horn of Africa, North Africa and the Indian Subcontinent. The literal meaning of the Arabic word *hawala* is to assign the responsibility of something to someone based on trust. During the early days of Islamic rule in the Middle East, it was unsafe for travellers to carry a large sum of money or valuable items because of the threat of theft. To prevent this problem, hawala was introduced [Thompson, 2013].

According to this system, a person approaches a hawala broker in his city (let us suppose, A) and deposits a sum of money that he instructs to hand over to someone in another city (let us suppose, B). Along with the money, the depositor provides a passcode that the withdrawer must present to verify his authenticity. The broker then contacts his peer in B City and instructs him to pay the sum to the nominated person. He also passes on to his peer the passcode for the verification of the authenticity of the withdrawer. Separately, the depositor also passes on the same information to the withdrawer located in B City. The withdrawer finally meets the broker in B City, proves her legitimacy by mentioning the passcode and collects the money. An execution of a hawala transaction is shown in Figure 8.2. It is evident from the figure that assets do not move through the transfer process. Instead, the brokers negotiate between them to continue working as a pair and execute transactions in such a way that the balance stays even on each end. The Ripple protocol takes the concept to the next level and makes it possible to transfer assets over the digital medium.

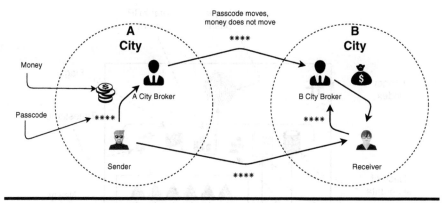

Figure 8.2   The execution of a hawala transaction.

8.3.2 XRP Ledger

The Ripple protocol provides the required distributed systems to the brokers to seamlessly transfer assets. It is comprised of server nodes connected to a peer-to-peer network. Each server in this network acts as a broker. Brokers' computers run software called "rippled" (always written with a lower-case *r* at the beginning) that powers them to connect with the network and take part in the exchange process. Globally distributed rippled servers host the ledger that contains all the transactions.

Ripple uses a distributed ledger instead of a blockchain. Although its distributed ledger has many features similar to a blockchain, it is perhaps called a ledger because of also storing state data such as accounts and balances. The name of Ripple's distributed ledger is XRP Ledger. It contains an index of the ledger, a unique hash, the hash of its parent ledger, transaction hashes, state data hashes, total ripple count, flags, and actual transactions and state data as shown in Figure 8.3 [Ripple, 2018].

The XRP Ledger has a new ledger version every several seconds. A close analogy of a "version" can be a page of a ledger book. When the network agrees on the contents of a specific version, it becomes validated. The contents of a validated version of the XRP Ledger are cryptographically secured and can never be changed.

A ledger version has two identifiers. The first identifier is its ledger index, which is a sequence number counted incrementally. For example, if the current ledger version has a ledger index of 100, the previous ledger index should be 99 and the next 101. The second identifier is a ledger hash generated based on the contents of that version.

The rippled servers keep proposing transactions to apply to the ledger. In doing so, they create several candidate ledger versions with different contents. These candidate versions have the same ledger index but different ledger hashes. Amongst the candidates, only one can become validated, and the remaining are discarded; hence there always exists exactly one validated ledger hash for each ledger index.

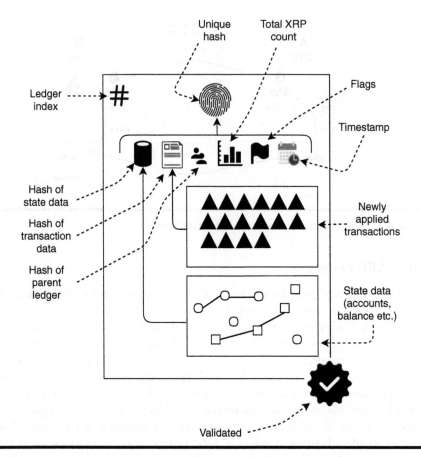

Figure 8.3   A page of the Ripple ledger showing its various components.

8.3.3 Transactions

In the Ripple protocol, the user-level changes to the ledger are the results of transactions. Transactions may occur due to making payments, changing account settings or trust lines, and offering to trade. Transactions are the only way to authorise changes to an account or to change anything else in the ledger. Each transaction authorises one or more changes to the ledger and is cryptographically signed by an account owner.

Each ledger version also contains a set of transactions and metadata about those transactions. The included transactions are those that have been applied to the previous version to create the new instance. The set of transactions incorporated in a version enables users to audit the ledger. For example, if an account balance is different in ledger N+1 than that of in ledger N, this must indicate ledger N+1 contains the transactions responsible for the change.

Applications working with rippled APIs must distinguish between candidate transactions proposed for inclusion in a ledger and validated transactions which are included in a validated ledger. Only transaction results found in a validated ledger are immutable. A candidate transaction may or may not ever be included in a validated ledger.

Ripple has a phenomenal transaction time giving this protocol an edge over existing renowned blockchain platforms. As opposed to the Bitcoin transaction time that may take up to an hour to complete a single transaction, Ripple is competent in making payments in a minute.

8.4 Consensus Mechanism: RPCA

Ripple protocol uses the Ripple Protocol Consensus Algorithm (RPCA) to reach a consensus amongst the nodes to validate the versions of the XRP Ledger. The RPCA is a Byzantine agreement (BA) algorithm where a set of previously selected trusted nodes communicate with each other to reach a consensus. Previously we learned that Ripple Ledger is comprised of a series of interconnected ledger versions. Nodes running rippled decide amongst themselves using this algorithm when to give the verdict to a version that it is validated. It cannot be changed or modified afterwards.

8.4.1 Components

Before we discuss how the algorithm works, it is necessary that the components are properly defined. Each node in this protocol is called a "server" that runs rippled. It is different than Ripple's client–server, which lets users send or receive payments or assets. The "ledger" refers to the master ledger that keeps all the transactions. An "open ledger" is the current operating status of a server where each maintains its open ledger. Transactions initiated by end users of a given server are applied to that server's open ledger. The "last-closed ledger" means the version that got validated last.

"Unique Node List" or simply UNL is a special list maintained by each server (let us suppose s). Only the votes of the members of the UNL of s (an arbitrary node) will be considered when determining consensus as opposed to every node on the network. UNL represents a subset of the network that can be considered collectively 'trusted' from the point of view of s. It must be realised that every member of UNL may not be trusted individually but collectively. s views those not defrauding the network. At the beginning, Ripple provides s with a short list to start with. This list later grows as s becomes active in the ledger validation process. Figure 8.4 shows the initial list that Ripple provides to all new servers in a text file. Ripple keeps changing this initial list but never disclosed the algorithm behind it or if there is any specific method in place at all.

```
←  →  C    🔒 https://ripple.com/ripple.txt

[accounts]
r3kmLJN5D28dHuH8vZNUZpMC43pEHpaocV

[validation_public_key]
nHB1FqfBpNg7UTpiqEUkKcAiWqC2PFuoGY7FPWtCcXAxSkhpqDkm
nHUpwrafS45zmi6eT72XS5ijpkW5JwfL5mLdPhEibrqUvtRcMAjU
nHUBGitjsiaiMJBWKYsJBHU2shmYt9m29hRqoh8AS5bSAjXoHmdd
nHUXh1ELizQ5QLLqtNaVEbbbfMdq3wMkh14aJo5xi83xzzaatWWP
nHUgoJvpqXZMZwxh8ZoFseFJEVF8ryup9r2mFYchX7ftMdNn3jLT

[domain]
ripple.com

[ips]
54.84.21.230 51235
54.86.175.122 51235
54.186.248.91 51235
54.186.73.52 51235
184.173.45.38 51235
198.11.206.26 51235
169.55.164.29 51235
174.37.225.41 51235

[validator_list_sites]
http://vl.ripple.com

[validator_list_keys]
ED2677ABFFD1B33AC6FBC3062B71F1E8397C1505E1C42C64D11AD1B28FF73F4734

[authinfo_url]
https://id.ripple.com/v1/authinfo
```

Figure 8.4   Unique Node List (UNL) in Ripple.

8.4.2 *Consensus Process*

The RPCA takes a procedural approach and helps servers to validate an open ledger. The consensus process in Ripple moves in rounds where each round confirms an open ledger. Before the beginning of a new round of the consensus process, each server takes all valid transactions it encountered but have not already been applied to a validated ledger. This includes both new and unsuccessful transactions from a previous consensus round.

The server then makes these transactions public in the form of a list known as the *candidate set*. There is a mandatory 2-second window for all nodes to propose their initial candidate sets in each round of consensus. It not only introduces a lower bound for each consensus round but also guarantees all nodes with reasonable latency to have the ability to participate in the process.

Once the participating servers propose their candidate sets, everyone amalgamates the candidate sets of other servers on their UNL and votes on the correctness of all transactions. Transactions that receive more than a minimum percentage of yes votes are considered for the next voting phase, while transactions that do not receive enough votes will either be discarded or included in the candidate set for the next round.

The final step of consensus goes through another voting phase for the previously selected transactions. It requires a minimum percentage of 80% of a server's UNL agreeing on a transaction to get selected. All transactions that meet this require-ment are applied to a ledger to become the last-closed ledger. Figure 8.5 shows the consensus process of Ripple in brief [Schwartz et al., 2014].

8.4.3 Correctness

For a UNL of n nodes in the network, the consensus protocol will maintain cor-rectness so long as $f \le (n - 1)/5$, where f is the number Byzantine failures. In fact, even in the face of $(n - 1)/5 + 1$ Byzantine failures, correctness is still technically maintained. The consensus process will fail, but it will still not be possible to con-firm a fraudulent transaction. Indeed it would take $(4n + 1)/5$ Byzantine failures for an incorrect transaction to be confirmed. The proof of the Byzantine fault tolerance of the RPCA can be found in Schwartz et al. [2014].

As the votes are recorded in the ledger for each round of consensus, nodes can be flagged and removed from the network for some common, easily identifiable mali-cious behaviours. These include nodes voting no on every transaction and nodes that consistently propose transactions which are not validated by the consensus.

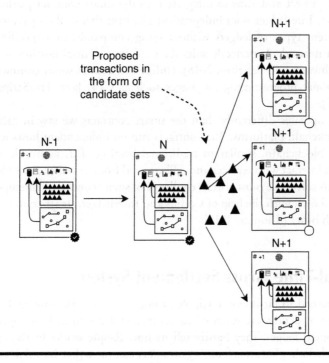

Figure 8.5   The consensus process of Ripple.

Ripple provides a curated default UNL to all new servers in a text file as shown in Figure 8.4. Ripple keeps changing this initial list but never disclosed the algorithm behind it or if there is any specific method in place at all. It, however, claimed that this default list guarantees even a naive server to participate in the consensus process and achieve correctness with extremely high probability.

Ripple also uses a network split-detection algorithm to avoid potential forks in the network. While the consensus algorithm certifies that the transactions on the last-closed ledger are correct, it does not prohibit the possibility of more than one last-closed ledger existing on different subsections of the network with poor connectivity. To try to identify if such a split has occurred, each node monitors the size of the active members of its UNL. If this size suddenly drops below a pre-set threshold, it indicates the possibility of having a split in the network.

8.5 Codius and Interledger

Ripple Labs is the developer of the *Codius* smart contract platform. The development of this smart contract was initiated in 2015 but put to a halt due to the lack of a neutral hosting platform. Later when *Interledger* became available, Ripple revived the Codius project and aims to integrate it as the smart contract platform for its XRP Ledger. Interledger is an independent platform that enables payments across many different types of ledgers without tying companies to a specific currency or payment network. It perfectly suits the need for a neutral hosting platform for Codius [Schwartz and Pestritto, 2018]. Unlike Ethereum's smart contract, Codius uses traditional programming languages such as C++, Java, JavaScript and C# [Njui, 2017].

Codius operates differently than the smart contracts we saw in Ethereum or similar blockchain platforms. The contracts run on independent hosts without an underlying blockchain, similar to traditional hosting. This approach allows the contracts to interact with services and APIs to read from or write to any blockchain. Thus Codius solves the most critical challenge of smart contracts "interoperability". Figure 8.6 shows, with the help of Codius and Interledger, smart contracts making calls to each other [Thomas, 2018].

8.6 Real-Time Gross Settlement System

We have learned so far how the Ripple protocol works at the low level. Although these technical details are essential to comprehend the underlying operations of this distributed ledger, they hardly tell us how Ripple works in the real world. Unlike blockchain platforms focusing on smart contracts that are value-agnostic by nature where developers decide what they should be used for, Ripple is a financial

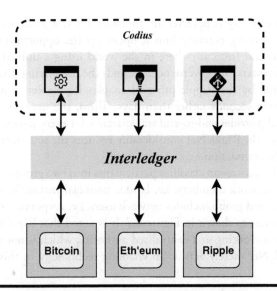

Figure 8.6   The cooperation between Codius and Interledger.

network and a real-time gross settlement system (RTGS). The primary objective of the Ripple protocol is to ensure real-time gross settlements in a few minutes. In doing so, it uses high-level components such as *RippleNet*, *xCurrent*, *xRapid* and *xVia*. The following introduces these components and explains how they are used in payment processing by the Ripple protocol.

8.6.1 RippleNet

The current practice of cross-border banking transactions is centralised, inefficient and expensive. The payment networks are fragmented between transacting institutions resulting in slow processing time and high fees that are ultimately passed down to the user. Ripple identified this payment network as a clear misfit for the growing demand for low-cost payments across the globe and came up with RippleNet. It was conceived to tackle the inefficiencies in the existing practice and change the landscape of cross-border international payments.

RippleNet is a global network of banks and financial institutions interested in sending and receiving payments through the use of Ripple's distributed financial technology. RippleNet is designed to produce real-time and low-cost payments by acting as a decentralised global network of banks and financial institutions. By eliminating the fragmentation in payment processing, RippleNet can deliver a frictionless experience for global payments. Members of RippleNet using the same technology and remaining within the same standard framework of payment rules and standards overcome the inefficiencies that a fragmented payment system produces.

The benefits of using RippleNet are fourfold. First, it gives access to a single global market, meaning entering into it opens up the opportunity to send and receive money to and from anywhere in the world using a unified framework of standard rules, formats and governance. Second, the underlying distributed ledger technology offered by the Ripple protocol enables RippleNet members to make transactions within seconds rather than days. Third, the network minimises the risk of failure and provides end-to-end transparency for every payment executed on the platform. Fourth, RippleNet considerably reduces the settlement fees and the overall cost of the transaction.

The RippleNet ecosystem classifies participants into two groups. The first group is comprised of network members, i.e. banks, financial institutions and payment providers. The second group includes network users, i.e. corporates, consumers and other similar entities as shown in Figure 8.7. It is noted that RippleNet in the figure looks as if it is working as a centralised authority, which is not the right interpretation. RippleNet merely acts as an enabling technology in this decentralised ecosystem.

8.6.2 xCurrent

xCurrent is an enterprise solution for Ripple that is responsible for facilitating the prompt settlement and end-to-end tracking of cross-border payments between RippleNet members. Four key components constitute xCurrent: Messenger, Validator, ILP Ledger and FX Ticker.

The Messenger is an API whose role is to establish links between transacting banks to serve the beneficiaries. It is the tool that initiates a transaction by exchanging beneficiary and transaction information. The role of the validator is to confirm the success or failure of a payment request cryptographically, while the ILP Ledger enables interoperation between different ledgers and payment networks. The last component is the FX Ticker that provides the rate of exchange between any pair

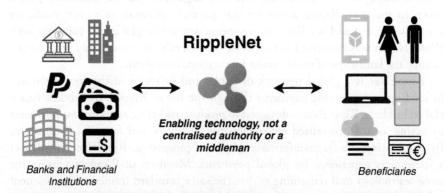

RippleNet

Enabling technology, not a centralised authority or a middleman

Banks and Financial Institutions

Beneficiaries

Figure 8.7 The RippleNet Ecosystem.

of ledgers. It also coordinates transfers on ILP Ledgers for settlement, ensures the validity of an FX quote and transfers the payment amount to the beneficiary bank's ILP Ledger [Asolo, 2018].

8.6.3 xRapid

xRapid is another settlement solution developed by Ripple that aims to makes payment even faster. From the description of xCurrent, it is understandable that this tool of the RippleNet does not need to use XRP cryptocurrency and is fully capable of working directly between fiat currency pairs. The reliance on fiat currency, however, introduces a chance of delay in case of finding an appropriate match between two rare currency pairs. The introduction of xRapid eliminates that possibility of delay by using XRP as the bridge currency; hence this tool is considered the most correlated aspect of Ripple protocol with XRP. The more partners use xRapid, the usage of XRP increases.

The operation of xRapid can be explained as follows: A financial institution first connects directly to digital asset exchanges in both the originating and destination partners. Then the originating currency is exchanged into XRP, which provides the necessary liquidity to power the final payment, and following the completion of that step, in seconds the XRP is exchanged into the destination currency in the second digital asset exchange. Once this transaction takes place, the funds are sent out on the local rails of the destination country for payout. The transaction is tracked end-to-end, and the result is a cross-border payment that is cheaper and faster than even xCurrent [Brown, 2018].

8.6.4 xVia

xVia is an API tool for the Ripple protocol that connects RippleNet with Enterprise Resource Planning (ERP), a software that allows an organisation to use a system of integrated applications to manage the business and automate many back-office functions related to technology, services and human resources. The tool is designed for corporates with large offices and not intended for the use of retail customers transferring money. It allows extending the capability of RippleNet within the ecosystem of ERP to facilitate services from both parties.

8.7 Partners

The success of RippleNet heavily depends on the participation of the partners in the network. It is not only because they act on behalf of clients, but they acting as the server nodes in making the Ripple protocol work and achieve consensus. Due to this reason, Ripple Labs continuously pushes for more partners to join the network. Table 8.1 is a list showing some of the notable partners of Ripple who have been

Table 8.1 Notable Partners of Ripple

Name	Type	Country	xCurrent	xRapid	xVia
Bank of England	Central bank	UK	Testing	—	—
Mitsubishi Corp.	Trading	Japan	Testing	—	—
American Express	Card	USA	Testing	—	—
Western Union	Transfer	USA	Testing	Testing	—
MoneyGram	Transfer	USA	Testing	Using	—
Cambridge Global	Transfer	Australia	Using	Testing	—
UAE Exchange	Transfer	UAE	Using	—	—
InstaRem	Transfer	Singapore	Using	—	Using
Deloitte	Consultancy	UK	Using	—	—
Accenture	Consultancy	Ireland	Using	—	—
Bank of America	Bank	USA	Using	—	—
Standard Chartered	Bank	UK	Using	—	—
MUFG Bank	Bank	Japan	Using	—	—
DBS Group	Bank	Singapore	Using	—	—
Santander Bank	Bank	Spain	Using	Testing	—
NAB	Bank	Australia	Using	Testing	—
Westpac	Bank	Australia	Using	Testing	—
Bank of Montreal	Bank	Canada	Using	Testing	—
BBVA	Bank	Spain	Using	—	—
Credit Agricole	Bank	France	Using	—	—
Nordia	Bank	Sweden	—	Using	—
Scotia Bank	Bank	Canada	—	Using	—
Bank Leumi	Bank	Israel	Using	—	—

(*Continued*)

Table 8.1 (Continued)   Notable Partners of Ripple

Name	Type	Country	xCurrent	xRapid	xVia
Rak Bank	Bank	UAE	Using	—	—
CBW Bank	Bank	USA	Using	—	—
Saldo	Bank	Mexico	Using	—	—
UBS	Bank	Switzerland	Testing	—	—
Credit Suisse	Bank	Switzerland	Testing	—	—
RBC	Bank	Canada	Testing	—	—
Barclays	Bank	UK	Testing	Testing	—
JP Morgan	Bank	Singapore	Testing	—	—
HSBC	Bank	UK	Testing	—	—
RBS	Bank	UK	Testing	—	—
Commonwealth Bank	Bank	Australia	Testing	—	—
ANZ	Bank	Australia	Testing	—	—
Macquarie Group	Bank	Australia	—	Testing	—
Intesa Sanpaolo	Bank	Italy	—	Testing	—
FairFX, RationalFX, Exchange4Free	Foreign exchange	UK	—	—	Using

using or testing RippleNet to send and receive money for the beneficiaries they serve. The list specifically indicates which tool – xCurrent, xRapid or xVia – they use while engaging in RippleNet. The list of all partners along with some vital information regarding Ripple and XRP can be found in the portal Rippl.Info.*

8.8 Summary

This chapter presented Ripple, one of the most popular distributed ledgers available in the industry. Instead of focusing on smart contracts, the Ripple protocol

---

* The portal is publicly accessible using the following URL: www.rppl.info.

emphasises developing asset transferring facilities in a decentralised environment. As such, the chapter aimed at providing descriptions of Ripples technical details keeping this use-case in mind. The description included introducing its token XRP, the architecture and the consensus mechanism, followed by an introduction to the partnering companies that have been using this protocol. The discussion of how blockchain can be used to develop alternative financial networks will continue to the next chapter where a similar protocol, *Stellar*, will be discussed.

Chapter 9

Stellar

If Ethereum revolutionised the path towards the smart contract, there is no doubt that Ripple deserves similar credit for popularising alternative and decentralised financial networks using blockchain technology. Established atop the foundation of Bitcoin, Ripple extended the capacity of this virtual currency by introducing mainstream partners in the network. Stellar, originally a hard fork from Ripple's distributed ledger, continues to develop on the same use-case introduced by its predecessor. The chapter presents the Stellar protocol, its native cryptocurrency Lumens, technical details of its underlying operation and its alliance with major industry partners. Because of the similarities between Stellar and Ripple, the emphasis in this chapter is to frequently compare both protocols, particularly while describing specific technical details to distinguish their performances.

9.1 What Is Stellar?

Stellar is a distributed ledger for exchanging money or tokens using blockchain technology. It aims to facilitate the cross-asset transfer of value at a fraction of a penny. The goal of Stellar is to become an open financial system that gives people access to low-cost financial services. Some of Stellar's service use-cases include remittances, micropayments, mobile branches, mobile money and distributed exchange. The co-founder of Ripple, Jed McCaleb, and Joyce Kim founded this blockchain in 2014. The non-profit Stellar Development Foundation (SDF) is responsible for the well-being of the Stellar ecosystem.

The Stellar protocol was originally a hard fork in the Ripple protocol. It was a moment of turmoil and debate surrounding Ripple due to Joyce Kim claiming to find a flaw in the initial Ripple protocol. Ripple Lab's CTO Stefan Thomas later contested this claim in favour of Ripple. In the wake of this drama, SDF was established, and a new consensus algorithm replaced the former in the fork creating 'Stellar-core'.

While sharing many affinities with other blockchain networks, Stellar does operate differently. Its peer-to-peer network is comprised of multiple servers communicating with each other every two to five seconds. Each of these servers keeps a copy of the public ledger that logs all transactions on the network. The ledger itself gets updated every few seconds.

Whenever an order pops up on the network, the Stellar protocol determines the best exchange rate for the transaction. While this could be as simple as converting one currency to another, the algorithm is capable of creating conversions passing through multiple currencies if the result is more beneficial for both parties. The Stellar protocol applies a small fee for each transaction, charged in its native cryptocurrency Lumens (XLM).

9.2 Token: Lumens (XLM)

Lumens, abbreviated as XLM, is the native token of Stellar. At the time of the launch in 2014, it was called 'stellar' but later renamed to its current designation. The Stellar protocol is designed to create all tokens at the genesis block; hence it is a 100% pre-mined cryptocurrency.

9.2.1 Generation and Distribution

At the genesis block of the Stellar network, 100 billion tokens were created as specified in the protocol. SDF is given the responsibility to ensure the fair distribution of the tokens and to look after the well-being of the network.

Following the formation, SDF was made responsible for 95 billion tokens that it will distribute over time around the world. SDF intends to distribute XLM tokens in the following manner:

- 50% via the Direct Sign-up Program. This program is an effort to make Lumens easily accessible to millions of individuals and communities across the globe. Using a simple web-based sign-up form, individuals could apply for Lumens.
- 25% via the Partnership Program to early adopters and contributors to the Stellar ecosystem, and to those who help extend the network's reach to underserved or financially excluded populations.
- 20% via the Bitcoin Program to be distributed for free to holders of Bitcoin (19%) and XRP (1%).

SDF retains the right on the remaining 5% of tokens that it holds to support the operational costs of the foundation and which it will not ever distribute to the public.

9.2.2 Price and Market Cap

Lumens had been trading below $0.002 in the exchanges until May 2017 when its value started to rise during the cryptocurrency bull run of the year. Initially, the price gained by more than 400% but soon nosedived to around $0.001 despite other major cryptocurrencies taking an active part in the rally.

The price of the XLM again started to rise in October and hit an all-time high price of $0.85 on 4 January 2018 demonstrating an 84,900% gain in three-and-a-half-months time. Following the cryptocurrency market crash of 2018, the price came down to around $0.10 in twelve months (Figure 9.1).

XLM is one of the fastest growing cryptocurrencies, and despite the volatile price, it remains one of the top 10 cryptocurrencies by market capitalisation.

9.2.3 Role of XLM in the Protocol

XLM has two roles in Stellar protocol. First, it works as a bridge currency. While discussing the application of Stellar, we learn that this protocol can enable multi-currency transactions in the network. Such a transaction requires a matching pair of currencies such as USD/GBP. In the absence of such a pair, XLM can step in and create a bridge in the form of USD/XLM and XLM/GBP to settle the payment.

The second role of XLM is to work as an anti-spam mechanism. In order to prevent denial-of-service (DoS) attacks that would inevitably occur on the Stellar

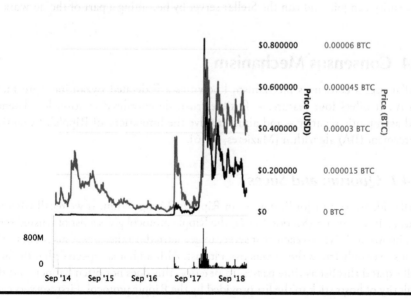

Figure 9.1 The price chart of XLM against USD (black) and BTC (grey).

network, a small fee of 0.00001 XLM is associated with every transaction that occurs on the network. This fee is small enough to affect the cost of a transaction but large enough to prevent bad actors from spamming the network. This is a common practice for its predecessor Ripple as well. However, Ripple does not give this fee to anyone; it destroys it. This makes XRP more scarce and increases the value of this token. Stellar takes a different approach and instead of destroying the tokens, puts it into a pool known as the 'inflation pool' and releases the tokens later at a rate of 1% each year through this pool to the holders of XLM token.

9.3 Architecture

Like other distributed ledgers, Stellar is a peer-to-peer network meaning it does not depend on any single entity. The idea is to have the participation of as many independent servers as possible in the Stellar network so that it will still run successfully even if some servers fail.

Stellar was a hard fork from Ripple, and therefore, the architecture looks similar. It is a distributed ledger where records are maintained like an accounting ledger book, as we saw for Ripple in the previous chapter. The Stellar ledger records a list of all the balances and transactions belonging to every single account on the network. A complete copy of the global Stellar ledger is hosted on each server that runs the Stellar software.

The architecture of this protocol is more flexible and more decentralised than its predecessor. Unlike Ripple where servers need to go through an approval process, any entity can join and run the Stellar server by becoming a part of the network.

9.4 Consensus Mechanism

Stellar uses a consensus mechanism known as a Federated Byzantine Agreement (FBA). It offers four features – flexible trust, decentralised control, low latency and asymptotic security – and aims to solve the limitations of Ripple's Byzantine Agreement (BA) algorithm [Mazieres, 2016].

9.4.1 Quorum and Slices

Stellar identifies a major limitation in Ripple's BA algorithm. If we recall what we learned in Chapter 8 (Section 8.4.2), the Ripple protocol gives a list of trusted servers, known as UNL, to each host server to get started. In the consensus process, the host server only trusts the servers from its list. Although it is expected that the host will expand this list as time passes, in practice, this does not often happen and the majority of hosts stick to the list provided by the Ripple protocol. First, servers cannot automatically join the Ripple network. They need to go through an approval process. This approach already introduces a sense of centralisation. On top of that, when the suggested UNL becomes the de facto trusted list for the majority of hosts, centralisation becomes a pivotal part of the process.

Stellar's FBA algorithm aims to solve this problem by allowing servers more flexibility. Unlike Ripple, this protocol preserves a simple entry passageway for the servers to get into the network without going through formal approvals. Once in, the servers then decide their group of trusted servers based on a concept called 'quorum slice'. A quorum is said to be a set of servers (nodes) sufficient to reach an agreement, while a quorum slice can be defined as the set of servers sufficient to convince another server of the validity of a record. Because the latter is a subset of the former, it is called a 'slice'.

Figure 9.2 shows four quorums: A, B, C and D. Quorums are formed based on the decisions of individual servers as to how they decide to trust other members. For example, n1, n2, n3 and n4 all trust one another. So they form a quorum together (Quorum A). Amongst the servers, n3 also trusts n10 and n11, but n1, n2 and n4 do not directly trust these two servers; hence they are not part of the Quorum A, but with n3 they form another quorum, D. Similarly B and C are formed.

Now let us try to understand the slices. It is easily visible from Figure 9.2 that A has three slices: (n1, n2), n3 and n4. A slice is the intersection of two quorums such as n3 between A and D, n4 between A and B, and n6 and n7 between B and C. These slices play an essential role in Stellar. If we recall, in Ripple at the time of voting, servers only accept votes from its trusted server from the UNL. However, in Stellar, slices continue to extend the boundary of trust as the network grows. For example, n1, n2 and n4 in quorum A do not generally trust n10 and n11. However,

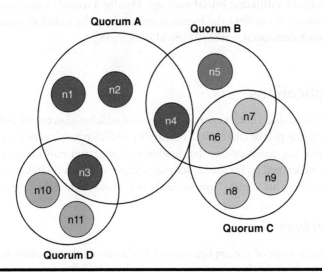

Figure 9.2 Quorum and slices as formed in the Stellar network.

as they trust n3 which trusts n10 and n11, the other servers of A now trust all servers of D.

By comparing Ripple's UNL with the quorum slice of Stellar, we observe that Stellar is more flexible in terms of allowing its servers to trust others. In this protocol, unlike Ripple, participating servers are free to decide other servers they trust, without any restrictions. Using slices, the boundary of this trust gets bigger helping the consensus algorithm to reach an agreement even quicker than its predecessor.

9.4.2 Agreement

An agreement in the FBA algorithm is achieved through federated voting. It is the method by which the participating servers in Stellar agree on a decision. It begins with initial voting, a process said to be the assurance from a server that for a specific decision it gives an affirmative verdict with the confirmation of not voting in favour of a contradictory decision. The server, however, can change its vote if enough of the other participating servers that it trusts vote for another decision.

The voting may go through three other phases: (1) acceptance, a phase where a server accepts a decision based on the decision of a contradictory statement accepted by a server from the quorum slice; (2) ratification, where all members of a quorum vote to accept a statement; and (3) confirmation, when the network agrees and confirms on a decision.

Through voting, participating servers ultimately agree on a particular decision once a sufficient threshold of messages is processed across the network. Servers propagate acceptance messages across the network from servers within their quorum. These messages could influence other servers to accept the decision even if they had accepted a different initial message. Finally, a round of confirmation messages is broadcast to confirm the message, concluding the round of voting with an agreement on a decision [Curran, 2018; Majuri, 2018].

9.5 Applications

Stellar is a decentralised currency transfer protocol which allows cross-border transactions between any pair of currencies. This ability of Stellar helps to build a number of use-cases involving currency transfer, foreign exchange and multi-currency transactions. We have learned so far the underlying technical details of Stellar and comprehended its working principles. Now we see how it works with real-world applications.

9.5.1 Anchors

Before we learn some of the applications of Stellar network, it is essential to understand anchors first. Anchors are entities in Stellar that people trust to hold their deposits and issue credits into the Stellar network for those deposits. Anchors are real financial companies based in different parts of the world. SDF makes the effort to keep partnering with anchors as the network grows. These anchors act as a bridge between different currencies and the Stellar network. All money transactions in the Stellar network, except XLM, occur in the form of a credit issued by anchors. The role of anchors, therefore, is twofold:

- They take the deposit and issue the corresponding credit to the client's account address on the Stellar ledger.
- Clients can make withdrawals by bringing credits they issued. The distributed ledger technology provides with the trust that the anchor will honour their deposits and withdrawals of credit it has issued.

The concept of an anchor is not new. For example, to use PayPal, users need to deposit money from their bank account. Following the successful deposit of the fund, PayPal gives users credits that they can use to buy products. Full or some of the unused credit users may retreat by filing a withdrawal request to PayPal that soon becomes real money in users' bank account. Anchors perform the same function in Stellar. However, the difference is that all actors (users and participating companies) including anchors are operating on the same network so that they can all transact with one another. This ability makes it easy for people to send and exchange different anchor credits with each other. Table 9.1 lists the anchors that Stellar currently has a partnership with.

9.5.2 Distributed Exchange

Stellar can be used as a distributed exchange and global marketplace for providing and accepting offers to buy and sell currencies. An offer on Stellar network can be viewed as a public commitment to exchange one type of credit for another at a predetermined rate. The ledger stores the offers that clients make and put it on the market for someone else to accept if the other party agrees to accept the rate.

Stellar maintains 'orderbooks' for all currency–issuer pairs. Offers from clients go to the relevant orderbooks that others can look up. For example, a client willing to exchange GBP/Barclays for BTC/Bitstamp must look at that particular orderbook in the ledger to see what people are buying and selling. This enables people to not only buy and sell currencies in a foreign-exchange-like manner but to also seamlessly convert currencies during transactions.

9.5.3 Multi-Currency Transactions

The multi-currency transaction is a powerful application of Stellar. The protocol allows its clients to send any currency they hold to anyone else in a different currency through the built-in distributed exchange. People can receive any currency through an anchor they add.

Table 9.1　List of Anchors on the Stellar Network

Name	Currency	Region
Stronghold	Multiple	Global
TransferTo	Multiple	Global
Clic	Multiple	Global
NaoBTC	BTC	Global
Euro Change	EUR	Global
Tempo	EUR	Europe
Anchor	CAD	Canada
Novatti	AUD	Australia
KlickEx	Multiple	Pacific Region
RippleFox	CNY	China
Sendx	SGD	Singapore
Lala World	SGD	Singapore
Money Match	RM	Malaysia
Pundi	Rp	Indonesia
Secure LC	XIM	Hong Kong
Moin	KRW	Korea
Coins.ph	PHP	Philippines
Clock Pesa	TZS	Tanzania
Celluland	NGN	Nigeria
Flutter Wave	GHS, KSH, NGN	Ghana, Kenya, Nigeria

If someone wants to send euros (EUR) using a US dollars (USD) balance to a recipient, Stellar automatically submits an offer to the distributed exchange to perform the underlying exchange on behalf of the client. In this operation, what Stellar is good at is finding the best exchange rate for the transactions so that the client sending money can enjoy the maximum benefits. Stellar performs such transactions in three possible ways:

1. *Conversion through an offer*: The straightforward option for Stellar is to find a direct offer on the internal USD/EUR exchange. If someone is waiting to buy EUR for USD, Stellar automatically makes the exchange between the two parties.

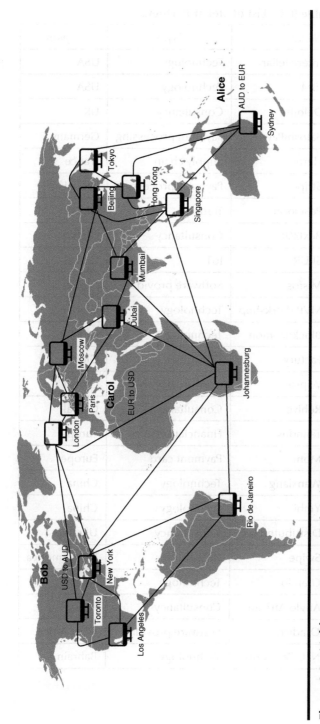

Figure 9.3 Multi-currency transactions in Stellar.

Table 9.2   List of Stellar Partners

Name	Type	Region
Inter/stellar	Technology	USA
IBM	Technology	USA
Deloitte	Consultancy	UK
SatoshiPay	Payment processing	Germany
Hijro	Supply chain	France
Stripe	Payment processing	Global
Poseidon	Trading	Global
Bext360	Consultancy	Global
SPUR	IoT	Global
Misfos	Software provider	Global
MVP Workshop	Technology	Global
Blockdaemon	Technology	Global
Factury	Consultancy	Global
Wipro	Consultancy	Global
Rehive	Consultancy	Global
Telindus	Financial service	Europe
Moni	Payment card	Europe
Wanxiang	Technology	China
Yinbi	Technology	China
Distributed Lab	Consultancy	Ukraine
Swipe	Fintech	Latin America
Gramio	Technology	Africa
Anglo African	Consultancy	Africa
Oradian	Software provider	West Africa
NEC Payments	Technology	Bahrain

2. *Conversion through compound offers*: If a direct offer does not remain available but a compound offer can be obtained out of multiple offers, Stellar takes the opportunity and settles the payment. Let us look at a more complex example in Figure 9.3 showing the Stellar network across global financial hubs. The figure shows that Alice from Sydney has an offer for EUR in exchange for Australian dollars (AUD). Meanwhile, Bob from New York places an offer for AUD but in exchange for USD. So in order to settle this payment, Stellar utilises the offer from Carol who wants to buy USD in exchange for EUR. What Stellar does next is:
   - First, it sells Alice's AUD for USD to Bob.
   - Second, it sells the USD to Carol for EUR.
   - Finally, it settles the EUR payment with Alice.
3. *Using XLM as the bridge currency*: If a direct or a compound offer cannot be found, Stellar uses its native cryptocurrency XLM to settle the payments. For a USD/EUR exchange, it first looks for offers on the network asking for USD in exchange for XLM. It simultaneously looks for an offer asking for XLM in exchange for EUR. The network makes those exchanges and completes the currency transfer request.

9.6 Partners

The success of the Stellar ecosystem depends on the participation of financial institutions in the network. These institutions are committed to supporting this new and inclusive global financial infrastructure.

SDF continually seeks to introduce new partners to use Stellar. Its effort saw many reputed institutions in addition to small and emerging financial firms joining and using the network. The network includes financial institutions, payment aggregators and technical specialists. Earlier, in Table 9.1, we learned about the partnership of Stellar with anchor companies. Table 9.2 lists some of the notable names that partnered with Staller and have been using the network for making payments and currency transactions on behalf of users or their companies.

9.7 Summary

This chapter presented Stellar, one of the leading distributed ledgers in the industry. The description included introducing its token XLM, the architecture, consensus mechanism, applications, and a brief introduction to the partnering companies and entities that have been making this protocol operational. The chapter concludes the third part of the book and wraps up the discussion of how to utilise blockchain technology to build alternative and decentralised financial networks.

ADVANCED LEDGERS AND APPLICATIONS

IV

ADVANCED LEDGERS AND APPLICATIONS

Chapter 10

Purpose-Built Distributed Ledgers

It has been only a decade since blockchain came into being, but this technology had evolved promptly from its origins. Distributed ledgers in the present day are very different than what we saw in Bitcoin. The initial proposal of Nakamoto indicated his interests in features like public availability, regulation-free and pseudonymity; however, the current trend identifies them unnecessary for many applications. Nowadays, private networks are becoming popular and industry users do not care much about the pseudonymity of the transactions. It is rather important to them that the blockchain ensures trust and enables applications with the traits necessary for the use-cases. As such, the demand for purpose-built distributed ledgers tailored to perform specific tasks is skyrocketing. This chapter takes the opportunity to present some of those platforms that have earned a reputation from both industry and academia. The chapter also briefly discusses some emerging blockchains that have the potential to disrupt the industry in the future.

10.1 Purpose-Built Ledgers and Blockchains

Existing public ledgers such as Bitcoin and Ethereum are not fast enough to provide adequate support to applications that require a response in the fraction of a second. These platforms also have scalability issues and it is difficult to browse through their data. There are initiatives to build high-level protocols to work with Bitcoin or similar blockchains such as *Lightning Network* that operate on top of Bitcoin-like distributed ledgers to enable fast transactions between participating nodes [Poon and Dryja, 2016]. Despite such efforts, seamless communication with the blockchain and scalability remain bottlenecks. Ethereum demonstrates better performance than Bitcoin but it still not considered good enough for many use-cases. Storing data on these blockchains is also a key concern due to the size and sensitivity of the materials. As blockchain has been becoming mainstream and industries are willing to adopt this new technology, the demand for purpose-built platforms is rising amid these problems.

A use-cases–specific distributed ledger opens the door to customising the platform depending on the requirements of the distinct applications at the blockchain level. It not only improves the performance but also allows introducing extra levels of security and authentication to the platform. Such an approach also aids in storing and managing data on the blockchain.

In order to give readers the idea of how these purpose-built blockchains and distributed ledgers work, the chapter identifies six areas, namely the *Internet of Things (IoT), supply chain, network connectivity, cybersecurity, private network* and *blockchain framework,* and discusses one platform from each area as shown next:

1. *IOTA*: A distributed ledger specifically designed to support IoT applications. Although there are several distributed ledgers available in the market that supports IoT use-cases, this ledger is chosen due to its unique nature of not using a blockchain-like data structure, and for a consensus mechanism that is very different from existing approaches.
2. *OriginTrail*: The author of its white paper claimed this platform to be the world's "first purpose built protocol for supply chains based on blockchain". It is also one of the most reputed blockchain platforms proposed for the supply chain industry. Despite having an even more popular platform supporting this area (VeChain), the chapter picks OriginTrail to show how multiple mainstream blockchains can be utilised to develop purpose-built ledgers. Its layer-based architecture is also suitable to show the interactions between application and blockchain.
3. *Moeco*: This is a one-of-a-kind blockchain platform that enables network connectivity for IoT devices in a unique way. There is no known reputed alternative for this platform in the market.
4. Naoris: This is perhaps the world's first cybersecurity initiative to provide a purpose-built application for this domain. Like Moeco, it is also one of a kind and there are no reliable alternatives available in the market.
5. *HydraChain*: This is a blockchain platform used for deploying private networks. Created by one of the largest public blockchain projects, Ethereum, to facilitate a permissioned blockchain, HydraChain is an excellent example of how a private distributed ledger can be built and managed.
6. *Hyperledger*: This a framework to develop blockchain platforms. It is unique in nature and focused solely on the blockchain technology instead of promoting tokens. Hyperledger is an initiative that is considered highly valuable by the industry as well as the scholarly community.

The chapter, in addition to those six distributed ledgers, also briefly discusses some emerging platforms providing support to use-cases such as medical services, drug manufacturing and quality assurance.

10.2 Internet of Things: IOTA

IOTA is a distributed ledger designed for the Internet of Things (IoT). It provides secure communications and payments between IoT devices and will soon have a smart contract service called *Qubic*. Unlike using a Hashcash-like proof-of-work, it uses *Tangle*, a consensus-building data structure made of a directed acyclic graph (DAG). Its transactions are fast, free of cost and scalable [Popov, 2018].

10.2.1 Overview

The communication between two IoT devices in IOTA is called machine-to-machine (M2M) communication. IOTA uses Tangle to solve the double-spending problem alongside solving both the scalability and transaction fee issues faced by most distributed ledgers including Bitcoin. By requiring the sender in a transaction to perform an approval of two transactions, IOTA turns its users into miners; hence the act of making a transaction and verifying transactions are coupled on this platform. There are no dedicated miners; instead, those making transactions are the actor affecting the system. Scalability, fast transactions and the ability to validate an unlimited number of transactions simultaneously make IOTA suitable for the use-cases working with IoT devices. In the near future, IOTA plans to introduce Qubic, this platform's smart contract feature capable of providing general-purpose, cloud or fog-based permissionless multiprocessing on Tangle.

10.2.2 Technical Details

Tangle is a consensus-building system that, instead of employing a blockchain, uses an orderly approach of verifying transactions to reach the consensus. Each machine (network member) in IOTA that submits a new transaction needs to verify two other transactions on the network before it gets verified. This approach ensures reaching the consensus out of a web of verifications.

Tangle removes the need for miners on the platform. Each machine willing to execute a transaction must actively participate in the network consensus by approving two past transactions. This way each transaction links to the two transactions it verified, and over time, it will be linked to future transactions that verify it as shown in Figure 10.1. For each verification, the verifier performs a small "proof of work" linking the transactions into the overall Tangle. This approach solves the scalability problem, as the network no longer relies on building blocks for a blockchain.

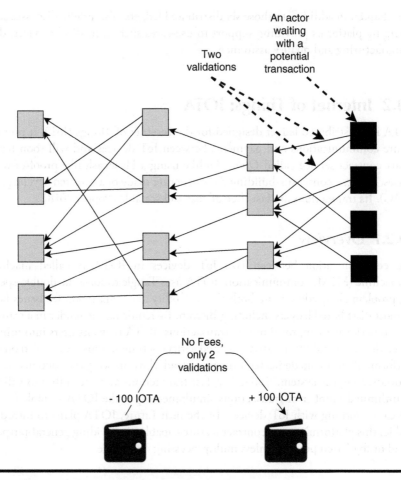

Figure 10.1   Tangle, consensus mechanism of IOTA.

Because every new machine on the network contributes its computing power to the network at the time of submitting a transaction, the cost of using the network is as good as the electricity consumed by the machine for verifying the required two transactions. As Tangle eliminates the need for block mining, the network released the entire volume of coins immediately after launch. Therefore, the task of verifying transactions on IOTA has no relation to creating new tokens and the role is limited to fulfilling the consensus condition only.

Tangle makes the IOTA network even more distributed than a blockchain network. With blockchain, the network is distributed amongst the miners on the blockchain, while with Tangle the network is distributed amongst every participating node. The latest addition in IOTA is Qubic, which is a protocol specifying IOTA's solution for quorum-based computations, outsourced computations and smart contracts. This protocol is expected to empower machines operating on IOTA with the ability to develop and run contracts.

We learned earlier that Bitcoin-like blockchain protocols are vulnerable if someone can accumulate 51% of the total computing power on the network. IOTA is less secure and theoretically more vulnerable than those protocols, as it requires only 34% or higher than one-third of the network's computing power to launch an attack on this platform. However, implementing a 34% attack using Tangle is complicated, as the attacker still has to discover the next verified transactions of the network before leveraging the 34% advantage. If the network grows big, the difficulty increases. Nevertheless, the IOTA network is not still big enough to avoid such attacks; hence, it uses a *coordinator* in its initial implementation to combat this threat and ensure the early Tangles are not compromised. IOTA plans to eliminate the coordinator once the network becomes strong enough in future.

10.2.3 Applications

The application domain of IOTA is data communication and storage for the Internet of Things. Most use-cases utilising this blockchain will enable IoT devices to fetch data from the data sources and store them on this platform. It can be used to develop applications related to smart cities, supply chains and regular monitoring of use-cases. It is expected that there will be more opportunities with IOTA in the near future when it implements smart contract functionality Qubic. This upgrade will open the opportunity to build decentralised applications on the platform. Once activated, developers will be able to host IoT applications like communications, public transport information hubs and interactive maps on the platform.

10.2.4 Alternatives: IBM Watson and Waltonchain

There are several blockchain platforms available in the market that are alternatives to IOTA. Amongst them, IBM Watson and Waltonchain are two renowned projects. *IBM Watson* is a massive initiative by technology giant IBM to connect IoT with the blockchain technology. In doing so, IBM has been using the Hyperledger framework, another project conceived by IBM in collaboration with Linux, to build the platform. We learn more about Hyperledger later in this chapter.

Waltonchain, on the other hand, was mainly developed to serve the supply chain industry, but it can be used as a dedicated IoT platform as well. It is named after Charles Walton, the inventor of RFID* technology and the project aims to advance his vision for the ubiquitous deployment of RFID technology in the form of IoT.

---

* Radio frequency identification (RFID) uses electromagnetic fields to identify and track tags containing electronically stored information attached to objects automatically.

10.3 Supply Chain: OriginTrail

OriginTrail is a decentralised and permissionless blockchain–supported data-sharing platform for integrating blockchain technology with digital supply chains. Working along with IoT technology, it enables the supply chain industry with data immutability and integrity in ensuring the quality of products [Rakic et al., 2017].

10.3.1 Overview

OriginTrail presents a stacked blockchain platform for vendors and clients involved in supply chains to exchange data seamlessly in a trusted environment.

It connects sensors and IoT devices to work with a broader ecosystem and allows developing DApps to read, write, access and verify facts about products and services throughout their life cycle. The platform implements the Electronic Product Code Information Service (EPCIS) framework to facilitate the layered, extensible and modular design across the entire structure. Its ecosystem consists of four layers (Figure 10.2). The first layer is called the blockchain layer that provides the necessary blockchain technology support, while the second and third layers integrate data and networking functionalities. The final layer hosts DApps to interact with blockchain and data via the network layer.

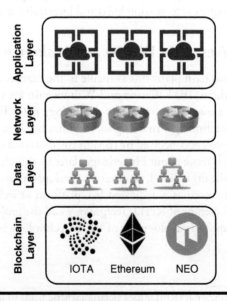

Figure 10.2   Layers of the OriginTrail platform.

10.3.2 Technical Details

OriginTrail itself is not a fully functional blockchain, rather operating over existing blockchains, it seeks to extend capabilities to a great extent. Early implementations of this platform used to utilise Ethereum only. However, now OriginTrail comes with support for a wide range of distributed ledgers including NEO and IOTA at its blockchain layer. This layer is responsible for providing data integrity in supply chains by incorporating blockchain as a data-sharing platform. It stores information on the immutable ledgers in the form of data fingerprints since the arrival of data throughout its life cycle.

An off-chain decentralised peer-to-peer network known as OriginTrail Decentralised Network (ODN) implements the data and network layers. The nodes in ODN are of two types: Data Creators (DC) and Data Holders (DH). DC nodes are responsible for incorporating supply chain data into the network and replicating it over a particular number of DH nodes, while DH nodes ensure the immutability and storage of the corresponding data.

The current version of OriginTrail implements the proof-of-work (PoW) mechanism that runs above the Ethereum blockchain. The consensus mechanism involves two key aspects: maintaining accountability and matching and validating the authenticity of the claims. The chain of accountability on this platform is maintained through the approval of each stakeholder by the previous and the following supply chain stakeholders. The matching, on the other hand, is performed by verifying dynamic batch information including batch identifiers, timestamps and other metadata such as transactional, compliance and sensor data. The information can also be verified by the auditing and compliance organisations providing their confirmations.

10.3.3 Applications

OriginTrail is designed to serve the supply chain industry by providing information about products throughout their life cycle. It can be used to develop applications giving users information about the place, location or area from where a product originates; hence ensuring the provenance. The application can also have information about the product's journey from the field or factory to the market and who are involved in producing this product. Applications ensuring the quality of a product can also be built using IoT devices measuring temperature and similar data to find out if the product is still in good condition despite having a long journey from the field and factory to the market and so on.

10.3.4 Alternatives: VeChain and OpenChain

There are several blockchain platforms available that are developed to support supply chain use-cases. For example, *VeChain* is a blockchain platform particularly designed for the supply chain industry. It enables manufacturers to share product data with vendors and consumers. It aims to inform both parties who are engaged in bringing a product to market and who purchase it with necessary information including the origin. *OpenChain* is another alternative blockchain to OriginTrail that seeks to build trust in the supply chain industry by providing a platform that forces participating companies of all sizes from all sectors to meet the defined specifications.

10.4 Connectivity: Moeco

Moeco is a blockchain platform envisioned by its creator as the "DNS of things". This platform integrates several network standards and offers connectivity to billions of devices globally through participating gateways. It is particularly built to suit IoT technology in a cost-efficient way. The goal of the Moeco blockchain system is to deliver data packages. As a decentralised system, there is no central authority ensuring the payment against any service provided by the gateway owners; hence the need for a blockchain transpired. Moeco works as a facilitator between vendors and gateway owners to establish connectivity for IoT data transmissions and delivering the payments [Moeco, 2018].

10.4.1 Overview

Moeco uses a crowdsourcing approach to enable existing networks and private gateway owners in its infrastructure. Anyone having the communication connectivity can become a gateway service provider. For example, someone with a wireless router at home or a smartphone with the internet connectivity can join as a gateway provider and start serving vendors, who are business providers owning sensor devices, to facilitate their sensor devices looking for connectivity. The permissionless decentralised architecture makes Moeco convenient for its users, both gateway owners and vendors. The platform takes care of payment and billing processes and ensures data delivery. The vendors pay for connectivity, while the gateway owners receive money for each connection made through their gateway.

10.4.2 Technical Details

The goal of the Moeco blockchain system is to deliver data packages. As a decentralised system, there is no central authority ensuring the payment against any service provided by the gateway owners; hence the need for a blockchain transpired. Moeco works as a facilitator between vendors and gateway owners to establish connectivity for IoT data transmissions and delivery of payments. Figure 10.3 shows the architecture of the platform where vendors look for connectivity in exchange of a small fee that they pay to the gateway owners. The blockchain is the technology

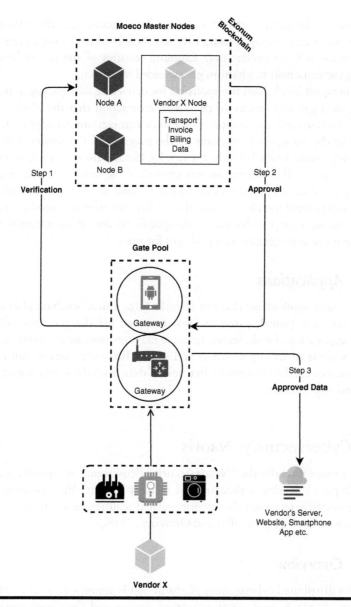

Figure 10.3   The architecture of the Moeco platform.

that ensures this service in a decentralised way. There is no central authority, rather the vendors themselves approve each connection and make arrangement for the payments before sending data to their servers.

This system utilises two blockchains, namely transport blockchain and invoice blockchain. The data package transportation and payment validation are both taking place in the Moeco network based on the Exonum blockchain framework, while the payment is arranged using ERC-20 Moeco tokens in the Ethereum network. Because it is an overlay over Exonum, features of the parent blockchain including the consensus mechanism get extended to Moeco.

The transport blockchain is responsible for delivering data packages in Moeco. In doing so, a gateway creates an encrypted transaction that the vendor's master nodes validate, decrypt and accepts. Once some transactions get approved, a block is signed in the transport blockchain by the majority of the master nodes. They concurrently create a new block in the invoice blockchain that holds records representing invoices. The gateway owners generate these invoices to the vendors for the transport of the transactions that they expedited in the network earlier. If an invoice has remained unpaid for more than n days (an arbitrary number of days set by the platform), master nodes remove the specific vendor's devices from the system and gateways stop processing data packages for them.

10.4.3 Applications

There are many applications that can be built using this blockchain platform. The base use-case is to provide gateways for sensors and IoT devices. This will lead to building applications for ski resort, resource management, smart traffic flow, agricultural, various smart city use-cases and so on. These use-cases do not require a blockchain to store data but need a free flow of data from the source sensor to their servers and applications.

10.5 Cybersecurity: Naoris

Naoris, or more formally the "Naoris Security Ecosystem", is arguably one of the first attempts to develop a decentralised security system. The distributed ledger takes the initiative to standardise security-related requirements within the realm of blockchain technology [Carvalho and Oravcova, 2018].

10.5.1 Overview

Naoris is a distributed cybersecurity platform that is agnostic to a device or operating system; hence, it works atop networked devices and their operating systems. It starts operating by uniquely identifying devices using smart proof of existence (SPoE). SPoE is a technique through which a cryptographically unique fingerprint of every digital device can be generated and stored into the blockchain that forever identifies those devices. Naoris is designed to run as lightly as possible across systems as a DApp. Naoris suggests the usage of an environment where critical domains and businesses will be able to support verifiable and trusted distributed resilience, integrity and availability.

10.5.2 Technical Details

The goal of Naoris is to ensure cybersecurity decentrally; as such, this system relies on identity verification through an approach known as Distributed Identity Validation Authority (DIVA). DIVA works in cooperation with SPoE to establish unique sources of truth to achieve genuinely attributable behaviour regarding data sources, devices or other digital assets. Each device can easily be a participant in a living, breathing ecosystem focusing on maintaining security and integrity of systems and digital assets across various networks (Figure 10.4).

Naoris's virtual and hardware-based appliances may act as confederated secure validator nodes allowing clients to participate in the effort of securing local and far away environments. This blockchain uses the delegated proof of stake (DPoS) as its consensus mechanism. The procedure is divided into two steps: first, electing the block producers and, second, building the blocks. It gives each nominal token holder the ability to observe and understand what is going on within the system creating a demand for delegate standing or reputation. If a user does not have excellent standing within the community, he is unlikely to be elected, as token holders may attempt to elect people that operate in line with the needs of the system. Within this principle of DPoS consensus, Naoris can build one irreversible block every second.

Byzantine fault tolerance is introduced to classic DPoS in this blockchain by allowing most block producers to sign all of the blocks in such a way that no single block producer would be allowed to sign two blocks with the same timestamp

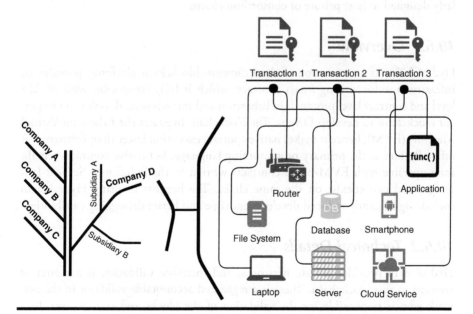

Figure 10.4 Architecture of the Naoris blockchain ecosystem.

or the identical block elevation. Once about five manufacturers sign a block, it is deemed irreversible. Any Byzantine producer intending to subvert the environment would have to build and sign cryptographic proofs. However, because individual producers are restricted to signing a limited number of blocks, such an attempt would reveal the abuse showing repeated signing at identical timestamps or block heights.

10.5.3 Applications

Naoris is designed to fight against cyberthreats and ensure securities of the cyberspace of the participating organisations. Its use-cases, therefore, fall within the cybersecurity regime covering various aspects of threats and retreat. This blockchain ecosystem accepts inputs in the form of scripts through the API. The management of a participating organisation can set up various rules regarding the security strategy of the environments they want to keep track of for numerous reasons such as compliance, best practice, patch-levels and so on.

10.6 Private Network: HydraChain

HydraChain is an open-source blockchain platform jointly developed by Brainbot Technologies and the Ethereum project. It is an extension of the Ethereum platform which adds support for creating *permissioned distributed ledgers*. It is particularly designed to host private or consortium chains.

10.6.1 Overview

HydraChain, as an extension of the Ethereum blockchain platform, provides an infrastructure for writing smart contracts which is fully compatible with all API level and contract level protocols in Ethereum and extends several tools from its parent blockchain to develop DApps. The blockchain bypasses the Ethereum Virtual Machine (EVM); hence it makes native contract execution faster than Ethereum. It offers Python as the primary programming language, but native contracts remain inter-operable with EVM-based contracts written in the Solidity or Serpent languages and can coexist on the same chain. The benefits of using HydraChain include significantly reduced development time and better debugging capabilities.

10.6.2 Technical Details

HydraChain provides private networks, and therefore validation is a matter of concern in this blockchain. There is a registered accountable validator in the network who is responsible for the validation of the blocks and transactions. In a HydraChain network, all the blocks are not allowed to enter the network without validation. It means a block will be added to the network only when the validators sign it. Once a block enters into a network, it becomes persistent, and there will be no reverts. Figure 10.5 shows the block-building process in HydraChain.

HydraChain has a restriction in creating blocks where new blocks are only created if there are pending transactions necessary to be processed. It creates new blocks when putting a transaction on hold does not remain an option. A validator needs to sign the block before it is allowed to be added to the network. As the validators are registered, a KYC* is used for the participants to make sure that the

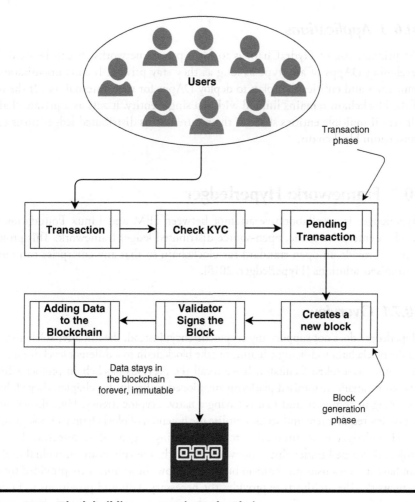

Figure 10.5   Block-building process in HydraChain.

---

* "Know your customer", alternatively known as "know your client" or simply KYC, is the process of a business verifying the identity of its clients and assessing potential risks of illegal intentions for the business relationship.

transaction takes place between registered participants only. HydraChain provides the ability to customised blockchain features such as transaction cost, gas limits, genesis allocation and block time.

The average block time in an Ethereum blockchain is 10 minutes, meaning it will take 10 minutes for a new block to be added to the blockchain. However, with HydraChain, this block time is not applicable due to its on-demand block-building character. So while creating a private blockchain, the administrator can set the block time according to their need.

10.6.3 Applications

The primary use of HydraChain is to form private networks. It can be used for developing DApps of any type as long as they stay private. It suits organisations, companies and entities that plan to deploy DApps for their internal use. If the use of the blockchain remains limited within a single entity, it acts as a private chain, whereas if multiple entities share it, the nature of this distributed ledger turns to a consortium blockchain.

10.7 Framework: Hyperledger

Hyperledger is a collaborative attempt between IBM and Linux Foundation to build an enterprise-grade, open-source distributed ledger framework. This project aims to provide an open standard for blockchain so that any enterprise can build customised solutions [Hyperledger, 2018].

10.7.1 Overview

Hyperledger does not support any cryptocurrency; instead, the initiative solely focuses on the blockchain technology. It aims to take blockchain to a different level disjointing its relation as a token facilitator. If we recall the previous blockchain protocols from Bitcoin to small, customised platforms mentioned earlier in this chapter, they all have one thing in common, and that is having a native cryptocurrency. Hyperledger steps out of that requirement and seeks to utilise the potential of blockchain technology only.

Hyperledger is an umbrella project providing a general architecture for any project developed under this framework. As such, the rule is an individual project can have its consensus mechanism but must follow the architecture provided by the framework. The architecture provides the necessary APIs and provisions to fit customised features including a consensus algorithm to make the blockchain operational. As an umbrella, several active projects are running under its hood. Fabric, Burrow, Sawtooth, Iroha and Indy are amongst the notable projects.

Fabric is the most popular platform from this group. It is a permissioned blockchain infrastructure with modular architecture which enables configuring different types of consensus algorithms. It also supports execution of smart contact (known as *Chaincode* in Fabric) and membership services provided by a Certificate Authority managing X.509* certificates, which are used to authenticate the identity of the members and their roles in the blockchain.

Amongst the other projects, Burrow provides Ethereum Virtual Machine support in Hyperledger, while Iroha focuses on mobile applications. Sawtooth, conceived by another technology giant, Intel, includes a dynamic consensus enabling hot swapping consensus algorithms in a running network. The Indy platform supports independent identities on distributed ledgers and provides the necessary tools, libraries and reusable components for implementing digital identities rooted on blockchains or other distributed ledgers.

10.7.2 Technical Details

Projects using Hyperledger can have an individual consensus mechanism but need to follow the architecture defined by the framework. The architecture of Hyperledger is arranged in layers:

1. *Consensus layer*: Responsible for the agreement of nodes about how to create and maintain the ordering of the blocks and how to confirm the correctness of the transactions in the blockchain.
2. *Smart contract layer*: Responsible for processing transaction requests and determining if transactions are valid by executing business logic.
3. *Communication layer*: Responsible for peer-to-peer message transport between the nodes that participate in a shared ledger instance.

There are several components in this framework such as data store abstraction, crypto abstractions, identity services, policy services and a wide range of APIs. Amongst these components, the identity services enable the establishment of a root of trust during setup of a blockchain instance; the enrolment and registration of identities during network operations; and management of changes like drops, adds and revocations. It is also responsible for providing authentication and authorisation features for the blockchain. The policy services ensure the management of various policies specified in the system, such as the endorsement policy, consensus policy and group management policy. Although there are a number of ongoing Hyperledger projects, the following discusses the architecture of Fabric to show an instance of how this framework can be used to implement a platform.

Hyperledger Fabric contains three nodes, namely the orderer node, the peer node and the client node. Each type of node is associated with some organisation

---

* The X.509 is a standard defining the format of public key certificates. These certificates are used in many Internet protocols, including TLS/SSL. They are also used in offline applications, like electronic signatures.

and has its certificates and private key. These nodes interact with each other to maintain the network, while end users communicate with them to get in touch with the blockchain as shown in Figure 10.6.

The client node acts on behalf of users in creating transactions. The peer node is responsible for maintaining the ledger and receiving ordered update messages for committing a new transaction to the ledger. There is a special type of peer node called "endorser", which endorses transactions by checking whether they fulfil

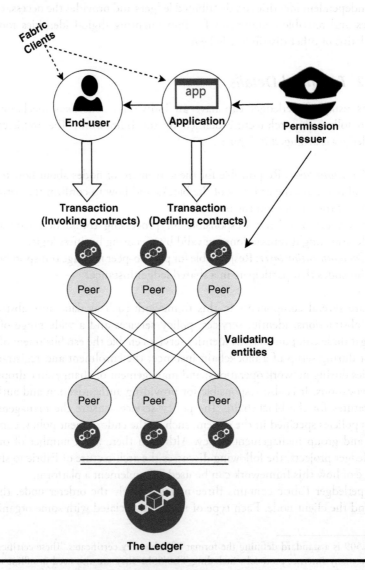

Figure 10.6   The architecture of the Hyperledger Fabric.

necessary and sufficient conditions. The orderer node provides a communication channel to the client and peer that can be used to broadcast transactions.

Being a permissioned blockchain, Hyperledger Fabric can support a considerable number of transactions. The number, however, will depend on the use-case and how it is deployed. For example, developers can use the *Max Message Count* to control the maximum number of transactions/messages to permit in a block. Similarly, they can control the block size with *BatchTimeout* and *BatchSize* parameters in the configuration file based on their use-case. Fabric uses modular architectural design to support different consensus mechanisms to be plugged in. Currently, Fabric supports only two consensus mechanisms: SOLO and Kafka. Although Hyperledger does not provide a token, there are provisions to implement one if need be.

10.7.3 Application

Hyperledger is a framework for creating blockchain platforms. It is possible to use this framework for building almost anything users wish; hence it is value-agnostic by nature. However, this distributed ledger is increasingly becoming popular for building private networks making it suitable for hosting DApps for organisations, companies and consortiums. IBM Watson, the blockchain platform developed to support IoT uses-cases, is one of the most notable examples of the implementation of the Hyperledger framework.

10.8 Emerging Distributed Ledgers

The chapter so far discusses some of the notable purpose-built distributed ledgers available in the market. The list, however, is not limited to those only, and new ledgers have been continuously coming. In this section, we learn about emerging distributed ledgers that have the potential to disrupt the industry in the near future.

10.8.1 Medical Services: MediChain and MediLedger

MediChain is a purpose-built platform for the medical industry. As a medical blockchain big data platform, it brings dispersed patient data together to improve diagnosis and treatment for individuals and allows analysing of big data in the search for new treatments and cures. The objective of MediChain is in twofold: first, it gives access to medical information coming from different systems and hospitals. It even allows individuals to view and control their own information. Second, in addition to acting as a data placeholder, it seeks to help scientists make important decisions as to how to prevent, treat and cure conditions that currently remain untreatable. In doing so, MediChain aims to extract clues to medical breakthroughs hidden in the mass of data that exists about patients, treatments and outcomes [Medichain, 2018].

MediLedger is another blockchain initiative jointly developed by LinkLab and Chronicled. It works with pharmaceutical companies to make prescription services easy and hassle-free for patients. The platform aims to unite rival pharmaceutical manufacturers and wholesale dealers for improved tracking and tracing functionality when it comes to making a prescription for a patient.

10.8.2 Drug Development: BlockPharma

BlockPharma is a French start-up that aims to introduce transparency and accountability in the drug manufacturing industry. Drugs are sensitive products that can cause death to someone if they do not provide what they promise to. As such, this platform uses blockchain technology to fight counterfeit drugs. It comes with an app that helps to track the origins of a medication giving patients the liberty to know where their medicine is produced, who produced and how it reached them.

10.8.3 Quality Assurance: Ambrosus

Ambrosus is a blockchain platform designed focusing on two industries: food and pharma. It uses a combination of sensors, RFID chips and QR codes to track movement, temperature and tampering. The data is then uploaded to the blockchain for security and to share data amongst counterparties in a trust-minimised way. This blockchain is expected to be used for the quality control and assurance of food, drugs and similar products in the factories, warehouses and customer-facing outlets.

10.8.4 Sharing Economy: Slock.it

Slock.it is a platform developed atop the Ethereum blockchain aiming to establish a genuinely decentralised sharing economy to enable direct interactions between producers and consumers of IoT smart objects. The principle of a sharing economy is to allow people to share their unused or rarely used physical or virtual resources, such as rooms or flats, cars, electricity or even time, for financial incentives. The traditional approach requires much human intervention with a big issue of trust and transparency. The existing applications of a sharing economy such as Uber and Airbnb are not decentralised. They rely on their monopolistic, centralised providers who charge a considerable fee, yet security, trust and transparency issues are prevalent in such applications. Slock.it aims to address these issues by providing a platform consisting of IoT smart objects, software and blockchain.

10.8.5 Genomic Data Collection: Nebula Genomics

Nebula Genomics is a blockchain platform to manage genomic data. Pharma and biotech companies spend billions of dollars each year on acquiring genomic information for scientists to determine what causes diseases and how to cure them.

However, there is not enough of this information, as it is fragmented and there are no standards of data acquisition. This blockchain platform aims to get rid of intermediaries, giving people control of their genomic data. It helps to cut the costs and ensure data security while allowing buyers to easily acquire standardised information from both individuals and genomic databases.

10.9 Summary

This chapter presented a wide range of purpose-built distributed ledgers available in the industry. The goal of this chapter was to introduce readers to application-specific ledgers and give an idea of how blockchain technology has been evolving. It discussed areas like the Internet of Things, supply chain, cybersecurity, connectivity, private networks and blockchain frameworks, and will act as the basis of the next chapter where the book elaborately discusses use-cases and applications of blockchain technology.

Chapter 11

Applications of Blockchain

The blockchain has been the subject of much debate in recent times both in and outside the scientific community as to what can be and what cannot be done using this disruptive technology. Interestingly, the world seems to get divided into two while discussing blockchain. Academics, industry leaders, developers – every group has opinions on this technology criticising or praising its ability to change the existing digital infrastructures and practices. Many inspiring words have been told in favour of this technology, while critics respond brutally to dissect its possible flaws and give their verdicts against its potentials. As the hype continues to skyrocket, many of these arguments proved to be impulsive indicating that useful use-cases can only be developed through systematic analysis of the sectors and identifying the genuine need for this technology in making those sectors better. This chapter takes the opportunity to look at the possibilities of how blockchain can be turned into real applications using educated assumptions. In doing so, it first classifies the use-cases based on roles, domains and categories, and thereafter presents detailed accounts of potential use-cases with the mention of existing blockchains in the market.

11.1 Hype or Hope?

Is blockchain technology hype? Bitcoin was the first application developed using this technology. This achievement encouraged researchers to move forward and many new use-cases have been considered, and many if not all became thriving applications. Bitcoin alone contributed to developing a series of financial services that include cost-effective money transfers, payment processing using Bitcoin and money exchanges. Once this first wave of applications became stable, developers looked for use-cases outside the financial industry. It is now anticipated that many non-profit, government and business use-cases can benefit from the distributed ledger technology. The presence of a blockchain in a product or service could drastically change the quality of the outcome where trust plays an important role. As such, blockchain platforms providing the underlying trust infrastructure are becoming popular, and industries are becoming more interested in adapting this technology to build new products or improve their current upshots.

The question, however, remains unanswered. The popularity of blockchain does not mean it is as good as it sounds. Any powerful application of this technology capable of changing our lives or society is yet to be seen. The absence of such an application does not reckon it is worthless either. When it comes to demonstrating the tangible benefits of the blockchain technology that many expect to change the world, it is still in its very early days of development, and the initial viable applications will likely arrive no sooner than half a decade. In fact, blockchain as a technology has just passed the peak of the Gartner hype cycle and is now progressing towards the next phase.

The Gartner hype cycle identifies five overlapping stages in a technology's life cycle as shown in Figure 11.1 and described next:

1. Technology trigger
2. Peak of inflated expectations
3. Trough of disillusionment
4. Slope of enlightenment
5. Plateau of productivity

Amongst these stages, the second is the most hyped period that unnecessarily affects the development of a new technology. Blockchain must have travelled through this when Bitcoin reached its all-time-high price in December 2017. As Bitcoin and other cryptocurrencies saw a sharp decline in price, most people started to lose interest, and only those with a genuine intention of using this technology to build exciting applications remain in the picture; hence it is in the trough of disillusionment. The next period is the slope of enlightenment where we should witness the potentially groundbreaking applications built around this technology.

Possibly the biggest irony of blockchain is that people find it difficult to put their trust in the technology that is used to establish trust in the digital medium. This scepticism arose partly due to the price hike of Bitcoin and its subsequent fall. Many experts quickly compared blockchain technology with the Dutch Tulip mania in the 17th century, the Mississippi Bubble in the 18th century, the UK Canal and Railway mania in the 19th century and the dot-com bubble of 2000. What seems to be very unfortunate for this technology is that most people could not imagine blockchain beyond Bitcoin and cryptocurrencies. Even comparing

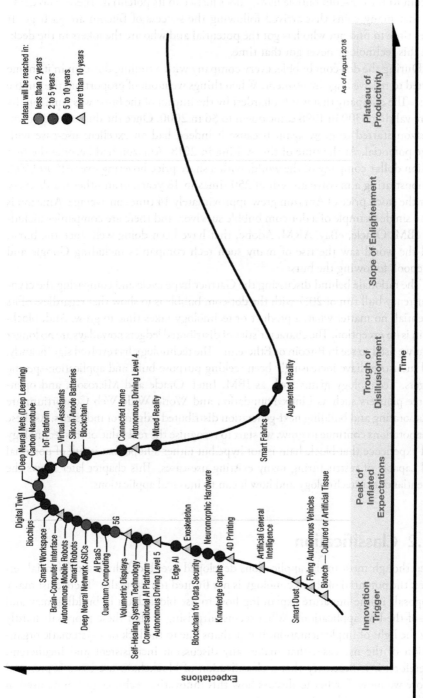

Figure 11.1   Gartner hype cycle for emerging technologies (August 2018).

Bitcoin to the dot-com bubble hardly does justice to its potential. There is no denying that many coins that arrived following the success of Bitcoin are garbage. It takes time to find out who has got the potential and who are the jokers in the deck, and this technology never got that time.

During the dot-com bubble, every company with a trailing dot-com in its name started to receive huge investment. When things went out of proportion, the bubble burst. The company that was hit hardest by the impact of the burst was Amazon. Its share valuing $300 in 1998 came down to $6 in 2000. Once the dust settled down, Amazon started to grow again because it indeed had an excellent use-case with huge potential. At the time of this writing in 2018, Amazon had become the first trillion dollar company of the world, with a share price hovering over $1500 USD, demonstrating a massive growth of 250 times in 18 years, or in other words every year the stock price of Amazon grew approximately 14 times on average. Amazon is just a single example of a dot-com bubble survivor, and there are companies including IBM, Oracle, eBay, ARM, Adobe, that have been doing well since the burst, and the world saw the rise of many such tech companies including Google and Facebook following the burst.

The rationale behind discussing the Gartner hype cycle and comparing the cryptocurrency bull run of 2017 with the dot-com bubble is to show that regardless of its potential, no matter what, a product or technology takes time to grow. And, blockchain is no exception. The characteristics of distributed ledgers nowadays are no longer what we used to see in Bitcoin or Ethereum. The technology has evolved significantly, and industries have increasingly been seeking purpose-built and application-specific ledgers. Technology giants such as IBM, Intel, Oracle and Microsoft, and opensource pioneers such as Linux Foundation and World Wide Web Consortium are collaborating and building next-generation distributed ledgers for industries. As these collaborations continue to grow, we start to recognise the real value of this technology and experience that blockchain is not hype but rather a hope that is full of potential and capable of restructuring many existing use-cases. This chapter later shows the potential of this technology and how it can fit into real applications.

11.2 Classification

Even though most initial applications developed over blockchain are financial services, the potential of this technology is not limited to that realm. There exist many proposals in the literature explaining how to use blockchain in building new and out-of-the-box applications. What seems surprising is that these proposals hardly saw the light of implementation. It is perhaps due to the lack of a systematic organisation of the use-cases that makes any discussion inconsistent and incoherent. Therefore, it is necessary that a classification of blockchain use-cases is prepared before we move further to discuss how this innovative technology can be used in building real-world applications.

11.2.1 Classifying the Domains

An attempt to organise the likely use of blockchain technology requires an in-depth analysis of what this technology can bring to a typical use-case and how its inclusion enhances the quality of an application developed using a particular use-case. In doing so, it appears to be a wise approach to identify the possible technological overlap and high-level domains first. This can be followed by showing how all or part of those findings can be incorporated into the use-cases.

To start, we first identify the role of blockchain in a use-case. There are other cutting-edge technologies around blockchain, and sometimes they overlap. So our approach will be to identify if blockchain is the leading or sole contributor to the use-case or plays a supporting role. If the role is in a supporting capacity, we identify if that role is a joint venture. In doing so, we also identify *artificial intelligence* (*AI*) and the *Internet of Things* (*IoT*) as the key technologies that closely collaborate with blockchain.

Next, we identify super domains. While playing a standalone role, blockchain can be used for developing use-cases in citizen services, business and finance, and marketplaces. In a joint venture, partnering with IoT, blockchain has the potential to contribute to supply chain use-cases, while with AI, blockchain technology can improve safety and security use-cases. In a supporting capacity, blockchain has the ability to contribute to smart city use-cases where both AI and IoT also play a significant role. So in summary, what we get here is as follows:

- ■ Roles and domains
  - − Standalone
    - • Citizen services
    - • Business and finance
    - • Marketplace
  - − Joint venture with AI or IoT
    - • AI
      - ■ Safety and security
    - • IoT
      - ■ Supply chain
  - − Supporting role with AI and IoT
  - − Smart City

11.2.2 Classifying the Categories

Having identified the roles and domains, we have constructed the foundation of the classification. In this section, we pick each domain and identify possible categories for the use-cases. Figure 11.2 shows how the higher-level domains are broken into lower-level categories. The figure demonstrates that each domain holds some categories that we will break down further into use-cases within their realm hereafter in this chapter.

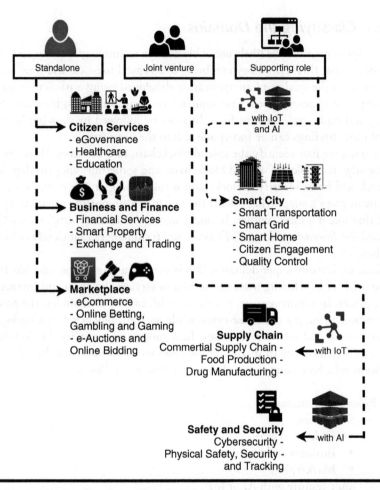

Figure 11.2   A classification of blockchain domains and categories for potential use-cases.

11.3 Citizen Services

Citizen services can be defined as the services that a state, its local offices and their partnering organisations provide to the citizen. This domain can be divided into three broad categories, namely *e-governance*, *healthcare* and *education*. It is likely that the applications from these categories will overlap as they all intend to serve the citizen. We learn more about this while discussing the potential use-cases soon.

11.3.1 e-Governance

The state is a complex centralised system. It is slow to react and continues to resist change. The development of a country usually depends on the decisions originating from the core. As such, bureaucracy plays a considerable role, often in a counter-productive manner, in providing services related to citizen welfare. Decentralised e-governance has the potential to overcome several hurdles that the state faces being centralised.

Blockchain technology is competent in solving the problems of security, harmonisation and settlement of data for the state management system. A distributed ledger is a novel tool for the enhancement of transparency of the budgetary process and the reduction of corruption factors. It removes the need for human involvement from many areas, and the system operates within the approved terms of smart contracts serving as the basis for operations.

Blockchain can play a pivotal role in making government decentralised, transparent, more accountable and active. This technology can be used to develop services such as generating citizen ID, marriage registration, birth certificate registration, notary, asset registration, degree validation and so on. There are already blockchain platforms in practice providing some of these services, including, for example, *Borderless*, a blockchain-based civil administration platform. *e-Auction*, another blockchain platform, presents necessary assistance to process auctions for the lease and sale of state property. The Credits platform provides the tools required to ensure blockchain-based interaction between citizens and the state where operations can be conducted using smart contracts and native cryptocurrency.

Arguably the most revolutionary application of e-governance could be the blockchain-based voting system, which does not exist yet. The architecture of the blockchain is a ready-made solution for such a case because blockchain is immutable, and without consensus, even sitting government cannot change the outcome of an election. The casting of votes may incorporate the use of biometric identifications such as fingerprints or retina scan, further derived from other blockchain applications providing citizen ID cards and birth registrations (Figure 11.3).

11.3.2 Healthcare

Quality healthcare service implies ensuring patients' health management at an excellent level at all times. This includes both medical well-being and bureaucratic processes. Unfortunately, in many countries regulations are making the delivery of quality healthcare even more tedious and lengthy. The primary issue in the healthcare sector is the gap between multiple parties involved in its operation.

Generally, the healthcare system operates like a triangle, where doctors, patients and providers occupy each of the angles. The role of doctors and medical personnel in this situation is solely giving the required treatments, while provider, such as an insurance company or a government, pays for the care. The patient is the individual who seeks medical assistance. Because patients' data and information remain scattered across different departments in the existing system, coordination is a big challenge that severely affects the quality of the medical service as well. For example, booking a pathological test or a surgery often requires the availability of

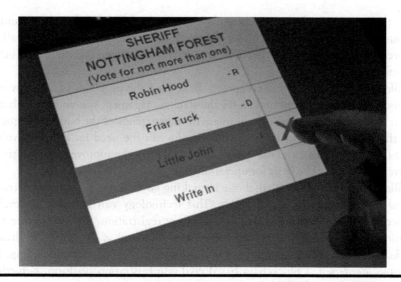

Figure 11.3 An electronic voting machine sarcastically showing the voting options for the Sheriff of Nottingham Forest from the Robin Hood folklore. Even the sitting Sheriff of Nottingham, the main antagonist, cannot change the outcome of the result should blockchain technology be used in this public voting.

facilities and resources, and identifying the right patients based on their circumstances. Despite having computers and mobile phones at every healthcare facility these days, exchanging the necessary data in a secure, privacy-friendly and seamless manner to obtain the best possible results is yet to be achieved.

The situation gets even worse when the question for payment arrives, particularly for services that are covered by private insurances. The dispute between insurance providers and patients is arguably one of the most common medical complaints in countries where governments do not pay for healthcare. Patients often complain about hidden terms and conditions that deprive them of the healthcare cost. It makes them vulnerable and helpless despite paying the premium on a regular basis.

Blockchain can produce a massive breakthrough in the healthcare ecosystem by either solving or playing a role in the solutions to the problems mentioned earlier. It can introduce specific changes in healthcare management that give power back to the people. Blockchain-based data sharing enables multiple parties to securely access and use information required to make better decisions and patients will have control over their data.

Furthermore, insurance powered by smart contracts will remove the need for a middleman. If a patient truly deserves to get paid, the provider will have no capacity to stop the payment. The smart contract will show the terms and conditions to the patients before the agreement gets initiated and will execute the payment request based on what it shows, no matter if there lives a hidden condition somewhere on the paper that the provider carefully kept out of sight of the patient.

There are already many blockchain platforms available in the market that specifically provide services related to healthcare. Some of these platforms offer medical data-sharing services while some cover the total care system. *MediChain*, *TrustedHealth*, *Doc.AI* and *CareX* are amongst the notable platforms already in use in the healthcare industry.

11.3.3 Education

The existing education system is mainly scattered where educational institutions operate standalone. They maintain an old tradition of carrying trust through badges and certificates. It used to work when there were fewer institutions, and people recognised the certificate issued by a specific university or school. However, as time passed by, people started to lose faith in paper certificates due to the availability of handy technology that can produce fraudulent documents. Instead, it became a new trend for the bearers of certificates, transcripts and other educational records to establish the authenticity of their papers. Sometimes they need to send documents to another school or an employer using official email of the providers, while some test scores such as the IELTS, GRE, GMAT or TOEFL need to come directly from the issuers by post. What seems to be the biggest irony in the education sector is that even the educational institutions that once proudly developed the convention of issuing certified documents now do not trust them.

In a world where trust is such a rare asset, blockchain can play an essential role in developing applications to authorise degree certificates that others can easily rely upon. Instead of operating individually, if the educational institutions jointly form a consortium blockchain using Ethereum, NEO or EOS, the practice will undoubtedly improve. If they start managing their certificates and transcripts on the blockchain, it would be much simpler and more accessible for students to provide their credentials to another party without having to go through the issuer again and again. Although it is yet to see institutions take such initiative, there exists plenty of proposals of such applications in the literature.

The use of a consortium blockchain as mentioned will not be restricted to issuing blockchain-based qualifications. The admission process at schools and universities will have the benefit of accessing data to decide who to offer positions and in which subjects. The current practice is very inefficient, as in most countries students need to apply individually for the courses they like to study. As such, they may end up applying for a degree that they do not qualify while fail to recognise a more suitable program that matches their credentials. With the help of blockchain, a UCAS*-like

---

* The UCAS Tariff, formerly called UCAS Points System, is used to allocate points to post-16 qualifications. Universities and colleges may use it when making offers to applicants. A points total is achieved by converting qualifications such as A levels (and many others) into points, making it simpler for course providers to compare applicants.

system but more widespread, decentralised and reliable can be developed for major levels such as undergraduate, masters and doctoral.

Blockchain technology can also be used in education for managing students registrations, badges, identity cards and other services that involve trust and security concerns. Last but not least, fees and funding can also be arranged using this disruptive technology. Offering automatic bursaries based on results, confirmation of payment of fees to clear registrations, deciding recipients of scholarships – all could benefit from smart contracts that would reduce human resource, involve less hassle and introduce more transparency in the process.

11.4 Business and Financial Services

The blockchain was initially conceived to develop financial applications. As such, it is no surprise that there will be a good many use-cases covering this domain. For the convenience of our discussion and to present the use-cases coherently, the domain is split into three broad categories: *financial services*, *smart property* and *trading and exchange*.

11.4.1 Financial Services

Traditional financial applications tend to be slow, error-prone and disjoint. This nature often necessitates intermediaries to intervene in reconciling the process and resolving disagreements. This practice costs stress, money and time that can be avoided or at least mitigated using blockchain-based services.

The asset management industry where asset managers and their analyst teams trade, balance and rebalance assets can benefit from blockchain technology. The current practice incorporates broker, custodian and the settlement managers to keep records, creating inefficiencies and room for error. The distributed ledger simplifies the process and removes the need for unnecessary intermediaries; hence speeding trading and rebalancing activities.

Insurance, where the processing of claims can be a daunting and endless procedure, could be another great use-case. Because processors must deal with a wide range of fraudulent claims, room for error is enormous. Use-cases such as smart city and the Internet of Things might help in establishing trust between users and the policy providers as well as building transparent and accountable management.

Cross-border payments, remittance, interbank money transfers and regular payment facilities are some other applications already available in some countries. Many blockchain platforms such as *Abra*, *Align Commerce* and *Bitspark* facilitate some of these services, while Ripple and Stellar are designed to enable bank and financial services to use blockchain technology to enhance the quality of their services.

11.4.2 Smart Property

Smart property is a type of service powered by the smart contract features of block-chain technology. It has the potential to revolutionise the traditional lending system. For example, hard money lenders providing loans and mortgages to customers with poor credit charge high interest rates to recover potential losses even before the contract starts. It stresses borrowers and often put them into bankruptcy.

Smart property can help lenders and borrowers settle ownership using smart contracts. Depending on the terms of the agreements, when borrowers pay a part of the mortgage or the full value, the properties will be transferred to their name. This system undercuts the risk and reduces the paperwork and bureaucratic process while allowing strangers to avail loans at a lower rate. In this use-case, home is just an example where the property can be a piece of land, a car, a factory, a smartphone or laptop and so on. Ethereum, NEO and EOS can be used to develop applications based on this use-case.

11.4.3 Exchange and Trading

Money exchange and trading platforms are natural fits for blockchain technology. These applications are part of the oldest use-case that blockchain addressed in Bitcoin – transferring funds between parties in a decentralised environment.

The current practice in the money exchange industry is heavily centralised. A person willing to exchange foreign currency needs to go through a broker who acts to maximise his or her profits only. It happens because other people who want to exchange their currency cannot see the whole network; hence they remain oblivious to potential offers that might make both parties winners. Trading of stocks and other financial instruments similarly involve middleman in the form of intermediaries, agents or brokers that costs people large fees and gives less decision-making power when buying or selling assets.

Blockchain technology has the potential to remove the middleman and connect these people to exchange their funds or assets at a better rate and by paying fewer fees. There are several high-level protocols including the *Lightning Network* that use Bitcoin or similar blockchain to facilitate bidirectional payment channels without delegating custody of funds. Ripple and Stellar are two notable distributed ledgers aim to build real-time gross settlement systems for exchanging and trading financial assets. Hundreds of companies have already been using these services offered by these two protocols, while many users are individually availing their services for exchanging foreign currencies, assets and other financial instruments through bids and offers.

11.5 Online Marketplace

The online marketplace is an excellent example of how digital technology can change our day-to-day practices. The products we buy from a real market can now be purchased in a couple of mouse clicks or smartphone taps from the internet. Because of the advancement of the supply chain industry (we learn more about this later), delivery of that product is no longer a problem either; hence, it is no surprise that the world's biggest public limited company, Amazon, is an online marketplace. Involving blockchain in this domain can significantly enhance the quality of services. The following discusses how blockchain and marketplaces can work together by dividing this domain into three broad categories, namely *e-commerce*; *online betting, gambling and gaming*; and *e-auctions and online bidding*.

11.5.1 e-Commerce

Blockchains are a natural fit for e-commerce, as they are designed for storing transactional data. This data, however, does not have to be financial. It can be any action needing a permanent record. It may include payment, but can be extended to a diverse range of operations involving order fulfilment.

Key advantages of using blockchain as the underlying platform for e-commerce sites include the visibility of the operation, transparency and automated dispute resolution. Because each block in the blockchain links to the previous block, it creates a visible chain of events showing the process of fulfilling past orders. Buyers can easily identify reliable sellers, while sellers can refuse to process orders depending on the reputation of the sellers. If a dispute still occurs, it can be resolved through an escrow account without involving someone from outside.

For example, let's suppose a customer places an online order on a blockchain-powered e-commerce site. Each step in the ordering process such as order placement, payment, fulfilment and shipping each add a new block to the chain with the time that the action was performed. The seller, however, does not instantly receive the payment; rather once the buyer confirms receiving the parcel as ordered, the blockchain releases the payment to the seller; otherwise, the buyer needs to return the parcel to get a refund.

At the moment, e-commerce sites such as Amazon, eBay and Alibaba offer an arrangement like this, but it is not reliable and hassle-free and involves the involvement of a third-party to addresses disputes adding extra costs. Blockchain, being decentralised and immutable, demonstrates the ability to revolutionise this industry by removing the need for a middleman. Contracts in Bitcoin have already implemented a form of e-commerce although for the wrong reasons for selling drugs, firearms and other illegal products (Chapter 16 further discusses the criminal activities of Bitcoin users). It is, however, the intention, not the technology that is wrong. To get the best out of blockchain, smart contract-based decentralised applications (DApps) will be necessary. NEO and EOS are two platforms that from the beginning targeted the e-commerce industry and developed architecture capable of handling thousands of transactions per second on a regular basis. It is no exaggeration that amongst the many potential applications discussed in this chapter, this use-case is amongst the most powerful ones.

11.5.2 *Online Betting, Gambling and Gaming*

The gambling industry itself has been going through a period of transformation for the last one and half decades, and the arrival of blockchain technology could not be better timed. As consumers continue to seek new and convenient opportunities to play, pay and receive rewards, this disruptive technology has a lot to offer.

Many gambling websites have already started accepting Bitcoin and other major cryptocurrencies as a form of payment alongside regular electronic options. It not only makes the process convenient but also offers benefits that include allowing users to gamble online anonymously without creating accounts or handing over documentation, and collect winnings more securely avoiding cash.

More coins like *Casinocoin* made exclusively for the gambling industry are expected to show up and offer benefits like lower fees and near-instant deposit times. Improving the cost-efficiency of financial transfers is a direct cost-saving for online sites that will enhance their profit margin and make players pay less by bypassing cash-handling commissions. These benefits of the gambling industry can be extended to the gaming and betting industry, as they generally have a common business use-case.

Making payment convenient and anonymous is certainly a significant transformation, but possibly the most prominent change expected to take place in these industries is blockchain-based infrastructure that users can rely upon. There are thousands of cases available where online gambling, gaming and betting companies tricked their users to gain an unfair advantage by depriving users of their actual winnings. Due to trust playing a massive role in these industries' online version, blockchain can be handy to develop DApps on Ethereum, NEO or EOS that people can trust. The popularity of such practices may lead to developing stand-alone blockchain platforms for gambling, gaming and betting industries.

11.5.3 *e-Auctions and Online Bidding*

Auctions and biddings are modes of securing possessions of goods and services by offering valid prices and challenging counter-offers with even higher but reasonable prices. It is a practice that has been in our societies for centuries. Government contracts given to private companies almost always go through auctions, while private possessions are commonly sold to the public through open bidding processes. The touch of digitisation even made the scope bigger, and now people can bid from their homes. This paradigm shift helps us observe governmental contracts going on e-auctions sites managed by public offices, and private properties being sold online using bidding marketplaces such as eBay, LiveAuctioneers, eBid and thesaleroom.com.

The general practice for governmental e-auctions is that bidders need to secretly provide a quote for a service or contract they seek to win followed by their statement of how they aim to achieve their goals. Amongst the viable bidders, the best quote wins.

There are many government auction portals where companies can bid to win contracts for construction works, telecommunication license, communication routes and so on. These are expensive contracts where maintaining the confidentiality of the bid is critical; otherwise, any competitor company having information about others' quotes can easily win the bid by placing their price marginally higher than the original highest bid. If such a thing happens, it is not only unfair for the participating companies, but also for the governments or entities, who called for the auction as they may not get the most appropriate quote from the bidders.

The eBay-like personal bidding sites also have trust issues, as it is a centralised system and administrators and officials of the platform may have access to the bidding information. In these systems, someone can set a maximum amount for auto-bid that remains hidden until someone gradually moves close to it and outbid the amount by offering counter-bids. A bidding stake smaller than auto-bid will always be defeated. Knowing the information about this auto-bid can help to win paying less in an unfair way.

The sensitivity of the information and a possible lack of trust in e-auction and online bidding sites make blockchain an ideal candidate to solve their problems. Smart contracts–based DApps can securely get the job done for governmental e-auction without the presence of a middleman and centralised control. The blockchain platform EOS is already providing customised support for building such applications, while *Auctionity* is a real-time auction platform for selling personal stuff that can mitigate trust issues for eBay-like platforms (Figure 11.4).

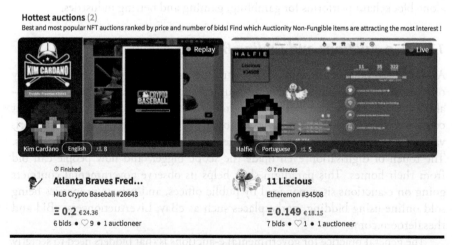

Figure 11.4   A blockchain-based auction website for individuals to buy and sell goods through live bidding. It is an example of a decentralised bidding platform where bidding information is secured through blockchain.

11.6 Supply Chain, Production and Provenance

Supply chain management (SCM) is the process of managing the flow of goods and services. It involves the movement and storage of raw materials, work-in-process inventory and finished goods from the point of origin to the point of consumption. The goods can be food, medicine or even non-edible products like clothes [Kozlenkova et al., 2015]. So we can quickly identify three broad categories forming the supply chain domain: *commercial supply chain, food production* and *drug manufacturing*.

11.6.1 Commercial Supply Chain

In the era of the international economy, carrying products and services from producers to consumers presents a complex network of events. From electronic devices to vehicles to food and clothing, most of the commodities we use have moved through several countries and many providers before they reach us. This web of transactions may abolish traces of the origin of the products, making consumers unaware of the sources and selling parties of the particulars that brought the goods from production to the retail marketplace. This lack of transparency could be dangerous, as it can bring catastrophic outcomes, including mishandling and fraudulent behaviour. As such, the blockchain-based supply chain could have been an excellent solution to this problem.

Distributed ledger technology could be used in supply chain management to reduce fraudulent transactions and optimise supply chain activities. From production to guarantees and repairs to recalls, it helps tackle the complex interconnection of data and puts everything into one database that can be used by all approved parties to retain the accuracy of information at all times. Food safety, drug safety and production, cold chain monitoring and origin tracking are amongst the most important use-cases where blockchain can play an important role. Many blockchain-based solutions such as *Skuchain, Provenance, Agri-Digital, Walmart, FishCoin* and *AnyLedger* have been designed to improve efficiency and transparency in this sector.

11.6.2 Food Production

Blockchain technology could play a vital role in reconstructing the food industry by increasing efficiency, transparency and collaboration throughout the food system. The ability to establish trust (or users' inability to cheat) makes blockchain an ideal technology to fit the bill for food supply chain and provenance use-cases. When used with sensors and precision delivery systems connected to a network, as with the Internet of Things, blockchain can be used to gather a wealth of data and employ it in the field of tracing origins and managing food systems.

If adopted, consumers could be able to trace the source of their salad ingredients in seconds. Shippers could see if a lorry is full before scheduling a delivery, while

Figure 11.5 Supermarkets in the United Kingdom often claim their beef is of British and Irish origin. Using blockchain technology, this can be verified in a few taps on smartphones.

shoppers could determine the temperature of the food during its journey. Grocery stores could check if a carton of eggs is cage-free, while the consumer could verify if the beef of a burger is really of the origin stated on the label. For example, burger chains and supermarkets in the United Kingdom and Ireland claim that their beef is of British and Irish origin (Figure 11.5). Using the blockchain technology, users could verify this claim in seconds.

The Walmart–IBM blockchain has made many headlines in recent time claiming to be the first implementation of such a system using blockchain. Although it operates only in Walmart and more particularly with the leafy green food supply chain, its success is likely to translate this initiative into hundreds of other foods and products in the future. Walmart also insists that the technology will be used to serve consumers fairly and justly. Because the technology tells the companies of the origin of the foods, if a consumer gets sick, government investigators will have a reliable spot to start the investigation. Instead of chasing a paper trail for months, the authority can get to the source of a particular food within seconds. This practice ultimately results in strict regulations, fewer sick people and more confidence in the food system [Splitter, 2018]. *OriginTrail*, *VeChain* and *Waltonchain* are some of the blockchain platforms that can be used in building applications based on this use-case.

11.6.3 Drug Manufacturing

The pharmaceutical industry is one of those that must maintain strict quality control regulations where blockchain can potentially play a vital role. The drug manufacturing process begins at the research and development division of each organisation that designs and develops new drugs before sending them for trials on mice or suitable creatures. During the first 3 to 4 years, this process continues to run and record the outcomes for the next phases. The second phase of drug testing is commonly known as human trial. At this stage, the medicine must be safe enough to run the trial on human subjects. How reliable a medicine is at this stage depends on the research and experiments conducted earlier. It is therefore essential to keep the records unaltered, and blockchain enters into the business at this point. Because of its immutable nature, recording every step of the drug development in blockchain ensures the medicine is adequate for human trial and subsequently patient trial in the third phase of its life cycle [Khurana, 2018].

In the US, the Food and Drug Administration (FDA) requires a drug to go through a further 13-month scrutiny period before it endorses it. In other parts of the world, the practice is similar, if not exactly the same. During that period, the authority needs to review the past trials, and blockchain data can be a good starting point. It is not only going to increase the reliability of the data but also introduce a high degree of transparency and accountability in the process resulting in better drug development practice. *BlockPhrama* and *Ambrosus* are two blockchain platforms that can be used for this use-case.

11.7 Safety and Security

As the physical world meets its digital counterpart, information has been turning out to be vital assets for many organisations. Keeping this information safe, secure and authentic is no easy job, and the challenges have been mounting every day. Where there is business, there will be interactions; hence complete lockdown of the system remains no longer a solution either. The following discusses how blockchain can be involved in the mix to develop applications capable of dealing with modern security challenges and help organisations fight back to prevent cyberattacks and possible security breaches.

11.7.1 Cybersecurity

Cyberspace is a continually changing area that is a highly disputed and one-of-a-kind environment. It deals with a diverse range of crowds establishing interactions between them to achieve specific goals. As such, its security involves a considerable amount of trust to run the system. It is, however, a fact that trust is a delicate asset that is difficult to outsource without incurring massive risk; hence cyberspace remains an open target for attackers who wish to gain unfair advantages by appropriating the loopholes of an organisation. As the amount of attacks and expertise of malicious actors continues to increase, the need for a new paradigm of security measures becomes paramount.

Within the context of cybersecurity, blockchain has two roles to play. First, we already know that blockchain is immutable, or in other words, a piece of information written in the blockchain remains there forever. This is a powerful feature that can contribute immensely to the development of security applications. Second, blockchain is inherently distributed and decentralised. The use of this technology will result in breaking down the traditional centralised architecture and transform it into a decentralised system.

A corporate or critical environment would have been an ideal model to benefit from the blockchain technology. In a setup like this, having a central point of governance produces the risk of the total collapse of the system, while malicious actors may use such structure to gain access to data and information stored at a central location. Decentralisation can play a role here by distributing access and responsibilities amongst multiple branches but managing them through consensus. Decentralised storage, record-keeping and peer-to-peer sharing would remove the chance of central failure. Furthermore, identifying the malicious actors and their intentions through activity tracking would help to proactively defend against attacks on the system.

In addition to a regular company or organisation, nuclear power stations, electrical infrastructure, power production units, banks and trading exchanges are few areas that could benefit from the use of blockchain technology. Instead of outsourcing trust, blockchain operates in a trustless environment that ensures the exact operation of its affiliates. If anyone tries to bend the rules, it will be quick to discover the breach and act against such exercises using this technology. *Naoris*, *BlockStack*, *MaidSafe* and *Safecoin* are some blockchain platforms that developed decentralised applications suitable for providing cybersecurity solutions to large corporations and organisations.

11.7.2 Physical Safety, Security and Tracking

Safeguarding cyberspace is not always enough for many organisations that deal with sensitive information, materials and services such as government offices, military and police barracks, nuclear power plants, power grids, hospitals and laboratories. These kinds of organisations need to become proactive to protect their assets from the outsiders as well as malicious insiders.

It is essential for organisations to ensure the safety of physical assets like paper files, radioactive materials, firearms, lethal drugs and so on. Blockchain could enable organisations to manage individuals' records of activity, and access to physical assets and infrastructure in an immutable format that nobody can change or alter, even the person having the highest authority in the organisation. It is also vital that the movement of sensitive materials or information is also registered in the blockchain to record their trails.

For instance, in a nuclear power plant, the radioactive materials must be taken care off in such a way that no one can misuse them. Keeping records in a blockchain of individuals having access to them as well as tracking information about the materials themselves as to how and when they changed hands and form helps identify any malicious behaviour relatively quickly. Sensitive paper files in military and government offices or lethal drugs in a pharmaceutical laboratory can be of similar importance where blockchain-based applications can come to the rescue. Platforms like *HydraChain*, *Hyperledger Fabric* and *Waltonchain* would be suitable for building these applications.

11.8 Smart City

The concept of a smart city has numerous definitions depending on the context and meaning of the word *smart*. Sometimes it refers to being intelligent, while occasionally it indicates the ability to generate and exchange real-time data. In general, a smart city incorporates people, technology and data to provide better services and living experiences for its citizens [Cocchia, 2014]. It is now widely anticipated that the foundation of future cities will be built atop IoT, AI and blockchain technologies.

A few years ago, technological giant Cisco envisioned a world where every object would have connectivity and various degree of sensing ability that it named the Internet of Things. Although that height has not been achieved yet, some 50 billion IoT devices could be found communicating by 2020 [Cooney, 2017]. Real-time data from IoT devices and immutable historical storage on blockchain is jointly going to create vast opportunities for the researchers and developers who would get an extra edge to look at the smart city use-cases from a new perspective called data-to-decision, which ties up sensor data with AI in making real-time decisions [Miller and Mork, 2013]. Smart Dubai is arguably the first blockchain and IoT-powered initiative in building a city that ticks almost all boxes of a smart city, and many other cities including Singapore, Hong Kong and several Chinese cities are ready to follow suit [Khan et al., 2017].

The following discusses how blockchain platforms, IoT and AI will work together to obtain decisions for making city life better for its citizens in the near future. The discussion divides the domain into five categories, namely *smart home*, *smart transportation*, *smart grid*, *citizen engagement* and *quality control*.

11.8.1 *Smart Home*

A smart home is a residence that incorporates advanced automation systems to provide the occupants with monitoring and authority over the building's functions in the form of controlling lighting, temperature, multimedia, security, window and door operations, and the washing machine, dishwasher and other appliances.

Smart homes make the use of IoT devices for sensing data and AI to make decisions. Blockchain technology by joining the workforce of IoT–AI can play a central role in making homes smart. A distributed ledger working as a shared data storage platform can enable multiple devices and appliances to communicate with one another and provide machine-learning algorithms with the necessary data stream to compare and make decisions.

There are two subgroups of the smart home use-case, namely smart appliance and smart security, that could benefit most in the presence of a blockchain. For example, if the design of a smart home requires the washing machine to switch on during midday when solar panels provide sufficient energy to run the appliance, the decision-making module of the smart home looks for solar generation data to compare with other information such as time of the day and availability of the machine in the blockchain. A similar example can be imagined where a security alarm decides to go off in response to a vibration that it identifies as an act of an intruder. The decision needs to come from analysing a wide range of data that the blockchain can provide.

11.8.2 Smart Transportation

Managing the transportation system has been a great challenge for many modern cities. The growing population caused by births and migration from rural areas keeps increasing the size of city communities and creates demand for more vehicles to be deployed on the streets, making the smart management of public and private transport inevitable. As such, blockchain-based and IoT-integrated transport system management certainly provide supports for better commuting and driving experience.

IoT-integrated citizen tracking in a smart city plays a pivotal role in this case. It will be able to facilitate many applications and services to use machine-learning algorithms in various areas such as designing timetables for metro trains and public buses, anticipating commuter demand in different parts of the city, assigning drivers' shifts, identifying appropriate onboard advertising for public transports and so on. Instant and pre-booked taxis, on the other hand, could also benefit from the same data to decide where to be present in the absence of public services. Besides, all forms of vehicles leave trails of their movement that can be captured using off- and on-vehicle sensing devices for providing services such as real-time traffic updates, adjusting the duration of traffic signal lights and suggesting alternative routes. Monitoring a vehicle's fitness, road taxes and other regulatory requirements can also be implemented within this scope.

As IoT plays its part, blockchain can be introduced to share and access data on the fly in the presence of the data stored in a consortium blockchain shared between approved parties. Although many of the modern cities already have some of these tracking and data-sharing facilities in existence, due to the presence of bureaucratic red tape accessing this data is either difficult or expensive in the contemporary state of affairs. Blockchain-based solutions make this process simpler, faster and easier by moving central authority to individual stakeholders and empowering them with the ability to register, write and access data with ease.

11.8.3 Smart Grid

The blockchain-based smart grid is a conceptual application having the real potential of changing the way we consume power. It works as if trading energy amongst our peers rather than purchasing it from the power companies. It would track and connect a network of electricity generation and usage through solar panels or windmills, giving its customers the option of choosing the greenest energy at an affordable rate.

Distribution of energy through peer-to-peer sharing not only allows users to see the origin of their power but also excessive energy from overproduction can be fed back into the network eliminating the need for exporting to the grid at a reduced rate. The demand for renewable energy continues to grow when people notice, access and choose the sources of their power, making clean energy more available to consumers.

Solar panels and energy bills are expensive, but when we remove the exploitative structure of the energy business and the inaccessibility of clean energy, real possible solutions start to show up. As digital and energy technologies evolve alongside one another, consumers will have the power to take control of their energy needs.

11.8.4 Citizen Engagement

A smart city looks after its citizens not only by providing services such as transportation and utilities, it also improves citizens' lifestyles by engaging them in activities and recreation. Public parks, libraries, museums, sports, cinemas, shopping centres, etc. are various forms of citizen engagement commonly found in modern cities.

The availability of real-time and historical data could improve the quality of the citizen engagement experience and introduce new perspectives. It paves the path for libraries to suggest books or museums to invite visitors to the collection that might be of their interest. People visiting parks and gyms may form objective-aimed challenges between them to enhance their workout experience. Shopping centres, cinemas, theatres, spas, etc. could give customers more specific offers tailored to their interests based on AI-analysed outputs from the data.

Citizen engagement is an ideal use-case for IoT and blockchain to work tightly in achieving specific goals. The real-time data can be collected using IoT-enabled sensors installed at public spaces, whilst blockchain provides the backbone of historical information that aids machine learning or similar methods to make recommendations (e.g. books, exhibitions), form groups (e.g. workout challenges), suggest products (e.g. clothes, movies, foods) and so on.

11.8.5 Quality Control

Ensuring regulatory compliance is the key to healthy living in a city. Foods, medicines, appliances, services – everything needs monitoring for quality-control purposes [Garau, 2018]. Because failure to comply with the recommended standard could potentially create health and living hazards, it is necessary that smart cities remain in total control of continuous monitoring to identify breaches as soon as possible. As such, smart cities can engage IoT and blockchain together to introduce a higher degree of transparency in quality control in food and hygiene, medical and pharmaceutical products, appliances, services and so forth.

There are strict food regulations in modern societies concerning preparation, preserving, temperature control, hygiene maintenance and timely disposal of expired food. As such, each of these activities could benefit from advanced IoT-integrated sensor devices that are capable of monitoring temperature, humidity, availability of unwanted foreign substances and so on. With the help of more sophisticated and advanced technologies, medicine and medical products are now easily monitored. There are already methods in place using sensors and robots to control the quality of appliances such as seating chairs in cinemas and auditoriums, escalators in shopping malls and similar locations, theme park equipment, etc.

Last but not least, the quality of services mainly in the absence of humans such as ATMs and parking ticket machines are also easy to observe these days. However, despite these technologies already being in existence, due to the lack of connectivity and a seamless flow of data turned the stakeholder off and many exciting applications remain to be implemented. Blockchain and IoT could be the much-needed bridge between sensors and historical data for AI-powered applications to make real-time decisions. Having choices, interests and preferences of citizens in an immutable blockchain would enable approved parties to offer suggestions or recommendations when an individual comes across public places and passes through IoT-integrated sensors.

There are many blockchain platforms already in operation that support various aspects of IoT. *IOTA* is a blockchain platform that can hold and share data between parties. One of the drawbacks of a public ledger is that its response time is not very fast. In that case, a private network can effectively improve performance. There are several private networks such as *HydraChain* and *Hyperledger Sawtooth* that can be utilised within an urban community without using a public ledger. *Moeco* is another blockchain platform that allows conventional smart devices to act as a gateway for IoT applications and people on the go can exchange data with the help of this blockchain.

11.9 Summary

This chapter took the opportunity to look at the possibilities of how blockchain can be turned into real applications using educated assumptions. In doing so, it first classified the use-cases based on roles, domains and categories, and then presented detailed accounts of potential use-cases with the mention of existing blockchains in the market on many occasions. With this chapter, the core technical discussions on the blockchain technology of the book come to an end. The remainder of the book concentrates on the social science aspects of blockchain technology but will be developed on the foundation of these technical discussions.

CRYPTOCURRENCY V

Chapter 12

Evolution of Money: From Barter to Bitcoin

It is a fact that all cryptocurrencies including Bitcoin are network protocols. It might be difficult to grasp how on Earth a network protocol becomes a currency. The answer to this question lies in the concept of money. A network protocol becomes a currency just like a piece of paper becomes US dollar or British pound sterling. To understand the underlying philosophy of cryptocurrency, knowing the origin of money, its functions and the evolution of the monetary system are essential. This chapter provides the basis for this requirement. The discussion presented hereafter is not a comprehensive discourse on the mentioned topic but will help readers relate the concept of cryptocurrency with regular money and comprehend how the monetary system works. In addition to briefly introducing money to readers, the chapter covers topics as early as from the age of bartering through commodity and representative money to contemporary money commonly known as fiat currency before introducing digital money and cryptocurrency.

12.1 Money

Perhaps the most common element that we regularly use in our day-to-day lives is money. Despite the Bible warning us that "the love of money is the root of all evil", it is no exaggeration that in modern societies "money makes the world go round". That said, it still seems somewhat deceptive that a piece of paper or a metallic object pays more than what it is worth in the name of money. This scepticism makes us think that there must have been a missing piece of a jigsaw puzzle hidden somewhere; otherwise, the entire idea makes no sense. In reality, there is indeed one missing piece, and that is an assurance given to the bearers confirming their ability to avail anything of the value of the amount written on the paper or inscribed on the metal in exchange for the object. In our contemporary world, this assurance is *actual* money. A government of a country generally grants this assurance on which people rely. Therefore, money can be defined as follows:

> *Any item or verifiable record accepted as payment for goods and services and repayment of debts in a particular country or socio-economic context is called money [Mishkin, 2007].*

12.1.1 Functions of Money

English economist William Stanley Jevons in his 1875 book *Money and the Mechanism of Exchange* identified four functions of money [Jevons, 2014]. Modern economists later agreed upon those functions and authors of macroeconomics textbooks also adapted Jevons's view. Many modern textbooks list all four functions as Jevons stated, while some rearrange them into three [Milnes, 1919]. The following briefly elaborate on these functions.

1. *Medium of exchange*: Money is a widely accepted token giving its bearer the right to exchange for goods and services. Because of this function, money acts as an intermediary instrument and avoids the limitations of barter that requires one to have precisely matched goods or services with what the other has to offer.
2. *Measure of value*: Money can measure the value of an item and provide the ability to compare things against each other such as goods, services, assets, liabilities, labour, income and expenses. This function of money is also known as a *unit of account*.
3. *Standard of deferred payment*: Money is a widely accepted method to value a debt; thereby allowing goods and services to be acquired now and paid for in the future. This is the function that some textbooks incorporate into the previous two.
4. *Store of value*: Money can be saved, retrieved and exchanged at a later time. More generally, a store of value is anything that retains purchasing power into the future.

12.1.2 Properties

The previous discussion revealed four functions of money. In order to fulfil these functions, money needs to have some specific properties that the following attempts to quickly review.

- *Fungibility*: It is perhaps the most important property of money. This property implies that individual units must be capable of mutual substitution; hence, it gives money the ability of interchangeability.
- *Durability*: This property means that money can be used again and again. It is the ability to withstand repeated use. Money, regardless of its form, changes hands and moves from one person or entity to another until the collapse of a system or is officially terminated.
- *Portability*: It means money must be portable from one place and person to another. This is the ability that allowed money to evolve from its primitive forms.
- *Divisible*: Money needs to be divisible so that it can be broken into small units. This property gives money the ability to be exchanged precisely.
- *Cognisability*: This property implies that the value of money must be easily identified. When using as a medium of exchange, both parties must quickly recognise the value without any dispute.
- *Stability of value*: The value of money needs to be stable so that bearers can use it for the various functions. If the value of money remains highly volatile, it would have been challenging to decide upon a price while purchasing or selling goods and services.

12.1.3 Money Supply

The money supply is the total value of monetary assets available in an economy at a specific time. There are several ways to define money, but standard measures usually include currency in circulation and demand deposits [Brunner, 1987].*

Money supply plays an essential role in regulating and managing an economy. For example, an increase in the money supply generally lowers interest rates, which in turn, generates more investment and puts more money in the hands of consumers, thereby stimulating spending. Businesses respond by ordering more raw materials and increasing production. The increased business activity raises the demand for labour. The opposite can occur if the money supply falls or when its growth rate declines.

The money supply within a jurisdiction has relation to prices as well. This relation between money and prices is historically associated with the quantity theory of money. There is strong empirical evidence of a direct relation between money-supply growth and long-term price inflation, at least for rapid increases in the amount of money in the economy. For example, Zimbabwe that saw extremely rapid increases in its money supply also saw extremely rapid increases in prices; a phenomenon commonly known as *hyperinflation*. This is one of the reasons for the reliance on a monetary policy as a means of controlling inflation.

---

* Demand deposits, also known as bank money or scriptural money, are funds held in demand deposit accounts in commercial banks.

12.1.4 Central Bank

A central bank is an institution that manages the currency, money supply and interest rates of a state as well as oversees the commercial banking system. In contrast to a commercial bank, a central bank possesses a monopoly on increasing the monetary base in the state and also generally controls the printing and coining of the national currency, which serves as the state's legal tender. A central bank also acts as a lender of last resort to the banking sector during times of financial crisis. Most central banks also have supervisory and regulatory powers to ensure the solvency of commercial banks and the prevention of reckless or fraudulent behaviour of those institutions. Functions of a central bank include:

- Implementing monetary policies
- Setting the official interest rate to manage both inflation and the country's exchange rate
- Controlling the nation's entire money supply
- Playing the role of the government's banker and the bankers' bank, i.e. "the lender of last resort"
- Managing the country's foreign exchange and gold reserves and government bonds
- Regulating and supervising the banking industry

12.2 Origin and Early Forms

Money, being an integral part of the human civilisation, has a long history of evolution. Modern money that we encounter daily emerged from some very primitive forms dating back thousands of years. Early societies traded and financially interacted with one another using various forms of money and money-like systems that eventually evolved to our present-day money.

12.2.1 Barter: The Origin of Money?

How money came into being is a matter of debate. Economists and anthropologists have been arguing with each other for ages on this but never reached an agreement. Economists believe there exists plenty of reason for an age-old system called *barter* to be the motivation for the creation of money. Anthropologists, on the other side of the table, deny this claim and instead blame the 18th century Scottish philosopher and professor at the University of Glasgow Adam Smith, who is widely regarded as the father of the modern economic theory, for popularising the barter economy as the precursor to money, which anthropologists find a fairy tale that never existed.

If we are to accept the story told by the economist, barter was in use as long ago as one hundred thousand years. According to this system, goods and services are directly exchanged for other goods and services without the use of a money-like medium of exchange. In order for an exchange to occur, participating entities must have the need for what the other possesses. For example, if someone requires rice and wants to exchange meat, she or he must find a suitable match looking for meat in exchange for rice.

Although modern economists accept the fact that there remains a lack of evidence for past societies being dependent on barter-like methods, the mention by Aristotle in *Politics* stipulates the Greek were aware of bartering long before Adam Smith discussed it in his book *The Wealth of Nations* [Plato, 2007]. Smith identified the inefficiency of bartering as the motivation for the emergence of money. He argued that markets emerged out of the division of labour, hence individuals began to develop specialisation. This practice resulted in a growing dependency on one another for subsistence goods. Although goods were first exchanged by barter, soon the limitations of this system were exposed and necessitated a replacement by a more convenient approach [Smith, 1982].

The example of meat and rice was a classic case of barter in the early societies, but as needs turned intricate, the demand for more complex goods became inevitable. Let suppose a man having lots of wood in his possession gets sick and is in need of medicine. He must find an individual with the ability to treat him with medicine, and most importantly that individual must require wood. To make their lives more comfortable in the event of such a complicated situation, people in early societies started stockpiling particular goods, such as salt or metal, that they thought no one would refuse. Smith found this practice the origin of money and claimed that because markets pre-existed the state, the creation of money was not state-tied.

Anthropologists have a different view on the origin of money and refute Smith's conclusion. They are confident that money is a creation of governments because when something resembling a barter-like system occurred in stateless societies, it was almost always between strangers, not fellow villagers. With this argument, anthropologists generally conclude that barter cannot be used to explain the origin of money without the state.

French sociologist Marcel Mauss in his book *The Gift* strengthened this argument pointing that earlier economic contracts predating money were not to act in one's economic self-interest, instead the transaction was fostered through the processes of reciprocity and redistribution, not barter. American anthropologist and professor at the London School of Economics David Graeber in his book *Debt: The First 5,000 Years* suggested that those people whom we know of using barter-like systems were already familiar with money and such cases are not a lot in number. British anthropologist and professor at the University of Cambridge Caroline Humphrey in one of her 1985 academic papers boldly dismissed the concept of a barter economy stating all available ethnography suggests that there never existed a concept like barter predating money; hence it points to governments as the creators of this concept.

12.2.2 Commodity and Representative Money

Economists and anthropologists may not agree about the origin of money; however, they do accept that the first form of money was *commodity money*. It is the type whose value comes from a commodity that it is made of. In addition to having intrinsic value, commodity money can also have value in its use as money. It was either for self-convenience or backed by the state; people started stockpiling valuable commodities having importance in the various contexts of life. Later these commodities became mediums of exchange or money.

After the domestication of cattle and the start of cultivation of crops in 9000–6000 BC, livestock and plant products were used as money followed by the use of products such as salt, peppercorns, large stones, decorated belts, shells, , cocoa beans, cowries and barley in a later period. Since the beginning of the Bronze Age around 3300 BC, precious metals such as gold, silver and copper became popular forms of money.

The invention of commodity money was a step forward towards the next stage of civilisation, as it removed the need for finding an appropriate pair while trading. Nevertheless, the system remained inconvenient because of the difficulties faced by the bearer of money while transacting, transporting and storing commodity money. As such, early societies worked out a method that kept the benefits of commodity money but introduced a convenient alternative to carry it. This new form of money is known as *representative money*. It did not require the bearer to carry the commodity while trading; rather something more convenient could be used as a representative of the original commodity kept securely at a designated location. Hence, representative money can be defined as a medium of exchange that represents something of value but has little or no value of its own. In order to be a genuine form of representative money, there must always be something valuable supporting the face value represented.

The Mesopotamian civilisation developed a large-scale economy based on commodity and representative money. The city-state of Sumer around 2150 BC developed the shekel, a coin-like currency representing a weight of barley held at the warehouse. Shekels had a variety of values depending on the era, government and region, and ultimately represented precious metals, most notably electrum, silver and gold (Figure 12.1). The use of shekels was so mainstream in the early societies that their mention can be found in the Hebrew Bible in the Book of Genesis (chapter 23, verse 15–16):

> Listen to me, my lord; the land is worth four hundred shekels of silver, but what is that between you and me? Bury your dead (15). Abraham agreed to Ephron's terms and weighed out for him the price he had named in the hearing of the Hittites: four hundred shekels of silver, according to the weight current amongst the merchants. (16)

Figure 12.1 **A Carthaginian shekel made of a naturally occurring alloy of gold and silver commonly known as electrum from 310–290 BC, bearing the image of Tanit, consort of Ba'al Hammon, the chief god of Carthage.**

12.2.3 *Coinage*

As the evolution of money continued, early societies that mastered metallurgy used metal ingots, silver bullion and unmarked bars for exchange. In the Late Bronze Age, standard-sized ingots as shown in Figure 12.2a and tokens such as knife money were used as currency to store and transfer value, particularly in China during the Zhou dynasty from about 1000 BC. The first manufactured coins appeared separately in India, China and the cities around the Aegean Sea between 700 and 500 BC. While the Aegean coins were heated and hammered with insignia, the Indian coins from the Ganges River Valley were punched metal disks, and Chinese coins were cast bronze with holes in the centre.

Most of the early coins included no writing but had an image of a symbolic animal. This makes the dating of these coins challenging that relies primarily on archaeological evidence. Furthermore, early coins were not standardised in weight, and their earliest usage was of ritual objects such as badges or medals issued by priests, not as a currency.

The first ruler known to have officially set standards of weight and money was Pheidon, the King of Argos in the Mediterranean. There remains sufficient evidence that minting occurred in the late 7th century BC amongst the Greek cities of Asia Minor, spreading to the Greek islands of the Aegean and the south of Italy by 500 BC. The first known stamped money with the mark of some authority in the form of a picture or words is credited to an electrum stater of a turtle coin made of 67% gold and 23% silver, manufactured at Aegina island about 700 BC. The earliest inscribed coins are those of Phanes, dated to 625–600 BC from Ephesus in Ionia, with the legend "I am the badge of Phanes" or just bearing the name "of Phanes" as shown in Figure 12.2b. Some of these coins were found in the foundation deposit of the Temple of Artemis at Ephesus, the earliest known deposit of electrum coins.

Despite the early developments of coins across Asia Minor, all modern coins are considered to be descended from a single kingdom of this region, the Kingdom of Lydia around 600 BC. King Alyattes of Lydia is frequently

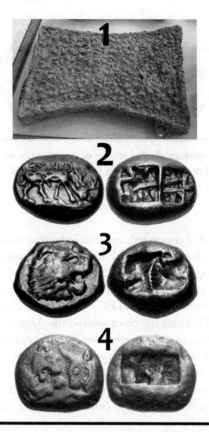

Figure 12.2 **(a) An oxhide ingot from Crete. Late Bronze Age metal ingots were given standard shapes, such as the shape of an "ox-hide", suggesting that they represented standardised values. (b) The earliest inscribed coinage, an electrum coin of Phanes from Ephesus, 625–600 BC. (c) Coin of Alyattes of Lydia (620–564 BC). (d) Gold Croeseid, minted by King Croesus circa 561–546 BC.**

credited to be the originator of coinage who built a workforce skilled in metallurgy and circulated coins made of electrum during his rule as shown in Figure 12.2c [Ramage, 2000].

Croesus, the son of Alyattes and the new king of Lydia following the death of his father, introduced the world's first bimetallic monetary system when he issued Croeseid, as shown in Figure12.2d, the first true gold coins with a standardised purity for general circulation [Metcalf, 2016]. Because electrum is a naturally occurring material that contains 54–63% gold with the remainder silver, the coins came in a variable mix of gold and silver. This unpredictability of the composition of the coins significantly hampered development and as a solution to this problem, pure gold and silver coins were developed. The ancient Greek historian Herodotus wrote referring to the Lydians during the rule of Alyattes and Croesus:

"So far as we have any knowledge, they were the first people to introduce the use of gold and silver coins and the first who sold goods by
retail" [Metcalf, 2016].

Cyrus the Great, who founded the Achaemenid Empire (the First Persian Empire)
in 550 BC, was unfamiliar to coinage in his realm where people were reliant on barter and silver bullions. It was only when he invaded Lydia in 546 BC and defeated
Croesus did he come across the Lydian coinage system. He quickly adapted it for
the whole empire, a move that massively helped to rapidly spread the coins in the
6th and 5th centuries BC, leading to the development of Ancient Greek coinage,
Achaemenid coinage, and further to Illyrian coinage. All modern coins are considered to be the descendants of one of these coinages.

12.2.4 Banknotes

The development of the banknote began in the Tang dynasty in China during the
7th century with local issues of paper currency. Before the use of paper money,
the Chinese used coins that were circular, with a rectangular hole in the middle
enabling several coins to be strung together on a rope. Merchants in China found
that their strings of coins were too heavy to easily carry around. They solved this
problem by leaving the coins with a trustworthy person who gave the merchants
a slip of paper recording how much money they had with that person. Someone
could regain the money by showing this paper to that person. This receipt of deposit
eventually resulted in paper money called *jiaozi*.

By 960 AD during the rule of the Song dynasty, due to the shortage of copper for striking coins, China issued the first generally circulating notes. A note
is a promise to redeem later for some other object of value, usually spices. These
banknotes, however, were limited to regional zones of the empire due to geographic
limitations and were valid for use only in a designated and temporary limit of
3 years. The geographic limitation changed between the years 1265 and 1274 AD
when the late Southern Song government finally produced a nationwide standard
currency of paper money backed by gold or silver. Kublai Khan, the founder of
the Mongol-led Yuan dynasty, conquered the Song Empire around 1279 AD and
issued paper money known as *chao*. It was the first paper currency to be used as the
predominant circulating medium in the history of China (Figure 12.3).

There are mentions of the use of various forms of paper-like alternative money in
Europe as early as the 10th century. According to a travelogue of a visit to Prague in
960 AD by Ibrahim ibn Yaqub,* small pieces of cloth were used as a means of trade,
with these cloths having a set exchange rate versus silver. By the next 200 years,

---

* Ibrahim ibn Yaqub was a 10th century Hispano-Arabic traveller, probably a merchant, who
  may have also engaged in diplomacy and espionage.

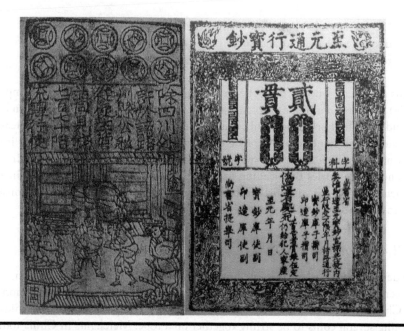

Figure 12.3 A Song dynasty *jiaozi*, the world's earliest paper money (left) and a Yuan dynasty banknote with Chinese and Mongol words (right).

the Knights Templar* started issuing banknotes to pilgrims around 1150 AD. The practice was pilgrims needed to deposit their valuables with a local Templar preceptory before embarking, when they received a document indicating the value of their deposit. They could use that document upon arrival in the Holy Land to retrieve their funds in an amount of treasure of equal value.

Chinese paper money of Mongol became known in Europe through the accounts of famous travellers, such as Marco Polo and William of Rubruck in the 13th century. Marco Polo in his book *The Travels of Marco Polo* dedicated a whole chapter titled "How the Great Kaan Causeth the Bark of Trees, Made Into Something Like Paper, to Pass for Money All Over his Country" to the paper money of the Yuan dynasty. He wrote:

> All these pieces of paper are, issued with as much solemnity and authority as if they were of pure gold or silver … with these pieces of paper, made as I have described, Kublai Khan causes all payments on his own account to be made; and he makes them to pass current universally over all his kingdoms and provinces and territories, and whithersoever his

---

* The Knights Templar was a highly trained, well-equipped and highly motivated elite fighting force from the 12th century.

power and sovereignty extends ... and indeed everybody takes them readily, for wheresoever a person may go throughout the Great Kaan's dominions he shall find these pieces of paper current, and shall be able to transact all sales and purchases of goods by means of them just as well as if they were coins of pure gold.

In medieval Italy and Flanders, because of the insecurity and impracticality of transporting large sums of cash over long distances, money traders started using receipt-like promissory notes to the original depositor. Although sometimes these receipts are seen as a predecessor to regular banknotes in Europe, they were merely bills of exchange.

The real need for banknotes became apparent during the mid-17th century due to the price revolution, when relatively rapid gold inflation was causing a reassessment of how money worked. The goldsmith-bankers of London began to give out these receipts as payable to the bearer of the document rather than the original depositor; hence the note could be used as currency based on the security of the goldsmith, not the account holder of the goldsmith-banker.

This pivotal shift changed the simple promissory note into an agency for the expansion of the money supply. As these receipts were increasingly used in the money circulation system, depositors began to ask for multiple receipts to be made out in smaller, fixed denominations for use as money. The receipt soon became a written order to pay the amount to whoever had possession of the note that eventually became the modern banknotes.

The first short-lived attempt at issuing banknotes by a central bank was in 1661 by Stockholms Banco, a predecessor of Sweden's central bank Sveriges Riksbank. However, the bank went bankrupt 3 years later after rapidly increasing the artificial money supply through the large-scale printing of paper money.

The first bank to initiate the permanent issue of banknotes was the Bank of England, now the central bank of the United Kingdom. Established in 1694 to raise money for the funding of the war against France, the bank began issuing notes in 1695 with the promise to pay the bearer the value of the note on demand. They were initially handwritten to a precise amount and issued on deposit or as a loan. There was a gradual move towards the issuance of fixed denomination notes, and by 1745, standardised printed notes ranging from £20 to £1,000 were being printed. Fully printed notes that did not require the name of the payee and the cashier's signature first appeared in 1855.

The Scottish economist John Law helped establish banknotes as a formal currency in France after the wars waged by Louis XIV left the country with a shortage of precious metals for coinage. In the United States, there were early attempts at establishing a central bank in 1791 and 1816, but it was only in 1862 that the federal government of the United States began to print banknotes [Weatherford, 1998; Davies, 2002; Ferguson, 2008].

12.3 Fiat Money

Fiat money is legal tender whose value is backed by the government that issued it or parties engaging in exchange agree on its value. The US dollar is fiat money, as are the British pound, euro and many other major world currencies. The concept of fiat money is very modern and was conceived less than half a century ago.

12.3.1 Gold Standard

The gold standard is when a country binds the value of its money to the amount of gold it owns; hence it guarantees that one could redeem its currency for its value in gold. Anyone holding that country's paper money could present it to the government and receive an agreed upon amount of gold from the country's gold reserve. That amount of gold is called "par value".

The United States, for example, used a gold standard for most of the late 19th and early 20th century. A person could exchange US currency – as well as many public and even some private debts – for gold as late as 1971. This period is commonly known as the "gold standard era" when US dollar bills used to read

> "This certificate is a legal tender in the amount thereof in payment of all debts and dues public and privates. *X* **dollars in gold coin payable to the bearer on demand**" **(Figure 12.4).**

12.3.2 US Dollar Standard

Following the two world wars, in 1944 an agreement commonly known as Bretton Woods agreement established the rules (Bretton Woods system) for commercial

Figure 12.4 Gold standard dollar bill of 1928. The bottom reads "20 dollars in gold coin payable to the bearer on demand."

and financial relations amongst the United States, Canada, Western European countries, Australia and Japan. It replaced the gold standard with the US dollar standard and made this currency the global currency. The agreement also created the World Bank and the International Monetary Fund to monitor the new system.

From 1944 to 1971, the Bretton Woods agreement fixed the value of US$35 to 1 troy ounce of gold. Other currencies were pegged to the US dollar at fixed rates. The US promised to redeem dollars in gold to other central banks. Trade imbalances were corrected by gold reserve exchanges or by loans from the International Monetary Fund.

12.3.3 Nixon Shock and Creation of Fiat Money

The Bretton Woods system collapsed in what became known as the *Nixon Shock*, a series of economic measures undertaken by US President Richard Nixon in 1971, the most significant of which was the unilateral cancellation of the direct international convertibility of the US dollar to gold.

While Nixon's actions did not formally abolish the existing Bretton Woods system of international financial exchange, the suspension of one of its key components effectively rendered the Bretton Woods system inoperative. Even though Nixon publicly stated his intention to resume direct convertibility of the dollar after reforms to the Bretton Woods system, all attempts proved to be unsuccessful by 1973 when the system was replaced by the current regime based on freely floating exchange rates between the major currencies. This marked the beginning of the modern fiat currencies that are not backed by any commodity.

12.4 Digital Money

Digital money is a type of currency that is available in digital form in contrast to physically structured money such as banknotes and coins. It is also frequently referred to as electronic money. The classification of this type of money is complicated due to the availability of a variety of money or money-like instruments in digital and other forms. Figure 12.5 shows an attempt to do a taxonomy of money by Morten Bech and Rodney Garratt [Bech and Garratt, 2017]. Their efforts demonstrate how complex a monetary system can be and how digital money overlaps with other forms of currencies. Thus, for the convenience of discussion, this chapter divides digital money into two broad categories: centralised and decentralised.

12.4.1 Centralised Digital Money

This category of digital money is controlled by a centralised entity, usually a central bank. This controlling entity retains the power to launch, abolish or alter the course of this money. Most centralised digital monies are generally the digital identity of physical

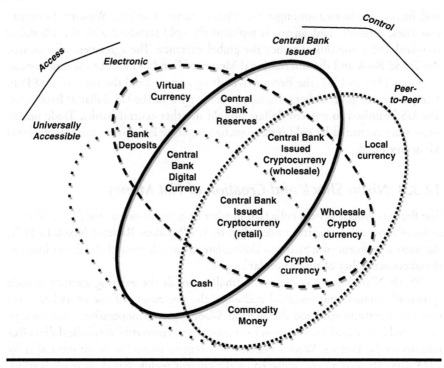

Figure 12.5   A taxonomy of money showing the position of cryptocurrency and virtual currency within the major categories.

money. For example, someone may make transactions using mobile banking apps or using banknotes. He or she is effectively using the same money in different forms.

More recently, since the inception of cryptocurrency, countries have been thinking of launching state-backed cryptocurrencies. Venezuela launched a cryptocurrency, the petro, and Sweden has been developing something similar, the e-krona, which will be equivalent to its national currency, the krona. It is too early to predict how these currencies will operate in the crypto-universe, but there is no doubt that they will be regulated to some extent.

12.4.2 Decentralised Digital Money

This category of digital money stays outside the control of the central bank, a centralised authority or any influence of a body. The most famous example of such money is the regular cryptocurrencies operated over a decentralised peer-to-peer network and run by the principles set out inside the algorithm such as Bitcoin, Ethereum or Ripple.

There is also another kind of decentralised digital money called *virtual currency*, which stays unregulated and outside the jurisdiction of the central bank. The terms *virtual currency* and *cryptocurrency* are often used synonymously, but they have some differences. For example, the definition of virtual currency implies that it retains its status within its dedicated community. In that sense, cryptocurrencies are all virtual currency. However, a condition for money to be called a virtual currency is the lack of universal accessibility. Cryptocurrencies once had this property, but due to the establishment of trading exchanges, crypto-ATMs and so on, most large cryptocurrencies are now easily accessible. Although hundreds of cryptocurrencies still cannot be easily accessed, as time passes, it is expected that cryptocurrencies will separate themselves from virtual currency and establish a new group by making them more available to the people.

12.5 Cryptocurrency

Cryptocurrency is perhaps the most advanced stage of the evolution of money since barter systems. It is digital and decentralised in nature and can act as a medium of exchange [Chohan, 2017]. A 2018 study identified six conditions that an asset must fulfil to be called cryptocurrency:

1. The system does not require a central authority; its state is maintained through distributed consensus.
2. The system keeps an overview of cryptocurrency units and their ownership.
3. The system defines whether new cryptocurrency units can be created. If new cryptocurrency units can be created, the system defines the circumstances of their origin and how to determine the ownership of these new units.
4. Ownership of cryptocurrency units can be proved exclusively cryptographically.
5. The system allows transactions to be performed in which ownership of the cryptographic units is changed. A transaction statement can only be issued by an entity proving the current ownership of these units.
6. If two different instructions for changing the ownership of the same cryptographic units are simultaneously entered, the system performs at most one of them [Lansky, 2018].

Hence, a formal definition of cryptocurrency will be as follows:

> *A cryptocurrency is a digital money system designed to work as a medium of exchange that uses strong cryptography to secure financial transactions, control the creation of additional units and verify the transfer of assets decentrally using distributed ledger technology, typically a blockchain, that serves as a public financial transaction database.*

As of December 2018, the number of cryptocurrencies available over the internet was over 1600 and the quantity has been growing. Bitcoin is currently the largest cryptocurrency by market capitalisation followed by Ripple and Ethereum. Table 12.1 lists

Table 12.1   List of Notable Cryptocurrencies

Year	Name	Founder	Hash	Consensus
2009	Bitcoin	Satoshi Nakamoto	SHA256	PoW
2011	Namecoin	Vincent Durham	SHA256	PoW
2011	Litecoin	Charlie Lee	Scrypt	PoW
2012	Peercoin	Sunny King	SHA256	PoW/PoS
2013	Dogecoin	Jackson Palmer, B. Markus	Scrypt	PoW
2013	Gridcoin	Rob Halford	Scrypt	PoS
2013	Primecoin	Sunny King	1CC/TWN	PoW
2013	Ripple	Chris Larsen, Jed McCaleb	ECDSA	RPCA
2013	Nxt	BCNext	SHA256	PoS
2014	Auroracoin	Baldur Odinsso	Scrypt	PoW
2014	Dash	Evan Duffield, Kyle Hagan	X11	PoW/Service
2014	NEO	Da Hongfei, Erik Zhang	SHA256	dBFT
2014	MazaCoin	BTC Oyate Initiative	SHA256	PoW
2014	Monero	Monero Core Team	CryptoNight	PoW
2014	NEM	UtopianFuture	SHA3-512	PoI
2014	PotCoin	Potcoin core dev team	Scrypt	PoS
2014	Titcoin	Edward Mansfield, R. Allen	SHA256	PoS
2014	Verge	Sunerok	Scrypt	PoW
2014	Stellar	Hard fork from Ripple	ECDSA	SCP
2014	Vertcoin	Bushido	Lyra2RE	PoW

(Continued)

Table 12.1 (Continued)   List of Notable Cryptocurrencies

Year	Name	Founder	Hash	Consensus
2015	Ethereum	Vitalik Buterin	Ethash	PoW
2015	Ethereum Classic	Hard fork from Ethereum	Ethash	PoW
2015	Tether	Jan Ludovicus van der Velde	Omnicore	PoW
2016	Zcash	Zooko Wilcox	Equihash	PoW
2017	Bitcoin Cash	Hard fork from Bitcoin	SHA256	PoW
2017	EOS	Dan Larimer	SHA256	DPoS

some notable cryptocurrencies along with information such as the founding year, founders, hashing algorithm and consensus mechanism.

12.6 Summary

This chapter presented a brief discussion on the origin of money, its functions and the evolution of the monetary system. The principal objective of the chapter was to give readers an understanding of how money works in our society to relate cryptocurrencies with that practice. It covered topics from the age of barter through commodity money to modern money, commonly known as fiat currency. It finally wrapped up with a discussion of various forms of digital money including cryptocurrency.

Chapter 13

Cryptocurrency Mining

Cryptocurrency mining is the method of verifying transactions and adding the records to the distributed ledger for various forms of cryptocurrency. The mining has increased both as a topic and activity as cryptocurrency usage has grown exponentially in the past few years. During the early days of Bitcoin, the use of a regular computer was sufficient; however, as the mining difficulty starts to grow, miners utilised graphics processing units (GPUs) to make the mining process faster and edge past competitors followed by using purpose-built machines. Cryptocurrency mining is no longer an amateurish job, rather it has become a booming industry attracting huge investment and involving large infrastructures dedicated to one task – finding a hash value! Chapters 3 and 4 of this book elaborated on mining algorithms and how the process works. This chapter takes the opportunity to discuss mining basics, hash rate, required hardware, pooled mining, reward sharing, countries famous for mining and criticisms against the proof-of-work mining process.

13.1 Mining

Boden is a city more than 900 km north of Stockholm in Sweden. In one of its airports, a massive aircraft hangar capable of holding a dozen helicopters is now full of computers. Forty-five thousand of them each with a whirring fan to prevent the internal machine from overheating. These machines have been tirelessly trying to solve so-called mathematical puzzles that would earn them 12.5 Bitcoin for each successful discovery. The venture is not so straightforward though, as they have to be quick enough to solve it first ahead of tens of thousands of participants around the world in this strange competition. Boden is just one of the many instances from around the globe. The competition those computers have been participating in is known as cryptocurrency mining and the computers are known as miners.

13.1.1 Evolution of Mining

Cryptocurrency mining is an ever-changing process that continues to evolve every few months. The mining landscape we saw in the example of Boden was not anything close to the mining practice a decade ago. It all began with central processing unit (CPU) mining using regular desktop computers. Soon miners figured out that graphics cards are even better at hashing; hence GPU mining kicked off.

It was still at a tiny scale, and one could run a very successful Bitcoin mining operation from his or her bedroom. This practice continued for some time until it was replaced by field-programmable gate arrays (FPGAs), which are integrated circuits designed to be configured by the customer or designer after manufacturing. The days of this hardware did not last long as mining difficulty increased and was soon replaced by a new generation of mining machines in the form of application-specific integrated circuits, or ASICs. These are specialised and purpose-built chips designed for hashing. The actual manufacturers of the equipment quickly realised that they could get a slice of the pie and so began to build big farms of those specialised mining rigs and some gathered miners around the world through the cloud to mine together. A few of them even stopped selling their products outside the pool.

The evolution of mining did not stop there. It was not profitable to mine alone from home in the current landscape. It cost money in the form of electricity consumption and damaged the computer. A concept called pool mining has taken over the job where miners share their processing power over a network to form a giant computing platform exclusively for mining and later split the reward between them using a variety of methods. These pools are so big that without joining one of them, earning anything from Bitcoin or similar cryptocurrency mining is impossible in the current practice.

13.1.2 Mining Process

Each time a user makes a transaction a cryptocurrency miner is responsible for ensuring the authenticity of information and updating the blockchain with the transaction. The mining process itself involves competing with other miners to solve mathematical puzzles with cryptographic hash functions associated with the block containing the transaction data. The first miner to find the desired hash gets the chance to build the block.

Mining is a vital condition for the survival of the blockchain. It prevents malicious participants of the network from altering the blockchain data. Because of this process, a group of miners operating decentrally in a network can collaborate and coordinate between themselves in making key decisions such as verifying transactions and building blocks.

In Bitcoin, a block is mined approximately every 10 minutes by solving a mathematical problem that is moderately difficult but easy to verify, based on a cryptographic hashing algorithm. The answer to this problem is called the proof of work (PoW). This proof shows that a miner did spend a significant amount of time to solve the problem and is not an adversary with an intention to gain improper benefits from the blockchain. Later altcoins and next-generation platforms such as Ethereum adapted this approach.

13.1.3 Difficulty

The difficulty is the measure of how difficult it is to find a new block compared to the easiest it can ever be. The rate is recalculated every 2016th block to a value such that the previous 2016 blocks would have been generated in exactly one fortnight (2 weeks) had everyone been mining at this difficulty. This is expected yield, on average, one block every 10 minutes. As more miners join, the rate of block creation increases. As the rate of block generation increases, the difficulty rises to compensate, which has a balancing of effect due to reducing the rate of block creation.

13.1.4 Rewards

Mining utilises the concept of *incentivisation*. Because the miners act as record-keepers by verifying the transactions, it is only fair if they get something in return. The mining process establishes the basis for the requirements. Each time a block is built, the quickest miner who solves the problem first receives a reward in exchange for its service; most of the time some newly generated native currency, fees or both. For example, each miner gets 12.5 Bitcoins (BTC) for building a block in Bitcoin's blockchain that is created afresh by the protocol. This reward may vary over time depending on the algorithm of the protocol. Bitcoin is designed to half the reward following a formula set inside its core. There will be a time when miners will only get the transaction fees; no reward for mining Bitcoin in future.

13.2 Hash Rate

A hash is the output of a hash function. The ability to generate it fast has a knock-on effect on the cryptocurrency mining and is considered the single most crucial element in the mining process.

13.2.1 Understanding Hash Rate

Previously in Chapters 3 and 4, we learned that mining involves finding a hash value associated with the block a miner builds. Tens of thousands of miners around the globe attempt to find this hash value. They generate the hash of the block header and compare it to see if it is the one that matches the criteria set by the protocol. If not, they increase the "nonce" in the header and generate the hash again. This process continues to go on until one miner discovers the hash fulfilling the conditions, for which he or she receives the reward and has the honour to build the next block.

This process tells us that finding the hash is indicative of the ability to compute fast; hence it is related to a parameter called *hash rate*. In plain words, the hash rate is the speed at which a machine is capable of operating within the context of Bitcoin or similar cryptocurrency, i.e. generating hashes.

13.2.2 Calculating Hash Rate

The hash rate is calculated in hashes per second (h/s). Depending on the number of hashes, this unit is accompanied by prefixes such as *mega-*, *giga-* and *tera-*. For instance, a machine having a speed of 60 h/s will be able to make 60 discoveries each second while building a block. Kilohash (KH/s) is used for 1000 hashes, mega-hash (MH/s) for 1000 kilohashes, gigahash (GH/s) for 1000 megahashes, terahash (TH/s) for 1000 gigahashes, petahash (PH/s) for 1000 terahashes and so on.

It is also notable that the hash rate for a machine is not a constant parameter. Because of the algorithmic differences leading to a different number of computing operations in hash functions, the hash rate for a machine varies for different cryptocurrencies. For example, a mining machine for Bitcoin has a different hash rate than that of Ethereum.

13.2.3 Hash Rate and Profits

The hash rate has a direct relationship with the profits a miner can earn. For example, while mining Bitcoin, a miner can earn 12.5 BTC until 23 May 2020. It is the hash rate that increases the possibility of earning this reward after building each block. Although the process does not follow a pattern and someone may discover the desired block by calculating fewer hashes than others, the hash rate remains the only variable in the mix that can be altered to increase the chances of winning the next reward. Amongst a certain number of miners, it will be likely that the miner having the greatest hash rate will win more than others.

13.3 Mining Hardware

Cryptocurrency mining is competitive and requires powerful hardware to compete with other miners in the network. Due to electricity playing a pivotal role in this process, it is a waste of energy and computer hardware to attempt to mine Bitcoin-like cryptocurrency if one does not have the appropriate tools to get to the battlefield of mining.

13.3.1 Non-Specialised Hardware

Non-specialised hardware is those that can be used for general-purpose computing, at least partially. Regular CPUs such as laptops and desktops; GPUs, or more commonly graphics cards used generally in gaming computers; and FPGAs used for designing customised devices through hardware programming are examples of non-specialised hardware.

This non-specialised hardware is capable of generating a hash rate in the range of mega- and gigahash for Bitcoin, but is no longer sufficient to compete with the other Bitcoin and similar cryptocurrency miners given the difficulty level of the mining. However, these devices are still used in Ethereum mining. If we recall from Chapter 5, the consensus algorithm of Ethereum is designed to suit regular computers rather than specialised hardware. Due to this constraint, Ethereum mining still retains some traditional approaches at least device-wise. Nonetheless, mining hardware companies have been trying hard to figure out how to design specialised hardware, and some are already in the market. The success of this hardware will depend on the level of competition they can create. If the performance remains the same, miners will opt to buy non-specialised hardware instead of those expensive devices.

Even though some specialised hardware is now considered less or not profitable in the absence of cheap electricity for mining Bitcoin, profit aside, mining can also be attempted even using small USB miners. Figure 13.1 shows four generations of mining hardware used in Bitcoin and similar cryptocurrency mining.

Figure 13.1   Mining hardware (clockwise from top left): CPU, GPU, FPGA and ASIC.

Table 13.1 Price and Hash Rate Comparison of the Latest Bitcoin-Mining ASICs (as of January 2019)

Name	Hash Rate	Company	Price
Dragonmint 16T	16.0 TH/s	Halong	$2729
Antminer S9	14.0 TH/s	Bitmain	$3000
Antminer R4	8.6 TH/s	Bitmain	$1000
Antminer S5+	7.722 TH/s	Bitmain	$2300
Antminer S7	4.73 TH/s	Bitmain	$500
Antminer S5	1.155 TH/s	Bitmain	$299

13.3.2 Specialised Hardware (ASICs)

An application-specific integrated circuit (ASIC) is a specialised hardware and an integrated circuit (IC) customised for a particular application. Examples of such chips include a digital voice recorder, a handheld computer and special transmission protocol in addition to high-efficiency cryptocurrency miners. Although Nakamoto intended for Bitcoin to be mined on desktop computers using CPUs, Bitcoin miners discovered they could get more hashing power, at first from graphics cards and then ASICs.

There are many ASIC miners available in the market made by several mining-hardware producing companies (Table 13.1). Amongst them, Dragonmint 16T, Antminer S9 and Antminer R4 are the most powerful and most expensive in the market (as of January 2019). More reasonably priced device includes Antminer S7 and Antminer S5, although the latter is no longer profitable for mining Bitcoin.

Three large companies dominate the current mining hardware market. They are as follows:

- *Halong Mining*: The newcomer in the industry producing the best mining tool available in the market. It produces Dragonmint T16, the most potent mining hardware currently in use with a hash rate of 16 TH/s.
- *Bitmain Technologies*: Based in China, the most dominant ASICs-building company in the industry. It has been producing the Antminer line for Bitcoin mining for a long time. The company also operates a mining pool.
- *Bitfury*: It is one of the largest producers of Bitcoin mining hardware and chips. Based in the US, it is also one of the largest Bitcoin pools. Its hardware, however, is not available for purchase outside the pool as of writing.

13.3.3 Profitability Factors

It is necessary that the profitability factors are carefully analysed before buying hardware to mine cryptocurrencies. Profitability factors give the potential miners tentative information on how much they could earn by mining a particular crypto-currency. The price of the hardware needs to be deducted from the earnings to get a tentative per-year earning from the mining initiative.

For instance, if the electricity costs $0.03 per kWh and the hash rate of an ASIC is 16 TH/s and costs 1480 watts to achieve that feat, depending on the price of Bitcoin, we can get an estimation from the Bitcoin Mining Profit Calculator.* As shown in Figure 13.2, it is going to generate no profit if the price of Bitcoin is $3728 or less. With our example conditions, to see a positive earning from the mining the price needs to be at least more than $3729; this still does not give a profit as the miner needs to subtract the cost of the device from the mining income to figure out the net profit.

13.4 Pooled Mining

Pooled mining has been a popular concept in cryptocurrency mining that helps to tackle the growing difficulties of the mining process. It is generally organised by a company that then makes the necessary arrangement to accumulate miners and distribute rewards amongst them. China is the most popular destination for pooled mining due to a large number of miners who reside there.

13.4.1 Pooled Mining Basics

Pooled mining is a mining approach where multiple generating clients contribute to the generation of a block, and then split the block reward according to the con-tributed processing power. Pooled mining effectively reduces the granularity of the block-generation reward, spreading it out more evenly over time.

With increasing generation difficulty, mining with lower-performance devices can take a very long time before block generation, on average. For example, with a mining speed of 1000 KH/s, at a difficulty of 14484 (which was in effect at the end of December 2010), the average time to generate a block is almost 2 years.

To provide a more inviting incentive to lower-performance miners, several min-ing pools, using different approaches, have been created. With a mining pool, a lot of different people contribute to generating a block, and the reward is then split amongst them according to their processing contribution. This way, instead of waiting for years to generate 50 BTC in a block, a smaller miner may get a fraction

---

* There are several mining calculators available online that can be accessed freely. The calculator used in this book can be accessed using the following URL: www.buybitcoinworldwide.com/mining/calculator/.

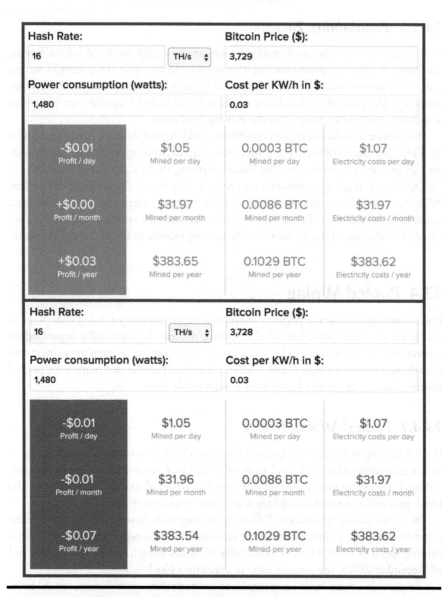

Figure 13.2   Profit estimation from Bitcoin mining.

of a Bitcoin on a more regular basis. The mining pool awards a share of the obtained reward to the clients who can present a valid proof of work.

13.4.2 Mining Pools

The concept of pooled mining began in 2010 when *Slush Pool* launched the first ever pooled mining initiative by the name "Bitcoin Pooled Mining Server". The company is currently owned by Satoshi Labs, a Czech-based tech company. Slush Pool is the sixth largest pool, as of early 2019, and mined more than 15,000 blocks in the Bitcoin network with a total hash power of about 7.3%.

In the current cryptocurrency mining landscape, most large pools are from China with five of them grabbing the top five spots. *BTC.com* and *AntPool* are two Beijing-based Bitcoin pools operated by the world's largest Bitcoin hardware manufacturer, Bitmain Technologies. Amongst the pools, they retain the top two positions interchangeably. During early 2019, together they held more than 30% hash power.

F2Pool, commonly known as the Discus Fish mining pool in the world of Bitcoin mining, is the third largest pool in the Bitcoin network with 11.3% hash power, while *BTC.TOP* is one of the fastest growing pools launched only in 2017 that holds the fourth spot with a hash power of 7.8%. *ViaBTC* is a newly launched mining pool that mines Bitcoin, Litecoin and BitcoinCash. It takes the fifth spot with about 7.7% hash power, although these latter positions are so close that they frequently change over time.

Amongst the pools based outside China, Slush Pool (Czech Republic), Eligius (US) and Bitfury (Georgia) are renowned but very small in size. Figure 13.3 shows the standing of the pools during early 2019 based on data calculated by Blockchain. com. The relative hash power of the pools is a rough estimation and for various reasons will not be 100% accurate. This standing also changes over time as new

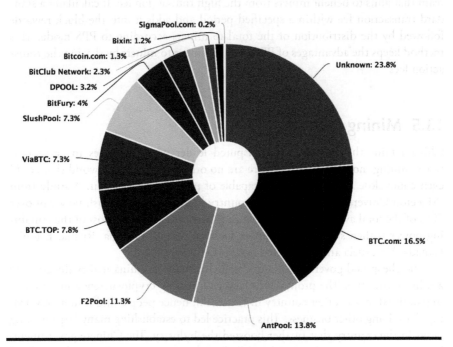

Figure 13.3   Standing of the mining pools during early 2019.

hardware hits the market and miners switch pools due to benefits and advantages. The large portion of "Unknown" blocks are not attacks on the network but rather indicate that the data provider was unable to determine the origin.

13.4.3 Reward Sharing

The problem with pooled mining is that steps must be taken to prevent cheating by the clients and the server. Currently, there are several different approaches used. For example, the *slush* approach, introduced by the Slush Pool, follows a score-based method. Older shares, from the beginning of the round, have a lower weight than more recent shares, which reduces the motivation to cheat by switching between pools within a round.

The *pay-per-share (PPS)* approach offers an instant even payout for each share that is solved. The payout is offered from the pool's existing balance and can be withdrawn immediately without having to wait for a block to be solved or confirmed. The possibility of cheating the miners by the pool operator and by timing attacks is thus eliminated. This method results in the least possible variance for miners while transferring all risk to the pool operator. The resulting possibility of loss for the server is compensated by setting a payout lower than the full expected value.

The *full pay-per-share (FPPS)* is another approach introduced by the BTC.com team that aims to benefit miners from the high transaction fee. It calculates a standard transaction fee within a specified period and adds it into the block rewards followed by the distribution of the total to miners according to PPS mode. This method keeps the advantages of PPS and pays more to miners by sharing the transaction fees.

13.5 Mining Nations

China retains the title of the undisputed leader when it comes to cryptocurrency mining, notably Bitcoin. There are no other nations in the world that could even come close to what China is capable of producing every year. A study from Princeton University found that the country holds the mining hash power of over 70% of the total available in the network [Kaiser et al., 2018]. Most of the remaining power is then shared by countries such as Iceland, Georgia, Russia, Estonia, Canada, Venezuela and the United States [Lielacher, 2018].

The cheap and government-subsidised electricity in China makes the country a mining paradise. The profitability factor of mining cryptocurrency in China is unparalleled to any other country in the world; hence people find it more rewarding than doing other business. This practice led to establishing many large mining pools in the country that further boosted the industry. The Chinese government, however, is not very comfortable with this practice due to misuse of subsidised electricity, and the crackdown on mining rigs in late 2017 was considered an action motivated by this concern.

There is no denying that two small countries, Iceland and Georgia, are the surprise entries in this list of mining nations. This is due to their geographical location and weather. Russia, Canada and Northern parts of the Scandinavia are also popular destinations for mining cryptocurrency for the same reason. It is because of the availability of the cold weather in those regions that helps cool down the mining rigs. It is just not the device that consumes the energy; cooling equipment also consumes a significant portion that those regions close to the North Pole can save. Mining sites, particularly in Iceland (Figure 13.4), also have the opportunity to produce less pollution than the coal-burning sites located in China, for they have access to geothermal and hydroelectric power plants, both cheaper and more environmentally friendly alternatives to coal. These advantages have led to mining companies relocating there from all around the globe. To put it in context, it was reported that Iceland was set to consume more electricity by the mining companies than households in the country in 2018 [Zuckerman, 2018].

13.6 Criticism of PoW Mining

The PoW-based cryptocurrency mining that consumes enormous energy has been the subject of severe criticism from renewable energy experts since the early days of Bitcoin. Although PoW is central to the security of the blockchain, it is often seen as a colossal waste of electricity by the people outside the community [NewScientist, 2017; Coppola, 2018].

Figure 13.4 A mining farm operated by Genesis Mining in Iceland.

Experts have been trying to put the consumption in context by comparing with known instances. In 2017, *The Guardian* reported that the yearly energy consumption of Ireland is less than what the Bitcoin network consumed and produces the same annual carbon emissions as one million transatlantic flights [Hern, 2017, 2018]. Despite those comparisons, how big this waste is remains complicated to express on a scale that can compare it with potentially anything. Such a scale became available when a study published in *Nature* put Bitcoin mining in the same context of precious metal mining. The study found that the amount of energy required to mine one dollar's worth of Bitcoin is more than twice that required to mine the same value of copper, gold or platinum [Krause and Tolaymat, 2018]. Figure 13.5 shows the energy consumption for mining cryptocurrencies compared to precious metals on the dollar scale.

China, being the most famous mining destination for Bitcoin, put more criticism in this mix. Chinese miners often use cheap coals to mine cryptocurrency, which severely damages the environment. Because the whole mining process is unregulated, there is no authority to ensure the cleanliness of the energy or enforce mining rigs to use renewable energy for these purposes.

Nevertheless, the landscape has been changing in recent times as a trend can be observed where mining companies are willingly using renewable energy, perhaps to reduce the cost [Kim, 2018b]. This move came amid the cracking down of mining rigs in China by the government, which encouraged many Chinese mining pools to move their operations to Europe. This geographical relocation was met with a piece of good news in the form of Bitcoin's difficulty which was set to decrease, not increase, for the first time since December 2011. Many new cryptocurrencies, meanwhile, avoided PoW and adopted a more energy-efficient way to establish consensus in the network, while Ethereum, one of the largest industries for PoW

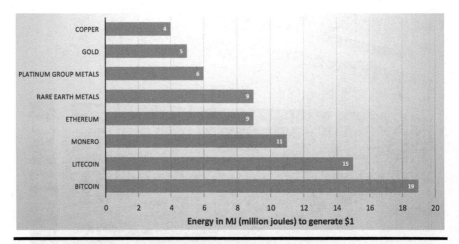

Figure 13.5   Energy consumption for mining cryptocurrencies compared to precious metals.

mining, already has been in the process of moving to an alternative consensus mechanism with proof of stake.

13.7 Summary

This chapter presented the cryptocurrency mining from the industry and operational perspective rather than discussing algorithms. It briefly presented some important key concepts such as mining difficulty, incentivisation, hash rate and its relation with the choice of hardware. The chapter then went on to present the required hardware, pooled mining approach, reward-sharing methods, mining pools and their hash power, popular destinations for mining and criticisms of this process due to excessive energy consumption that is often viewed as a misuse.

Chapter 14

Cryptocurrency Wallet

The concept of the cryptocurrency wallet is misleading as it never holds the token. We already learned that Bitcoin and similar cryptocurrencies have no virtual existence; hence they do not reside on the blockchain or our computers. The blockchain stores only the transactions, while our computers may have the client software to interact with the blockchain. The ownership of the tokens is determined based on the transactions triggered by the private–public key pair. Therefore, a place to keep these key pairs can be the closest analogy for a real wallet. This chapter takes the opportunity to discuss various types of cryptocurrency wallets from the personal wallet to cold storage used by exchanges. The key objectives of this chapter are to establish the importance of wallets within the context of cryptocurrency and show why their safeguarding is necessary. The chapter also helps users understand how to pick a suitable wallet for their tokens.

14.1 Wallet

A wallet is a place to store the required public and private key pairs that give access to cryptocurrency. Because transactions between two or more bearers determine the owners, the public key acts as the medium of receiving tokens, while the private key gives the right to spend those tokens by granting access. It is, therefore, no exaggeration to say that the keys are the actual representative of the tokens, and losing the keys, particularly the private key, means losing the tokens.

A wallet can be of different types: software, hardware, physical or even a brain wallet. The type of wallets might also differ depending on their actions such as a multi-signature wallet, a receive-only wallet, a cold-storage wallet and so forth. Wallets have been subject to various attacks since the inception of cryptocurrency and users need to safeguard their tokens by increasing the securities of their wallets. This involves encrypting keys or storing them using multiple private keys.

Some users keep their keys offline, while some go as far as memorising their keys removing any form of physical or digital existence.

A wallet closely works with a piece of software that allows spending the funds. Sometimes this software itself acts as the wallet by storing the keys, yet seldom does its role remains limited to giving access to the blockchain. In any case, this software lets users spend the funds, interact with the blockchain and request payments. This software may reside on the user's computer or can be a web application.

The public–private key pair plays a pivotal role in sending and receiving funds. Reviewing the structures of the keys and the transaction process is essential to understand the importance of wallets and their safeguarding.

14.1.1 Private Key and Address

In Bitcoin and similar cryptocurrencies, the address represents the hash of the public key, while the private key is a 256-bit number. The following shows a Bitcoin and an Ethereum address and their corresponding private key. Please note that these are sample addresses and private key pairs. Readers must not send tokens to these addresses as they may lose their money.

Bitcoin address and private keys:
19BEJfwj7Ej5s6uy3uiKGvRuygjrujNRhG
L1FGnCmpU9kGVHAKnU5TunkeiB7exsUdWjBKwn3cH3HsqsuUWLmS
Ethereum address and private keys:
0xC2D7CF95645D33006175B78989035C7c9061d3F9
3a1076bf45ab87712ad64ccb3b10217737f7faacbf2872e88fdd9a537d8fe266

14.1.2 Transferring Funds

The transfer of funds is achieved using the key pair. Let us retrace a bit. We learned in Chapter 4 that Bitcoin's address is a hash representation of a public key. It is called "representation" because it does not contain the key, but rather its hash value in a particular format with other metadata. Notable cryptocurrencies including Ethereum and Ripple also follow this convention.

This address is the key to receive funds. For example, Alice requested Bob to send her a payment using this address. Bob in response will transfer the funds to this address by inserting it into the transaction request. Once miners verify the transaction and include it in a block, the fund gets locked and only the private key of the associated address can redeem it.

Alice must have the private key in her wallet that she will use to access the transferred fund. She uses her private key to generate a digital signature where her public key acts as the message. It accompanies a hash of the message encrypted by the private key. Alice sends this message as an instruction to redeem the funds.

The protocol then verifies the signature. A valid signature designates the public key to be the counterpart of a private key that possibly qualifies to redeem the fund. It is, however, not readily made available to Alice. She must pass through one last drill. The hash of this public key is then compared with the hash of the address. If that matches, the protocol unlocks the funds for Alice to redeem in a new transaction. This example explains the importance of keeping the keys secure. It is illustrated in Figure 14.1 describing the steps of transferring and accessing funds.

14.2 Types of Wallets

There is no hard and fast rule for a wallet. It is just a storing place for the keys. People can be innovative in making their wallets as long as they securely store the keys. However, they must bring in the keys to a software wallet connected to the

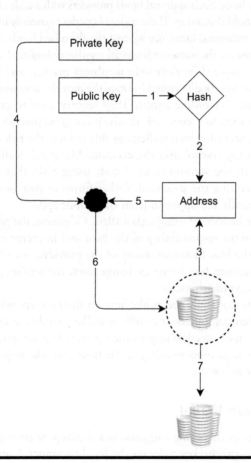

Figure 14.1   A typical fund transfer of major cryptocurrencies.

internet to interact with the blockchain and spend the funds. These kinds of wallets are called hot wallets, while the wallets that remain offline are called cold wallets. The following discusses some ordinary wallets that can be found in regular use.

14.2.1 Web Wallet

A web wallet is an online account with an external provider where users deposit their keys to interact with the blockchain to access their funds. Web wallets are also known as hosted wallets or cloud wallets. Using a web wallet requires granting the host to manage the funds on behalf of their users. Giving the responsibility of the private keys means conferring them with access to the funds; hence any security breach on their server would immensely affect users. It is therefore essential to choose the right web wallet provider that the users can trust.

One way to pick a reputed wallet provider is to examine their approval from the local financial regulatory body. Such approval binds providers with a code of conduct that they must practice to uphold this status. These codes of conduct generally include maintaining high cybersecurity measures, insurance against the deposited funds and regular inspections. Table 14.1 presents the names of financial regulatory bodies of some countries and territories that are renowned for their strict regulatory practice, and having recognition from one or more of these bodies would indicate the provider is somewhat reliable.

Web wallets are like online banks. They require users to create one or more forms of authentication to access their funds. It is a good practice to use two-factor authentication for accessing web wallets, as this reduces the risk of suffering hacking attacks and losing control over the account. Many web wallets connect users' mobile phones with the account to send code using SMS that requires inserting at the time of providing the password. Other forms of two-factor authentication include sending emails and approval from the mobile app.

There are some benefits of using web wallets. Of course, the principal advantage is that the keys are the responsibility of the host and in events of security threats, insurance covers the loss. However, many of the providers are also exchanges that can give low transactions fees, better exchange rates, and fee-free portfolios to manage and invest in cryptocurrencies.

Some providers store only the public keys on their servers, while users store the private keys on their computers or in offline wallets. In this setup, usually called a hybrid web wallet, users need to import their private keys temporarily to the server to spend funds. It helps users to mitigate the trust and take responsibility for their keys while using a web wallet.

14.2.2 Software Wallet

A software wallet, as the name suggests, is a desktop or smartphone application to store the public–private key pairs on the local computer. Sometimes the blockchain itself may provide the wallet. For instance, the Ethereum blockchain provides

Table 14.1 Major Financial Regulatory Bodies

Country	Authority	Abbreviation
United Kingdom	The Financial Conduct Authority	FCA
United States	Securities and Exchange Commission	SEC
Australia	Australian Securities and Investments Commission	ASIC
Canada	Investment Industry Regulatory Organization of Canada	IIROC
Ireland	Central Bank of Ireland	CBI
Germany	Federal Financial Supervisory Authority	BaFin
France	Autorite des marches financiers	AFM
Denmark	Financial Supervision Authority	DFSA
Austria	Financial Market Authority	FMA
Belgium	Financial Services and Markets Authority	FSMA
Netherlands	Financial Markets Authority	AFM
Luxembourg	Commission de Surveillance du Secteur Financier	CSSF
Switzerland	Financial Market Supervisory Authority	FINMA
Singapore	Monetary Authority of Singapore	MAS
Hong Kong	The Financial Commission	FinCom
UAE	Dubai Financial Services Authority	DFSA
Cayman Islands	Cayman Islands Monetary Authority	CIMA
Cyprus	Cyprus Securities and Exchange Commission	CySEC

Mint, a wallet application that acts as client software for Ethereum accounts and resides on the users' computers. Bitcoin Core, the client software for Bitcoin, also has a wallet. Web wallet providers may also allow users to install software wallets at their computers. Such software may store the private keys, while the web server contains corresponding public keys and only imports private keys at the time of spending funds.

Software wallets are subject to many security perils. These wallets usually have internet connectivity, allowing adversaries to launch attacks from the outside. Even if the attackers fail to seize the keys, damage to the hard drive or losing the software database means users can no longer access the funds unless they have the keys stored somewhere else. Unlike web wallets, these are not protected by insurance and copies of the keys are not stored safely at multiple locations on the server.

Software wallets, however, can be handy if managed carefully. Keeping a backup in the form of a paper wallet (we learn about this soon) at a secure place removes the risk of losing the keys in the event of physical damage to the computer, while encrypting the keys using a robust algorithm can safeguard them from the hacking attacks. One of the principal benefits of this type of wallet is the ability to generate keys at the local machine with ease. It also assists in managing funds locally without disclosing the keys to a third party.

14.2.3 External Storage Media

Both web wallets and software wallets are forms of hot wallets that remain connected with the internet. Despite taking precautionary measures, these wallets endure potential threats from outside attackers. One way to remove such a threat is to use cold wallets that do not have internet connectivity. There are several cold wallets available in practice, and external storage media is one of them.

The external storage media wallet utilises storage like USB flash drives or optical drives. These storage media safely store private keys in a place that is not reachable by hackers. It is still advisable to encrypt the keys on the storage media to protect them from offline attacks like attempts to copy the keys from the device.

The weak link of such a wallet is the moment of importing the keys to the software or web wallet intending to spend some of the funds. To mitigate this risk, the best practice is not to accumulate a large amount of funds under a single key; instead, manage them separately so that later individual keys can be imported to spend the linked funds. It alleviates the risk of losing all funds at once in the event of an attack.

14.2.4 Paper Wallet

A paper wallet is a piece of paper where private keys are stored in printed form. It is then kept in a safe place to prevent physical theft. A paper wallet is one of the safest ways to deposit keys, as it not only curtails the likelihood of potential online attacks but also eliminates the digital existence of the keys.

To distinguish the key pairs, generally, public keys are printed alongside their corresponding private keys. Because public and private keys are long hexadecimal numbers in the printed form, the software creating the paper wallet also generates a QR code for the convenience of reading the number from the wallet. Figure 14.2 shows a sample paper wallet generated using www.bitaddress.org.

Figure 14.2   A typical paper wallet.

As the external storage media, keys on a paper wallet need transferring to a software or web wallet before users can spend the funds. This process of importing keys is a point of vulnerability that users must take care of. Storing the wallet in a secure physical location is also of utmost necessity, otherwise the whole point of using a paper wallet becomes worthless.

14.2.5 Hardware Wallet

A hardware wallet is a device that stores private keys and associated transactions. These wallets offer arguably the safest possible digital option that users may avail. Unlike an external storage medium, the private keys of a hardware wallet never leave the device. The device of a hardware wallet is specially designed to communicate with the client software of the blockchain and spends the funds by generating the digital signature locally within the wallet; hence the hardware wallet remains protected from attacks launched at web or software wallets.

Hardware wallets often come in the shape of flash drives with a screen to display the transactions. These wallets utilise the USB port of computers to connect with the client. Users can observe the transactions the wallet executes on the screen and some sophisticated wallets may also provide extra buttons to grant further permission to proceed or abort. It is a common requirement for a hardware wallet to enter a PIN before accessing the data. Figure 14.3 shows a hardware wallet interacting with the Bitcoin blockchain to spend some funds.

Trezor and *Ledger* are the two most popular hardware wallets available in the market. Because of the sensitivity of the data that these wallets intend to store, manufacturers put in every effort to make them secure in every possible way. These wallets come in a secured box having a safety seal on it confirming that the product has not been tampered with. Inside, the device comes with a USB cable to connect with computers, several recovery seed cards and full instructions for users as to how to use the device to store and use private keys associated with cryptocurrencies. As of December 2018, they cost just below $100 each.

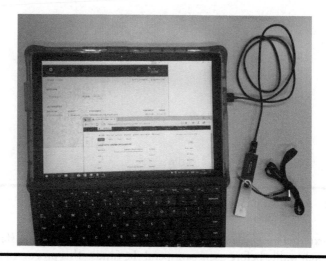

Figure 14.3   An actual Bitcoin transaction from a web-based cryptocurrency exchange to a hardware wallet. (Source: Image created by FlippyFlink, who released it under the creative commons license CC BY-SA 4.0.)

14.2.6 Brain Wallet

A brain wallet is not a wallet of any form, but a technique to store private keys in the users' mind. A private key is a large number, for instance, the length of a Bitcoin private key is 256 bits. It is difficult for an ordinary individual to memorise such a long number, hence it is rarely attempted. The technique is to generate the hash of a password in the size required. Because Bitcoin private keys are 256 bits long, SHA256 can be utilised for this blockchain.

A brain wallet stores the password in the brain and does not require keeping backups as long as the user can remember the passphrase. Like a paper wallet, it does not constitute an actual wallet, and the keys need importing to a web or software wallet for accessing funds.

The brain wallet is subject to brute-force attacks that could lead to stealing the funds. If the password is not strong enough, this kind of wallet is as vulnerable as a simple email password against the brute-force attacks of hackers. It is, therefore, essential for the users to pick the password carefully with a high degree of entropy [Goodin, 2012].

The rule of thumb for creating a strong password is to have at least 12 characters including numbers, symbols, and lower- and upper-case letters. The password must not have dictionary words or a combination of words that can be quickly identified, and rely on obvious substitutions such as "H0use" for "House" [Hoffman, 2018]. A password fulfilling these requirements is challenging for users to memorise, and a little technique may help. In order to remember a password of that complexity, the right way is to generate the password from a memorable sentence. For example, "The first house I rented in Dublin is 5 Vernon Avenue in Clontarf, and the rent was $440 per month". We can turn this into a strong password by taking the first letter of each word. This gives us "TfhIriDi5VAiCatrw$4pm". It would take about 3 sextillion years for a hacker to break this password applying a brute-force attack using a desktop computer.*

14.3 Special Wallets

There are some particular types of wallets in use that are not common amongst regular users. Organisations such as exchanges and online sellers that deal with a considerable amount of funds generally use these wallets. The primary objective of these wallets is not usability but security. These wallets are designed in such a way that stealing funds would require tremendous efforts both online and offline.

14.3.1 Multi-Signature Wallet

Multi-signature wallets are those that require multiple keys to access the funds. Let us recap what we learned in Chapter 4. The concept of multi-signature refers to requiring more than one key to authorise a transaction. It is available in all major blockchains and generally used to divide up responsibility for possession of cryptocurrencies such as Bitcoin, Ether and XRP. Standard transactions on a blockchain network are "single-signature transactions". It is because transfers in these transactions require only one signature– from the owner of the private key associated with the token address. However, Bitcoin and most major networks support much more complicated transactions that require the signatures of multiple people before the funds can be transferred. These are often referred to as M-of-N transactions.

Typically, all types of multi-signature wallets require M-of-N signatures. Let's suppose we have configured a multi-signature wallet for 3-of-5 authorised signatures. This means a transaction would only become valid when at least three out of five authorisers sign it. Multi-signature wallets are useful to securely protect funds and prevent loss of funds in the event of losing keys. This type of wallet is generally used by exchanges, companies and organisations that need to store a large amount of funds in a single wallet.

14.3.2 Cold-Storage Wallet

Cold storage in the context of cryptocurrency refers to keeping a reserve of tokens offline. This is often a necessary security precaution, especially dealing with large amounts of funds. For example, a cryptocurrency exchange typically offers an instant withdrawal feature and might be a steward of hundreds of thousands of

---

* Interested readers may use the website www.howsecureismypassword.net to examine their passwords.

tokens. To minimise the possibility that an intruder could steal the entire reserve in a security breach, the operator of the exchange follows a best practice by keeping the majority of the reserve in cold storage, or, in other words, not present on the web server or any other computer. The only amount kept on the server is the amount needed to cover anticipated withdrawals. The remaining amounts are kept offline.

There are several options available to implement cold storage. A paper wallet, hardware wallet or external storage device can store the keys. This wallet is then stored at a secured location. Deep cold storage refers to storing the offline wallet in a safe deposit box, insured locker and so on to add a further layer of protection. Cold storages usually contain a multi-signature wallet, making it extremely difficult for hackers to steal the funds.

Figure 14.4, generated using bitinfocharts.com, shows the five wealthiest Bitcoin addresses collecting tokens in December 2018 that would have been more than $11 billion at the all-time-high price of Bitcoin. It is no surprise that all of them are cold storage for the world's five largest cryptocurrency exchanges, and three out of five wallets are multi-signature.

14.3.3 Receive-Only Wallet

A receive-only wallet is a unique wallet that refers to the ability to receive funds but not spend them. These wallets do not hold private keys; they only include the public keys to generate addresses. This wallet is a good idea if the recipient is a seller or an exchange where a large volume of in-flow is regularly expected. The funds of a receive-only wallet can be transferred to a more appropriate wallet or cold storage later.

14.4 Deterministic Wallet

A deterministic wallet is a wallet that can generate many addresses and their associated private keys from a shared private key. Deterministic wallets have several advantages over regular wallets. For instance, regular wallets need to backup every user who creates a new address. In contrast, a deterministic wallet requires only one backup when the wallet is set up. The backup size of a regular wallet grows over time as new addresses are added to it. Some wallets come with a large size – for example, the Bitcoin Core Wallet generates 100 addresses in advance by default. On the other hand, the backup of a deterministic wallet has a small constant size, as only the master password needs to be backed up.

14.4.1 Type-1 Wallet

Type-1 deterministic wallets can be derived from brain wallets. The process begins with a password and a counter. Let suppose the password is "TfhIriDi5VAiCatrw$4pm", which we created in the discussion of brain wallet.

	Address	Balance △1w/△1m	% of coins	First In	Last In
1	3D2oetdNuZUqQHPJmcMDDHYoqkyNVsFk9r 3-of-6 wallet: Bitfinex-coldwallet	138,661 BTC ($503,717,903 USD)	0.7947%	2017-01-05 12:34:15	2018-12-23 15:06:43
2	352USv8Cih1Bq81XnzB2C9VLMQBh55Y4uV wallet: Binance-coldwallet	109,232 BTC ($396,811,885 USD)	0.6261%	2018-11-20 10:14:20	2018-12-10 14:00:27
3	3Cbq7aT1tY8kMxWLbitaG7yT6bPbKChq64 3-of-5 wallet: Huobi-wallet	108,135 BTC ($392,824,327 USD)	0.6198%	2017-09-08 17:41:05	2018-12-25 02:49:38
4	3Nxwenay9Z8Lc9JBiywExpnEFiLp6Afp8v 3-of-5 wallet: Bitstamp-coldwallet	107,848 BTC ($391,784,018 USD)	0.6181%	2015-10-16 15:43:06	2018-12-16 14:54:11
5	16rCmCmbuWDhPjWTrpQGaU3EPdZF7MTdUk wallet: Bittrex-coldwallet	107,203 BTC ($389,440,147 USD)	0.6144%	2016-02-27 18:00:09	2018-12-18 23:19:13

Figure 14.4   The five wealthiest Bitcoin addresses. It is no surprise that all of them are cold storage for the world's five largest cryptocurrency exchanges.

A counter n is appended at the end of the password before hashing it to yield the private key:

$$priv = H(pw \mid n) \tag{14.1}$$

This private key is then used to create the public key and subsequently the address:

$$B = priv.A \bmod p \tag{14.2}$$

The explanation of Equation 14.2 is presented in Section 2.4 in Chapter 2, where A is the generator of the elliptic curve, B is the public key and p is the order of the prime field under which the elliptic curve operations are performed.

The addresses generated by a type-1 deterministic wallet are impossible to relate to one another by anyone who does not know the master password. Like brain wallets, type-1 deterministic wallets are sensitive to brute-force attacks and should not be used unless the master password has been generated with enough entropy.

14.4.2 Type-2 Wallet

Type-2 deterministic wallets separate the roles of the generation of private keys and the generation of addresses. Unlike type-1 wallets, it does not rely on a master password (pw) but only rather utilises an extra component called a master private key (mpk). These two components together generate the private key:

$$priv = mpk + H(pw \mid n) \tag{14.3}$$

This wallet splits the elliptic curve cryptography (ECC) private key into two parts: a public key and a password:

$$B = privA \bmod p \tag{14.4}$$

From Equation 14.3,

$$B = mpkA + H(pw \mid n)A \bmod p \tag{14.5}$$

$$B = B_{mpk} + H(pw \mid n)A \bmod p \tag{14.6}$$

Equation 14.6 shows the generation of the public key not involving the corresponding private key. Instead, the process uses a master public key in combination with a master password.

Type-2 deterministic wallets increase security because of the separation of the roles of the *mpk* and the *pw*. The *mpk* is a regular ECC private key randomly generated and backed up following standard procedures. The compromise of this key does not necessarily mean the loss of the funds, hence it can be shared amongst many users. Businesses such as online portals with customer-facing servers can benefit from the key-split. The administrator can give the servers a copy of the B_{mpk} and the *pw*. Servers then use them to generate new addresses for receiving payments from customers. As the servers do not keep a copy of the private keys for those addresses, the funds will not be subject to any attack. The attacker can only identify the location of the funds stored but not be able to steal them.

14.4.3 HD Wallet

A HD wallet, or hierarchical deterministic wallet, is a type of cryptocurrency wallet that is amongst the most popular wallet in use at the moment. Its popularity is partly because of the convenience it provides and partly due to its security. Its mathematical foundation is based on the deterministic wallets described earlier; however, it comes with a set of extra features that enhances the security and the usability of this wallet to a great extent.

A HD wallet derives addresses form a hierarchy starting with a secret. It follows the convention of type-2 wallet where public and private keys are derived separately. The novelty introduced by HD wallets is that it stores the generated addresses in a tree structure such that a node has visibility of its descendants but not of its ascendants. There are two types of nodes in the tree: private nodes that hold the private keys to the sub-tree originating from them, and public nodes that hold only the public keys to their sub-tree. In addition to the private and public keys, each node includes an additional 32-byte field called the chain code. The goal of the chain code is to add additional entropy to each node. Thus revealing an address does not automatically reveal the tree derived from that node.

While using an HD wallet, the backing up of the seed key is mandatory. It is also recommended that the users should keep this backup safely stored somewhere

Table 14.2 Major Wallet Providers

Name	Control	Anonymity	Usability	Type	Tokens
Bitcoin Core	User	High	Difficult	Desktop	BTC
Ethereum Mist	User	Medium	Average	Desktop	ETH
Ledger Nano S	User	Medium	Difficult	Hardware, desktop	Most major coins
Trezor Wallet	User	Medium	Average	Hardware, mobile desktop	BTC, ETH, altcoins
CoinPayments	Third party	Medium	Easy	Mobile	All major coins
Guarda	User	High	Easy	Mobile, web desktop	Most major coins
Multiwallet	Third party	High	Easy	Mobile, web	Most major coins
Coinomi	User	Medium	Easy	Mobile	Most major coins
Exodus	User	High	Easy	Desktop	Most major coins
Satowallet	Third party	Low	Easy	Mobile, web desktop	BTC, ETH, most altcoins
Jaxx	User	High	Average	Mobile, web desktop	BTC, ETH, most altcoins
Citowise	User	High	Easy	Mobile	BTC, ETH, most altcoins

(Continued)

Table 14.2 (Continued)   Major Wallet Providers

Name	Control	Anonymity	Usability	Type	Tokens
UberPay	User	Medium	Easy	Mobile	BTC and major altcoins
KeepKey Wallet	User	Medium	Difficult	Hardware, mobile desktop	BTC, ETH, LTC, BCH, DOGE, DASH
Qbao Network	User	High	Easy	Mobile	ETH, ERC-20, QTUM, QRC20
MT	Third party	Medium	Easy	Web	BTC, ETH, MTRC
Blockchain	Third party	Low	Easy	Mobile, web	BTC, ETH, BCH
CoolWallet S	User	High	Average	Hardware, mobile	BTC, ETH, XRP, LTC, BCH
Kimera	Third Party	High	Average	Web	BTC, ETH, XRP, XLM, LTC, BCH, ADA, ERC-20
Enjin	User	High	Easy	Mobile	BTC, LTC, ETH

so that the wallet can be restored in the event of theft or damage. Moreover, the excellence of HD wallets is that taking a backup only once allows users to recreate all the addresses mathematically as explained earlier.

14.5 Wallet Providers

There are plenty of wallet providers available in the market. Some of them provide hardware wallets, while some offer only desktop and mobile wallets. Desktop versions come in Windows, Linux and MacOS operating systems, while mobile versions offer Android and iOS. However, it depends on the providers if they wish to cover all or a part of these operating systems. The permitted coins is another criterion that users must keep in mind, as not all providers allow storing all available tokens. Some providers charge fees, while many keep the service free of charge by monetising their business through advertisements or partnering with other services.

Many blockchains come with their wallets, for example the Bitcoin Core wallet and Ethereum Mist wallet. These wallets are often very reliable but not user-friendly. It is a good idea to start exploring from native wallets, but using a commercial HD wallet will be the best option. These wallets come with many extra features and provide user-friendly interfaces, and are often on multiple platforms allowing users to access their funds from smartphones, laptops or desktop computers.

Comparing the underlying technology, permitted tokens and services offered by the providers, users may pick and choose whom they want to take the wallet from and whom they will ignore. Table 14.2 provides a list of wallet providers comparing them using five criteria: control, anonymity, usability, type and supported tokens. The first two wallets on the list are the official Bitcoin and Ethereum wallets, while the remaining are third-party commercial providers.

14.6 Summary

This chapter took the effort of presenting the theories and underlying principles of cryptocurrency wallets. It offered broad discussions on how the concept of a wallet works, various types of wallets, the construction of deterministic wallets and recommendations for some wallet providers. One of the key objectives of the chapter was to help readers pick a suitable wallet for their tokens for secure storage to supplement the discussion of Chapter 15 that talks through the trading and investment methods using cryptocurrencies.

Chapter 15

Cryptocurrency Trading and Investment

A cryptocurrency is an investment instrument that investors can use to obtain a return. Unlike a stock or a bond, it is a notably different kind of investment tool that involves not only business and financial aspects but also a technological perspective. To determine how good a cryptocurrency is, understanding its underlying principles and potential to serve specific uses-cases are essential. The first eleven chapters of this book elaborate on this front. This chapter takes the liberty to present the investment outlook of this technology focusing on practical aspects such as distinguishing the asset classes and knowing the possible investment options. The principal objective of this chapter is to provide some basic understanding of investment so that investors having no or little prior experience can find a place to begin. With that objective in mind, the chapter first introduces the asset classes and continues to explain portfolios such as funds, exchange-traded funds (ETFs) and indices before discussing the exchanges and platforms. Finally, the chapter briefly discusses various investment strategies and possible ways to implement those in the current landscape of the cryptocurrency market. Nevertheless, investment as a discipline is a vast topic and it is impossible to elaborately cover everything within a few pages; hence, this is not attempted in this chapter.

15.1 Investment

The process of investment is distributing money in the expectation of some benefit in the future such as investment in financial assets, durable goods, real estate, factories, product development or research. Amongst these, financial assets are particular types of investments where the benefit is called a *return*. The return may consist of a profit from the sale of property or an investment, or investment income including dividends, interests, rental income or a combination. The projected economic return is the appropriately discounted value of future returns [Arnold, 2014].

Investors generally expect higher returns from riskier investments, while making a low-risk investment will usually earn a low return. In this context, the risk–return ratio, which is a measure of return in terms of risk for a specific time period, gives an idea about a particular investment and its associated risks. Investors who are not experienced often seek advice from experts to adopt a particular investment strategy and diversify their portfolio in order to statistically reduce overall risk. The expert who builds the portfolio is known as a portfolio manager or fund manager [Kroijer, 2017].

The types of investments are complex and challenging to group together. It is, however, necessary to assemble various types of investments into smaller collections so that they can be analysed carefully with a view to reducing risks and maximising returns. As such, generally, the whole investment domain is divided into two groups, namely *traditional investments* and *alternative investments*. Traditional investments refer to putting money into well-known assets such as bonds, cash, real estate and equity shares. On the other hand, alternative investments means asset classes other than stocks, bonds and currency; hence they include tangible assets such as precious metals, art, wine, antiques, coins, and stamps, and some financial assets such as commodities, private equity, distressed securities, hedge funds, carbon credits, venture capital, financial derivatives and, more recently, cryptocurrencies.

There are several classifications of investment instruments available in the market, and an investor or a portfolio manager needs to decide what to use.

The following discusses the most widely used instrument classes with a view to identifying where cryptocurrency fits in.

15.1.1 Financial Instruments

A financial instrument is a monetary contract between multiple parties that can be created, traded, modified and settled. Examples of financial instruments include a contractual right to receive or deliver cash (bond) and evidence of an ownership interest in an entity (stock/share). Bonds and stocks are collectively known as "security" in the financial industries.

The *bond* is a debt security under which the issuer owes the holders a debt and, depending on the terms of the bond, is obliged to pay the interest or to repay the principal at a later date, termed the maturity date. Interest is usually payable at fixed intervals: semi-annual, annual or sometimes monthly. Very often the bond is negotiable; that is, the ownership of the instrument can be transferred in the secondary market. Once the transfer agents at the bank stamp the bond, it becomes highly liquid on the secondary market. Bonds are available to purchase from governments as well as from the corporations. In that sense, the former is known as a government bond, while the latter is called a corporate bond.

The *stock* of a corporation is all of the shares into which ownership of the corporation is divided. In the US, the shares are commonly known as "stocks", while in the UK "share" is the term frequently used. A single share of stock represents fractional ownership of the corporation in proportion to the total number of shares. This typically entitles the stockholder to that fraction of the company's earnings, proceeds from the liquidation of assets after the discharge of all senior claims such as secured and unsecured debt, or voting power, often dividing these up in proportion to the amount of money each stockholder has invested. Not all stock is necessarily equal, as certain classes of stock may be issued, for example, without voting rights, with enhanced voting rights, or with an absolute priority to receive profits or liquidation proceeds before or after other classes of shareholders. Stocks are launched through a process commonly known as the initial public offering (IPO). An IPO is underwritten by one or more investment banks that also arrange for the shares to be listed on one or more stock exchanges; hence a privately held company becomes a public limited company.

15.1.2 Commodities

A commodity is an economic good or service that has full or substantial fungibility, which means the market treats instances of the good as equivalent or nearly so with no regard to who produced it [Smith, 1982]. Most commodities are raw materials, basic resources, agricultural, or mining products, such as iron, gas, petroleum, coal, sugar, or grains like rice and wheat. Goods that are grown are called *soft commodities*, while mined commodities are known as *hard commodities*. Commodities can also be mass-produced unspecialised products such as chemicals and computer memory.

The price of a commodity good is typically determined as a function of its market as a whole. Well-established physical commodities have actively traded spot and derivative markets. The wide availability of commodities typically leads to smaller profit margins and diminishes the importance of factors such as brand name other than price.

15.1.3 Currencies

A *currency* in the most specific use of the word refers to money in any form when in use or circulation as a medium of exchange, especially circulating banknotes and coins. A more general definition is that a currency is a system of money or monetary units in common use especially for people in a nation. Under this definition, US dollars, British pounds, European euros, Russian rubles and Indian rupees are examples of currency. These various currencies are recognised as stores of value and are traded between nations in foreign exchange markets, which determine the relative values of the different currencies. Currencies in this sense are defined by governments, and each type has limited boundaries of acceptance [Peter, 1965].

15.1.4 Derivatives

A derivative is a contract that derives its value from the performance of an underlying entity. This underlying entity can be an asset, index, cryptocurrency and so on. Derivatives can be used for many purposes, including insuring against price movements (hedging), increasing exposure to price movements for speculation, or getting access to otherwise hard-to-trade assets or markets. Some of the more common derivatives include forwards, futures, options, swaps, contracts for difference, and variations of these such as synthetic collateralised debt obligations and credit default swaps [Hull, 2006].

A *forward contract*, or simply a *forward*, is a "non-standardised" contract between two parties to buy or to sell an asset at a specified future time at a price agreed upon today. The party agreeing to buy the underlying asset in the future assumes a *long position*, and the party agreeing to sell the asset in the future assumes a *short position*. The price agreed upon is called the delivery price, which is equal to the forward price at the time the contract is entered into. In contrast, a *futures contract*, or simply futures, is a "standardised" forward contract, a legal agreement to buy or sell something at a predetermined price at a specified time in the future between parties not known to each other. The asset transacted is usually a commodity or financial instrument. The predetermined price the parties agree to buy and sell the asset for is known as the forward price. The specified time in the future, which is when delivery and payment occur, is known as the delivery date.

An *option* is a contract which gives the buyer, who is the owner or holder of the option, the right but not the obligation to buy or sell an underlying asset or instrument at a specified strike price prior to or on a specified date depending on the form of the option. The strike price may be set by reference to the market price of the underlying security or commodity on the day an option is taken out, or it may be fixed at a discount or a premium. The seller has the corresponding obligation to fulfil the transaction, to sell or buy, if the buyer exercises the option. An option that conveys to the owner the right to buy at a specific price is referred to as a call, while an option that conveys the right of the owner to sell at a specific price is referred to as a put. A *swap*, on the other hand, is a derivative in which two counterparties exchange the cash flow of one party's financial instrument for those of the other party's financial instrument. The benefits in question depend on the type of financial instruments involved. For example, in the case of a swap involving two bonds, the benefits in question can be the periodic interest payments associated with such bonds and so on.

Finally, a *contract for difference* (CFD) is a contract between two parties, typically described as the "buyer" and "seller", stipulating that the seller will pay to the buyer the difference between the current value of an asset and its value at contract time; however, if the difference is negative, then the buyer pays instead to the seller. In effect, CFDs are derivatives that allow traders to take advantage of prices moving up (known as long positions) or prices moving down (known as short positions) on all underlying financial instruments. They are often used to speculate on markets. A CFD is a tool of leverage with its own potential profits and losses. It allows an investor to enter the global trading market without directly dealing with shares, indices, commodities or currency pairs.

15.1.5 Status of Cryptocurrency

Deciding which class of investments cryptocurrency belongs to is challenging. The status of this new instrument is disputed as there is no clear official regulation available for most countries; various departments and authorities define it based on their interpretation. Decisions from the courts, opinions of renowned magazines and actions of regulatory authorities often contradict one another. Some identify cryptocurrency as currency, while some consider it a commodity. Because there are some similarities between IPOs and the process of raising funds for pre-mined cryptocurrencies, known as initial coin offerings (ICOs), this new instrument is sometimes compared to stocks as well. However, there is still no global agreement as to where to put cryptocurrency, and it remains to be a matter of debate. Chapter 17 elaborates on this matter.

15.2 Portfolio

A portfolio is a collection of investments held by an investment company, hedge fund, financial institution or individual. More particularly, it refers to any combination of financial assets such as stocks, bonds, currencies and commodities. A portfolio is tailor-made and can be customised. Individual investors may hold portfolios or have them managed by financial professionals, hedge funds, banks and other financial institutions. It is a generally accepted principle that a portfolio is designed according to the investor's risk tolerance, time frame and investment objectives. The monetary value of each asset may influence the risk–return ratio of the portfolio.

15.2.1 Funds

A fund or an investment fund is a form of investing money alongside other investors in order to benefit from the inherent advantages of working as part of a group. These advantages include the ability to hire professional investment managers, which may potentially be able to offer better returns and adequate risk management. It also benefits from lower transaction costs and increases the asset diversification to reduce some unsystematic risk. A fund can be of several types such as a mutual fund, closed-end fund or special-purpose acquisition company (SPAC). A mutual fund is an open-ended investment where anyone can enter or exit at anytime. A closed-end fund, however, restricts the duration of the investment to a specific period, while an SPAC allows investors to invest in private equities.

A fund can be constructed using any asset class such as stocks, bonds, currencies, commodities or even real estate. More recently, cryptocurrency has become a lucrative asset class, and professional fund managers have been looking at this instrument to build funds entirely using cryptocurrencies and blockchain technologies. CryptoFundResearch is an organisation that collects and shares data related to cryptocurrency funds. According to CryptoFundResearch, the first cryptocurrency fund became available in the market in 2013. Within the next 5 years, over 700 such funds were established with more than 100 new funds joining the fray in 2018 alone. Recently, Bitcoin Market Journal* surveyed those funds and published a report along with a score out of five. Table 15.1 lists a collection of those funds with their name, their assets under management (AUM), the founding year and the score.

15.2.2 Indices

An index is a measurement of a section of a particular financial asset such as stock. It is usually computed from the prices of the selected assets taking a weighted average. Indices are tools used by investors and financial managers to describe the market and to compare the return on specific investments. Two of the primary criteria of an index are that it is investable and the method of its construction should be transparent. The American S&P 500, the Japanese Nikkei 225 and the British FTSE 100 are some renowned stock indices.

The rise of the cryptocurrency market creates a provision for creating crypto indices. The idea has been hovering in this industry for some time, but no serious attempt was taken until recently. A survey in the market indicated that there are at least four operational indices available while several are at the proposal level waiting to be launched.

- *Bloomberg Galaxy Crypto Index* (BGCI): Founded by the data giant Bloomberg, BGCI is designed to measure the performance of the largest cryptocurrencies traded in US dollar. The index is market capitalisation weighted and includes cryptocurrencies such as Bitcoin, Ethereum, Monero, Ripple and Zcash. Its constituents are diversified across different categories of digital assets, including stores of value, mediums of exchange, smart contract protocols and private assets.
  URL: www.bloomberg.com/quote/BGCI:IND

---

* Publicly accessible using the following URL: www.bitcoinmarketjournal.com.

Table 15.1   Renowned Cryptocurrency Funds

Name	AUM	Year Founded	Score
Polychain Capital	$1.04b	2016	4.10
Pantera Bitcoin Fund	$810m	2013	4.00
Pantera Long Term ICO Fund	$810m	2017	3.10
Galaxy Digital Assets	$500m	2017	3.70
Alphabit Fund	$480m	2017	3.00
Altana Digital Currency Fund	$450m	2014	3.30
Crypto Currency Fund L.P.	$200m	2017	2.70
BlockTower	$150m	2017	3.00
MetaStable Capital	$60m	2014	2.60
1confirmation	$30m	2017	1.70
AltaIR Capital	$20m	2010	3.20
Abstract Ventures	$12m	2016	1.90
Amentum Investment Management	$10m	2017	1.60
Aenigma Capital	$10m	2018	1.60

Source: Bitcoin Market Journal.

- *Cryptocurrency Index 30* (CCi30): Launched on 1 January 2017, the CCi30 is a rules-based index designed to measure the overall growth as well as the daily and long-term movement of the blockchain sector. By tracking the 30 largest cryptocurrencies by market capitalisation, it serves as a tool for passive investors to participate in this asset class and as an industry benchmark for investment managers. The founders claimed that the CCi30 had been designed with five main characteristics namely diversified, replicable, transparent, providing in-depth coverage of the entire sector and presenting the best risk-adjusted performance profile possible.

  URL: www.cci30.com
- *Crpto20*: The index was launched by Invictus Capital in 2017 and has been traded on a number of platforms since the beginning of 2018. It was established through an ICO and constructed over Ethereum blockchain. The index tracks 20 cryptocurrencies while itself an ERC-20 coin.

  URL: www.crypto20.com

■ *CRypto IndeX* (CRIX): CRIX is an academic initiative to build a comprehensive cryptocurrency index. Led by Professor Wolfgang Hardle from the School of Business and Economics at Humboldt University in Berlin, the index was constructed following the Laspeyres derivation method and holds 55 cryptocurrencies (Figure 15.1).
URL: www.thecrix.de

15.2.3 ETFs

An exchange-traded fund (ETF) is an investment fund traded on stock exchanges, much like stocks. An ETF holds assets such as stocks, commodities or bonds, and generally operates with an arbitrage mechanism designed to keep it trading close to its net asset value, although deviations can occasionally occur. Most ETFs track an index, such as a stock index or bond index. ETFs may be attractive as investments because of their low costs, tax efficiency and stock-like features.

ETFs entirely based on cryptocurrency are a grey area that most national authorities around the world have been against due to the volatility of these assets. Cameron and Tyler Winklevoss* first took the initiative of creating such an ETF when they submitted the request to register a Bitcoin-based ETF called Winklevoss Bitcoin Trust in 2013. Despite putting tremendous effort into negotiating with the Securities and Exchange Commission (SEC) to get the request approved, the ETF

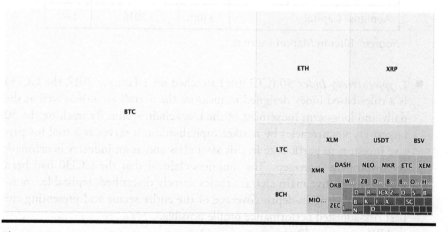

Figure 15.1   Cryptocurrency distributions in CRIX Index.

---

* They are famously known as the Winklevoss twins who gained their fame during their Harvard University time through a legal dispute with Mark Zuckerberg concerning the social media sites ConnectU and Facebook for which they received more than $20 million in compensation. They later went on to become one of the most active advocates of Bitcoin and the underlying technologies.

Table 15.2 Renowned Blockchain ETFs

Symbol	Name	AUM
BLOK	Amplify Transformational Data Sharing ETF	$113.44m
BLCN	Reality Shares Nasdaq NexGen Economy ETF	$77.41m
LEGR	First Trust Indxx Innovative Transaction & Process ETF	$41.47m
KOIN	Innovation Shares NextGen Protocol ETF	$9.83m
BKC	REX BKCM ETF	$5.22m
GFIN	Goldman Sachs Motif Finance Reimagined ETF	$5.16m
BKCH	AdvisorShares Sabretooth ETF	$2.70m
BCNA	Reality Shares Nasdaq NexGen Economy China ETF	$2.42m

Source: Blockchain ETF List, www.etfdb.com/themes/blockchain-etfs/.

was denied in 2017. This negotiation, however, created the grounds for further discussion, and several entities including some ICOs took the opportunity to push for launching their ETFs in the near future [Pihl, 2019].

Nevertheless, the ETFdb, a website specialised for indexing all available ETFs around the world, identified some stock ETFs involving blockchain-related companies that can be considered the closest possible investment opportunities of this kind at the moment. Table 15.2 is prepared based on ETFdb's listing.

15.3 Exchanges and Platforms

Unlike stocks and bonds, investing in a crypto-asset is much easier. Chapter 14 describes how cryptocurrencies can be stored in a wallet. An investor willing to invest in a particular cryptocurrency can buy the tokens and store them in the wallet depending on his investment strategies. However, like any other regular product in our life, people generally randomly sell stuff in the middle of nowhere. There needs to be a marketplace where they meet and make the trade. Trading exchanges and platforms are places where investors can buy the desired tokens. Nowadays, many modern exchanges also provide wallets or keep the purchased asset at their disposal with insurance and higher security. The following introduces cryptocurrency exchanges and platforms for investing in indices, funds and derivatives.

15.3.1 Cryptocurrency Trading Exchange

A cryptocurrency exchange is a place that allows customers to trade cryptocurrencies for other assets, such as conventional fiat money or other digital currencies. A cryptocurrency exchange can be a market maker taking the bid–ask spreads as a transaction commission or may charge flat fees. The exchanges can send cryptocurrency to a user's cryptocurrency wallet, while some can convert cryptocurrency balances into anonymous prepaid cards which can be used to withdraw funds from ATMs worldwide.

A regular cryptocurrency trading exchange is a typical market maker that allows clients to join and exchange their assets. For example, Alice has some Bitcoin that she wants to exchange for Ether, and Bob, having some Ether, wants to buy Bitcoin. A trading exchange, acting as a middleman, can help them. Alice must first put a bid for Ether in exchange for her Bitcoin. If Bob finds that bid reasonable enough, he will accept the offer. The trading exchange then sends Ether to Alice and Bitcoin to Bob. In the whole process, the exchange is likely to charge a fee. Some exchanges do not charge fees but take a percentage from one or both parties.

There are many cryptocurrency exchanges globally operating at the moment. Some of these exchanges are infamous for criticisms and allegations of wrongdoing, while many operate within the regulatory norms of the countries they are based in. Amongst the notable exchanges, the following have gained the reputation of providing the best service to their customers.

- Binance – www.binance.com

  Binance is a global cryptocurrency exchange established by Chinese-Canadian businessman Changpeng Zhao and currently based in Malta. It is considered the biggest cryptocurrency exchange in the world in terms of trading volume and provides a platform for trading more than 100 cryptocurrencies.
- Bitstamp – www.bitstamp.net

  Bitstamp is a UK- and Luxemburg-based exchange that primarily focuses on the major cryptocurrencies. It allows trading using US dollars (USD), euros (EUR), Bitcoin, Litecoin, Ethereum, Ripple, Bitcoin Cash and so on. The exchange offers an API to allow clients using custom software to access and control their accounts on their platform.
- Huobi – www.huobi.com

  Huobi was originally founded in China by Leon Li, a Chinese businessman and computer engineer. In 2017 when China banned cryptocurrency exchange and ICOs, Huobi relocated its business to Singapore. It is now a publicly listed company on the Hong Kong stock exchange.
- Coinbase – www.coinbase.com

  Coinbase is a US-based exchange founded in 2012 by Brian Armstrong and Fred Ehrsam. It is considered the most user-friendly cryptocurrency exchange and very popular amongst new users. It offers Bitcoin, Bitcoin Cash, Ethereum, Ethereum Classic and Litecoin with fiat currencies to exchange.

▪ Bittrex – www.bittrex.com

Bittrex is a US-based cryptocurrency exchange headquartered in Seattle, Washington. Three former security professionals from Microsoft led by Bill Shihara founded the company in 2013. It is one of the largest exchanges for cryptocurrency trading allowing a wide range of tokens including Cardano, ZCash, Tether, Endor, Tron, Siacoin and Komodo in addition to all the major cryptocurrencies.

15.3.2 Derivative Trading Exchanges

A derivative trading exchange is a place (within the context of this book) where derivative instruments related to cryptocurrencies are sold. The derivative products that are usually traded at these exchanges are CFDs.

While investing in CFDs, an investor does not hold the underlying cryptocurrency but steps into a contract to get paid for the price differences between the current price and the future price. There are two fundamental differences between trading a real cryptocurrency and a CFD. While the former is a natural asset traded based on the changes of its value, the latter is a leveraged product and can be purchased as both a *buy* and *sell* position.

Leverage is the increased buying power allowing an investor to pay less than full price for a trade. It is expressed as a ratio; for example a 2:1 leverage means that an investor would be able to hold a position that is twice the value of the trading account. If the investor has 25,000 in a trading account with 2:1 leverage, he or she would be able to purchase 50,000 worth of cryptocurrency. Nonetheless, it magnifies the losses on the same scale making it a very risky investment.

CFDs also allow investors to purchase either a buy or sell position. This means a CFD product gives the opportunity to make a profit regardless of the price movement of a cryptocurrency. For example, if Alice thinks that the price of Bitcoin will go up, she may purchase a buy position for Bitcoin. If the price does go up, she makes a profit on the differences. Similarly, if she predicts that the price will go down, she may purchase a sell position. If the price goes down as predicted, despite the real asset losing its value, Alice will make a profit on the differences. Figure 15.2 shows a screenshot from an exchange offering Bitcoin CFD. It provides the opportunity for the investor to decide between buy and sell positions and picking a leverage.

The following are some well-known exchanges for offering cryptocurrency CFD products.

▪ eToro – www.etoro.com

Founded in Israel but now registered in Cyprus and headquartered in London, eToro is one of the most renowned exchanges for both real and CFD products. It provides CFDs for all asset classes described earlier in addition

Figure 15.2 **An exchange offering Bitcoin CFD.**

to cryptocurrency. They coined the term "social trading" which allows beginners to learn through discussion in a social media–like environment. They also introduced a mechanism called "copy trading" that newcomers can use for investment by copying (following) positions of experienced traders. The FCA, the financial regulator of the UK, is responsible for regulating eToro in addition to other regulators from the EU.

■ BitMEX – www.bitmex.com

BitMEX is a cryptocurrency exchange that provides both real and derivative products. It was co-founded by Ben Delo, who made his fortune from Bitcoin and is reported to be the United Kingdom's youngest self-made billionaire [Urwin, 2018]. Unlike many other trading exchanges, BitMEX only accepts deposits through Bitcoin, which can then be used to purchase a variety of other cryptocurrencies. BitMEX specialises in sophisticated financial operations trading with leverage. Like many of the exchanges that operate through cryptocurrencies, BitMEX is currently unregulated.

■ Plus500 – www.plus500.co.uk/

Plus500 is an online trading exchange offering CFD products across more than 2000 securities and multiple asset classes including cryptocurrencies. The company is headquartered in Israel and has subsidiaries in the UK, Cyprus, Australia and Singapore. Plus500 is regulated by the FCA and listed on the London Stock Exchange where it is a constituent of the FTSE 250 Index.

15.3.3 Investment Platforms

An investment platform acts like an exchange, but at a greater capacity, and hosts indices, ETFs and funds. If a platform provides only indices and funds, their execution does not happen in real-time; hence the operation differs from a regular exchange. However, providing ETFs requires exchange-like platforms which are difficult to distinguish from a regular exchange. Because cryptocurrency is a new product in the market, such platforms are not very popular in this domain. The following four platforms are mentioned as examples so that the reader may have a starting point:

- HitBTC – www.hitbtc.com
- p2pb2b – www.p2pb2b.io
- Fork Delta – www.forkdelta.app
- Dflowx – www.dflowx.com

15.4 Investment Strategy

An investment strategy is a set of rules, behaviours and procedures designed to guide an investor to select the right investment type appropriate for an individual. Some choices involve a trade-off between risk and return, while most investors fall somewhere in between accepting some risk for the expectation of higher returns. The volatility of cryptocurrency makes it a risky investment; therefore, it requires enough diversification. The following presents some strategies that are well recognised amongst the investment community and can be applied to cryptocurrency investments.

15.4.1 Day Trading

Trading is the process of buying and selling financial instruments to make a profit. Traders use financial instruments such as stocks, bonds, ETFs, commodities (oil, gas, gold and so on) and more recently cryptocurrencies to take advantage of the gap between the buying and selling price to make a profit.

Day trading is the process of buying and selling financial instruments within the same trading day such that all positions are closed before the market closes for the trading day. Traders who trade in this capacity with the motive of profit use market speculation; hence they are called speculators. The methods of quick trading contrast with the long-term trades underlying buy-and-hold and value-investing strategies. Day traders exit positions before the market close to avoid unmanageable risks, negative price gaps between one day's close and the next day's price at the open.

Day trading was once an activity that was exclusive to financial firms and professional speculators. Many day traders are bank or investment firm employees working as specialists in equity investment and fund management. Day trading gained popularity after the deregulation of commissions in the United States in 1975, the advent of electronic trading platforms in the 1990s, and with the stock price volatility during the dot-com bubble. However, the rise of cryptocurrency makes day trading open to amateurs through exchanges dedicated to trading cryptocurrencies.

15.4.2 Buy and Hold

Buy and hold, also called position trading, is an investment strategy where an investor buys financial instruments and holds them for a long time with the goal that it will gradually increase in value over a long period. This approach is founded based on the view that in the long run financial markets give a reasonable rate of return even while taking into account a degree of volatility. Buy and hold says that investors will never see such returns if they bail out after a decline. This viewpoint holds that market timing, the concept that one can enter the market on the lows and sell on the highs, does not work; hence, attempting such timing gives negative results, at least for small or unsophisticated investors. It is, therefore, better for them to buy and hold for a more extended period.

An advantage of the buy-and-hold approach is that it is cost effective. Generally, costs such as brokerage and bid/offer spread are incurred on all transactions separately, and because buy and hold involves the fewest transactions for a given amount invested in the market, it incurs fewer fees should all other conditions remain equal.

Taxation law also has some effect on this approach. Tax for long-term capital gains may be lower in many jurisdictions, and tax may be due only when the asset is sold and often never if the person dies. Warren Buffett, chairman of Berkshire Hathaway and one of the three richest people in the world, is an example of a buy-and-hold advocate who has built his fortune by investing in companies at times when they were undervalued.

15.4.3 Value Investment

Value investment is an investment paradigm that involves buying securities that appear underpriced by some form of fundamental analysis [Graham, 1949]. The various forms of value investing derive from the investment philosophy first taught by Benjamin Graham and David Dodd at Columbia Business School in 1928, and subsequently developed in their 1934 book titled *Security Analysis* [Graham and Dodd, 1934].

Warren Buffett has argued that the essence of value investing is buying stocks at less than their intrinsic value. The discount of the market price to the intrinsic value is what Benjamin Graham called the "margin of safety". For the last 25 years, under the influence of Charlie Munger, Buffett expanded the value-investing concept with a focus on "finding an outstanding company at a sensible price" rather than generic companies at a bargain price.

15.5 Investing in Cryptocurrencies

The current practice of cryptocurrency investment can be broadly divided into two types: self-investment and guided investment. The former is the process where the investor makes the investment decision and executes the order, while the latter involves an expert to decide and execute the order on behalf of the investor where an expert may mean an experienced trader, a fund manager or even an index.

15.5.1 Self-Investment

Self-investment is the most common practice in the current cryptocurrency industry. On the contrary to the stock, bond or commodity investment where well-established funds, ETFs and indices are available for investors to choose from, the cryptocurrency landscape provides minimal options concerning those choices driving investors to decide and execute investment for oneself. The self-investment approach may involve all three strategies mentioned in Section 15.4.

■ Day trading: Investors can buy and sell cryptocurrencies in the form of either real asset or CFD products from the exchanges mentioned in Section 15.3. Day trading involves some strategies such as *trend following, contrarian investing, range trading* and *scalping*. It is beyond the scope of this chapter to discuss all these strategies, but interested readers may self-learn more on this using these keywords.

Day trading is risky due to the volatility of the cryptocurrencies where inexperience traders are likely to get caught up by the *FIMO*, or the *fear of missing out*. When the price of a cryptocurrency keeps rising, new investors could feel that they might be missing on the profit and make the impulse decision of buying a stake. In most cases, following such an irrational purchase, investors are likely to find themselves in a losing position as the price starts to drop soon. The rational behaviour, however, would be the opposite: buy when the market goes down and sell when prices rise.

Inexperienced investors also often lose money when the price drops sharply. In those situations, they panic and sell their asset only to find that the market reverses and they repurchase the same asset at a higher price. It is commonly known as *panic selling*. Instead of making such a sale, holding on to their asset generally earns them more profit.

■ Buy and hold: Within the context of self-investment, buy and hold is an approach where investors develop their portfolio by investing in a range of cryptocurrency. In the current cryptocurrency landscape, finding all desired assets in one exchange is difficult. Investors may invest through multiple exchanges and later virtually track their portfolio using smartphone apps or web applications independent of the exchanges.

The buy-and-hold approach requires sufficient knowledge to identify the appropriate cryptocurrencies. This knowledge, however, cannot be developed overnight. The skill set of investors usually gets better as they spend more time in the industry and have more experience. In self-investment, it is necessary that investors remain well informed through the reading of newspapers, journals and relevant materials to understand the market trend and new products.

- Value investment: This is an approach through which investors invest in assets having the potential to grow in future. Buying tokens from ICOs can be a way to make some value investment. As we know, all cryptocurrencies have something to offer, a use-case. While evaluating a project before the token sale, understanding this use-case is essential because the real potential lies here. Moreover, due to the lack of regulations, many fraudulent actors target this industry to make some quick money; hence, investors need to be careful when investing through ICOs. Chapter 16 will elaborate more on the investment and scam issues concerning ICOs.

15.5.2 Guided Investment

Guided investment is the process of employing experts to act on behalf of investors. In the current landscape of cryptocurrency, options are limited to seek help from an expert due to two reasons: first, the availability of such smarts is very slim and second, there are hardly enough platforms to support funds, ETFs and indices that the experts design and maintain. Despite those limitations, this chapter identified some investment opportunities in Section 15.2 and platforms hosting them in Section 15.3.

- Day trading: While investing through guidance, day trading looks like an option off the table. However, eToro makes it possible by introducing an option called "copy trade" that allows following experience traders and copying their trading activity. For instance, Figure 15.3 shows a list of experienced traders on the platform. Investors can look at their risk factors; returns from the last 1, 3 or 6 months; and number of copiers to decide if they want to copy

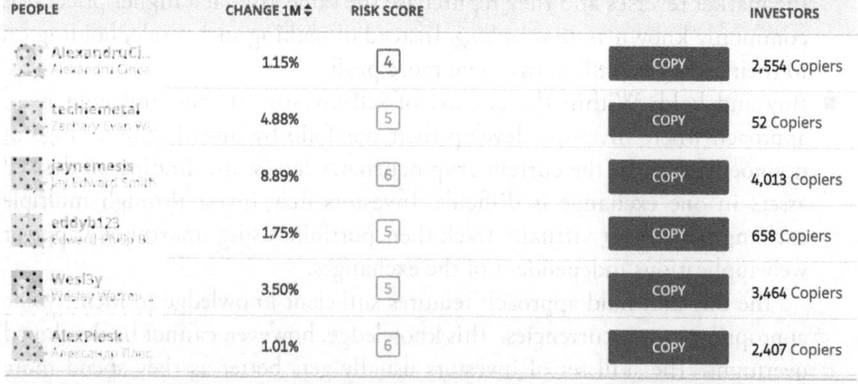

PEOPLE	CHANGE 1M	RISK SCORE		INVESTORS
AlexandruCi... Alexandru Cinca	1.15%	4	COPY	2,554 Copiers
techiemetal Zachary Evan Wi...	4.88%	5	COPY	52 Copiers
jaynemesis Jay Edward Smith	8.89%	6	COPY	4,013 Copiers
eddyb123 Edward Philip B...	1.75%	5	COPY	658 Copiers
Wesl3y Wesley Warren ...	3.50%	5	COPY	3,464 Copiers
AlexPiesk Александр Плес	1.01%	6	COPY	2,407 Copiers

Figure 15.3 eToro gives the option to copy experienced traders.

them. Their full portfolio is available to view (not displayed in Figure 15.3), which can also help investors to make decisions. It is also possible for the investors to make a portfolio of the traders they copy.

■ Buy and hold: This is the approach that most fund managers take. Investors willing to utilise this strategy can buy funds, ETFs or follow an index by creating a portfolio on one or more exchanges. Section 15.2 gives an idea about where to invest. Funds and ETFs are generally available to buy from the platforms by paying a small fee, while investing in indices can be either platform managed or self-managed. Some of the platforms mentioned earlier offer C20 where investors can put their money in. However, if investors do not want to pay a fee but like to follow an index, they can create a portfolio as mentioned in the self-investment section for themselves by tracking an index of their choice. In this approach, they must make sure that they keep an eye on the tracked index so that any change in the index can be quickly introduced in the self-managed portfolio. In addition to funds managed by specialised and independent managers, some cryptocurrency exchanges are now coming with their portfolios which investors may consider investing.

■ Value investment: It is a recent trend that companies are making portfolios combining ICOs. So instead of investing in a particular ICO, experts are gathering investments in a pool to diversify the risk by putting that money across an extensive collection of ICOs. A similar approach can be found in pooled mining where experts are collecting investors' money to develop large mining rigs and later pay investors a return monthly, bi-annually or annually. It is challenging to find these investment approaches for new investors, but networking with members of the community can help to get to the investment ladder.

15.6 Regulation and Tax Affairs

The cryptocurrency industry is mostly unregulated at the moment; however, regulation is likely to arrive soon. It is a necessity when investing in stocks and bonds to provide identification and proof of address in Europe, Canada, Australia, the United Kingdom and the United States. This regulation is highly likely to be extended for cryptocurrency in future. Many exchanges already willingly adapted these rules and ask for identification documents, bank details and proof of address when opening an account for trading or managing a cryptocurrency wallet.

Investments generally generate returns, and investors are liable to pay taxes on their capital gain. Cryptocurrencies are a grey area at the moment, and many jurisdictions have not thought out a proper tax law for the investors investing using crypto-assets. However, cryptocurrency investment through CFD products is covered by well-established law, and investors must pay tax in due time.

Many countries provide the opportunity to make some tax-free investments, often in the form of a threshold on the capital gain. If someone does not cross that threshold, he or she does not have to pay taxes. Countries also offer specially designed investment pots that are either tax-free or come with some conditions and fulfilling those requirements gives the holder tax benefits. Examples include *individual savings accounts*, or more commonly known as *ISAs* in the United Kingdom, where investors are allowed to put a specific amount of money each year (declared by the government at the beginning of each fiscal year) to trade or invest for which they are not liable to pay taxes. This pot provides a tax-free investment opportunity in addition to the regular tax-free threshold which is calculated on the investment outside this container. Investors are, therefore, strongly recommended to consult a professional accountant to discuss their tax affairs and explore the available options open to them in their countries.

15.7 Summary

This chapter presented the investment principles and methods that can be utilised in cryptocurrency investment. The chapter aimed to provide some basic understanding of investments so that investors having no or little prior experience can find a place where they can start. It began with introducing the asset classes and continued to explain portfolios such as funds, ETFs and indices before discussing exchanges and platforms. Finally, the chapter discussed investment strategies and possible ways to implement those in the current landscape of the cryptocurrency market. The readers also must note that the literature presented in this chapter is for guidance purposes only and is not formal investment advice. The author of this book is not a qualified investment adviser approved by any financial conducting authority of any jurisdiction; hence he is not legally allowed to offer investment advice to retail clients.

Chapter 16

Initial Coin Offerings (ICOs)

The *initial coin offering*, or more commonly *ICO*, is the established method of securing funds for potential projects in the blockchain industry. Investors generally put their money into a project looking at its prospects by buying pre-mined tokens through ICOs. Although ICOs are not regulated and there is no hard and fast rule as to how to arrange an ICO, over time the industry established some conventions such as publishing a white paper and promoting ICOs through events. The method worked well until 2017 when during the cryptocurrency bull run a lack of regulation made ICOs a favourite tool for fraudulent actors to cheat and commit scams. This, in turn, led regulatory authorities to intervene and crack down on projects creating a lot of buzz and chaos making the process substantially infamous to the public. This chapter takes the opportunity to look at the whole landscape involving ICOs beginning with their history, how they came into being, selling of pre-mined tokens, the advantage and disadvantages of investing through ICOs, and issues related to regulation and scams surrounding this new crowdfunding approach.

16.1 Overview

An ICO is a type of funding using cryptocurrencies. Mostly the process is arranged by crowdfunding, but private ICOs are becoming more common. In an ICO, a quantity of cryptocurrency is sold in the form of *tokens* to venturers or investors in exchange for fiat money or other cryptocurrencies such as Bitcoin or Ethereum. The tokens sold are promoted as future functional units of currency if or when the ICO's funding goal is met, and the project launches.

The primary objective of investors to buy tokens through ICOs is to invest money on the potential of a future product. Each cryptocurrency holds a use-case that associates specific services. If the investors find the use-case lucrative enough to become a successful product in future, they take the calculative risk of buying a token that has just originated or not been launched yet. Once launched and popular, the token value is expected to grow giving investors their foreseen return.

16.1.1 The Creation of ICOs

It is sometimes assumed that Ripple Labs was the first company that acquired capital using the token sale, although not through a formal ICO. When Ripple Labs developed the Ripple protocol in early 2013, 100 billion XRP tokens were created at the genesis block. The company sold a fraction of these tokens in private to generate a working capital that helped it to survive during the early days. Nevertheless, Ripple is not an ICO-dependent distributed ledger where selling tokens is their vision or intention. Ripple has a defined policy of giving away tokens to charities and partner companies instead of selling those in exchange for fiat money or another cryptocurrency.

The first formal ICO took place in July 2013 when *Mastercoin* managed to attract a good many people to buy its token MSC. Mastercoin is a successful attempt to build a new protocol layer on top of Bitcoin. While Mastercoin allows implementing exclusive features like design and creating contracts, the underlying Bitcoin acts as the primary means of providing the foundation. The founder of Mastercoin sold this use-case to investors who purchased MSC believing in its potential. Some $1 million gathered from the token sale was later used to develop the product.

Neither Ripple nor Mastercoin made ICOs famous; this is credited to Ethereum that took the community by surprise when it raised $2.3 million (3700 BTC at that time) in the first 12 hours of its token sale in 2014. Vitalik Buterin, the creator of Ethereum, initially proposed changes so that Bitcoin can have a smart contract-like feature. Failing to convince the Bitcoin community, he and a group of developers who supported the idea arranged the crowdsale in mid-2014. Ethereum became the centre of attention again in 2016 when a decentralised autonomous organisation called The DAO, a set of smart contracts developed on the platform, raised a record $150 million in a crowdsale to fund the project. The event was surrounded by controversy, dispute and scepticism as an unknown hacker took $50 million in Ether soon after the event. It sparked a debate in the crypto-community about whether Ethereum should perform a contentious *hard fork* to reappropriate the affected funds. As a result of the dispute, the network split in two. Ethereum continued on the forked blockchain, while a new token Ethereum Classic continued on the original blockchain.

The Ethereum blockchain went live on 30 July 2015 with 72 million coins *premined*, more than 70% of the total circulating supply available in 2018. Unlike

Bitcoin that is a mined token, Ethereum intentionally took this path of creating tokens in advance so that can be sold to obtain more funds for the project. This approach is often considered greedy by the Bitcoin community, and Vitalik Buterin is credited for popularising the pre-mining concept [Chong, 2018].

16.1.2 How Do ICOs Work?

An ICO is a crowdsale; hence it requires promoting the event to the right community. The team behind a new project typically announces the event on various cryptocurrency forums, social media sites and sometimes in the mainstream media. The announcement comes with a URL linking to the project's website presenting information such as a white paper of the project, goals, timeline of the development phases, and the team involved and their experience to potential token buyers. The promotional materials also pinpoint the key features of the product that the developer primarily sells alongside other ICO details.

Bitcoin and Ethereum are amongst the most popular methods of collecting funds. Sometimes organisers create a global address that shows all the incoming funds of the crowdsale. It is, however, not rare to have a separate and unique address created for individual investors to collect the funds. The best practices dictate that all funds ultimately be held in a publicly announced multi-signature address to establish transparency and fairness in the process.

The duration of an ICO may vary. Generally, the crowdsale of an ICO runs for a few weeks to raise as much money as possible. Occasionally, ICOs have a fixed cap that requires achieving the target before the event may end. There are exceptional cases when ICOs ran for a significantly longer period. For instance, *block.one*, the company behind the EOS blockchain ran the ICO for a year raising $4 billion using ERC-20 tokens for the project.

Once the ICO comes to an end, and the organiser launches the project, the ICO tokens get listed at the cryptocurrency exchanges to trade against other cryptocurrencies. The price of these tokens typically reflects the overall market sentiment of that token, the value of the product and its potential to grow.

16.2 Token Creation

ICOs come with a token (coin). The money that a project registers comes from the sale of the token an ICO offers; hence the name "initial coin offering". The following discusses the nature of the token and the platforms that offer token-creation services.

16.2.1 Token

The purpose of arranging an ICO is to raise money for a future project selling its pre-mined tokens to investors. Because the project stays at a proposal stage, by the time the token sale takes place, usually the proposed blockchain is not ready meaning there will be no tokens on the blockchain for sale. This situation leads to a catch-22 problem. Luckily, there are many platforms available in the current market that can assist the teams behind ICOs to create a temporary token and put it on sale even before launching the native blockchain.

EOS is one of the notable examples. At the time of its ICO, the project did not commence and, naturally, the EOS token was not ready for sale. Block.one, the company behind the ICO, instead used the Ethereum platform for creating a token and gathered more than $4 billion from its crowdsale. When the EOS platform became ready for operation, the token was transferred to its native blockchain.

Possibly the next question hovering around the mind of the readers would be, what is this temporary token? A token is a set of standards defined by the platforms representing a value in Ethereum, Bitcoin or other cryptocurrencies. At the time of an ICO, the project team creates this token and assigns a price tag against it. During the crowdsale, investors can buy the token in exchange for the indicated cryptocurrency. The token can be then stored in a wallet and kept for future usage. Once the native blockchain is ready, the team will make the necessary arrangement to transfer the token to its blockchain.

16.2.2 Platforms

Many platforms offer token creation; amongst them, Ethereum is the most popular. This blockchain platform not only popularised pre-mining and ICOs but also came up with a token-creation mechanism that projects willing to offer ICOs could easily use. The tokens that can be created on the Ethereum platform are called ERC-20 tokens. "ERC-20" is basically a set of standards defining the underlying rules of a token. These rules help to create, access and store the token seamlessly [Blockgeeks, 2017]. These standards are elaborately described in Chapter 5, Section 5.7.

Another popular token-creation platform is *Waves*. It is a cryptocurrency project launched by the Russian entrepreneur Alexander Ivanov in 2016. The blockchain platform itself was an ICO and raised $16 million to become one of the largest projects in terms of funds raised through crowdfunding in 2016. Soon it became one of the most popular ICO-hosting platforms. Tokens created on the Waves platform need explanation as to why they were created and how they are relevant to the project. Because no one can easily create a token on Waves and go for an ICO, investors can rely more on these projects [Waves, 2017].

As of April 2018, 82.35% of ICOs created their tokens using the Ethereum platform. Nearly 9% of tokens are custom-made, while 2.50% tokens are created on Waves making it the second most used platform for ICOs. All other platforms created 5.53% tokens combined. A small portion of tokens (0.89%) are created using Bitcoin forks [BlockchainHub, 2018].

16.3 Understanding ICOs

The success of the Ethereum ICO made it possible to generate funds from the initial coin offerings for the development of blockchain projects by releasing some or all of the native tokens. Because it has become a new form of investment, a growing interest in this type of investment can be observed. However, not all ICOs are suitable for investment as many scams can be in disguise. It is therefore essential to understand the nature and the characteristics of the ICOs to foresee the expected growth of the investment.

16.3.1 ICOs vs IPOs

ICOs have been compared to initial public offerings (IPOs) of companies (Table 16.1). There are some striking similarities, such as both of them are used to sell a stake and raise money, and both have investors who see the potentials and risk their capital to make a profit. However, there are notable differences as well. Early supporters and enthusiasts mostly invest in ICOs. This approach makes ICOs more like "kickstarter campaigns" with the backers having a substantial financial stake

Table 16.1 ICOs vs IPOs

ICOs	IPOs
ICOs are organised by enthusiasts and start-ups in a bid to raise money for a new idea or technology.	IPOs are organised by established companies to sell their company stocks.
ICOs are not bound by regulations.	IPOs are heavily regulated.
ICOs are short in duration, although some exceptions are available such as ICO of EOS.	IPOs generally take a longer time, often up to 6 months.
The team, group or company behind the idea generally promote and arrange the ICOs.	IPOs are arranged by an investment bank that also takes care of the legal and regulatory requirements tied with the offering.
ICOs are open to the public.	IPOs are not generally open rather exclusive in nature.
ICOs have a short, corrupt and sordid history surrounded by scams and frauds.	IPOs have a solid long history dating back to 1602 when the Dutch East India Company offered shares of the company to the public in order to raise capital.

in the project. ICOs are also not regulated or registered with any government, and, generally, there exist no investor protections.

A company willing to issue an IPO must produce a legal document called a prospectus. This document is a legal announcement that includes vital information about the company and the IPO. There are some legal bindings that this document needs to meet some standards of transparency. On the other hand, ICOs do not require such legal documents. Although most ICOs publish a white paper where everything about the project and its purpose is explained, it is not a necessity, and groups organising the ICOs are not obligated to create this document.

The IPO is a long process taking up to 6 months in order to meet all legal requirements. Processing ICOs can be very fast, and the duration may depend on the nature of the project. When a company or a group issues a white paper and a smart contract, it can start with the crowdsale. The duration of the crowdsale depends on the project and targeted cap, and usually takes up to 1 month.

ICOs became a controversial issue in 2018 when South Korea and China banned new offerings in their jurisdictions. It led to new ICOs to be marketed as "crowdsales" instead of ICOs in order to avoid the legal requirements associated with the securities sale. These ICOs use legal disclaimers and language to participants mentioning that ICOs are not securities. It is, however, unclear whether this is sufficient for global jurisdictions to treat it differently from a securities sale and the matter has not been prosecuted in a court of law as of this writing.

16.3.2 Signs of Good and Bad ICOs

Before investing through ICOs, investors must look out for some common signs telling them the nature of those ICOs. There are signs warning investors to stay away from certain ICOs that can be bad investments or scams, while some ICOs demonstrate specific characteristics giving investors the required confidence to go ahead.

It is almost always a warning if the ICO proposal does not have a well-written and well-documented white paper. People backing a project must know what they have been talking about, and a good white paper will be their representative. A lack of such a document indicates the lack of seriousness of the team for the project. And, if the team is not serious enough, it is not worthy of placing a stake on them. Most scams set a goal that is unrealistic and unachievable. They often fail to introduce the key people involved in the project or the justification of their involvement or demonstrate their experience in the areas the project is interested in. The absence of trust and transparency, and handling the token sale mysteriously are always a red alert for investors.

It is, however, not the case that all ICOs are bad. While researching for potential projects where investors can put their money, ICOs having hype and discussions in the community are good to start with. Investors must also look at the white papers and try to understand the use-case those ICOs have been addressing. The key people backing the projects and their experiences are parameters that can standout good ICOs. A realistic goal with a defined problem that potentially has a robust solution is a strong indication of a good ICO. It is difficult to filter good use-cases amongst the scams and bad ones, however, once done, investment in ICO can be very lucrative.

16.3.3 Advantages and Disadvantages

Investing in ICOs has both advantages and disadvantages. It is essential for investors to realise the challenges and the difficulties associated with ICOs before buying tokens. Arguably the most significant advantage of the ICO is that it is open to the public. Anyone willing to purchase tokens can get involved without going through much hassle. Generally, tokens are sold at a lower price giving investors the chance to have a good return. However, some disadvantages must not be overlooked either – for example, regulation and risk. Unlike IPOs, ICOs are not regulated, and therefore chances of losing the money are high. The investment itself is very risky due to the nature of the projects and the people who run it. Enthusiasts or start-ups run most blockchain projects, and almost always their use-cases try to solve something new making them risky. Table 16.2 lists some key advantages and disadvantages of investing in ICOs.

Table 16.2   Key Advantages and Disadvantages of ICOs

Advantages	Disadvantages
ICOs are open to the public where anyone can invest by purchasing tokens.	It is easy to manipulate the token sale and the market as a whole.
The process of buying tokens is simple and straightforward. Most ICOs accept Bitcoin and Ethereum to buy tokens, giving investors the freedom of staying within the cryptocurrency ecosystem.	ICOs are unregulated. It means fraud can happen anytime, and people backing the project may not comply with what they promise at the time of token sale.
ICOs increase the chances of buying tokens at a very lower price.	The unregulated token sale encourages scams to get involved more in the market.
Generally, ICOs do not have a minimum or maximum purchase cap, and the investors can buy the number of tokens of their interest.	People associated with ICOs are mostly enthusiasts with no proven track record.
Because start-ups and enthusiasts mostly run the blockchain project, investors having a good stake can get more involved in the project and play a role in shaping the blockchain industry.	It is risky to rely on enthusiasts and the promise they make even if they have the genuine intention to make the project a success.

16.4 ICOs in Number

The first reported ICO of Mastercoin took place in 2013 followed by Ethereum and Karmacoin in 2014 and 2015 respectively. The number of ICOs suddenly jumped in 2016 when 54 major ICOs raised more than $103 million. In 2017, the number of major ICOs hit 92 raising a mammoth total of $1.25 billion. The following discusses the numbers in more detail and identifies the biggest winners and losers from the ICOs in recent time.

16.4.1 Amount Raised

During the cryptocurrency bull run in 2017, ICOs suddenly became very popular attracting hundreds of thousands of investors. In addition to 92 major ICOs, many other small projects raised money throughout the year. It is anticipated that about 552 ICOs raised more than $7 billion. Amongst the most successful ICOs, Filecoin raised $257 million, Tezos $232 million, Paragon $183 million, Finney $157 million and Bancor $153 million. The ICO Watch List, an organisation dedicated for collecting and providing ICO-related data, publishes all notable ICOs and the amount they register during the crowdsale. Their data is accessible using the URL www.icowatchlist.com.

A joint report published by the consulting firm PwC and the Swiss Crypto Valley Association stated that in 2018 despite the market crashes and price collapse, ICOs became more popular. A total of 537 ICOs registered a volume of $13.7 billion during the year [Diemers et al., 2018]. The ICO Watch List reports EOS to be the most successful project of the year raising $4.1 billion. The amount is by far the most substantial sum an ICO ever registered. Amongst the other thriving ICOs, Telegram raised $850 million, tZero $250 million and Elastos $94 million in 2018.

The United States is the jurisdiction where the largest number of ICOs are created totalling 370 to date. Russia and the United Kingdom are the next two most popular nations for ICOs with 231 and 187 respectively. Singapore and Switzerland also attracted a significantly large number of projects, more than 250 ICOs between them. Estonia, Singapore and Cyprus are the top 3 countries with most ICOs per million people. Statistics show that in 2017, a total of $956 million was raised in Russia, $778 million in the US, $258 million in Singapore, $131 million in the UK and $35 million in Estonia.

There were 4 months in 2017 when the registered amount crossed the $300 million mark with September being the most successful raising $537 million. In 2018, the most prosperous month was June that raised $4.1 billion, although it is mainly due to the closure of EOS that ran for almost a year.

16.4.2 Breakdown by Industry

According to the ICO Watch List, the network and telecommunication industry attracted the most significant sum raised by ICOs. A total of $4.6 billion was registered for projects proposing use-cases related to communications. Blockchain platform and smart contract projects gathered the second largest total of $1.6 billion followed by industries like finance ($453 million), drug and health ($276 million), payment networks and wallet providers ($262 million), and commerce/retail ($193 million).

Although the network and telecommunication industry attracted more than half of the registered fund, only 16 projects (2.3% of the total ICOs) accumulated that capital ensuring those companies a robust financial backing during the early stage of their life cycles. Thirty-eight blockchain platform companies, 5.5% of the total ICOs, claimed almost 20% funds, while the financial industry saw 84 companies (12.2%) claiming the third largest share. Table 16.3 presents the funds raised so far according to industries.

16.4.3 Biggest Winners and Losers

The price of the token does not necessarily always reflect the real value of the use-case, but it is indeed an indication of how a company has been doing. During the ICOs, investors buy tokens expecting growth in future. Some projects ensure substantial return while many fail to grow at all.

A 2018 report compiled by BlockchainHub evaluated projects that came into being through ICOs in 2017 and found that as of 13 April Spectrecoin was the biggest winner returning 37,175% of investors' money. Storj.IO is another project that saw 9822% growth followed by Qtum (5525%), Populous (4891%) and Omisgo (4832%). Amongst the biggest losers, Useless Ethereum Token, an ICO created to mock Ethereum, saw its value go down by 99.74%. LevierCoin, Dimcoin, iDice and BlockCAT all lost more than 95% of their stake [BlockchainHub, 2018].

16.5 Scams and Criticisms

The successful launch of the Ethereum platform encouraged other projects to raise capital using ICOs. Many major blockchain platforms and companies benefited from the idea and successfully secured the required funds to get started. However, this also paved the path for bad actors in the industry having fraudulent intentions to steal investors' money. The crypto start-up *Giza* is one ideal example. It raised $2.4 million using a fake ICO involving more than a thousand investors in 2018 [McQuaid, 2018]. Other examples include the US Securities and Exchange Commissions (SEC) freezing $15 million from *PlexCoin* that it accumulated using an ICO promising a 1354% return [Palmer, 2018]. Another blockchain platform called *Benebit* raised around $4 million in 2017 using fake photos for the administrative team and just walked away with the money afterwards [Sedgwick, 2018b].

Table 16.3   ICOs by Industry (as of 2018)

Industry	% Of Projects	Total Raised
Network/communications	2.32%	$4,640,447,641
Blockchain platform	5.50%	$1,688,474,628
Finance	12.16%	$453,615,006
Drugs/health	3.76%	$276,868,999
Payments/wallets	6.66%	$262,955,940
Commerce/retail	5.64%	$193,172,700
Content/advertising	2.75%	$120,550,000
Gaming/AR/VR	4.92%	$120,172,361
Media/content	3.91%	$117,510,000
Data/computing/AI	4.92%	$117,370,000
Social network	2.03%	$112,110,000
Funding/VC	3.04%	$98,920,000
Energy/utilities	2.03%	$90,000,000
Security/identity	3.33%	$80,060,000
Asset management	5.35%	$72,916,240
IoT	3.76%	$66,508,616
Prediction market	3.91%	$62,703,450
Jobs/marketplace	2.75%	$48,724,150
Entertainment	3.76%	$36,580,000
Industry/logistics	2.32%	$34,279,663
Real estate	2.75%	$28,410,000
Betting/gambling	4.34%	$22,370,000
Education	1.16%	$13,900,000
Insurance	1.16%	$7,397,480
Music/arts	0.43%	$1,360,000

Scams and frauds using ICOs make regulatory bodies around the world take strong legal actions against the companies involved. US authorities acted on more than 750 legal cases during the first half of 2018 alone. Amongst these cases, notable ongoing lawsuits include those against Ripple Labs alleging it raised funds through the unregistered sale of XRP to retail investors and against UK-based *Bitconnect* for failing to disclose material facts that caused its value to drop [Castillo, 2018]. *Airfox* and *Paragon* are two companies that are currently under investigation by the SEC. It appears that the SEC, instead of launching random crackdowns, using these two cases to prepare future templates for ICO enforcement in the US [Palley, 2018]. The authorities in China and South Korea banned ICOs fearing that investors in the country would lose money to scams.

ICOs and token sales also became notoriously popular when Bitcoin and other cryptocurrencies had a rollercoaster ride in the exchanges in 2017. At the start of October coin sales from ICOs of that year were worth $2.3 billion, more than ten times as much as in all of 2016. By the time the year hit November, there were around 50 offerings a month with the highest-grossing ICO being Filecoin raising $257 million, of which $200 million was raised within the first hour of the token sale. Companies raised more than $7 billion via ICOs in 2017 where 20 ICOs made 37% of that amount. By February 2018, an estimated 46% of the 2017 ICOs had failed [Sedgwick, 2018a].

Joseph Lubin, co-founder of Ethereum, claimed during an interview with CNBC in November 2017 that many ICOs are copycats that do not intend to offer any real value to investors. His statement was echoed by Brad Garlinghouse, CEO of Ripple Labs, who mentioned token sales operate in a grey area while waiting for regulation to catch up [Choudhury, 2017]. More recently, a study conducted by the ICO advisory firm Statis Group noticed that more than 80% of 2017 ICOs were scams. The study took into consideration the life cycle of the project from the proposal stage to the most mature phase of trading on a crypto exchange [Alexandre, 2018].

The number of scams involving ICOs became so frequent in 2017 that internet giants Google and Facebook had to ban all advertisements concerning cryptocurrencies. As of 2018, Facebook had partially lifted the ban allowing only credible companies to post ads through a separate approval process [McLean, 2018], while Google also lifted the ban but for the US and Japan only [Marshall, 2018].

16.6 Summary

This chapter presented the whole landscape of ICOs. The goal of this chapter was to introduce readers to this new crowdfunding process and explain how it works. In doing so, the chapter first discussed how ICOs came into being following the renowned pre-sell of Ethereum tokens, and how tokens are created and sold in the absence of the proposed blockchain. It then continued to explain the differences between IPOs and ICOs as well as the advantages and disadvantages of investing using this method followed by discussions giving some historical breakdown of past ICOs and how fraudulent actors have been trying to misuse this crowdfunding technique. Along with Chapter 15, this chapter provided the basis for investing in cryptocurrencies and blockchain projects.

SOCIO-ECONOMIC LANDSCAPE VI

IV
SOCIO-ECONOMIC LANDSCAPE

Chapter 17

Economic Outlook of Cryptocurrency

A striking feature of cryptocurrency is its potential to act as an alternative form of money. Traditionally, money had either intrinsic value or derived value from government decree that acts as its foundation. Even when people use money electronically, the use of private ledgers and at least one trusted intermediary is necessary. Cryptocurrencies, however, employ user agreements, a network of users and cryptographic rules to achieve transfers of value. In this process, it uses blockchain technology to protect the public ledgers of accounts against manipulation allowing users to make valid transfers without a centralised and trusted intermediary. This revolutionary concept not only threatens to rival traditional money but also challenges the conventional practices of the use of money in our societies. This chapter presents the economic outlook of cryptocurrencies with takes on exploring how users, merchants, regulators and experts treat this virtual money as an economic tool. In doing so, the chapter looks at classifications, prices, volatilities and acceptance of cryptocurrencies in the society.

17.1 Classification

Cryptocurrencies are digital assets frequently referred to as currency, digital cash, virtual currency, electronic currency, digital gold and more commonly cryptocurrency. There is still no consensus as to how authorities classify them. While some describe them as "decentralised money", others state that they are "protocols" and "public ledgers containing entries." Despite these definitions having some form of facts and descriptions of the underlying properties in part, they are not complete reflections of cryptocurrency. This tendency of looking at cryptocurrencies from multiple points of view created confusion and led authorities and investors to classify them in three broad categories: currency, commodity and stock.

17.1.1 Currency

The phrase *cryptocurrency* suggests that it possibly resembles currency more than anything else. Although the question of whether Bitcoin and similar coins are currencies or not is disputed, however, *The Economist* magazine articulated that they have three useful qualities as currency: they are hard to earn, limited in supply and easy to verify [Boden, 2015]. In Chapter 12, we saw economists defining money as a store of value, a medium of exchange and a unit of account. Cryptocurrencies have some way to go to meet all these criteria. They do best as a medium of exchange; by the start of 2015, the number of merchants accepting Bitcoin had already passed half a million (Figure 17.1). All cryptocurrencies including Bitcoin, Ether and

Figure 17.1 A Bitcoin ATM at a shop in Wien Westbahnhof railway station, Vienna.

XRP have an exchange rate against most major currencies including the US dollar (USD), British pound (GBP) and euro (EURO), and it is possible for investors to make profits by buying and selling cryptocurrencies like other fiat currencies.

Classification of cryptocurrency by the United States government is unclear at the time of this writing with multiple conflicting rulings. Judge Amos L. Mazzant III of the United States District Court for the Eastern District of Texas stated in a 2013 ruling that "Bitcoin is a currency or form of money" [Hill, 2013]. However, an opposite verdict came 3 years later, in 2016, when Judge Teresa Mary Pooler of the Eleventh Judicial Circuit Court of Florida cleared Michell Espinoza in *State of Florida v. Espinoza* for money-laundering charges he faced involving his use of Bitcoin. Pooler stated, "Bitcoin may have some attributes in common with what we commonly refer to as money, but differ in many important aspects, they are certainly not tangible wealth and cannot be hidden under a mattress like cash and gold bars" [Hurtado and Nesmith, 2016]. Later the same year, a ruling by Judge Alison J. Nathan of the United States District Court for the Southern District of New York contradicted the *Espinoza* ruling stating, "Bitcoins are funds within the plain meaning of that term. Bitcoins can be accepted as a payment for goods and services or bought directly from an exchange with a bank account. They therefore function as pecuniary resources and are used as a medium of exchange and a means of payment" [Redman, 2016].

17.1.2 Commodity

Cryptocurrencies are sometimes considered commodities. A commodity is a single unit of a tangible asset – for example, gold, silver and oil. Commodities are dissimilar to stocks or bonds on the basis that who produces them does not matter. Across all marketplaces, such commodities remain mutually interchangeable. Further, commodities have a limited and fixed supply because unlike a stock certificate, one cannot just create another ton of timber. The pricing of commodities is entirely determined by supply and demand. These qualities readily describe Bitcoin and similar cryptocurrencies. Their algorithm has a fixed quantity at a predetermined rate that does not alter the inherent value, and like other commodities, they need to be sold to be profitable, implying that supply and demand determine the value [Bitcoin Exchange Guide Team, 2018].

The US government's Commodity Futures Trading Commission classifies cryptocurrency as a commodity, and the Internal Revenue Service classifies it as an asset [Redman, 2016], while the South African Revenue Service, the legislation of Canada, the Ministry of Finance of the Czech Republic and several others classify it as an intangible asset [Rangongo, 2018; Appel, 2014]. Leading newspapers also took the same stance. Back in 2013, *The Wall Street Journal* described Bitcoin as a commodity and *Forbes* described it as a digital collectable debunking its currency status [Chapman, 2013; Woodhill, 2013]. More recently, *The Guardian* described Bitcoin as digital gold [Usborne, 2017].

17.1.3 Stock

Although it is less common, many investors consider cryptocurrency as stock. This approach was universalised by initial coin offerings (ICOs) where groups and start-ups sell pre-mined tokens in a bid to raise working capital and in exchange give token holders the right to participate in the administrative activities of the blockchain. Because ICOs resemble many features that IPOs offer, they are considered similar. In reality, however, there are stark contrasts between ICOs and IPOs. Professor Meg Luo of the Villanova University School of Business while writing for *U.S. News and World Report* argued that investors buy stocks and bonds because they bring in future cash flows, interest and principal income in the case of bonds and dividend for stocks, and capital gains from a possible increase in price in the future. However, cryptocurrencies can only offer a return in the price increase. Her arguments also point to the fact that stock market prices tend to be low in volatility to achieve overall stability. When it comes to Bitcoin and cryptocurrencies, volatility seems to be an integral part of the ecosystem making them less likely to function similar to stocks [Luo, 2018].

17.2 Price of Bitcoin

The prices of Bitcoin and other cryptocurrencies have gone through various cycles of appreciation and depreciation with Bitcoin leading the volatility parade. Such behaviour of cryptocurrency pricing is referred to by many as bubbles and busts. *Forbes* suggested Bitcoin is a *classic bubble*, while *The Guardian* referred to it as the "Harlem shake of currency" stating that it is nothing but a bubble as early as in 2013 [Colombo, 2013' Moore, 2013].

Having reached its all-time high price of nearly $20,000 in December 2017, the value of Bitcoin sharply fell below $3000 within a year. Many pointed to this drop as the beginning of the end of Bitcoin and other cryptocurrencies. It is, however, interesting to find that the cryptocurrency giant had suffered even worse declines in the past.

On 17 March 2010, the now-defunct *BitcoinMarket.com* exchange first offered trading Bitcoin at $0.003. The value of Bitcoin rapidly rose in 2011 when the price of a single token moved from about $0.30 to $32 before returning to $2 – a massive growth of 10,566.66% followed by a 1500% decline. In the latter half of 2012 and during the 2012–13 Cypriot financial crisis, the price began to rise again reaching a high of $266 on 10 April 2013, before crashing to around $50. On 29 November 2013, the cost of one Bitcoin rose to an all-time peak of $1242 (2384% growth). Some evidence suggests that part of this peak in the price of Bitcoin was due to price manipulation [Gandal et al., 2018]. In 2014, the price fell sharply, and as of April remained depressed at little more than half its 2013 pricing facing a decline of about 265%. As of August 2014, Bitcoin was under $600.

In January 2015, noting that the Bitcoin price had dropped to its lowest level since spring 2013 – around $224, losing approximately 455% of its value – *The New York Times* suggested that the industry is bracing for the effects of a prolonged decline in prices and flashing warning signs [Ember, 2015]. The same year, Business Insider reported that deep web drug dealers were "freaking out" as they lost profits through being unable to convert Bitcoin revenue to cash quickly enough as the price declined and that there was a danger that dealers selling reserves to stay in business might force the Bitcoin price down further [Price, 2015]. Those predictions, however, did not prove to be correct rather 2016 saw Bitcoin price staying mostly stable between $600 and $780. As of January 2017, the price was $800 that ultimately hit nearly $20,000 within 12 months only to drop back to around $3000 by December 2018 where it had been hovering at the time of writing. This saw Bitcoin experiencing another massive growth of roughly 2400% followed by 566.66% decline. Figure 17.2 shows how the price of Bitcoin moved from 2008 to 2018.

17.3 Volatility of Bitcoin

In finance, volatility is the degree of variation of a trading price series over time as measured by the standard deviation of logarithmic returns. The volatility of Bitcoin's price has been a piece of prime news ever since. It attracted prominent figures from the financial and tech industries to comment on it. Many tried to predict the price while others warned potential investors of their disbelief in blockchain technology. Nevertheless, it has been observed numerous times that experts make harsh comments about Bitcoin and write off blockchain technology following massive crashes, but this virtual currency eventually revives and moves from one all-time-high to another in the end.

According to risk management expert Professor Mark T. Williams, as of 2014, Bitcoin has volatility 7 times greater than gold, 8 times greater than the S&P 500 and 18 times greater than the US dollar [Williams, 2014]. Attempting to explain the high volatility, a group of Japanese scholars pointed out that having no stabilisation mechanism is one of the causes behind the irregular movement of Bitcoin and other cryptocurrency prices [Iwamura et al., 2014]. The Bitcoin Foundation contends that high volatility is due to insufficient liquidity, while a Forbes journalist claims that it is related to the uncertainty of its long-term value and the high volatility of a start-up currency that people are still experimenting how to figure out how useful it could be [Wilkes, 2013; Lee, 2013].

A group of pro-Bitcoin venture capitalists, in 2014, argued that significantly increased trading volume is needed to decrease price volatility [Casey, 2014a]. This view was echoed in a statement made by Canadian and Dutch experts who stated that according to economic theory, the volatility of the price of Bitcoin would drop when business and consumer usage of this virtual currency increases. It is due to the usage

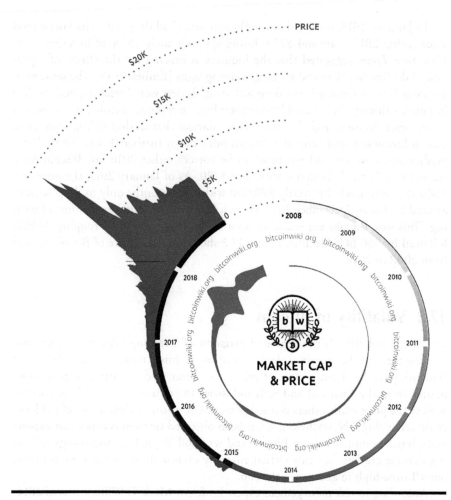

Figure 17.2 The historic price movement of Bitcoin. (Image courtesy of Bitcoin Wiki.)

for payments that reduce the sensitivity of the exchange rate to the beliefs of speculators about the future value of this virtual currency [Bolt and Oordt, 2016]. According to *The Wall Street Journal*, as of April 2016, Bitcoin is starting to look slightly more stable than gold [Yang, 2016]. On 3 March 2017, the price has surpassed the value of gold for the first time, and its price surged to an all-time high [Molloy, 2017].

A study in *Electronic Commerce Research and Applications*, going back through the network's historical data, showed the value of the Bitcoin network as measured by the price of Bitcoins, to be roughly proportional to the square of the number of daily unique users participating on the network. This is a form of Metcalfe's law and suggests that the network was demonstrating network effects proportional to its level of user adoption [Alabi, 2017].

17.4 Historic Price Predictions

Financial journalists, analysts, economists and investors have attempted to predict the possible future value of Bitcoin on several occasions. In April 2013, John Quiggin, professor of economics at the University of Queensland, stated in an article he wrote for *National Interest* magazine, "Bitcoins will attain their true value of zero sooner or later, but it is impossible to say when" [Quiggin, 2013]. A similar forecast was made in November 2014 by Kevin Dowd, professor of finance and economics at Durham University, in his article titled "Bitcoin is Bust: Why Investors Should Abandon the Doomed Cryptocurrency" [Dowd, 2014].

Mark T. Williams, professor of finance at Boston University and an expert in risk management, forecast in December 2013 that Bitcoin would trade for less than $10 by mid-2014 [Williams, 2013]. In the indicated period Bitcoin exchanged as low as $344 (April 2014) and during July 2014 the price was $609. In November 2014, David Yermack, professor of finance at New York University Stern School of Business, forecast that in November 2015 Bitcoin may be all but worthless [Macguire, 2014]. In the indicated period Bitcoin exchanged as low as $176.50 (January 2015) and during November 2015 Bitcoin's lowest price was $309.90.

However, not everyone has had a sceptical view of Bitcoin while predicting its value. In May 2013, Bank of America foreign exchange and rate strategist David Woo forecast a maximum fair price of $1300 for each Bitcoin token [Sharf, 2013]. Investor Cameron Winklevoss stated in December 2013 that the "small bull case scenario for Bitcoin is $40,000 a coin" [Stan, 2013]. By December 2017, Bitcoin reached half of this value before crashing to $3000 within a year. In December 2014, a year later following his comment that Bitcoin price would go down to $10 by mid-2014, Williams stated, "The probability of success is low, but if it does hit, the reward will be very large" [Sidel, 2014].

17.5 Price Movement of Major Cryptocurrencies

Bitcoin is the giant amongst the cryptocurrencies and tends to influence the price of others. It is highly unlikely that when Bitcoin goes bearish, other cryptocurrencies will not follow suit. This is the reason why experts talk about Bitcoin to indicate the whole industry. Nevertheless, there have been some instances when other cryptocurrencies tried to break away from the influence of Bitcoin and developed their pattern; although that did not last long. The following briefly presents a commentary of the price movement* of some of the major cryptocurrencies and the story behind how they came into being.

---

* All prices are taken from www.coinmarketcap.com, which is free and publicly available to access.

17.5.1 ETH

The ETH, spelt out as Ether, is the native cryptocurrency of the Ethereum platform. It is the fundamental token for the operation of its distributed ledger and gas payments.

The Ethereum platform went live on 30 July 2015 with 72 million tokens pre-mined. This accounts for about 70% of the total circulating supply in 2018. For the first 1½ years, Ether traded below $12. However, in May 2017, Ether experienced massive growth of 13,000% following in the footsteps of Bitcoin and hit its all-time-high price of about $1400 on 15 January 2018. In less than a year its value fell by 1455% and has been trading below $90 as of December 2018.

In 2016, following the theft of $50 million worth of Ether, Ethereum encountered a hard fork, splitting into two separate blockchains – the new version became Ethereum (ETH) with the theft reversed and the original continued as Ethereum Classic (ETC). As of December 2018, ETC was trading below $5.

17.5.2 XRP

XRP is the native cryptocurrency of the Ripple protocol. Unlike Bitcoin, this cryptocurrency along with the Ripple protocol is heavily promoted by Ripple Labs, the company that created the network. Due to having a strong use-case focusing on becoming a global financial network and securing a number of reputed partners to use the system, Ripple came under the spotlight in 2017 and briefly surpassed Ethereum to become the second largest cryptocurrency based on market capitalisation. Although Ethereum soon regained second place, later that year Ripple strongly captured the position again and as of December 2018, it has been holding on to it.

The XRP has been in the market since 2 February 2013. It was first traded in the cryptocurrency exchange on 4 August 2013 at a price of $0.01 that reached $0.05 on the 1 December 2013 delivering growth of 400% within 4 months of its launch. The value of XRP, however, soon returned to $0.01 and stayed below $0.05 for more than 3 years. On a couple of occasions, in 2013 and 2014, the price of this cryptocurrency refused to follow Bitcoin indicating a new trend for Ripple protocol. Despite those early signs, this did not happen until April 2017 when XRP broke away from the influence of Bitcoin and raised on its own. On 29 March 2017, XRP was traded at $0.01 and hit $3.20 on 5 January 2018. In less than 9 months XRP experienced incredible growth of 31,900.00%. Although this rapid growth of XRP coincided with Bitcoin's all-time high price, it did not strictly follow the pattern. There was a clear and unique trend for XRP that distinguished its journey than that of Bitcoin's. The massive crash of the cryptocurrency market in 2018 saw the value of XRP fall below $0.50, which Ripple has yet to recover from.

17.5.3 XLM

XLM, shorthand for Lumen, is the native token of Stellar. Originally Stellar was created from a hard fork from the Ripple network, but soon it established itself as one of the major cryptocurrencies. XLM was first introduced for trading by the Brazilian Bitcoin exchange *Mercado Bitcoin* on 5 August 2014 and many exchanges around the world soon follow suit. Since its inception, the price of XLM remained below $0.003 until April 2017 when cryptocurrency markets started to experience massive growth. Instead of following Bitcoin, XLM followed its predecessor XRP and reached an all-time high in January 2018. As of 4 April 2017, XLM has been trading at $0.003137, and in 9 months, it reached $0.93 experiencing an enormous growth of 29546.15%. As of December 2018, this cryptocurrency is now steadily trading at around $0.10.

17.5.4 NEO

NEO is the native cryptocurrency of the NEO blockchain platform. It was first traded in the cryptocurrency exchange on 9 September 2016 at a price of $0.18 in the name of *Antshares*. Later it was rebranded to its current name in June 2017. It is a pre-mined coin, and a total of 100 million NEO were created in the genesis block. Fifty million NEO were sold to early investors, with the remaining 50 million NEO locked into a smart contract. Each year, 15 million NEO tokens are unlocked for the NEO development team to fund long-term development goals and will never enter into the exchanges for trading. NEO tokens generate a slowly deflationary amount of GAS tokens, which are used to pay for transactions on the network. The inflation rate of GAS is controlled with a decaying half-life algorithm that will release 100 million GAS over approximately 22 years. More on this can be found in Chapter 6.

As of April 2017, NEO traded at $0.18 or below, but soon it joined the cryptocurrency bull movement and reached its all-time high of $196.85 on 15 January 2018. NEO is one of the few cryptocurrencies that revived close to its all-time high following the mid-January crash. Having seen its price hovering at around $100, NEO gained a price of approximately $160 by the end of the month. However, the resistance this cryptocurrency showed did not last long and crashed again. Later that year on multiple occasions, NEO again demonstrated strong resistance rejecting to follow the footsteps of Bitcoin, but ultimately came under the influence of Bitcoin by the end of the year. As of December 2018, NEO has been trading at around $7.

17.5.5 EOS

EOS is the native cryptocurrency of the EOS blockchain. It was established amid the cryptocurrency bull run of 2017 and officially launched following a yearlong

ICO that saw 1 billion pre-created tokens sell for a total of $4.2 billion. The EOS token was first traded at $1 but soon its value started to shoot high, and by January 2018 when all other cryptocurrencies hit their all-time high, it reached $18.16. It was a new all-time high for EOS, but not its best.

EOS is the only dominant cryptocurrency that broke away from the influence of Bitcoin and demonstrated its unique pattern for the first half of 2018. It is also the only cryptocurrency that hit another all-time high of $21.46 on 29 April 2018 when all other cryptocurrencies including Bitcoin had been struggling. However, following a series of cryptocurrency market crashes and the arrival of bad rumours and the news of strict government regulations for the industry, the latter half of 2018 saw EOS come under the influence of Bitcoin and follow this giant's movement. As of December 2018, EOS has been trading at below $3.

17.6 Reception

The acceptance of cryptocurrency as an economic tool does not depend only at the hands of users rather merchants who accept payments, investors who put more money into this industry to grow it further and governments who create the environment for everyone to use it play a vital role in this regard. The following analyses that how these three entities have been reacting to the arrival of this new kind of alternative money in our society.

17.6.1 Acceptance by Merchants

It has been a decade since the first cryptocurrency became available, but the use of this new type of alternative currency is rare with merchants outside the exchanges (Figure 17.3). Bitcoin's nature of taking around 10 minutes to process payments through the blockchain and hefty fees for small retail purchases makes it impractical to buy a cup of coffee or similar product on the go. The volatility of cryptocurrency is another challenge, as merchants frequently need to adjust the price through conversion with a fiat currency such as the US dollar.

Contrary to common belief, during the early days of Bitcoin and other altcoins, merchants were more willing to accept cryptocurrency but have become more restrictive in recent time. Statistics show that in 2017 and 2018 Bitcoin's acceptance amongst major online retailers included only 3 of the top 500 US online merchants, down from five in 2016. Another report by Bloomberg stated that the largest 17 crypto merchant-processing services handled $69 million in June 2018, down from $411 million in September 2017 [Kharif, 2018].

Cryptocurrency seems to be more suitable for large and delay-tolerant payments. Bitcoin started to be accepted for real estate payments in late 2017 when the first recorded sale of a house in exchange for Bitcoin happened in September. Texas-based Kuper Sotheby's International Realty brokered the deal using bitpay.

Figure 17.3   Bitcoin is accepted as a method of payment at a cafe in Delft, the Netherlands.

com to process the payment. Two months later, the first recorded sale of an apartment in the world and first real estate property in Europe was sold for Bitcoin in the Czech Republic. The Czech real estate agency HOME Hunters brokered the deal for a 3-room apartment for a Russian buyer without using payment service providers at all [Elkins, 2018].

Despite the challenges, many online and offline merchants still accept cryptocurrencies as payment. For example, Microsoft has been accepting Bitcoin in its online Xbox Store since 2014, while *Purse.io* is a platform that allows spending Bitcoin on Amazon. Overstock, one of the largest US internet retailers, and Expedia, one of the world's largest travel agencies, accept cryptocurrency for buying products and booking hotels and flights. In addition to many online merchants, there are hundreds of thousands of offline restaurants, hotels, supermarkets, car dealers and so on that accept cryptocurrency payment across the globe. CoinMap* in an interactive map provider that offers users information from these outlets worldwide (Figure 17.4).

17.6.2 Acceptance by Investors

There is a division between investors as to whether to put their money in the blockchain industry, particularly in cryptocurrencies. It looks like young and novice

---

* CoinMap is publicly accessible using the URL www.coinmap.org.

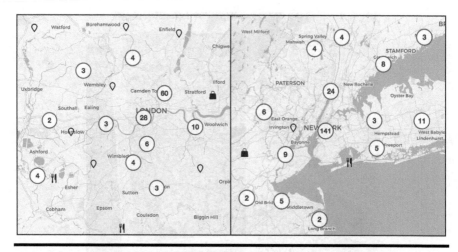

Figure 17.4   A map showing outlets accepting Bitcoin as a method of payment in London (left) and New York (right).

investors are more willing to invest in blockchain than the people having more experience. This division is echoed in the voice of Andreas Treichl, the CEO of Erste Group Bank AG, one of the largest financial services providers in Central and Eastern Europe, when he admitted in an interview with Bloomberg that he is not a "believer" in this technology and prevented his children from investing money in Bitcoin despite their strong wish. Distinguished investor Warren Buffet has been a long-time Bitcoin sceptic who claims this virtual money not to be a value-producing asset and a "real bubble".

Perhaps the most hostile reaction came from the CEO of JPMorgan Jamie Dimon who called Bitcoin a "fraud" and stated that if JPMorgan traders began trading in Bitcoin, he was going to fire them "in a second". It was remarkable that a year later he admitted that he regrets his comment and praised blockchain technology saying that "the blockchain is real. You can have crypto yen and dollars and stuff like that".

Regardless of the criticism, the blockchain industry has been experiencing massive growth despite the huge market crash that happened throughout the year 2018. Surprisingly, more than $13 billion was invested through ICOs alone during this period [Diemers et al., 2018]. It appears that large corporates such as IBM and Microsoft have taken initiatives to build blockchain products, while large exchanges such as Coinbase have recently released cryptocurrencies. It is still too early to comment on the future of this industry, but early signs are mostly positive outside the trading markets.

17.6.3 *Acceptance by Governments*

Government is perhaps the most important amongst the three entities, as their unwillingness to support the rise of cryptocurrency will only create chaos and turmoil. The arrival of decentralised Bitcoin was first treated as an attack on government-controlled monetary systems. South Korea's action on taking down cryptocurrency exchanges and China banning cryptocurrency mining were forms of retaliation from those governments against the revolt that Bitcoin-enthusiasts initiated a decade ago. However, blockchain has moved on from its original forms, and running unregulated is not the concern of most projects in recent times. The actions South Korea and China demonstrated hardly helped to develop this technology and only increased volatility in the market followed by a series of crashes [Kim, 2018a; Hsu, 2018].

Despite some governments taking a hard line, there are also a few nations that are friendly with this new technology. Sweden, Switzerland, Estonia, Malta, Dubai and Japan are jurisdictions that extended their hands to support the growth of ICOs and exchanges. Amongst them, Estonia attempted to adapt blockchain technology even before the arrival Bitcoin, while Switzerland has an entire city in Zug to nurture ICOs and start-ups related to this new technology. Sweden has been in preparation for launching its own digital money, and Dubai aims to become the first blockchain-powered government by 2020 [Adams, 2018; Billner, 2018; Jenkinson, 2018].

Blockchain technology is going through a crucial phase as the European Union and the United States are currently considering regulations for cryptocurrency as an asset, and for its underlying technology. As two of the largest geographical regions where cryptocurrency is mined, created and used, the regulations they put forward will significantly alter the future path of this technology in future. Chapter 19 will elaborate more on the topics of government regulations, actions and willingness to control this technology.

17.7 Summary

This chapter presented the economic outlook of cryptocurrencies. The ability of these virtual currencies to act as an alternative to regular money makes it essential to look at their utilities and acceptance in society. With that objective in mind, the chapter presented discussion related to the classification of cryptocurrencies followed by the movement and volatilities of prices; past predictions that ultimately proved to be wrong; and acceptance by merchants, investors and governments around the globe.

Chapter 18

Crime, Criminals and Cryptocurrencies

It is an unfortunate fact that the underworld recognised the potential of Bitcoin before learned society did. Renowned thriller writer Dan Brown in his bestselling novel *Origin* narrated an instance where a contract killer is contacted using a secured network and given the assignment of killing a person for which the killer receives payment in Bitcoin. This narrative of the novel may sound dramatic, but the reality is that an episode like this seems to be no longer fiction. Underworld syndicates have secured networks and a convenient payment method in Bitcoin to turn such a tale to an actuality. Criminal organisations and underworld crime syndicates have been using cryptocurrencies as early as 2011. They utilised cryptocurrencies like Bitcoin and altcoins to pave the path for payment in exchange for illicit goods and services. The use of virtual currency is also involved in financial crimes, cybercrimes and possibly the hiring of gangsters and hitmen for serious offences like murder and abduction. This chapter seeks to gather accounts on criminal activities using cryptocurrencies and present how criminals use this technology as a tool for committing crimes in a wide range of wicked and unlawful exercises. The chapter also offers some recommendations as to how such crimes can be tackled and how cryptocurrencies can become mainstream without limiting the benefits of blockchain technology.

18.1 Criminal Activities

Cryptocurrencies have a close tie with the underworld and crimes since their inception. Criminals promptly liked the concept and adapted Bitcoin when it first arrived, even before the learned society started releasing the true merit of this new technology. A 2014 study from the University of Kentucky examining Google search data found evidence that illegal activity drives interest in Bitcoin [Wilson and Yelowitz, 2018], while a 2018 study led by the University of Sydney found that 24 million Bitcoin users accounted for illicit activities and hold $8 billion worth of this token. This is an estimated amount of 25% of all Bitcoin users and 44% of all Bitcoin transactions [Foley et al., 2018].

There are markets to buy and sell goods and services online that are restricted to trade in a regular supermarket. Products like drugs, guns and fake banknotes are not possible to buy from the local supermarket; however, current technology allows people having Bitcoin to go online and buy stuff like this with a few mouse clicks on their computers. The misuse of cryptocurrencies does not stop there, and people use this technology to commit financial crimes, scams and market manipulation.

To present readers with a comprehensive but organised discussion on the subject of criminal activities relating to cryptocurrencies, the types of crimes are divided into three broad categories, namely *darknet-based crimes*, *financial crimes* and *fraudulent activities*. Later the chapter, having provided some background on the deep web, aims to address these categories by breaking them down further into more elaborate subcategories. The chapter also discusses potential approaches to preventing the misuse of cryptocurrencies.

18.2 Deep Web

It is a common criticism against Bitcoin that it acts as a method of payment for trading goods. However, there must have been a secret online market where the trades take place; otherwise, how does a buyer get to know about products and whom to make the payment. Under the surveillance of government authorities around the globe, maintaining such marketplaces seems to be impossible. Sadly, that impossible task has become possible due to the advancement of computer communication technology that enables criminals to set up black markets.

The World Wide Web (WWW, or simply the web) is not limited to what we access, browse and use for our day-to-day activity. There exists a world that remains unindexed by search engines and out of reach for most users; even the Google search engine robot cannot locate that part of the web. Computer scientist Michael K. Bergman coined a term for it – the *deep web* [Wright, 2009]. The contents of the deep web are hidden behind HTTP forms and mostly include common applications such as webmail and online banking. A direct URL or IP address is generally required to access these contents. Some of the contents need passwords or other forms of security access approvals.

Deep inside this deep web, there exists a small part called darknet (also known as dark web) that hosts black markets for trading illicit goods and illegal services. Although the purpose of having the darknet is not for criminal activities but for people who want to stay undetected such as whistle-blowers and people sharing contents in a secret group, it is no surprise that criminals found a sanctuary in it. The following sections briefly describe its architecture, required protocols and how Bitcoin became the last missing piece of a jigsaw puzzle to unleash darknet markets to their full potential [Henderson, 2017].

18.2.1 Darknet and Dark Web

Darknet and dark web are not the same but are closely related to each other and can be used synonymously. Darknet refers to the network, whereas the dark web collectively denotes the websites hosted on the darknet network. Using specially built secured communication protocols, such as *Tor* or *I2P*, users get access to the darknet and ultimately browse through the dark web to view its contents. These websites often require specific software, configurations and access approval.

A 2014 study at the University of Portsmouth found that the most commonly hosted type of content on Tor is child pornography, followed by black markets. The individual sites with the highest traffic in Tor are assigned to botnet operations where many internet-connected devices run bots to perform distributed denial-of-service (DDoS) attacks, steal data, send spam and allow attackers to access targeted devices. The study also noticed that darknet hosts many whistle-blowing sites and political discussion forums [Dredge, 2014]. More recently, a 2016 study conducted at King's College London produced a deep search in darknet and found that more than half of the live sites on Tor is involved in unlawful activities [Moore and Rid, 2016].

18.2.2 Onion Routing and Tor

Onion routing provides the basis of the darknet. It is an anonymous communication method over a computer network where messages are encapsulated in layers of encryption, analogous to layers of an onion. The encrypted data is transmitted through a series of network nodes called onion routers, each of which "peels" away a single layer, uncovering the next destination of the data. When the final layer is decrypted, the message arrives at its destination. The sender remains anonymous because each intermediary knows only the location of the nodes immediately preceding and following it [Reed et al., 2006].

Paul Syverson, Michael G. Reed and David Goldschlag at the US Naval Research Laboratory developed onion routing in the mid-1990s to protect US intelligence communications online. The technique was further improved by the Defense Advanced Research Projects Agency (DARPA) and patented by the US Navy in 1998.

Computer scientists Roger Dingledine and Nick Mathewson joined Syverson in 2002 to develop Tor (The Onion Router), the software and network protocol that makes the largest onion-routing network. Following the release of Tor source code under a free license by the US Navy, Tor became a non-profit organisation in 2006 with financial support from several organisations [Dredge, 2013].

Tor directs internet traffic through a free, worldwide, volunteer overlay network consisting of more than 7000 relays to conceal a user's location and usage from anyone conducting network surveillance or traffic analysis. Although Tor's intended use is to protect the personal privacy of its users, as well as their freedom and ability to conduct confidential communication by keeping their internet activities from being monitored, it is not widely used as a tool to form the largest part of the darknet. Besides Tor, there are other anonymous communication networks such as I2P (Invisible Internet Project), Freenet and Riffle that jointly form the whole of the darknet.

18.2.3 Bitcoin: The Missing Piece

The principal motivation for using Bitcoin and similar cryptocurrencies by darknet markets is perhaps their pseudonymous nature. Because Bitcoin allows its bearer to hide behind cryptographic addresses, despite the blockchain being an open platform where everyone can see the transfer of funds between parties, there is no way to identify who they are unless the parties willingly disclose their identity. This feature enables underground sellers and buyers to keep their identities private while trading and negotiating unlawful deals. Once payment is made to an address, the person having access to the private key of the address can only and secretly redeem the funds.

If the addressing of Bitcoin looks advantageous for trading illicit goods, the "escrow" function of the protocol presents criminals with a perfect underground eBay! Using the escrow, a third-party individual in disguise can step in between the buyers and the sellers and act as a regulator to make the smooth exchange of goods between the parties. For example, Alice purchases a gun from an underground market in exchange for 10 Bitcoins (BTC) from Bob. Carol can be the middleman who will have the final say on this trade. The transfer of the fund will be locked between the trio and Bob can only redeem the tokens when Carol gives the permission. Once Alice confirms that she received delivery of the gun, Carol would use her private key to allow Bob to redeem the tokens. In case of a dispute, the funds remain locked on the blockchain. The script of the Bitcoin also allows for complex operation between multiple parties in the form of an m-of-n contract. It means, to redeem funds, out of n signatory at least m individuals must agree upon a decision to release the funds.

Between 2006 and 2011, the darknet proliferated rapidly. When criminals found onion routing, Tor and similar networks, they found a place to hide in anonymity to discuss goods and services that they could not discuss in the real world. They, however, still lacked the last piece of the jigsaw puzzle that they have been solving. To make a trade happen, payment is mandatory, but there was no payment method. Following the arrival of Bitcoin in 2009, they found the missing piece of the puzzle, and black markets have been thriving ever since.

18.3 Darknet-Based Crimes

Darknet-based crimes are all connected to darknet markets, which are also referred to as crypto-markets. These markets act as the middlemen for trading prohibited goods and services in exchange for cryptocurrencies [Gayathri, 2013].

A darknet market can be more formally defined as a commercial website on the darknet accessible through Tor or similar software. Criminals and underworld sellers use these markets to trade illicit goods such as drugs, cyber-arms, weapons, counterfeit currency, stolen credit card details, forged documents, unlicensed pharmaceuticals and steroids. Modern markets even attempt to provide services such as cyberattacks and assassinations [Beckett, 2015].

18.3.1 Silk Road

Silk Road was the first darknet market established in 2011 that developed the model of a perfect online black market where buyers and sellers stay under the hood using anonymous networks with payments that are taken through cryptocurrencies such as Bitcoin as shown in (Figure 18.1). The approach became so popular that other markets such as Agora, Utopia and Evolution were introduced with the intention of selling illegal goods.

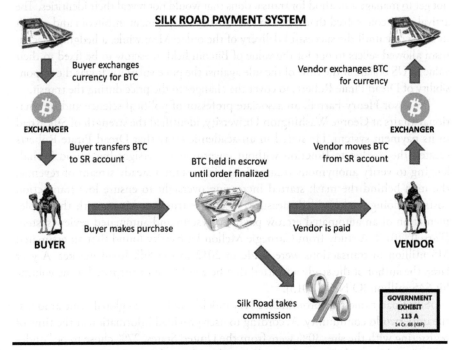

Figure 18.1   A flowchart depicting Silk Road's payment system submitted as evidence in a US court at the trial of the founder of Silk Road.

This market was constructed using Tor where users were able to browse the site anonymously and securely without potential traffic monitoring. The name of the market is inspired by the historical trading routes dating back to the Han dynasty of the third century BC between Europe, India, China and many other countries on the Afro-Eurasian landmass.

Silk Road was operated by the pseudonymous "Dread Pirate Roberts" who was known for advocating libertarian ideals and criticising regulation. The involvement of two other individuals, Variety Jones and Smedley, is considered a catalyst for the growth and success of the site. Initially, the number of new seller accounts was limited and allocated through auctions, however, a fixed fee was charged for each new seller account when the market got established.

Silk Road is most famous for trading drugs; at the height of its thriving phase, almost 70% of the total products were related to drugs [Chen, 2011]. The market used to group these products under the headings stimulants, psychedelics, prescription, precursors, opioids, ecstasy, dissociative and steroids/PEDs. From the inception of Silk Road, the creator and administrators instituted terms of service that prohibited the sale of anything whose purpose was to "harm or defraud" such as child pornography, stolen credit cards, assassinations and weapons of any type [Gayathri, 2013].

The success of Silk Road heavily relies on Bitcoin. It is because Tor, the technology behind the market, was already in place for some years, but buyers and sellers could not get to manage a method for transactions that would not reveal their identities. The arrival of Bitcoin solved that problem. Silk Road took payment in Bitcoin and took it in an escrow until the successful delivery of the order. Meanwhile, a hedging mechanism allowed sellers to opt for the value of Bitcoin held in escrow to be fixed to their value in US dollars at the time of the sale against the price volatility. It was the responsibility of Dread Pirate Roberts to cover the changes in the price during the transit.

Professor Henry Farrell, an associate professor of political science and international affairs at George Washington University, identified the strength of Silk Road in its payment system. He stated in an academic essay that Dread Pirate Roberts created the market to function without government oversight but found it challenging to verify anonymous transactions. To sustain a steady stream of revenue, the man behind the mask started increasing oversight to ensure low transaction costs. In doing so, he added measures to ensure trustworthiness with the implementation of an automated escrow payment system and automated review system [Farrell, 2017]. A study from Carnegie Mellon University found that an estimated $15 million in transactions were made in 2012 in the Silk Road market. A year later, the author of the study admitted that he would not be surprised if the volume hit $45 million [O'Neill, 2013].

Silk Road came into prominence very quickly and earned global fame amongst the underworld community. According to user-provided information at the time of registering with the site, 30% were from the United States, 27% chose to be "undeclared", and beyond that, in descending order of prevalence: the United Kingdom, Australia, Germany, Canada, Sweden, France, Russia, Italy and the Netherlands.

The activities on the Silk Road made authorities around the world anxious. The selling of illicit goods was not the only threat that this market possessed. It inspired many other markets to come into being and start trading even more notorious products including contract killing. This makes police and special forces in the US, Europe and Asia desperate to shut down the operation of this marketplace.

The Federal Investigation Bureau (FBI) of the United States had been trying to find the identity of the Dread Pirate Roberts but did not see much success after almost 2 years of investigation. In 2013, it received a massive clue from an Internal Revenue Service (IRS) tax inspector, Gary Alford, who while browsing through Google noticed the name Dread Pirate Roberts in the Bitcoin forum. The person in the forum tried to advocate for selling drugs in his post and left an email address Ross.Ulbricht@gmail.com to contact him. Alford had previously known that the nickname Dread Pirate Roberts is the administrator of Silk Road. He suspected that the Dread Pirate Roberts on Bitcoin forum might be the same person, and if so, Ross Ulbricht could have been his real name.

The tax inspector went on searching for the name and obtained the IP address that this email account used to use. His off-duty investigation eventually led him to a San Francisco address where a man named Ross Ulbricht resided. Initially, he was not taken seriously, but when the FBI heard of the address that matched with an address it found from a different source, Ross Ulbricht became the prime suspect of being the person behind the pseudonym Dread Pirate Roberts.

Following an FBI crackdown on 2 October 2013, Ross Ulbricht was arrested at Glen Park Library, a branch of the San Francisco Public Library and the website was shut down. Ulbricht was indicted on charges of money laundering, computer hacking, conspiracy to traffic narcotics and attempting to have six people killed. Prosecutors alleged that Ulbricht paid $730,000 to others to commit the murders, although none of the murders actually occurred, and Ulbricht ultimately was not prosecuted for any of the alleged murder attempts. He was convicted of eight charges related to Silk Road in the US Federal Court in Manhattan and was sentenced to life in prison without the possibility of parole.

18.3.2 Post-Silk Road Markets

Silk Road, as the first modern online black market, inspired other underworld syndicates to found new markets in the darknet. Some markets arrived as competitors, while many became successors once Silk Road was shut down. The following presents a brief commentary on those competitor and successor sites.

- *Silk Road 2.0 and 3.0*: Silk Road 2.0 came into being in November 2013 and is considered to be the direct successor of the original website. The management of the new market, however, had a difficult time from the beginning. At first, a technical glitch hit the market resulting in the theft of $2.7 million worth of Bitcoin from its escrow accounts. This vulnerability then led to chaos and uncertainty amongst buyers, despite the site refunding at least half of its affected users with the lost Bitcoins. Later that year, authorities including the Federal Bureau of Investigation, Europol, and Eurojust commenced *Operation Onymous*, an international law enforcement operation targeting darknet markets and other hidden services operating on the Tor network. The joint force as a part of this operation arrested Blake Benthall, allegedly the owner and operator of Silk Road 2.0 under the pseudonym *Defcon* and closed down the site [Cox, 2014]. Another site, Silk Road 3.0 was launched soon to capitalise on the brand. This market is still in operation and topped the Reddit darknet market list at the time of this writing.

■ *Evolution*: Evolution was another Silk Road–inspired darknet market operating on the Tor network. It was founded by an individual known as "Verto" and became one of the two largest drug markets alongside Silk Road 2.0 at the time of its height [Greenberg, 2014a]. Evolution was notoriously infamous for selling stolen credit cards data and other kinds of fraudulent materials and permits including passports. *WIRED* magazine in 2015 wrote about this market in the article "The Dark Web Gets Darker with Rise of 'Evolution' Drug Market" [Greenberg, 2014b]. There is an allegation that the growth of this market was helped by Operation Onymous that did not target this market. Speaking about why Evolution was not part of Operation Onymous, head of the European police cybercrimes division could not give a proper answer and escaped saying: "…because there's only so much we can do on one day" [DW-News, 2014]. In March 2015, roughly 4 months after the operation, the market went offline with administrators freezing its users' escrow accounts. It never came online again and later became apparent that the shut down was an exit scam with the operators of the site stealing approximately $12 million in Bitcoins held in its escrow [Woolf, 2015].

■ *Agora*: Agora operated as a darknet market in the Tor network from 2013 until its closure in August 2015. It was unaffected by Operation Onymous and had been one of the strongest competitors for the top spot amongst darknet markets. Once Evolution was closed in an exit scam in March 2015, Agora quickly replaced it as the largest market. In August 2015 Agora's admins released a PGP signed message announcing a pause of operations to protect the site against potential attacks that they believe might be used to deanonymise server locations. Unlike Evolution, the closure of Agora was not an exit scam, and most activities moved over to the darknet market AlphaBay making it the largest in the realm.

■ *AlphaBay*: Launched in December 2014, it was the next generation of darknet markets that became very popular. AlphaBay saw steady growth that made darknet informer Gwern Branwen, an independent researcher who oversees the website *Gwern*,* to place it in the top tier of markets regarding the

---

* The site is publicly accessible using the URL www.gwern.net.

6-month survival probability [Branwen, 2018]. By October 2015, AlphaBay was recognised as the largest darknet market by Dan Palumbo, research director at Digital Citizens Alliance [SC-News, 2015]. It was the first market that enabled contract functionality for the user to allow making engagements and agreeing to provide services in the future according to the terms of the contract. By the time the law enforcement authority seized this site in July 2017, AlphaBay had more than 400,000 registered users. It was ten times larger than the original Silk Road with over 369,000 listings and facilitated tradings worth $600,000 to $800,000 every day. It received payment in two cryptocurrencies: Bitcoin and Monero [Popper, 2017].

■ *The Farmer's Market* had initially been a regular website founded in 2006 and moved to the darknet in 2010. It took payment using PayPal and Western Union that led law enforcement authorities to track down the trading parties relatively quickly. Following a 2-year investigation, it was shut down in 2012.

■ Others: *Black Market Reloaded* and *Atlantis* were two competitor markets of the original Silk Road. The former gained notoriety amongst users because of not being restrictive on products like child pornography, stolen credit cards, assassinations and weapons of any type, while the latter took its place in history by accepting Litecoin, a cryptocurrency other than Bitcoin for the first time. During the blooming period of these markets, a lesser known site, *Sheep Marketplace*, came to prominence when its vendor stole $6 million worth of users' Bitcoins. The investigation to find the thief led to an approach for fighting against crimes involving Bitcoin-like cryptocurrencies. (The chapter later elaborates on this issue.) None of these markets is operational at the moment.

Despite the constant effort of authorities around the globe to close down darknet markets, these websites keep coming and get bigger in size. A 2015 study from Carnegie Mellon University claims the estimated size of the markets based on listings in 2015 nearly reaches $300,000 per day [Soska and Christin, 2015]. Another report by the Digital Citizens Alliance shows almost $50,000 of the trading involved drugs [*The Economist*, 2015]. Figure 18.2 illustrates the volume of drug sales on darknet markets from 2013 to 2015 until the rise of the AlphaBay market.

Modern darknet markets accept payment in multiple cryptocurrencies, and many prefer the model established by AlphaBay. Amongst them, *Dream, The Wall Street, Empire* and *Point* are a few that have been still operating. There are websites such as *Dark Web News** that gives nearly live status of existing darknet markets as shown in Figure 18.3.

---

* The site is publicly accessible using the URL www.darkwebnews.com.

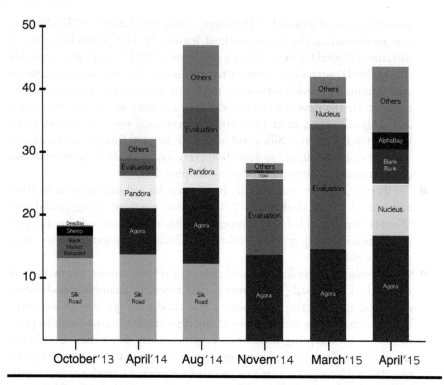

Figure 18.2 Digital Citizens Alliance reported that a trade volume of almost $50,000 involved drugs in the darknet markets from 2013 to 2015 (the Y-axis shows data in thousands).

18.3.3 Assassination Markets

An assassination is a prediction market where any party can place a bet using anonymous electronic money on pseudonymous remailers about the date of death of a given individual, and collect a payoff if they "guess" the date accurately. This would incentivise the assassination of individuals because the assassin, knowing when the action would take place, could profit by making an accurate bet on the time of the subject's death. Because the payoff is for accurately picking the date rather than performing the action of the assassin, it is substantially more difficult to assign criminal liability for the assassination [Harkin, 2009].

The concept originated from a broader theory called assassination politics, a term popularised by Jim Bell in his 1995–96 essay of the same name. He wrote:

> If only 0.1% of the population, or one person in a thousand, was willing to pay $1 to see some government slimeball dead, that would be, in effect, a $250,000 bounty on his head. Further, imagine that anyone considering collecting that bounty could do so with the mathematical

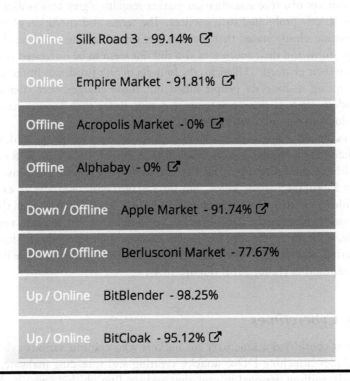

Figure 18.3 There are websites such as www.darkwebnews.com that gives nearly live status of the existing darknet markets.

certainty that he could not be identified, and could collect the reward without meeting, or even talking to, anybody who could later identify him. Perfect anonymity, perfect secrecy, and perfect security. And that, combined with the ease and security with which these contributions could be collected, would make being an abusive government employee an extremely risky proposition. Chances are good that nobody above the level of county commissioner would even risk staying in office.

[Greenberg, 2013]

At the time Bell wrote this, there was no technology in place to make it a reality. However, the arrival of Bitcoin now made it possible. The first market titled the "Assassination Market" came into being in 2013 when a self-described crypto-anarchist formed it using Tor. It used Bitcoin as bounties as well as the underlying prediction technology. Former US President Barack Obama, economist Ben Bernanke and former Justice Minister of Sweden Beatrice Ask were amongst the notables placed on the hit list. As of 2015, the site is not operational, but most of the deposited Bitcoins remained untouched [Greenberg, 2013].

The concept of a true assassination market remains a grey area as darknet marketplaces strictly prohibited such services. The terms and condition of Silk Road and Evolution clearly stated that services like assassinations could not be traded on the platform and their successors also did not seem to be interested in allowing hitmen on their platforms. Ulbricht, the founder of Silk Road, was initially charged for attempting to have six people killed but those charges were later dropped. Nevertheless, there is news emerging in recent times that darknet has possibly opened doors to commit such crimes.

The existence of any such marketplace hides so deep inside the dark web that it is difficult for a regular person to reach it. A British hacker in 2018 exposed a hitman-hiring site called *Besa Mafia* in the darknet that provides assassins starting from $5000 for a "basic killer", but for $30,000 one could hire an ex-military trained hitman with a sniper rifle on buildings [Miller, 2018]. Although there is no known history of using the darknet to kill any notable person, recently a man from Riverside, California, who appeared before a San Luis Obispo judge for his preliminary hearing, was charged for allegedly trying to hire a hitman from the darknet to kill his stepmother [Julio, 2018] (Figure 18.4).

18.3.4 Cybercrimes

Darknet is considered a sanctuary for hackers who commit various cybercrimes. This includes launching DDoS attacks, creating and spreading malware, stuffing credentials, sniffing personal information and sending phishing emails. Although traditionally hackers operate anonymously from the darknet to gain personal and financial benefits, the availability of cryptocurrency now popularises a concept

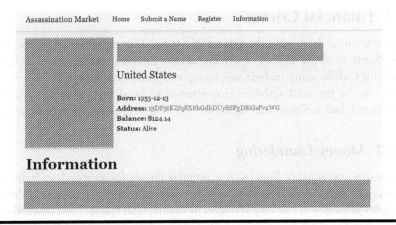

Assassination Market   Home   Submit a Name   Register   Information

United States

Born: 1953-12-13
Address: 13DF5tKZfq8X8hGdhDUySSPgD8iGsFv2WG
Balance: B124.14
Status: Alive

Information

Figure 18.4   A screenshot from the Tor Assassination Market showing the listing of an influential person from the United States and the prize money of the equivalent of about $1.7 million (as of December 2017). The name, picture and information about the person is removed for safety reasons.

called *hacker-for-hire*. Like hitmen, hackers are now available to be hired for providing a wide range of services to their would-be buyers.

A 2018 study by researchers at Positive Technologies on 25 sites on the dark web in Russian and English with a total registered user-base of about 3 million people analysed more than 10,000 hack-for-hire and malware-related postings. They found that the darknet-based cybercrime industry has been thriving with the demand for the creation of malware three times greater than the supply [Ashford, 2018].

The same research identified that the costs of cybercrime services across the deep web for compromising a site and obtaining full control over its web application costs as little as $150. Nonetheless, launching an attack on an organisation depends on the difficulty and may cost more than $4500, while the most expensive malware was for targeting banks' ATMs with prices starting at $1500. The leading type of malware available in the darknet is cryptocurrency miners (20% of the total), followed by hacking utilities (19%), botnet malware (14%), remote access Trojans (RATs) (12%) and ransomware (12%).

A less expensive but booming service is hacking social network accounts and emails. Almost two-thirds of the total hacker-for-hire requests from would-be buyers involve these requests. There are also super-cheap hacking services available such as hacking keyloggers would cost around $2.00, WiFi $3.00, Bluetooth $3.50 and malware for draining Bitcoin wallets $6.00.

Branded phishing attacks are by far another dominant cyberattack that enterprising hackers are selling. They offer pages that look like the pages of popular brands ranging from Apple and Netflix to Walmart. These fake websites cost about $2.00 each except for big outliers such as Apple for which darknet hackers charge approximately $5.00 on average [Migliano, 2018].

18.4 Financial Crimes

Cryptocurrencies have been the subject of financial irregularities on several occasions. Some of those instances involve actual financial crimes such as money launderings while many include suspicious and fraudulent activities. This section focuses on the financial activities that attempt to bend the law using cryptocurrency. Fraudulent activities such as scams will be discussed in the next section.

18.4.1 Money Laundering

Cryptocurrency, notably Bitcoin, is a popular choice for money laundering, the process of concealing the origins of money obtained illegally by passing it through a complex sequence of banking transfers or commercial transactions. Even though this is a lousy tool for committing such a crime, there are many instances around the world where cryptocurrencies are used in concealing the origins of money obtained illegally. The magnitude of money laundering varies from individuals laundering a small scale of money to as large as cryptocurrency trading exchanges getting involved in illegally handling millions of dollars.

Authorities including the European Banking Authority, the FBI and the Financial Action Task Force of the G7 had expressed concerns during the early days of Bitcoin that money launders could use this cryptocurrency. Their suspicion proved to be right when Charlie Shrem, an operator of a US Bitcoin exchange, was arrested for money laundering using cryptocurrency and subsequently sentenced to 2 years in prison for "aiding and abetting an unlicensed money transmitting business" in 2014.

More recently, Alexander Vinnik, wanted for money laundering by the US, France and Russia, and an alleged owner of the cryptocurrency trading exchange BTC-e, was arrested in Greece on $4 billion money laundering charges in 2017. This case quickly grabbed media attention because of the involvement of multiple countries, a plot to murder Vinnik in prison, and a report by Bloomberg finding a potential link between Vinnik and the Russian hacking group *Fancy Bear* [Chrepa et al., 2018].

The exchange, BTC-e, itself was also believed to be involved in criminal activities. It was founded in 2011 with its headquarters in Russia and had been operational until the US government seized its website in 2017. As of February 2015, this exchange handled around 3% of all Bitcoin exchange volume. It allowed trading between the US dollar, Russian ruble and euro currencies, and the Bitcoin, Litecoin, Namecoin, Novacoin, Peercoin, Dash and Ethereum cryptocurrencies until its closure [Guttmann, 2013].

US authorities also fined Bitfinex, one of the largest cryptocurrency exchanges of current times in 2016 for offering illegal off-exchange financed commodity transactions. They also found Bitfinex violating the Commodity Exchange Act by not registering as a futures commission merchant.

Authorities, however, did not always find their job as straightforward as these cases. They often faced difficulties dealing with this new technology as criminals tried to bend the rule misusing a grey area of the law involving cryptocurrency. As there is no correct definition as to if cryptocurrencies are money or not, it is sometimes difficult to convince a court of law that a crime has been committed.

A famous case, *State v. Espinoza*, became the topic of interest in the financial, law and tech industries. The case traces its root to 2014 when Michell Espinoza was unknowingly selling Bitcoin to undercover agents of the Miami Police Department and the US Secret Service. Though one of the undercover detectives had implied that the Bitcoin would be used to buy stolen credit card numbers, Espinoza continued with the sales charging transaction fees for the privilege. He was later charged with money laundering and illegal money transmission. When the case moved to court in 2016, Judge Teresa Mary Pooler of the Eleventh Judicial Circuit of Florida dismissed those charges stating that Bitcoin is not legal money; hence Espinoza could not be punished under existing Florida statutes. The judge stated:

> Bitcoin may have some attributes in common with what we commonly refer to as money, but differ in many important aspects, they are certainly not tangible wealth and cannot be hidden under a mattress like cash and gold bars.
>
> **[Hurtado and Nesmith, 2016]**

Interestingly, a few months later the same year, a ruling by Judge Alison J. Nathan of the United States District Court for the Southern District of New York contradicted the *Espinoza* ruling. The judge mentioned:

> Bitcoins are funds within the plain meaning of that term. Bitcoins can be accepted as a payment for goods and services or bought directly from an exchange with a bank account. They therefore function as pecuniary resources and are used as a medium of exchange and a means of payment.
>
> **[Redman, 2016]**

As Bitcoin becomes mainstream, an astonishing verdict came in January 2019 from Florida's Third District Court of Appeal. The court reversed Pooler's ruling on Espinoza's motion stating that:

> Based on the undisputed facts, Espinoza was acting as a payment instrument seller or engaging in the business of a money transmitter, either of which requires registration as a money services business under Florida law. Given the plain language of the Florida statutes governing money service businesses and the nature of Bitcoin and how it functions, Espinoza was acting as both.
>
> **[Benson, 2019]**

Despite those instances of money laundering, as authorities have more knowledge about this technology, cryptocurrencies are now conceived less risky for such crime. It is due to the public nature of the blockchain's transactions and discovery of potential methods to identify associated entities involved. A report by the UK's Treasury and Home Office reflected on this matter. Titled "UK National Risk Assessment of Money Laundering and Terrorist Financing", it identified that, of the 12 methods examined in the report, Bitcoin carries the lowest risk of being used for money laundering with the most common money laundering method being the banks [HM Treasury, 2017].

18.4.2 Market Manipulation

The rumours of manipulating the price of cryptocurrencies have been hovering since the inception of Bitcoin. Because of the volatility of these virtual currencies, it is challenging to detect if someone is actually trying to manipulate the price or if the volatility is organic. Nevertheless, there have been multiple studies recently that investigated past episodes and suggested that manipulation happened in part.

During the 2012–13 financial crisis in Cyprus, the Bitcoin price suddenly began to rise. It reached a high of $266 on 10 April 2013, before crashing to around $50 only to bounce back in November to hit the then all-time peak of $1242. A study from Tel Aviv University and the University of Tulsa found evidence that the part of this peak in the price was due to price manipulation [Gandal et al., 2018].

Researchers from the University of Texas, Austin investigated the involvement of the cryptocurrency exchange Bitfinex with Tether cryptocurrency in 2018. Their findings suggested that Bitfinex played a role in rising half of the price of Bitcoin during the bull run in late 2017. They asserted that purchases with Tether were timed following market downturns resulting in sizeable increases in Bitcoin prices [Griffin and Shams, 2018]. Bitfinex, however, denied this accusation.

More recently, the US Justice Department launched an investigation into possible price manipulation including the techniques of spoofing and wash trades. Traders in the US, UK and South Korea are likely to be investigated [Cornish, 2018]. Furthermore, the *Wall Street Journal* reported that US federal investigators also expressed their concern about numerous exchanges including Bitstamp, Coinbase, itBit and Kraken, and demanded trading data. Several of the exchanges initially refused to comply with this request but later afforded data only in limited amount. The Commodity Futures Trading Commission then summoned the data from the exchanges. No wrongdoing has been identified as of writing [Rubin et al., 2018].

18.5 Fraudulent Activities

Cryptocurrency has been the subject of various fraudulent activities in recent times. When the price of Bitcoin had been increasing in 2017, even people having no or little knowledge about the technology launched cryptocurrencies. This practice led to the creation of more than 1600 coins by August 2018. Most of these tokens are of little value and created with the intention of committing crooked ventures such as scams and selling tokens through false claims. During these pursuits, an initial coin offering (ICO) remained the principal tool for wicked actors to launch their exploits.

18.5.1 False Claims

The founding organisations behind several cryptocurrencies tried to promote their tokens by making false claims such as showing the potential of substantial return and being backed by currencies or commodities to make them so-called stablecoin.*

Tether Limited, the organisation behind the cryptocurrency Tether, claimed that fiat currencies backed its token, which was designed to always to be worth $1.00. The claim came when it rebranded Realcoin, the precursor to Tether originally launched in 2014 on the Bitcoin blockchain using Mastercoin's layer two protocol and founded by Brock Pierce, Reeve Collins and Craig Sellars as a Santa Monica–based start-up. After the rebranding, the company announced that it was entering private beta, which supported a "Tether+ token" for three currencies: USTether (US+) for US dollars, EuroTether (EU+) for euros and YenTether (JP+) for Japanese yen. The company remarkably claimed, "Every Tether+ token is backed 100% by its original currency and can be redeemed at any time with no exposure to exchange risk" [Casey, 2014b]. However, following a string of criticism, controversy and failure to meet all customer withdrawal requests in 2017, the company reportedly admitted that it was no longer 100% backed by actual dollars [Coppola, 2019]. At the time of writing, Tether was priced at $1.01 according to the CoinMarketCap.

Petro is another cryptocurrency that was claimed to be backed by one barrel of oil for each token. It was designed, promoted and launched by Venezuela's government. President Nicolas Maduro initially claimed on Twitter that the oil-backed cryptocurrency attracted $735 during the first day of its token sale in February 2018 but 6 months later admitted that Petro's worth might be determined solely by the market value [Browne, 2018].

There is another case where the US Securities and Exchange Commission (SEC) froze $15 million from *PlexCoin* that it accumulated using an ICO in 2017. Prior to the ICO, PlexCoin promised that it would return 1354% of the invested money, but it did not have any plan in place and now will be prosecuted for this false claim [Palmer, 2018].

---

* Stablecoins are cryptocurrencies designed to minimise the volatility of the price of the stablecoin, relative to some "stable" asset or basket of assets. A stablecoin can be pegged to a currency or exchange-traded commodities such as precious metals.

18.5.2 Scams

The successful launch of the Ethereum platform encouraged many to pre-mine tokens with a view to selling them for accumulating working capital of the respective platforms. Although it worked well for many major blockchains that emerged as giants in the industry offering diverse use-cases, there are hundreds of small blockchain platforms and cryptocurrencies that raised money from investors without having a clear idea of what they want to do. Many had fraudulent intentions. For example, Crypto start-up *Giza* raised $2.4 million using a fake ICO involving more than a thousand investors in 2018 [McQuaid, 2018]. Another blockchain platform called *Benebit* raised around $4 million in 2017 using fake administrative team photos and just walked away with the money afterwards [Sedgwick, 2018b].

ICOs and token sales became notoriously famous when Bitcoin and other cryptocurrencies had a rollercoaster ride in the exchanges in 2017. However, despite companies raising more than $7 billion via ICOs that year, by February 2018, an estimated 46% of those projects had failed, indicating that most of them were worthless and full of false claims [Sedgwick, 2018a].

Joseph Lubin, co-founder of Ethereum, claimed during an interview with CNBC in November 2017 that many ICOs are copycats that do not intend to offer any real value to investors. His statement was echoed by Brad Garlinghouse, CEO of Ripple Labs, who mentioned token sales operate in a grey area while waiting for regulation to catch up [Choudhury, 2017]. More recently, a study conducted by the ICO advisory firm Statis Group noticed that more than 80% of 2017 ICOs were scams. The study took into consideration the life cycle of the project from the proposal stage to the most mature phase of trading on a crypto exchange [Alexandre, 2018].

The number of scams involving ICOs became so frequent in 2017 that internet giants Google and Facebook had to ban all advertisements concerning cryptocurrencies. As of 2018, Facebook had partially lifted the ban allowing only credible companies to post ads through a separate approval process [McLean, 2018], while Google also lifted the ban but for the US and Japan only [Marshall, 2018].

18.6 Prevention

The proverb "prevention is better than cure" goes hand-in-hand with cryptocurrencies. Taking down darknet marketplaces and cracking down over money launderers do not help much in stopping criminal activities using virtual currency. Instead, bringing in useful regulation can put criminals off and discourage the commission of crimes in the first place. However, it must not be forgotten that regulation alone is not sufficient to deter crime. If the criminals leverage innovative technology to facilitate their activities, then law enforcement must hit back to identify and mitigate the hurdles that innovative technology may raise against them. In doing so, this book stretches importance on three grounds: *regulation, cooperation* and *participation.*

18.6.1 Regulation

Regulation is the first and perhaps the most important ground that helps to fight against criminal activities involving cryptocurrency. In an unregulated environment, bad actors find sanctuary, while a regulated industry will not only ensure removal of those unwanted actors but also restore the faith of consumers in this technology. The following discusses how regulation plays an important role in assisting police and security services to bring down those bad actors.

Regulation is very critical in stopping scams and fake ICOs. Unlike stocks and bonds that are financial instruments that investors rely on, there are no such rules in place at the moment that state how an ICO needs to be conducted, what the project can and cannot claim, and for how long it can run. Cryptocurrencies are defined variously at different jurisdictions making it more difficult to regulate as a financial instrument. This representation of the industry makes it urgent that financial authorities around the world get together to decide how cryptocurrencies will be dealt with globally.

Regulations may solve issues in ICOs and reduce scams, but fighting against the underworld and criminals laundering money need police and security services to join financial authorities to work together in making regulations related to cryptocurrency exchanges, trading and transactions. Contrary to popular opinion, it is not difficult to trace the person behind a Bitcoin (or similar cryptocurrency) address if proper regulations remain in place. A huge misconception amongst people is that Bitcoin is anonymous, which is not true; it is rather pseudonymous. All transactions to and from addresses are open and can enable authorities to link transactions together to locate perpetrators' addresses with the help of regulated information such as proof of identity, address and bank details.

A classic example of identifying the culprit following this approach is the case of the darknet market *Sheep Marketplace.* The market announced in 2013 that one of the site's vendors exploited a vulnerability to steal 5400 tokens, valued at about $6 million at the time. However, users through discussion on the site's forum identified that the administrator transferred 40,000 Bitcoins, seven times larger than the claimed stolen amount, to an account and blocked withdrawing of any money even a week before this claimed incident. Amid this discussion, when users found the forum being taken down, they became sure that the main culprit is none other than the administrator of the site who initiated an exit scam even before the alleged hack took place.

Victims of the theft then attempted to identify the thief by sending "tagged" Bitcoins to his accounts. Because of the public nature of Bitcoin transactions, they followed this money through the blockchain record of transfers. Soon a large amount of Bitcoin was noticed to be processed by Bitcoin Fog, a "tumbler" used to launder Bitcoins by shuffling them between many accounts for a small fee. Not long thereafter the last known wallet of the user who had been presumed to be the thief was found to be a wallet owned by BTC-e, the infamous Bitcoin currency exchange that US authorities recently seized. The money stayed in the wallet for some time until the thief paid for an expensive house entirely in Bitcoins revealing his identity in 2015. This led Czech police to arrest Tomas Jirikovsky, the creator of the Sheep Marketplace, who was later sentenced to serve nine years in prison for stealing Bitcoins from the market's users [Aliens, 2017].

This classic example teaches that identifying someone's address is not always enough to unveil the person behind the disguise. It is a good starting point, but there is a number of steps involved in finding the real person. One approach is to wait and observe. A bunch of Bitcoin in someone's wallet does not look like a profitable prospect unless he or she tries to exchange the virtual currency with fiat currency and withdraw the money from an exchange or buy something using cryptocurrency. This is the Achilles heel that can be capitalised on finding the person's identity. Regulated cryptocurrency exchanges can give information regarding who withdrew the money. Countries in the European Union have strong policies related to disclosing the name, proof of address and bank details to the exchanges. The Financial Conduct Authority (FCA) in the UK asks exchanges not only to collect this information but to also make sure it is up to date and not older than 6 months. Such regulations should not be a problem for investors who do not want to bend the rules and the regulations immensely help authorities to catch the offenders.

18.6.2 Cooperation

Cooperation is possibly second to regulation in terms of importance. Without cooperation between authorities, such an industry involving technology, finance and social issues cannot be kept safe. It was shown in the previous section how financial and security authorities can cooperate to make regulations to track down criminals. This cooperation is also essential across the border between authorities from different nations.

Because public blockchains are decentralised where transactions take place all around the globe, this makes life difficult for authorities to keep law and order and take actions against the offenders. Without cooperation between police and secret service forces across jurisdictions, these modern crimes are challenging to deal with. *Operation Onymous* is one of the most excellent examples of such cooperation between US and European authorities that took down the pioneering darknet market Silk Road.

These cooperations are also crucial to identify linked criminals and bring them to justice before committing something substantially massive. The structure of Bitcoin transactions, in this case, is a great source of clues. A darknet marketplace escrow address or an address used extensively to commit money laundering leaves traces of who are involved in the activities. Following the unveiling of one or a few heads from the cluster, the task of tracking down other heads does not seem to be difficult should the authorities have the required technology and the brainpower to operate innovative tools. One classic example is tracking down Variety Jones and Smedley who were the second in command of Silk Road's "Dread Pirate Roberts", the pseudonym of Ross Ulbricht.

If we recall, authorities failed to identify Variety Jones and Smedley at the time of taking down the Silk Road market. However, through linked transactions, they kept researching into these individuals' identities and found that Smedley's true identity could be Mike Wattier, an American web developer living in Thailand, and Variety Jones could be Roger Thomas Clark, a Canadian also living in Thailand. These findings led them to successfully arrest Clark in Thailand 2 years after seizing the marketplace. Clark has been facing extradition to the United States, while Wattier still remains at large. This example shows how cooperation between nations can help crack down on criminals [Cox, 2015].

18.6.3 *Participation*

Participation is perhaps the least most important amongst the three grounds discussed; however, it can help to restore trust amongst consumers of blockchain-based services and decentralised applications (DApps). Much negativity about this technology has already been spread that severely damaged its reputation. As such, consumers will have their faith back when they see reputed corporations have been using distributed ledgers either inside their business model or for their day-to-day activity.

As we progressed through the technical details of blockchain from Chapters 1 to 11, it was evident that the idea of distributed ledgers in the present day is very different than what Bitcoin proposed. The initial proposal of Nakamoto indicated his interests in features like public availability, regulation free and pseudonymity; however, the current trend identifies them as unnecessary for many applications. Nowadays, private networks are becoming popular, while industry users do not care much about the pseudonymity of the transactions. It is rather important to them that the blockchain ensures trust and enables applications with the traits necessary for the use-cases. IBM, Linux Foundations, Walmart and Microsoft are few companies that have been actively getting involved in this industry.

There is another aspect where reputed entities become nodes of the distributed ledger. Ripple and Stellar are two such ledgers that operate entirely based on approved nodes. No one can join their network without approval. This approach, however, does not make them centralised. They are fully decentralised at their core but allow established entities to get priorities. Large corporate and financial giants have already joined these networks to either use or test distributed ledger technology for their use.

The more known faces that come out and participate openly in the use of blockchain and related services will help the technology become mainstream. Such participation, in the end, sends a strong message that blockchain and cryptocurrencies are not for performing criminal and illegal activities but for improving the quality of lives and making the world a better place.

18.7 Summary

This chapter presented the criminal activities surrounding cryptocurrencies, one of the widely used criticisms against the blockchain technology. The chapter tried to be neutral in presenting facts and decoupling potential misunderstandings. It offered a thorough discussion on the activities regarding darknet markets, Silk Road and its successors, the role of the underground in misusing cryptocurrencies, financial and social crimes such as scams, and some recommendations as to how to potentially fight against such crimes. The objective of this chapter was to highlight the point that despite criminals using cryptocurrencies, it is only fair to fight against those crimes instead of suggesting to ditch this innovative technology as many experts and prominent figures did in the past, to be discussed in Chapter 20.

Chapter 19

Regulations, Laws and Practices

The blockchain industry has seen rapid growth in recent times as many new applications based on distributed ledger technology hit the market. However, the progress has not been undisrupted but rather surrounded by indecision, chaos and clampdowns as regulatory authorities had to deal with fraudulent and corrupt actors in the industry in the name of initial coin offerings (ICOs) and fake start-ups that walked away investors' money. Mining bans and shutting down exchanges in some countries crashed markets causing small investors to lose their stake. The fearful environment prevented many genuine blockchain start-ups from raising working capital to begin their product development. The state of affairs, however, might not have been this bitter had there been specific guidelines and regulations as to how the companies would operate. This chapter presents the current aspects of blockchain regulations, misuse of the industry by mischievous players, and how the industry and governments around the world have been evolving towards embracing new laws and regulations for business focusing on delivering blockchain applications, cryptocurrencies and ICOs.

19.1 Legality of Blockchain and Cryptocurrency

The legal status of blockchain technology is somewhat ambiguous around the globe. It is not illegal in most parts of the world, but the state of legality is not clear either. Because of the lack of proper laws, regulatory frameworks and clear definition of this new technology, confusion has been mounting at an alarming rate.

To put it in perspective, Judge Amos L. Mazzant III of the United States District Court for the Eastern District of Texas stated in a 2013 ruling that "Bitcoin is a currency or form of money" [Hill, 2013], while his colleague Judge Teresa Mary Pooler of the Eleventh Judicial Circuit Court of Florida cleared Michell Espinoza in *State of Florida v. Espinoza* of money-laundering charges he faced involving his use of Bitcoin on the basis that this virtual currency is not a currency. Pooler stated that "Bitcoin may have some attributes in common with what we commonly refer to as money, but differ in many important aspects, they are certainly not tangible wealth and cannot be hidden under a mattress like cash and gold bars" [Hurtado and Nesmith, 2016].

In the US, authorities sometimes consider virtual currency as a commodity, while other departments recognise it either as currency or an asset. Many countries in the world including China and South Korea see cryptocurrencies as a tool to commit crimes overlooking the fact that the underlying blockchain technology has huge potential to contribute to many sectors of society. The view of many governments, however, is not totally unjustified. While dealing with new technologies, authorities require time to become acquainted with the applications, understand them and decide appropriate regulations.

In the case of the blockchain, that did not happen. Because of the sudden rise in popularity of Bitcoin and cryptocurrencies, regulatory authorities never got that required time frame to determine guidance for this technology. This resulted in confusion amongst multiple departments of government leading some to take random and whimsical actions. However, as time passes, we can anticipate that the dust of chaos will settle, and governments around the globe will start preparing legal frameworks for this new and innovative technology.

19.2 Regulatory Issues

Despite the recent rapid growth of blockchain technology, blockchain-related industries are still largely unregulated in most countries. This is not perceived as an advantage by the people involved in the industry; rather their views are quite the opposite. The lack of regulation is often considered a weakness because consumers are not assured of standards. Sometimes the use of cryptocurrency is even regarded as a device or tool to facilitate criminal activities, making conventional businesses fearful and often unwilling to provide services using blockchain technology and cryptocurrencies. As such, to prove their credibility, many blockchain-related businesses are seeking regulations. On the other side of the coin, people having no genuine interest in this technology have been getting involved to make some quick money. These people have upset many regulatory bodies and law and order enforcement authorities leading to legal actions, crackdowns and potentially stricter policies for the industry.

19.2.1 Misuse of Pre-Mining and ICOs

The successful launch of the Ethereum platform encouraged many to pre-mine tokens with a view to selling them for accumulating working capital of the respective platforms. Although it worked well for many major blockchains that emerged as giants in the industry offering diverse use-cases, there are hundreds of small blockchain platforms and cryptocurrencies that raised money from investors without having a clear idea of what they were going to do. Amongst many had fraudulent intentions. For example, Crypto start-up *Giza* raised $2.4 million using a fake ICO involving more than a thousand investors in 2018 [McQuaid, 2018]. The US Securities and Exchange Commissions (SEC) has frozen $15 million from *PlexCoin* that it accumulated using an ICO in 2017. Prior to the ICO, PlexCoin promised that it would return 1354% of the invested money, but it did not have any plans in place [Palmer, 2018]. Another blockchain platform called *Benebit* raised around $4 million in 2017 using fake administrative team photos and just walked away with the money afterwards [Sedgwick, 2018b].

Scams and frauds using ICOs led regulatory bodies around the world to take strong legal action against the companies involved. During the first half of 2018, more than 750 legal measures had been taken against companies in the United States. It was the most prolific 24-month period of taking legal action against companies and individuals involved in investment and securities since the Private Securities Litigation Reform Act was enacted in 1995. Amongst the cases, notable ongoing lawsuits included those against Ripple Labs, alleging that the defendants raised "hundreds of millions of dollars" through the unregistered sale of XRP to retail investors, and against UK-based *Bitconnect*, alleging that the company "failed to disclose material facts" that caused its value to drop [Castillo, 2018]. *Airfox* and *Paragon* are two companies currently under investigation by the SEC. It appears that the SEC, instead of launching random crackdowns, is using these two cases to prepare future templates for ICO enforcement in the US [Palley, 2018].

During the 2017 cryptocurrency bull run, scams involving ICOs became so frequent that internet giants Google and Facebook had to ban all advertisements concerning cryptocurrencies. As of 2018, Facebook had partially lifted the ban allowing only credible companies to post ads through a separate approval process [McLean, 2018], while Google also lifted the ban but for the US and Japan only [Marshall, 2018].

19.2.2 Crackdowns on Mining and Trading

China, the producer of the most mined Bitcoin, made newspaper headlines in January 2018 when its government decided to crack down on miners. Although Chinese authorities reasoned this action was to prevent misuse of electricity, China's central bank viewed cryptocurrency as a potential tool for committing malicious acts like fraud and money laundering. Chinese authorities also cracked down on thousands of criminal cases associated with cryptocurrencies such as *Onecoin* and *Ticcoin* that they perceived as Ponzi schemes used to raise illicit funds. More recently authorities also shut down cryptocurrency trading exchanges and banned fundraising through ICOs in China [Hsu, 2018].

South Korea, another crypto-heaven in Asia, introduced stricter regulations for cryptocurrency exchanges following the recent cryptocurrency bull run. Previously individuals were allowed to make trades anonymously. This practice encouraged criminals to quietly slip into the system and take advantage of it in committing criminal activities and receiving payments. As of January 2018, the Korean government has banned exchanges that allowed traders to use anonymous bank accounts. South Korea's chief financial regulator went on to say that it may consider shutting down all domestic virtual currency exchanges. Although the threat of shutting down all domestic exchanges has not been implemented, the statement produced a considerable amount of noise in the cryptocurrency market causing a massive crash [Kim, 2018a].

19.3 Current Landscape

The current landscape of cryptocurrency and the blockchain industry is unsettled and noisy as of writing. Rumours of possible crackdowns often play an important role in crashing the market, while a lack of regulation makes investors less interested to get involved. Nevertheless, the year 2018 following the best cryptocurrency bull run of 2017 saw people with wicked intentions leaving the industry, paving the path for a redevelopment of the industry where regulation can be instituted.

19.3.1 Challenges

Although the blockchain industry seems to be genuinely willing to embrace regulations, the path to finding a solution is not straightforward and full of challenges. Public ledgers like Bitcoin and Ethereum are meant to be distributed and free from any centralised control, and having lots of strings attached to these ledgers significantly hinders the underlying fundamentals.

Government regulations usually seek to take control of the processes introducing some degree of central association. In the recent past, actions from authorities around the globe seemed to be random and whimsical, making the cryptocurrency market highly volatile. Any attempt to take control of the system using strength makes investors fearful and insecure. The role of investors is an integral part of blockchain technology and discouraging them from staying in the mix will only worsen the situation.

Therefore, the biggest challenge will be to find a balance between what extent regulatory bodies can intervene and what kind of freedom the technology still holds. Another critical challenge here is to accomplish this balance through peaceful conversations between the people serving the industry and government regulatory bodies. It is essential to avoid all unnecessary measures that could potentially cause noise in the market. The cryptocurrency market is already considerably volatile, and failure to keep it noise-free and operating normally could create additional hurdles in the process.

19.3.2 *Areas*

There are three notable areas where the industry urgently needs regulations. Amongst them, regulation for cryptocurrency usage is undeniably the most important. A lack of regulation as to how to facilitate cryptocurrency alongside fiat currencies prevents online portals, e-commerce sites and websites accepting cryptocurrency payments regularly. This is also the primary obstacle to setting up cryptocurrency kiosks in physical locations to take payments using virtual currencies. During the early days of cryptocurrency and blockchain technology, there was a rapid growth of the number of Bitcoin ATMs and kiosks in the US; however, as time passed, this growth significantly slowed. Outside the US, it is now rare to encounter kiosks taking payments in virtual currencies. One of the key reasons behind people being hesitant in using cryptocurrency as a method of payment, either online or offline, is this technology's infamous popularity of being a tool to commit criminal activities. Government regulations could partially eradicate the fear and encourage both consumers and business providers to adopt the technology.

The second most important area is ICOs. There is no denying that native tokens play an essential role in enabling start-ups. ICOs give them the opportunity to raise the initial funds to start with. Because of the lack of regulation and past scams, investors may feel hesitant to put their money in new blockchain platforms. The industry is still at a very early stage, and a lot of exciting applications are yet to arrive. Investment in companies at this stage is crucial, and regulations could quickly encourage new and existing investors to get more involved. Regulation is also necessary for companies that offer ICOs. A lack of regulation also means a lack of guidance. Unlike initial public offerings (IPOs), a company offering certain promises while publishing white papers for their ICO does not know the potential consequences. There have been instances where authorities charged reputed blockchain companies following their successful launches – the case against Ripple Labs is one of the most notable examples. If there exists a guideline explaining what a company can mention or promise and what it cannot, people involved in ICOs would feel more confident in describing their products to the investors.

The third area where immediate attention needs to be given is how far authorities can intervene in the governance of the blockchain. For example, a smart contract is meant to be free from third-party control allowing two parties to get tied up in a deal. It is the essence of a smart contract that without the intervention of a third entity, the contract can mature. Unnecessarily bringing in regulatory authorities in the governing process is likely to introduce bureaucracy that the technology tries to avoid. As such, it is imperative that regulations prescribe the design of the product but stay away from its seamless execution.

19.3.3 Blockchain-Friendly Nations

The US, South Korea, China and Japan are amongst the nations where most crypto-mining, trading and investment take place. This, however, does not imply they are the most friendly nations for the blockchain industry to grow. Amongst these four, only Japan is considered blockchain-friendly because of its existing policies and willingness to allow this industry to flourish. Japan has shown great support for blockchain technologies, putting it at the forefront of a technological revolution that encourages change, trust and business dealings in the financial and technological sectors in the country. It is no surprise that Mitsubishi UFJ Financial Group (MUFG), one of the world's largest banks, announced plans to open a cryptocurrency trading department for its retail and institutional investors. MUFG also expects to introduce a native token tied to the Japanese yen and facilitate peer-to-peer transactions, lower fees and reduce volatility. DMM group, another Japan-based corporation specialising in electronic commerce entertainment, launched DMM Bitcoin, a cryptocurrency exchange with support for a range of cryptocurrencies and pairs. This move came amid the changes the Japanese government has been introducing to encourage investors and people to get involved in blockchain technology. The changes removed unnecessary red tape from cryptocurrency trading and made Bitcoin a legitimate currency and payment method.

Sweden is the most friendly country for blockchain technology after Japan. Sweden recognises cryptocurrency as a crypto-asset and encourages investors to come forward and invest. Sweden is arguably the first country to launch exchange-traded funds (ETFs) using Bitcoin. Even the Swedish government has plans for its own central bank electronic currency, the e-Krona, although it is anticipated that the implementation of e-Krona would take several years [Billner, 2018].

Estonia, a country in Northern Europe, is often viewed as a Blockchain model for the world. Following the collapse of the Soviet Union in 1990, Estonia emerged as a digital society. Before the launch of Bitcoin, the Estonian government began exploring a similar technology called "hash-linked timestamping". As of 2012, Estonia adopted blockchain technology in national health, judicial, legislative, security and commercial sectors [Adams, 2018].

Venezuela is another blockchain-friendly country willing to adopt blockchain technology. The government of Venezuela is leading the charge for the mass adoption of cryptos in a bid to stabilise the Venezuelan economy and the plunging bolivar. It issued *Petro*, a new cryptocurrency backed by oil. However, because of the political unrest in the country, corruption and dictatorship, its genuine interest in this technology remains to be examined.

The United States, United Kingdom, Canada, Germany, the Netherlands, France, Russia, Singapore, Hong Kong, South Korea and China are not amongst the most friendly nations for blockchain technology, but they are not blockchain-sceptics either. Their actions against this technology came primarily to safeguard their citizens from fraud and potential crimes. There is no denying that most investors are coming from these nations and building exciting applications using this technology is likely to happen in these countries in the near future. The sooner these nations adopt regulations, the better for the growth of the blockchain industry.

19.4 Regulations for Blockchain Technology and Cryptocurrency

The regulatory scenario of blockchain was chaotic worldwide as of December 2018. The technology is still unregulated in most of the world. Hope, however, has been coming from smaller nations and territories that have been proactively dealing with blockchain start-ups for the last couple of years. Some bigger countries also have put forth proposals for regulations in 2018 that could be implemented by 2020. The following describes the legislative and regulatory outlook of blockchain technology, loosely based by continent.

19.4.1 The Americas

The situation regarding blockchain and cryptocurrency in the US is complicated. Although it is legal to use virtual currencies, their status remains confusing. The interpretation of the underlying technology powering cryptocurrency and blockchain platforms varies from agency to agency. As we have seen in Chapter 15, recent multiple judicial verdicts contradict one another other. US courts have sometimes referred to cryptocurrency as an asset and sometimes likened it to fiat currency; hence there lacks a clear definition to determine the true nature of the applications of this technology. The practice in the US at the moment is that the SEC requires registration of any virtual currency traded in the US if it is classified as a security and of any trading platform that meets its definition of an exchange. The Internal Revenue Service (IRS) treats virtual currency as property and requires the calculation of gains or losses upon exchange for tax purposes. There is no specific law to define ICOs in the US, but it looks like the SEC is set to prepare guidelines for companies willing to create ICOs.

Canada seemed to be ahead of its neighbour in preparing a draft regulation for blockchain technology companies, as the federal government had listened to many comments and opinions from the people involved in this technology before making the regulations. However, in August 2018, Canada postponed the announcement of regulations until the next year. The Canadian Blockchain Association took this move positively, commenting that because of the complexities of this new and evolving sector, the government's decision to move slowly will be beneficial for Canadian blockchain and cryptocurrency space [Willms, 2018].

On the south side of the US border, Mexico published a legal framework passing a law for fintech companies that includes cryptocurrencies in September 2018. The central bank, Bank of Mexico, is the regulatory authority of crypto-space in the country. The new law defines cryptocurrencies as *virtual assets* and gives the Bank of Mexico the right to determine which cryptocurrencies are appropriate for companies to offer, run and deal with. The framework states that companies willing to carry out transactions involving cryptocurrencies needs to request authorisation from the Bank of Mexico so that they can use those technologies associated with any of the virtual assets. The president of National Banking and Securities Commission (CNBV) of Mexico, Bernado Gonzalez, stated that the rules would apply to crowdfunded companies, online payments and cryptocurrencies. He went on asserting that the move would open the possibility for small- and medium-sized companies to obtain financing from the public through a collective funding platform without having to go to a traditional credit institution, indicating ICOs. In addition to these fintech regulations, Mexico is also due to publish general provisions for cryptocurrencies in 2019 [Helms, 2018b].

Venezuela is another nation in the region that has drafted regulations for blockchain technology and cryptocurrency. The Ministry for Communication and Information reported in November 2018 that the National Assembly of Venezuela approved a bill on cryptocurrency regulation and it is due to be passed in early 2019. The law validates Petro, Venezuela's oil-backed cryptocurrency, as a unit of commercial exchange within the country, and states that goods and services can also be purchased using this cryptocurrency [Berman, 2018].

Amongst the other Latin American countries, Argentina, Chile, Costa Rica, Paraguay, Panama and Uruguay do not have legal frameworks to regulate blockchain applications and cryptocurrencies. In Brazil, although there are no official regulations regarding cryptocurrencies, a legislative bill project is in development where cryptocurrencies are treated similarly to air-mile programs referring to them as "payment arrangements". The Colombian Central Bank warned investors against cryptocurrencies, and the Colombian Superintendency of Finance banned financial entities from operating using virtual currencies. Despite its efforts, Colombia remains one of the top four countries in Latin America with the highest blockchain operation volume. Other countries in that region are considered crypto-sceptics, as their government and authorities continuously warn investors to stay away from virtual currencies and blockchain applications [Kelemen, 2018].

19.4.2 Europe

In Europe, it is surprising that instead of so-called financial powerhouse nations, smaller countries and territories have been doing better in adapting blockchain technologies. Amongst them, Switzerland has already established itself as a world leader. As one of the most blockchain-friendly nations in the world, the Swiss government has been developing a blockchain space in Zug, dubbed Crypto Valley, for the last few years [Williams-Grut, 2018]. The country already regulates the use of cryptocurrency using anti-money laundering laws allowing citizens to make payments using cryptocurrency. Now regulatory bodies have been looking at ICOs and other blockchain-related areas. FINMA, Switzerland's independent financial-markets regulator, is working towards drafting guidelines and has already published a framework for ICOs [Keskin, 2018a]. Meanwhile, the State Secretariat for International Financial Matters (SIF) established a blockchain/ICO working group in collaboration with the Federal Office of Justice (FOJ). They are commissioned to review all legal frameworks, identify any need for action with FINMA and people involved in the blockchain industry, and to finalise a regulation soon [Keskin, 2018b].

Estonia, another blockchain-friendly nation in Europe, has been exploring opportunities related to this technology even before the arrival of Bitcoin. Eventually, its form of blockchain, commonly known as hash-linked timestamping, and the conventional type merged together creating a world-famous start-up ecosystem. Estonia already has a highly regulated financial sector supervised by the Estonian Financial Supervision Authority (EFSA), locally known as Finantsinspektsioon. EFSA is tolerant to not only cryptocurrencies but also a diverse range of blockchain applications. It has recently published a comprehensive legal framework overview of ICOs in Estonia. EFSA perceives that tokens might be considered securities according to the definition outlined in the state's existing Securities Market Act as well as in the Law of Obligations Act. In any case, they consider every ICO unique and assesses them by their characteristics [Liive, 2018].

Malta, the Southern European island country in the Mediterranean Sea, is also amongst the nations that have been trying to come to the forefront of blockchain technology and is already at a mature stage of implementing regulations in the state. The Cabinet of Malta has approved the Virtual Financial Assets Bill, providing a regulatory framework for cryptocurrencies and ICOs. Although the bill is due to be debated in the parliament before it gets passed, the Maltese government meanwhile launched the Malta Digital Innovation Authority in February 2018 to provide legal clarity for companies developing blockchain applications, cryptocurrencies and ICOs. These proactive moves of the lawmakers of the country have attracted blockchain companies to the jurisdiction; for example in March 2018, Binance, the largest cryptocurrency exchange by volume, announced its willingness to move a part of its operations to Malta [Nakamura, 2018].

Gibraltar, a British overseas territory, is one of the few jurisdictions in the world to have a regulatory framework already in place. The regulations are specially designed to improve blockchain businesses including cryptocurrency exchanges, wallet service providers and any company that stores or transmits value belonging to others using distributed ledger technology. The government of Gibraltar decided to regulate the blockchain industry in 2014 and invited private companies to work with the designated unit of the government to identify what the most appropriate form of regulation should be. This initiative led to delivering a principles-based regulatory framework appropriate for blockchain and cryptocurrency businesses that flexible enough to remain relevant as new technologies develop within the territory. The Gibraltar Financial Services Commission (GFSC) regulates the sector, having a team dealing exclusively with blockchain sectors.

On the western flank of Europe, the United Kingdom has the reputation of being one of the leaders in fintech innovation with its capital London as one of the most regulated, friendly and safe places to establish businesses. This reputation of the UK somehow does not go hand-in-hand when it comes to the cryptocurrency regulation. The country seems to be lagging compared to its European, Asian and North American competitors. The Financial Conduct Authority (FCA) regulates the financial industry in the UK. The FCA initially denied that it was the regulator for the blockchain technology, stating that the design of a crypto-asset primarily as a means of payment or exchange would not generally sit within the scope of FCA and whether an ICO falls within its administrative boundaries can only be decided case by case. However, it later partially changed its position, and as of July 2018, announced the acceptance of 29 companies in its regulatory sandbox; of those 11 are blockchain start-ups. This move by FCA is undoubtedly a positive sign for the UK that is expected to deliver required legal frameworks and regulations in the future [Stankovic, 2018]. The Netherlands, Germany and France are amongst the other European nations that have been planning to follow suit.

19.4.3 Asia

Most Asian nations seem to be blockchain sceptics, including almost all Persian Gulf nations, South Asia and many countries in Southeast Asia. Although Southeast Asia is one of the most active regions for cryptocurrency mining and trading, countries like China and South Korea have not put forth any clear regulations rather than their recent actions regarding clamping down on mining and exchanges, which made the market more volatile [Pavesic, 2018].

Surrounded by sceptical neighbours, only a few Asian countries have shown a keen interest in creating a blockchain-friendly ecosystem that will help start-ups, ICOs and trading exchanges to grow. One of those nations is Singapore, which does not have a regulation in place for blockchain technology at the moment, and surprisingly it does not want to constitute anything soon. Authorities in Singapore perceive regulations as red tape and intend to avoid having regulations as much as possible. The head of the Monetary Authority of Singapore (MAS), which serves as the central bank and financial regulator of Singapore, stated in a 2017 interview with Bloomberg that MAS would keep "an open mind" with no plans of regulating cryptocurrencies. Meanwhile, the government had already declared Bitcoin as a commodity and outlined the tax issues related to cryptocurrency trading and investment in the country [Chanjaroen et al., 2017].

Japan, being one of the most friendly blockchain nations, is also keen to establish a regulatory framework in the state. The Financial Services Agency (FSA), the financial regulator of Japan, published a draft report in December 2018 outlining new cryptocurrency regulations. The report contains measures in areas that are not currently addressed in existing laws such as hacking incidents, self-regulation, deemed dealers, privacy coins and margin trading [Helms, 2018a].

Another jurisdiction in Asia that is eager to become a crypto-friendly environment is the Chinese autonomous territory of Hong Kong. The Securities and Futures Commission (SFC), the regulator for securities in the region, stated in November 2018 that it has been setting guidelines for funds dealing with cryptocurrency with the intention to ultimately establish a formal regulatory environment for cryptocurrencies in Hong Kong [Suberg, 2018]. Amongst the Persian Gulf nations, only Dubai in the UAE has plans to develop a blockchain-friendly incubator for start-ups. In 2016, it established the DubaiCoin crypto-exchange making cryptocurrencies transactions and tradings legal. Now, it is possible to buy luxury cars and apartments using Bitcoin in the emirate. Nevertheless, Dubai has even bigger plans to become the first blockchain-powered government by 2020, and its authorities have been working on regulatory frameworks expected to become law by 2019 [Jenkinson, 2018].

19.4.4 Australia and Africa

Australia seems genuinely willing to provide the blockchain industry with the necessary conditions to grow. In 2018, the Australian government passed new laws for Digital Currency Exchange (DCE) providers. The laws were then enforced by AUSTRAC, Australia's financial intelligence agency and anti-money laundering and counter-terrorism financing (AML/CTF) regulator. These new AML/CTF laws for the first time cover regulation of service providers of Bitcoin and other cryptocurrencies. Nicole Rose, the CEO of AUSTRAC, following the implementation of this law, stated that the laws would strengthen the agency's compliance and intelligence capabilities to help DCEs implement systems and controls that can minimise the risk of criminals using them for money laundering, terrorism financing and cybercrime. Effective immediately, DCEs with a business operation located in Australia must now register with AUSTRAC and meet the government's AML/CTF compliance and reporting obligations.

On the African continent, cryptocurrencies have legal but unregulated status in South Africa, but the law of the state restricts their use. Because South African law only distinguishes currencies that exist in a physical form as legal tenders, payment transactions using cryptocurrencies are not plausible. The South African Reserve Bank (SARB), the central bank, has been formulating policies with regard to digital currencies. It published a white paper clarifying the possible status of cryptocurrency as "stores of value". If it becomes law in the future, this could convert cryptocurrency to legal tender; hence opening its usage to a greater extent. Any earnings from virtual currencies are taxable in South Africa, and investors need to ensure compliance with tax laws. In other African countries including Kenya and Nigeria, regulations do not recognise cryptocurrency as legal tender, and central banks usually do not encourage its citizens to invest in this industry due to the speculative nature of cryptocurrencies.

19.5 Summary

This chapter presented the current regulatory landscape of blockchain technology, cryptocurrency and ICOs around the globe. It briefly outlines how fraudulent actors misuse the system in the absence of a regulatory framework leading to government crackdowns and market crashes. The chapter then pointed out the challenges and areas needing urgent attention followed by identifying blockchain-friendly nations of the world. The chapter finally concluded with commentary on proposed regulatory frameworks and plans by governments of many countries that have been keen to establish an ecosystem within their jurisdiction to nurture this new and innovative technology.

Chapter 20

Criticism, Scepticism and Support

Blockchain technology has been the subject of critical discussions since its inception, with its first application Bitcoin being the primary target. Experts from both finance and tech industries, economists, academics, investors, journalists and public figures from various areas openly expressed their opinions against or in favour of this technology. During the 2017 cryptocurrency bull run, every day hundreds of news and opinion articles from around the globe used to arrive explaining flaws and possibilities of this technology. People predicted the values of Bitcoin and explained the similarities of its price hike with the Dutch Tulip mania to label it a bubble. Many of those comments proved to be wrong, while a large number of predictions are yet to be confirmed. This chapter aims to accumulate those criticisms, scepticism and supporting comments of blockchain technology with a view to present readers an orderly commentary aligned with the rise and fall of the price of Bitcoin. Although unsurprisingly, a large lump of these comments discussed Bitcoin and cryptocurrencies, efforts are also given to incorporate comments and criticisms on blockchain as a host of futuristic applications. Unlike the previous chapters, it is not written in a formal structure; rather the comments are organised as stated over the last decade.

20.1 Before It All Started

Nobel laureate in economics Milton Friedman made a remarkable prediction in 1999, a decade before the launch of the Bitcoin network. He stated:

> "The internet is going to be one of the major forces for reducing the role of government. The one thing that's missing, but that will soon be

developed, is a reliable e-cash: a method whereby on the internet you can transfer funds from A to B without A knowing B or B knowing A – the way in which I can take a $20 bill and hand it over to you, and there's no record of where it came from." – *Milton Friedman*

Date: 21/06/1999

Bitcoin Price: $0.00

Stance: Supportive

20.2 Early Days of Bitcoin

The price of Bitcoin remained below $20 until 2012. During this period, the discussion about the technology and this cryptocurrency was mostly confined amongst developers and enthusiasts. Later that year when the price began to rise, more people gathered, new cryptocurrencies were launched and people outside the community started to take an interest in the blockchain technology, particularly in Bitcoin. By the start of 2013, the price of Bitcoin hit more than $200, Litecoin and Ripple arrived on the landscape, and critics and sceptics began to become furious about this technology.

If Friedman noticed something coming that was going to change the world, his fellow Nobel laureate Paul Krugman saw evil in Bitcoin in December 2013 when the price hit more than $700.

"Bitcoin is evil. So far almost all of the Bitcoin discussion has been positive economics – can this actually work? And I have to say that I'm still deeply unconvinced." – *Paul Krugman*, Professor of Economics, City University of New York

Date: 28/12/2013

Bitcoin Price: $721.44

Stance: Critical

By the time we reached the year 2014, Bitcoin's price had begun to fall from its peak and undergone some severe volatile periods. Despite those agitations, leaders from tech industry giants overwhelmingly praised the underlying principles of blockchain technology.

"... (Bitcoin) is a remarkable cryptographic achievement. The ability to create something which is not duplicable in the digital world has enormous value." – *Eric Schmidt*, Chairman, Google (Alphabet Inc.)

Date: 03/03/2014

Bitcoin Price: $669.76

Stance: Supportive

"Bitcoin as a currency is working. There may be other currencies like it that may be even better. But in the meantime, there's a big industry around Bitcoin. People have made fortunes off Bitcoin; some have lost money. It is volatile, but people make money off of volatility, too." – *Richard Branson*, Founder and CEO, Virgin Group

Date: 10/09/2014

Bitcoin Price: $483.24

Stance: Supportive

"Bitcoin is exciting because it shows how cheap it can be. Bitcoin is better than currency in that you don't have to be physically in the same place and, of course, for large transactions, currency can get pretty inconvenient." – *Bill Gates*, Founder and Chairman, Microsoft

Date: 02/10/2014

Bitcoin Price: $376.86

Stance: Supportive

20.3 Bitcoin Grabs Attention

The years 2015 and 2016 are when blockchain technology started to grab attention. The arrival of Ethereum and smart contracts opened a new era that many other platforms decided to follow. This is the period when central banks around the world became concerned about the potential of cryptocurrency. Authorities from two Asian financial giants, Japan and Singapore, made thoughtful comments amid the continued volatility of the cryptocurrency market.

"Whether digital currencies will take off in a big way remains to be seen. But it is a phenomenon that many central banks are watching closely, including MAS. And if they do take off, one cannot rule out central banks themselves issuing digital currencies some day!" – *Ravi Menon*, Managing Director, Monitory Authority of Singapore

Date: 29/06/2015

Bitcoin Price: $255.53

Stance: Supportive

"Given that the development of financial services has been supported by ledgers as the basic infrastructure for information, the dramatic changes in how ledgers are kept may have the potential of significantly changing the structure of financial services."– *Haruhiko Kuroda*, Governor, Bank of Japan

Date: 23/08/2016

Bitcoin Price: $580.94

Stance: Supportive

20.4 Beginning of the Bull Run

The year 2017 is the most successful year for cryptocurrencies to date. The price of Bitcoin hit nearly $20,000 making people crazy about commenting on this topic. Remarks were launched from all possible directions from both critics and supporters. Critics and sceptics became extremely critical about this technology, while the "believers" praised its potential as usual.

> (*Addressing the audience at a cryptocurrency conference*) "I'm a believer. … I'm one of the few standing before you today from a large financial-services company that has not given up on digital currencies." – *Abigail Johnson*, CEO, Fidelity Investment

Date: 23/05/2017

Bitcoin Price: $2216.18

Stance: Supportive

"Digital currencies are nothing but an unfounded fad (or perhaps even a pyramid scheme), based on a willingness to ascribe value to something that has little or none beyond what people will pay for it. They are not real. Nobody has been able to make sense to me of these currencies." – *Howard Marks*, Co-Chairman and Co-Founder, Oaktree Capital Group

Date: 26/07/2017

Bitcoin Price: $2503.29

Stance: Critical

"It's a fraud. If a JPMorgan trader began trading in Bitcoin I'd fire them in a second. For two reasons: It's against our rules, and they're stupid. And both are dangerous." – *Jamie Dimon*, CEO, JPMorgan Chase & Co

Date: 12/09/2017

Bitcoin Price: $4179.95

Stance: Critical

"China doesn't recognize cryptocurrency as payment and forbids ICOs. ... Our views are absolutely similar. In our view, it's a sort of a financial pyramid that may collapse at any moment." – *Elvira Nabiullina*, Governor, Bank of Russia

Date: 14/09/2017

Bitcoin Price: $3391.25

Stance: Critical

"Bitcoin is a sort of tulip. It's indeed an instrument of speculation for those that want to bet on something that can go up and down 50 or 40 percent in a few days but certainly not a currency, and certainly we don't see it as a threat to central banking or monetary policy, that's for sure." – *Vitor Constancio*, Vice President, European Central Bank

Date: 22/09/2017

Bitcoin Price: $3615.10

Stance: Critical

"This is going to be the largest bubble of our lifetimes. ... Prices are going to get way ahead of where they should be. You can make a whole lot of money on the way up, and we plan on it." – *Mike Novogratz*, Former macro manager, Fortress Investment Group

Date: 26/09/2017

Bitcoin Price: $3908.25

Stance: Sceptical

"(Bitcoin is) certainly something more than just a fad ... The concept of anonymous currency is a very interesting concept – interesting for the privacy protections it gives people, interesting because what it says to the central-banking system about controlling that." – *James Gorman*, CEO, Morgan Stanley

Date: 27/09/2017

Bitcoin Price: $4154.27

Stance: Supportive

"Not so long ago, some experts argued that personal computers would never be adopted and that tablets would only be used as expensive coffee trays. So I think it may not be wise to dismiss virtual currencies. Countries with weak institutions and unstable national currencies may see growing use." – *Christine Lagarde*, Managing Director, International Monetary Fund

Date: 29/09/2017

Bitcoin Price: $4171.25

Stance: Supportive

20.5 Crazy Price Hike

It is notable at this stage that in September 2017, when the bull market began to jump at a great pace, authorities from several central banks and international organisations, who used to play the role of the observer, started to express their concerns. The centre of their criticisms was surrounded by possible money laundering allegations and criminal activities that news outlets had been breaking at a regular interval during that period.

"Bitcoin just shows you how much demand for money laundering there is in the world." – *Larry Fink*, CEO, BlackRock Financial Management

Date: 03/10/2017

Bitcoin Price: $4283.59

Stance: Sceptical

"Bitcoin's value is a function of supply and demand; it doesn't really do anything else. Blockchain is a great platform for future applications."– *Mark Cuban*, Billionaire venture capitalist

Date: 03/10/2017

Bitcoin Price: $4283.59

Stance: Supportive

"I think it will be an asset class that will work over time. ... I feel like it's a bit of a mania at the moment, but I think in the long term, it's a viable asset class." – *Kyle Bass*, Founder, Hayman Capital Management

Date: 06/10/2017

Bitcoin Price: $4339.40

Stance: Supportive

"People are more curious than really willing to invest. I don't think there's any meaningful desire by high net worth individuals to take big bets on this kind of phenomenon." – *Sergio Ermotti*, CEO, UBS Group AG

Date: 10/10/2017

Bitcoin Price: $4873.10

Stance: Critical

20.6 To Invest or Not to Invest?

As the price got beyond $5000, CEOs of the biggest investment banks were found divided in their opinions. While many decided to take a strong position against this technology, some openly expressed their support, and a few took a cautious stance indicating that they might not invest at that moment but had their faith in it.

"Bitcoin is an attempt to replace fiat currency and evade regulation and government intervention. I don't think that's going to be a success." – *Ben Bernanke*, Former Chairman, Federal Reserve

Date: 17/10/2017

Bitcoin Price: $5577.30

Stance: Critical

"Bitcoin critics are underestimating it. ... It's like a reserve form of money, it's like gold and it's just a store of value. You don't need to use it to make payments." – *Peter Thiel*, Co-Founder, PayPal

Date: 26/10/2017

Bitcoin Price: $5842.24

Stance: Supportive

"There ought to be a hard look at the policy of anonymous currencies, because the ability to track information of money flowing is one we use seriously against terrorism and as (a tool) against improper, illegal behavior." – *Brian Moynihan*, CEO, Bank of America Corp.

Date: 26/10/2017

Bitcoin Price: $5842.24

Stance: Critical

"People get excited from big price movements, and Wall Street accommodates. You can't value Bitcoin because it's not a value-producing asset. It's a real bubble." – *Warren Buffett*, Chairman and CEO, Berkshire Hathaway Inc.

Date: 29/10/2017

Bitcoin Price: $5753.71

Stance: Critical

"I don't have an investment in it, but I'm not willing to pooh-pooh it, and that's why I say I'm open to it." – *Lloyd Blankfein*, CEO, Goldman Sachs Group Inc.

Date: 02/11/2017

Bitcoin Price: $7057.82

Stance: Supportive

"From what we can identify, the only reason today to buy or sell Bitcoin is to make money, which is the very definition of speculation and the very definition of a bubble." – *Tidjane Thiam*, CEO, Credit Suisse Group AG

Date: 02/11/2017

Bitcoin Price: $7057.82

Stance: Critical

"I don't see why there is all this hostility to it. Bitcoin is not much different than gold because it doesn't have liability attached to it, by definition, like a security" – *Jeff Currie*, Global Head of Commodities Research, Goldman Sachs Group Inc.

Date: 29/11/2017

Bitcoin Price: $10,193.45

Stance: Supportive

20.7 $10K and Counting

Many critics of Bitcoin did not expect it to hit $10,000. While numerous supporters of the technology indicated that the price of the cryptocurrency is not what they looked at but rather the potential of the underlying technology, critics kept their focus on the price hike as criticisms continued to arrive starting the so-called potential bubble.

"In terms of Bitcoin, I would be pretty cautionary about it. I think that it's not a stable store of value … I would be, at this point, pretty skeptical of Bitcoin. I think it's really more of a speculative activity."– *William Dudley*, President, Federal Reserve Bank of New York

Date: 29/11/2017

Bitcoin Price: $10,193.45

Stance: Critical

"Bitcoin is successful only because of its potential for circumvention, lack of oversight, so it seems to me it ought to be outlawed. It doesn't serve any socially useful function." – *Joseph Stiglitz*, Nobel Prize–Winning Professor of Economics, Columbia University

Date: 29/11/2017

Bitcoin Price: $10,193.45

Stance: Critical

"We will discover that behind this Bitcoin scam, some funds were channeled maybe to finance terrorism and at that point, we will wake up and realize that this is not appropriate." – *Lorenzo Bini Smaghi*, Chairman, Societe Generale SA

Date: 30/11/2017

Bitcoin Price: $9653.92

Stance: Critical

"Digital currency is disruptive, it has a lot of potential but that doesn't tell us a lot about what these actual instruments are worth. Even the insiders in that industry don't really know where it's going and it's going to take some time. And for the average investor, you know, buyer beware because you need to do your homework and it's tough; there's a very high learning curve to figure out exactly what this all means." – *Jurrien Timmer*, Director of Global Macro, Fidelity Investments

Date: 30/11/2017

Bitcoin Price: $9653.92

Stance: Sceptical

"I'm not a Bitcoin believer. My kids think I'm really stupid … they could have made a lot of money and I didn't allow them to invest in it … It's fascinating but it will make central banks lose control, and they are not going to let this happen. At some point in time, maybe at $20,000, $25,000, $30,000, somebody will say 'Stop!'" – *Andreas Treichl*, CEO, Erste Group Bank AG

Date: 30/11/2017

Bitcoin Price: $9653.92

Stance: Critical

"It is not a stable store of value, and it doesn't constitute legal tender. It is a highly speculative asset, and the Fed doesn't really play any regulatory role with respect to Bitcoin other than assuring that banking organizations that we do supervise are attentive that they're appropriately managing any interactions they have with participants in that market." – *Janet Yellen*, Chair, Federal Reserve

Date: 13/12/2017

Bitcoin Price: $16,752.00

Stance: Sceptical

20.8 Nosedive

All major cryptocurrencies reached their all-time high either in December 2017 or January 2018. Bitcoin hit nearly $20,000 spot before it started to nosedive. The free fall of the cryptocurrency leader was soon followed by all other members, and the market met with a series of crashes throughout the year. Most comments arrived this year were of negative attitude, but some positive signs also shined sporadically.

"Having no clear fundamental value and largely unregulated markets, coupled with a storyline conducive to delusions of grandeur, makes this more than anything we can find in the history books the very essence of a bubble." – *Jeremy Grantham*, Co-Founder and Chief Investment Strategist, GMO

Date: 03/01/2018

Bitcoin Price: $15,055.23

Stance: Critical

Amongst the positives, the most remarkable comment was made by the JPMorgan CEO who previously called Bitcoin "a fraud" and stated he would not delay firing people in his organisation should he find them investing in this crypto-asset. Jamie Dimon considered changing his position about the blockchain technology and stated:

"I regret making comments saying Bitcoin is a fraud. The blockchain is real. You can have crypto yen and dollars and stuff like that." – *Jamie Dimon*, CEO, JPMorgan Chase & Co.

Date: 09/01/2018

Bitcoin Price: $14,554.08

Stance: Supportive

"The cryptocurrency trading that's going on actually worries me a little bit. I think it's going to end very badly, I really do. Some people are going to lose a lot of money and there's no reason that the prices should be going up at the rate that they're going up. There's no fundamental economic reason." – *F. William McNabb*, Chairman, Vanguard Group Inc.

Date: 17/01/2018

Bitcoin Price: $11,376.69

Stance: Critical

"I believe that we are heading into a new age in which blockchain technology is going to provide a significant level of a digital currency that is going to have a consumer application. And I believe that Starbucks is in a unique position to take advantage of that." – *Howard Schultz*, Founder and Chairman, Starbucks

Date: 25/01/2018

Bitcoin Price: $11,256.52

Stance: Supportive

"Cryptocurrencies like Bitcoin, we should be looking at these very seriously precisely because of the way they can be used, particularly by criminals." – *Theresa May*, Prime Minister, United Kingdom

Date: 25/01/2018

Bitcoin Price: $11,256.52

Stance: Critical

"We need better cross-border payments, ... because it's good for development, it's good for financial inclusion. So Bitcoin can help us, it can pay us a service by forcing us to upgrade our systems. That's a positive lesson. The international community still needs to understand and control these gateways between the shadow-currency universe and the regular financial system." – *Benoit Coeure*, Member of Executive Board, European Central Bank

Date: 26/01/2018

Bitcoin Price: $10,874.79

Stance: Supportive

As Bitcoin lost nearly half of its value within a short span of time, heads of many central banks or similar organisation quickly became very critical about cryptocurrencies and the technology empowering them.

"(Cryptocurrencies) ... are not really currencies at all. One should really, really be careful and be mindful of the fact that this is more like participating in a lottery or going to the casino. This is not banking as we know it." – *Stefan Ingves*, Governor, Riksbank (Central Bank of Sweden)

Date: 29/01/2018

Bitcoin Price: $11,206.99

Stance: Critical

"(Bitcoin is) ... a purely speculative asset. ... in no way a currency, or even a cryptocurrency. It is a speculative asset. Its value and extreme volatility have no economic basis, and they are nobody's responsibility. The Banque of France reminds those investing in Bitcoin that they do so entirely at their own risk." – *Francois Villeroy De Galhau*, Governor, Bank of France

Date: 30/01/2018

Bitcoin Price: $10,086.79

Stance: Critical

"We will not create a market because the mandate of Euronext is to power pan-European capital markets to finance a real economy, and Bitcoins have nothing to do with the real economy. Bitcoin is, at best, a crypto asset ... just like a piece of art, just like a diamond, just like a Pokemon card. Today people buy it because it goes up and because it's not as transparent as other assets." – *Stephane Boujnah*, CEO, Euronext NV

Date: 30/01/2018

Bitcoin Price: $10,086.79

Stance: Critical

"India doesn't consider cryptocurrencies legal tender and will take all measures to eliminate use of these crypto-assets in financing illegitimate activities or as part of the payment system while exploring the use of blockchain technology." – *Arun Jaitley*, Finance Minister, India

Date: 01/02/2018

Bitcoin Price: $9094.20

Stance: Critical

Soon after the price of Bitcoin fell below $10,000, economists and investment personnel became vocal to point out that it was a bubble and it had burst. As the price continued to drop, harsh comments showered the news outlets.

"Bitcoin is the mother of all bubbles and is also the biggest bubble in human history if you compare it to, say, the Mississippi bubble or the tech bubble or tulip mania or South Sea Bubble. Now it has crashed by about 60 percent compared to the peak of mid-December. It has crashed 30 percent in the last week and 10 percent today, and the fundamental value of Bitcoin is zero." – *Nouriel Roubini*, Chief Economist and Co-Founder, Roubini Global Economics Chairman

Date: 02/02/2018

Bitcoin Price: $8570.00

Stance: Critical

"We have seen historical instances where such a rush into certain investments has benefitted our economy and those investors who backed the right ventures. But when our laws are not followed, the risks to all investors are high and numerous – including risks caused by or related to poor, incorrect or non-existent disclosure, volatility, manipulation, fraud and theft." – *Jay Clayton*, Chairman, US Securities and Exchange Commission

Date: 06/02/2018

Bitcoin Price: $7764.60

Stance: Sceptical

"I never considered for one second having anything to do with it. I detested it the moment it was raised. It's just disgusting. Bitcoin is noxious poison." – *Charles Munger*, Vice Chairman, Berkshire Hathaway Inc.

Date: 14/02/2018

Bitcoin Price: $9287.96

Stance: Critical

"For many reasons the crypto-assets in your digital wallets are unlikely to be the future of money. But that is not meant to dismiss them. Their core technology is already having an impact. Bringing crypto-assets into the regulatory tent could potentially catalyze innovations to serve the public better." – *Mark Carney*, Governor, Bank of England

Date: 02/03/2018

Bitcoin Price: $11,029.95

Stance: Sceptical

"Cryptocurrencies are just Candy Crush. There are now more than 1,300, and it seems reasonable to assume all 1,300 are not of equal quality … the return-on-investment could be considerably lower than investors currently expect" – *Richard Bernstein*, CEO, Richard Bernstein Advisors LLC

Date: 18/04/2018

Bitcoin Price: $8187.53

Stance: Critical

"Bitcoin is a scam. In my opinion, it's a colossal pump-and-dump scheme, the likes of which the world has never seen. Cryptocurrency is best-suited for one use: Criminal activity. Because transactions can be anonymous – law enforcement cannot easily trace who buys and sells

– its use is dominated by illegal endeavors." – *Bill Harris*, Founding CEO, PayPal

Date: 24/04/2018

Bitcoin Price: $9449.88

Stance: Critical

By the time Bitcoin's price reached $6000, people started to lose interest in the topic. It was a period when most ICOs conceived the previous year had failed, and fraudulent actors in the industry began to leave. The frequency of comments about blockchain technology also got significantly reduced.

"Blockchain technology could change our world more than people imagine. … Bitcoin, however, could be a bubble." – *Jack Ma*, Founder and Chairman, Alibaba Group Holding

Date: 25/06/2018

Bitcoin Price: $6250.81

Stance: Sceptical

"I think of Bitcoin as a remarkable social phenomenon. It's an epidemic of enthusiasm. It is a speculative bubble. That doesn't mean that it will go to zero. Speculative bubbles recur. We had a bubble in Bitcoin in 2013, and it looked like it was done – it fell from 1,000 to 200 – but now look, it comes back." – *Robert Shiller*, Nobel Prize–Winning Professor of Economics, Yale University

Date: 26/06/2018

Bitcoin Price: $6181.63

Stance: Critical

(*Announcing that CFA institute will add topics on cryptocurrencies and blockchain to its Level I and II curriculums in 2019*) "We saw the field advancing more quickly than other fields, and we also saw it as more durable. … This is not a passing fad." – *Stephen Horan*, Managing Director, CFA Institute

Date: 16/07/2018

Bitcoin Price: $6661.85

Stance: Supportive

The announcement from the CFA Institute was a huge boost for the blockchain industry. This is the institute that offers CFA Charter, the most valued qualification in the investment industry and the institute itself is famous for overseeing the ethical issues and standards of the industry. Its decision to include blockchain technology in its curriculum cannot be an impulse move; rather it indicates the need for such a technology in future.

20.9 Summary

This chapter took the initiative of accumulating most major criticisms and support of cryptocurrency and blockchain technology received over its lifetime. It is quite evident from the commentary presented here that most comments are concentrated around the latest price hike of Bitcoin. This was the period when blockchain technology became the centre of attention to a wide range of experts, and media coverage was at its best to complement the scenario. Nevertheless, the discussion also tried to assemble comments from the early years and late 2018 to give readers a complete understanding of the criticisms, scepticisms and support that the technology receives from around the world.

Bibliography

Adams, C. (2018). Estonia, a Blockchain Model for Other Countries? Technical report, Invest in Blockchain.

Ahson, S. A. and Ilyas, M. (2008). *SIP Handbook: Services, Technologies, and Security of Session Initiation Protocol*. Taylor & Francis.

Akkoyunlu, E. A., Ekanadham, K. and Huber, R. V. (1975). Some Constraints and Tradeoffs in the Design of Network Communications. In *Fifth ACM Symposium on Operating Systems Principles*, Austin, Texas, pp. 67–74.

Alabi, K. (2017). Digital Blockchain Networks Appear to Be Following Metcalfe's Law. *Electronic Commerce Research and Applications*, 24:23–29.

Alexandre, A. (2018). New Study Says 80 Percent of ICOs Conducted in 2017 Were Scams. Technical report, Cointelegraph.

Aliens, C. (2017). Sheep Market Owner Gets Nice Years in Prison. Technical report, DeepDotWeb.

Andrews, G. R. (2000). *Foundations of Multithreaded, Parallel, and Distributed Programming*. Addison–Wesley.

Antonopoulos, A. M. (2010). *Mastering Bitcoin*. O'Reilly.

Appel, M. S. (2014). Canada: Can You Take a Security Interest in Bitcoin? Technical report, Mondaq.

Arnold, G. (2014). *The Financial Times Guide to Investing*. FT Publishing International.

Ashford, W. (2018). Dark Web Cyber Crime Markets Thriving. Technical report, Computer Weekly.

Asolo, B. (2018). RippleNet and Ripple xCurrent Explained. Technical report, Mycryptopedia.

Back, A. (1997). A Partial Hash Collision Based Postage Scheme. Technical report, Hashcash.org.

Bambrough, B. (2018). Ripple (XRP) Overtakes Ethereum as Second Largest Cryptocurrency on CEO's Bullish Bet. *Forbes*.

Bashir, I. (2017). *Mastering Blockchain*. Packt Publishing.

Bech, M. and Garratt, R. (2017). Central Bank Cryptocurrencies. BIS.

Beckett, A. (2015). The Dark Side of the Internet. Technical report, *The Guardian*.

Bellare, M. and Rogaway, P. (2015). Introduction to Modern Cryptography. Course notes.

Benson, J. (2019). Florida Appeals Court Overturns State v. Espinoza, Bitcoin May Be Money After All. Technical report, ETH News.

Berman, A. (2018). Venezuela: Parliament Approves Crypto Bill to Combat "Financial Blockade". Technical report, Cointelegraph.

Berners-Lee, T. (1996). The World Wide Web: Past, Present and Future. W3.org.

Billner, A. (2018). Now There are Plans for "e-Krona" in Cash-Shy Sweden. Technical report, Bloomberg.

Bitcoin Exchange Guide Team. (2018). Bitcoin Classification as a Commodity or a Stock: Top Crypto Assets Type? Technical report, Bitcoin Exchange Guide.

BlockchainHub. (2018). History and Evolution of ICOs. Technical report, BlockchainHub.

Blockgeeks. (2017). ICO Basics, to Invest or Not? Technical report, Blockgeeks.

Boden, S. (2015). The Magic of Mining. Technical report, *The Economist*.

Bolt, W. and Oordt, M. (2016). On the Value of Virtual Currencies. Bank of Canada Working Paper.

Branwen, G. (2018). Survival Analysis of Lifespans, Deaths, and Predictive Factors of Tor-Bitcoin Darknet Markets. Technical report, Gwern.

Brown, B. (2018). xRapid: Everything You Need to Know About Ripples Crypto Service. Technical report, Blockexplorer.

Browne, R. (2018). Venezuela's Oil-Backed Cryptocurrency Raised $735 Million in One Day, President Claims. Technical report, CNBC.

Brunner, K. (1987). Money Supply. In *The New Palgrave: A Dictionary of Economics*, edited by J. Eatwell, M. Milgate and P. Newman. Palgrave Macmillan.

Brutman, J., Layton, J., Sulmone, C., Stuto, G., Hopkins, G. and Creighton, R. (2018). The Revolution of Privacy: Fulfilling Satoshi's Vision for 2018 and Beyond. Technical report, Bitcoin Private white paper.

Buterin, V. (2013). A Next-Generation Smart Contract and Decentralized Application Platform. Technical report, Ethereum.

Carvalho, D. and Oravcova, M. (2018). Naoris: No Weak Link. Technical report, Naoris.

Casey, M. J. (2014a). Bloomberg to List Bitcoin Prices, Offering Key Stamp of Approval. Technical report, *The Wall Street Journal*.

Casey, M. J. (2014b). Dollar-Backed Digital Currency Aims to Fix Bitcoin's Volatility Dilemma. Technical report, *The Wall Street Journal*.

Castillo, M. (2018). Federal Class Action Lawsuits Against ICOs are Set to Double. Technical report, *Forbes*.

Chanjaroen, C., Tan, A. and Amin, H. (2017). Singapore Won't Regulate Cryptocurrencies. Technical report, Bloomberg.

Chapman, L. (2013). Coinbase to Push Bitcoin from Commodity to Currency. Technical report, *The Wall Street Journal*.

Chaum, D. (1985). Security without Identification: Transaction Systems to Make Big Brother Obsolete. *Communications of the ACM*, 28(10):1030–1044.

Chen, A. (2011). The Underground Website Where You Can Buy Any Drug Imaginable. Technical report, Gawker.

Chohan, U. W. (2017). Cryptocurrencies: A Brief Thematic Review. *Economics of Networks Journal*, 4 August.

Chong, N. (2018). Ethereum Co-Founder Vitalik Buterin Rebuts Criticism from Bitcoin Advocate. Technical report, News BTC.

Choudhury, S. R. (2017). Many ICOs Are Fraudulent, Say Men Behind Two Top Bitcoin Rivals. Technical report, CNBC.

Chrepa, E., Kharif, O. and Mehrotra, K. (2018). Bitcoin Suspect Could Shed Light on Russian Mueller Targets. Technical report, Bloomberg.

Cocchia, A. (2014). Smart and Digital City: A Systematic Literature Review. In *Smart City: Progress in IS*, edited by I. Dameri and C. Rosenthal-Sabroux. Springer, pp. 13–43.

Cocks, C. (2001). An Identity Based Encryption Scheme Based on Quadratic Residues. In *Cryptography and* Coding, edited by B. Honary. Lecture Notes in Computer Science, vol. 2260. Springer, pp. 360–363.

Colombo, J. (2013). Bitcoin May Be Following This Classic Bubble Stages Chart. Technical report, *Forbes*.

Cooney, M. (2017). Cisco's Jasper Deal – One Year, 18 million New IoT Devices Later, Challenges Remain. Technical report, *Network World Magazine*.

Coppola, F. (2018). Bitcoin's Need for Electricity is Its "Achilles Heel". Technical report, *Forbes*.

Coppola, F. (2019). Tether's U.S. Dollar Peg is No Longer Credible. Technical report, *Forbes*.

Cornish, C. (2018). Bitcoin Slips Again on Reports of US DoJ Investigation. Technical report, *Financial Times*.

Coulouris, G., Dollimore, J., Kindberg, T. and Blair, G. (2011). *Distributed Systems: Concepts and Design*, 5th edition. Addison–Wesley.

Cox, J. (2014). How Silk Road Bounced Back from Its Multimillion-Dollar Hack. Technical report, Vice.

Cox, J. (2015). FBI Says Suspected Silk Road Architect Variety Jones Has Been Arrested. Technical report, Vice.

Crocker, S. (1969). Host Software. Technical report, IETF Working Group.

Curran, B. (2018). What is the Stellar Consensus Protocol? Technical report, Blockonomi.

Damgard, I. (1989). A Design Principle for Hash Functions. In *Advances in Cryptology – CRYPTO'89 Proceedings*, edited by G. Brassard. Lecture Notes in Computer Science, vol. 435. Springer-Verlag, pp. 416–427.

Davies, G. (2002). *A History of Money: From Ancient Times to the Present Day*. University of Wales Press.

Davis, J. (2011). The Crypto-Currency, Bitcoin and Its Mysterious Inventor. The *New Yorker*.

Diemers, D., Arslanian, H., McNamara, G., Dobrauz, G. and Wohlgemuth, L. (2018). Initial Coin Offerings: A Strategic Perspective. Technical report, PwC in association with Crypto Valley.

Dierks, T. and Rescorla, E. (2008). RFC 5246 – The Transport Layer Security (TLS) Protocol. Technical report, IETF.

Diffie, W. and Hellman, M. (1976). New Directions in Cryptography. *IEEE Transactions on Information Theory*, 22(6):644–654.

Dowd, K. (2014). Bitcoin is Bust: Why Investors Should Abandon the Doomed Cryptocurrency. Technical report, Cityam.

Dredge, S. (2013). What is Tor? A Beginner's Guide to the Privacy Tool. Technical report, *The Guardian*.

Dredge, S. (2014). Study Claims More than 80 Sites. Technical report, *The Guardian*.

DW-News. (2014). Raids on Underground Darknet Websites. Technical report, DW.

Dwork, C. and Naor, M. (1993). Pricing via Processing, or, Combatting Junk Mail. In *Advances in Cryptology – CRYPTO'92*, edited by E. F. Brickell. Lecture Notes in Computer Science, vol. 740. Springer, pp. 139–147.

Dziembowski, S., Faust, S., Kolmogorov, V. and Pietrzak, K. (2015). Proofs of Space. In *Advances in Cryptology – CRYPTO 2015 Proceedings*, edited by R. Gennaro and M. Robshaw. Lecture Notes in Computer Science, vol. 9216. Springer, pp. 585–605.

Elkins, K. (2018). Here's the One Thing You Need to Buy a House with Bitcoin. Technical report, CNBC.

Ember, S. (2015). As Bitcoins Price Slides, Signs of a Squeeze. Technical report, *The New York Times*.

EOS (2018). EOS.IO Technical White Paper v2. Technical report, EOS.

Farrell, H. (2017). Why the Hidden Internet Can't Be a Libertarian Paradise. Aeon.

Ferguson, N. (2008). *The Ascent of Money: A Financial History of the World.* Allen Lane.

Ferguson, N., Schneier, B. and Kohno, T. (2010). *Cryptography Engineering: Design Principles and Practical Applications.* John Wiley & Sons.

Filali, I., Bongiovanni, F., Huet, F. and Baude, F. (2011). A Survey of Structured P2P Systems for RDF Data Storage and Retrieval. In *Transactions on Large-Scale Data- and Knowledge-Centered Systems III: Special Issue on Data and Knowledge Management in Grid and PSP Systems*, edited by A. Hameurlain, J. Kung and R. Wagner. Springer, pp. 20–55.

Floyd, S. (2018). How EOS Block Producers are Paid. Technical report, Eostribe.

Foley, S., Karslen, J. R. and Putnis, T. J. (2018). Sex, Drugs, and Bitcoin: How Much Illegal Activity is Financed Through Cryptocurrencies? Oxford Business Law Blog.

Franco, P. (2015). *Understanding Bitcoin.* Wiley.

Ganapati, P. (2008). Top Technology Breakthroughs of 2008. In *Wired Magazine*.

Gandal, N., Hamrick, J. T., Moore, T. and Oberman, T. (2018). Price Manipulation in the Bitcoin Ecosystem. *Journal of Monetary Economics*, 95:86–96.

Garfinkel, S., Spafford, G. and Schwartz, A. (1991). *Practical UNIX and Internet Security.* O'Reilly.

Garner, B. (2018). What is GAS? An Introduction to the NeoGas Crypto and What It Does Within NEO. Technical report, Coin Central.

Garau, C. and Pavan, M. V. (2018). Evaluating Urban Quality: Indicators and Assessment Tools for Smart Sustainable Cities. *Sustainability*, 10(3).

Gayathri, A. (2013). From Marijuana to LSD, Now Illegal Drugs Delivered on Your Doorstep. Technical report, International Business Times.

Ghosh, S. (2007). *Distributed Systems an Algorithmic Approach.* Chapman & Hall.

Goodin, D. (2012). Why Passwords Have Never Been Weaker and Crackers Have Never Been Stronger. Technical report, Ars Technica.

Graham, B. (1949). *The Intelligent Investor.* Harper & Brothers.

Graham, B. and Dodd, D. (1934). *Security Analysis.* McGraw-Hill.

Graves, R. (1957). *The Twelve Caesars.* Penguin.

Greenberg, A. (2013). Meet the "Assassination Market" Creator Who's Crowdfunding Murder With Bitcoins. Technical report, *Forbes*.

Greenberg, A. (2014a). Not Just Silk Road 2: Feds Seize Two Other Drug Markets and Counting. Technical report, *Wired*.

Greenberg, A. (2014b). The Dark Web Gets Darker with Rise of the 'Evolution' Drug Market. Technical report, *Wired*.

Griffin, J. M. and Shams, A. (2018). Is Bitcoin Really Un-Tethered? Social Science Research Network, 13 June.

Grigg, I. (2017). EOS – An Introduction. Technical report, EOS.

Guttmann, B. (2013). *The Bitcoin Bible.* Books on Demand.

Hankerson, D., Vanstone, S. and Menezes, A. (2004). *Guide to Elliptic Curve Cryptography.* Springer.

Harkin, J. (2009). *Lost in Cyburbia: How Life on the Net Has Created a Life of Its Own*. Knopf Canada.

Helms, K. (2018a). Japan Publishes Draft Report of New Crypto Regulations. Technical report, Bitcoin.com.

Helms, K. (2018b). Mexico Publishes Crypto Rules, Puts Central Bank in Charge. Technical report, Bitcoin.com.

Henderson, L. (2017). *Tor and the Deep Web: Bitcoin, DarkNet and Cryptocurrency*. Independent.

Hern, A. (2017). Bitcoin Mining Consumes More Electricity a Year than Ireland. Technical report, *The Guardian*.

Hern, A. (2018). Bitcoin's Energy Usage is Huge – We Can't Afford to Ignore It. Technical report, *The Guardian*.

Hill, K. (2013). Federal Judge Rules Bitcoin Is Real Money. Technical report, *Forbes*.

HM Treasury. (2017). National Risk Assessment of Money Laundering and Terrorist Financing 2017. Technical report, HM Home Office.

Hoffman, C. (2018). How to Create a Strong Password and Remember It. Technical report, How-to-Geek.

Hsu, S. (2018). China's Shutdown of Bitcoin Miners Isn't Just About Electricity. Technical report, *Forbes*.

Hull, J. C. (2006). *Options, Futures and Other Derivatives*. Prentice Hall.

Hurtado, P. and Nesmith, S. (2016). Florida State Judge Rules Bitcoin Doesn't Qualify as Money. Technical report, Bloomberg.

Hyperledger (2018). An Introduction to Hyperledger. Technical report, Hyperledger.

Iwamura, M., Kitamura, Y., Matsumoto, T. and Saito, K. (2014). Can We Stabilize the Price of a Cryptocurrency?: Understanding the Design of Bitcoin and Its Potential to Compete with Central Bank Money. Technical report, Institute of Economic Research.

Jenkinson, G. (2018). Dubai – The Blockchain Oasis of the UAE: From Public to Private Sector. Technical report, Cointelegraph.

Jevons, W. S. (2014). *Money and the Mechanism of Exchange*. Amazon.

Jimi, S. (2018). Blockchain: How Mining Works and Transactions are Processed in Seven Steps. Technical report, Coinmonks.

Jin, X. and Chan, S.-H. G. (2010). Unstructured Peer-to-Peer Network Architectures. In *Handbook of Peer-to-Peer Networking*, edited by X. Shen, H. Yu, J. Buford and M. Akon. Springer, pp. 117–142.

Julio, S. (2018). California Man to Stand Trial for Allegedly Hiring Hitman on the Dark Web. Technical report, Dark Web News.

Kahn, D. (1967). *The Codebreakers – The Story of Secret Writing*. Macmillan.

Kaiser, B., Jurado, M. and Ledger, A. (2018). The Looming Threat of China – An Analysis of Chinese Influence on Bitcoin. arXiv.

Kaliski, B. (1992). The MD2 Message-Digest Algorithm. Technical report, RSA Laboratories.

Kalodner, H. A., Carlsten, M., Ellenbogen, P., Bonneau, J. and Narayanan, A. (2015). An Empirical Study of Namecoin and Lessons for Decentralized Namespace Design. In *WEIS*.

Katz, Z. (2010). *Digital Signatures*. Springer.

Kelemen, A. (2018). A Glance at the State of Blockchain in Latin America. Technical report, Neu Fund.

Keskin, H. (2018a). An Overview of FINMAs Guidelines on ICOs. Technical report, Rigoblock.

Keskin, H. (2018b). Swiss Blockchain and Cryptocurrency Regulation. Technical report, Rigoblock.

Khan, M. S., Woo, M., Nam, K. and Chathoth, P. K. (2017). Smart City and Smart Tourism: A Case of Dubai. *Sustainability*, 9(12):2279.

Kharif, O. (2018). Bitcoin's Use in Commerce Keeps Falling Even as Volatility Eases. Technical report, Bloomberg.

Khatwani, S. (2018). NEO Cryptocurrency: Everything You Need to Know About China Ethereum. Technical report, CoinSutra.

Khurana, S. (2018). Drug Manufacturing: Blockchain in Pharmaceutical Industry. Technical report, Medium.

Kim, C. (2018a). South Korea to Ban Cryptocurrency Traders from Using Anonymous Bank Accounts. Technical report, Reuters.

Kim, E. (2018b). New Report Finds 80% of Bitcoin Mining Running on Renewable Energy. Technical report, Bitcoinist.

Konstantopoulos, G. (2018). Understanding Blockchain Fundamentals – Delegated Proof of Stake. Technical report, Plasma R&D.

Kozlenkova, I., Hult, G., Lund, D., Mena, J. and Kekec, P. (2015). The Role of Marketing Channels in Supply Chain Management. *Journal of Retailing*, 91(4):586–609.

Krause, M. J. and Tolaymat, T. (2018). Quantification of Energy and Carbon Costs for Mining Cryptocurrencies. *Nature Sustainability*, 1:711–718.

Kroijer, L. (2017). *Investing Demystified*. FT Publishing International.

Kurson, K. (2013). The True Value of Bitcoin and Ripple. Technical report, *Esquire*.

Lamport, L., Shostak, R. and Pease, M. (1982). The Byzantine Generals Problem. *ACM Transactions on Programming Languages and Systems*, 4(3):382–401.

Lansky, J. (2018). Possible State Approaches to Cryptocurrencies. *Journal of Systems Integration*, 9(1):19–31.

Larson, S. (2017). Bitcoin Split in Two, Here's What That Means. Technical report, CNN.

Lee, T. B. (2013). Bitcoin's Volatility is a Disadvantage, But Not a Fatal One. Technical report, *Forbes*.

Lielacher, A. (2018). The Top 7 Best Countries for Bitcoin Mining. Technical report, Bitcoin Market Journal.

Liive, R. (2018). Estonia is Striving to Be Center Stage in Cryptocurrencies and Blockchain. Technical report, Invest in Estonia.

Liu, A. (2015). rippled Feature Update: Nu.DB and Autobridging. Technical report, Ripple Labs.

Luo, M. (2018). Should You Invest in Bitcoin? Technical report, *U.S. News and World Report*.

Lynch, N. A. (1996). *Distributed Algorithms*. Morgan Kaufmann.

Macguire, E. (2014). Bitcoin: One Year on from Peak Price, What Does the Future Hold? Technical report, CNN.

Majuri, Y. (2018). Simply Explained: Stellar Consensus Protocol. Technical report, Medium.

Marshall, A. (2018). Google to Reverse Crypto Ad Ban for Exchanges Advertising in US, Japan. Technical report, Cointelegraph.

Martin, K. M. (2012). *Everyday Cryptography*. Oxford University Press.

Mazieres, D. (2016). The Stellar Consensus Protocol: A Federated Model for Internet-Level Consensus. Technical report, Stellar Development Foundation (SDF).

McLean, A. (2018). Facebook Holds ICO Ban but Allows "Approved" Cryptocurrency Ads. Technical report, ZD Net.

McQuaid, D. (2018). Cryptocurrency Scam Makes More than USD 2million After Ditching Investors. Technical report, *Daily Express*.

Medichain (2018). MediChain Health Breakthrough. Technical report, Medium.

Menezes, A. J., van Oorschot, P. C. and Vanstone, S. A. (2005). *Handbook of Applied Cryptography*. CRC Press.

Merkle, R. C. (1979). Secrecy, Authentication, and Public Key Systems. PhD thesis, Stanford University.

Metcalf, W. E. (2016). *The Oxford Handbook of Greek and Roman Coinage*. Oxford University Press.

Migliano, S. (2018). The Dark Web is Democratizing Cybercrime. Technical report, Hackernoon.

Miller, C. (2018). British Hackers Expose Secrets of Hitman-for-Hire Service Hidden on the Dark Web. Technical report, Metro.

Miller, H. G. and Mork,P. (2013). From Data to Decisions: A Value Chain for Big Data. *IT Professional*, 15(1):57–59.

Milnes, A. (1919). *The Economic Foundations of Reconstruction*. Macdonald and Evans.

Mishkin, F. S. (2007). *The Economics of Money, Banking, and Financial Markets*. Addison Wesley.

Moeco (2018). Moeco Whitepaper. Technical report, Moeco.

Molloy, M. (2017). Bitcoin Value Surpasses Gold for the First Time. Technical report, *The Telegraph*.

Moore, D. and Rid, T. (2016). Cryptopolitik and the Darknet. *Survival*, 58(1):7–38.

Moore, H. (2013). Confused About Bitcoin? It's the Harlem Shake of Currency. Technical report, *The Guardian*.

Nakamoto, S. (2008). Bitcoin: A Peer-to-Peer Electronic Cash System. Technical report, Bitcoin.org.

Nakamura, Y. (2018). World's Biggest Cryptocurrency Exchange is Heading to Malta. Technical report, Bloomberg.

Naumoff, A. (2017). Why Blockchain Needs Proof of Authority Instead of Proof of Stake? Technical report, Cointelegraph.

NEO (2014). NEO White Paper. Technical report, NEO.

NewScientist (2017). Bitcoin: What a Waste of Resources. Technical report, *New Scientist*.

Njui, J. P. (2017). Smart Contracts will Never Be the Same as Ripple (XRP) Revives CODIUS. Technical report, Ethereum World News.

O'Dwyer, K. J. and Malone, D. (2014). Bitcoin Mining and Its Energy Footprint. CIICT, Limerick, Ireland.

Olenski, J. (2015). What is ECC and Why Would I Want to Use It? Technical report, Global Sign.

O'Neill, H. (2013). How Big is the Internet's Most Notorious Black Market? Technical report, The Daily Dot.

Oram, A. (2001). *Peer-to-Peer: Harnessing the Benefits of a Disruptive Technologies*. O'Reilly.

Paar, C. and Pelzl, J. (2009). *Understanding Cryptography: A Textbook for Students and Practitioners*. Springer.

Palley, S. (2018). The SEC Cracks Down on Two ICOs, Creating a Template for Future Enforcement. Technical report, The Block Crypto.

Palmer, D. (2018). SEC Seeks Court Sanction Against PlexCoin ICO Founders. Technical report, CoinDesk.

Pavesic, N. (2018). Cryptocurrencies: South Korea's Winding Regulatory Path. Technical report, *Nikkei Asian Review*.

Percival, C. (2012). Stronger Key Derivation via Sequential Memory-Hard Functions. Technical report, Tarsnap.

Perrin, B. (1916). *An English Translation of Plutarch's Lives*. Harvard University Press.

Peter, B. (1965). *A Primer on Money, Banking and Gold*. Wiley.

Pihl, R. (2019). What is a Cryptocurrency ETF? Technical report, Toshi Times.

Pilkington, N. (2017). Investing in Ripple: The Next Big Thing? Technical report, The Market Mogul.

Plato (2007). *The Republic* (Penguin Classics). Penguin.

Poon, J. and Dryja, T. (2016). The Bitcoin Lightning Network: Scalable Off-Chain Instant Payments. Technical report, Lightning Network.

Popov, S. (2018). The Tangle. Technical report, IOTA.

Popper, N. (2017). AlphaBay, Biggest Online Drug Bazaar, Goes Dark, and Questions Swirl. Technical report, *New York Times*.

Prahalad, B. (2018). Proof of Work, Proof of Stake and Proof of Burn. Technical report, Hackernoon.

Price, R. (2015). Deep Web Drug Dealers are Freaking Out About the Bitcoin Crash. Technical report, Business Insider.

Quiggin, J. (2013). The Bitcoin Bubble and a Bad Hypothesis. Technical report, *The National Interest*.

Rakic, B., Levak, T., Drev, Z., Savic, S. and Veljkovic, A. (2017). First Purpose Built Protocol for Supply Chains Based on Blockchain. Technical report, OriginTrail.

Ramage, A. (2000). *Golden Sardis. In King Croesus' Gold: Excavations at Sardis and the History of Gold Refining*, edited by A. Rampage, P. T. Craddock and M. Cowell. Harvard University Press, p. 18.

Rangongo, T. (2018). Own Bitcoin or Ethereum? Sars is Coming for You. Technical report, Business Insider.

Raval, S. (2016). *Decentralized Applications: Harnessing Bitcoin's Blockchain Technology*. O'Reilly.

Redman, J. (2016). New York Judge Classifies Bitcoin as Money. Technical report, Bitcoin. com.

Reed, M. G., Syverson, P. F. and Goldschlag, D. M. (2006). Anonymous Connections and Onion Routing. *IEEE Journal on Selected Areas in Communications*, 16(4):482–494.

Reinke, E. C. (1992). Classical Cryptography. *The Classical Journal*, 58(3):114.

Ripple (2018). Ripple Documentation. Technical report, Ripple Labs.

Rivest, R., Shamir, A. and Adleman, L. (1978). A Method for Obtaining Digital Signatures and Public-Key Cryptosystems. *Communications of the ACM*, 21(2):120–126.

Rivest, R. L. (1990). Cryptography. In *Handbook of Theoretical Computer Science*, vol. A. Elsevier.

Rubin, G., Michaels, D. and Osipovich, A. (2018). U.S. Regulator Demands Trading Data from Bitcoin Exchanges in Manipulation Probe. Technical report, *The Wall Street Journal*.

SC-News (2015). Buying Drugs Online Remains Easy. Technical report, Southwest Coalition.

Scardovi, C. (2016). *Restructuring and Innovation in Banking*. Springer.

Schneier, B. (1996). *Applied Cryptography: Protocols, Algorithms and Source Code in C.* John Wiley & Sons.

Schwartz, D., Youngs, N. and Britto, N. (2014). The Ripple Protocol Consensus Algorithm. Technical report, Ripple Labs.

Schwartz, E. and Pestritto, V. (2018). Interledger: How to Interconnect All Blockchains and Value Networks. Technical report, Xpring/Medium.

Sedgwick, K. (2018a). 46% of Last Years ICOs Have Failed Already. Technical report, Bitcoin.com.

Sedgwick, K. (2018b). Benebit ICO Does a Runner with USD 2.7 Million of Investor Funds. Technical report, Bitcoin.com.

Shannon, C. E. (1948). A Mathematical Theory of Communication. *Bell System Technical Journal*, 27(3):379–423.

Shannon, C. E. (1949). Communication Theory of Secrecy Systems. *Bell System Technical Journal*, 27(4):623–666.

Sharf, S. (2013). Bitcoin Gets Valued: Bank of America Puts a Price Target on the Virtual Tender. Technical report, *Forbes*.

Shaughnessy, H. (2011). Solving the $190 billion Annual Fraud Problem: More on Jumio. Technical report, *Forbes*.

Sidel, R. (2014). How Mt. Gox Debacle Won Over a Bitcoin Convert. Technical report, *The Wall Street Journal*.

Singh, S. (2002). *The Code Book: The Secret History of Codes and Codebreaking*. HarperCollins.

Smith, A. (1982). *The Wealth of Nations* (Penguin Classics). Penguin.

Soska, K. and Christin, N. (2015). Measuring the Longitudinal Evolution of the Online Anonymous Marketplace Ecosystem. In *Proceedings of the 22nd UNIX Security Symposium*, pp. 33–48.

Splitter, J. (2018). What Can Blockchain Really Do for the Food Industry? *Forbes*.

Stan, S. (2013). Cameron Winklevoss: Bitcoin Might Hit USD 40,000 per Coin. Technical report, Mashable.

Stankovic, S. (2018). Cryptocurrency Regulation in the UK Cryptocurrency Regulation in the UK. Technical report, Crypto Briefing.

Steinmetz, R. and Wehrle, K. (2005). What is This "Peer-to-Peer" About? In *Peer-to-Peer Systems and Applications*, edited by R. Steinmetz and K. Wehrle. Lecture Notes in Computer Science, vol. 3485. Springer, pp. 9–16.

Suberg, W. (2018). Hong Kong Issues New Rules to Regulate Cryptocurrency Funds and Exchanges. Technical report, Cointelegraph.

Teodoro, N. (2018). Hacker Livestreams 51% Attack on Bitcoin Private. Technical report, Crypto Globe.

The Economist. (2015). Daily Chart: Silk Road Successors. Technical report. 29 May.

Thomas, S. (2018). Codius: Smart Contracts Made from Containers. Technical report, Coil/Medium.

Thompson, E. (2013). *Safer Corridors Rapid Assessment – Somalia and UK Banking*. Beechwood International.

Urwin, R. (2018). Wheres Wallet? Can You Spot Ben Delo, the UK's First Bitcoin Billionaire? Technical report, *The Times*.

Usborne, S. (2017). Digital Gold: Why Hackers Love Bitcoin. Technical report, *The Guardian*.

Vranken, H. (2017). Sustainability of Bitcoin and Blockchains. *Current Opinion in Environmental Sustainability*, 28:1–9.

Waves (2017). How to Run an ICO. Technical report, Waves.

Weatherford, J. (1998). *The History of Money*. Crown Publications.

Wilkes, T. (2013). Backer Defends Virtual Currency Bitcoin After Big Fall. Technical report, Reuters.

Williams, M. T. (2013). Bitcoin Will Crash to USD 10 By Mid-2014. Technical report, *Business Insider*.

Williams, M. T. (2014). Virtual Currencies – Bitcoin Risk. World Bank Conference, Washington DC, 21 October.

Williams-Grut, O. (2018). Here's What It's Like to Visit Crypto Valley – Switzerland's Picturesque Blockchain Version of Silicon Valley. Technical report, *Business Insider*.

Willms, J. (2018). Canada Delays Regulation of Cryptocurrencies and Blockchain Companies. Technical report, *Bitcoin Magazine*.

Wilmoth, J. (2018a). Bitcoin Gold Hit by Double Spend Attack – Exchanges Lose Millions. Technical report, CCN.

Wilmoth, J. (2018b). EOS ICO Approaches 4 Billion USD After Year-Long Crowdsale. Technical report, CCN.

Wilson, G. M. and Yelowitz, A. (2018). Characteristics of Bitcoin Users: An Analysis of Google Search Data. Social Science Research Network, 3 November.

Wirdum, A. (2017). Bitcoin Gold is About to Trial an ASIC–Resistant Bitcoin Fork. Technical report, *Bitcoin Magazine*.

Woodhill, L. (2013). Bitcoins are Digital Collectibles, Not Real Money. Technical report, *Forbes Magazine*.

Woolf, N. (2015). Bitcoin "Exit Scam": Deep-Web Market Operators Disappear with $12m. Technical report, *The Guardian*.

Wright, A. (2009). Exploring a "Deep Web" that Google Can't Grasp. Technical report, *The New York Times*.

Yang, S. (2016). Is Bitcoin Becoming More Stable than Gold? Technical report, *The Wall Street Journal*.

Yi, E. (2018). The EOS Worker Proposal System, Necessary, or Useless? Technical report, Blockgenic.

Zhang, E. (2014). A Byzantine Fault Tolerance Algorithm for Blockchain. Technical report, NEO.

Zhu, C., Li., Y and Niu, X. (2010). *Streaming Media Architectures: Techniques and Applications: Recent Advances*. IGI Global.

Zuckerman, M. J. (2018). Iceland – Crypto Mining Companies will Consume More Energy than Households in 2018. Technical report, Cointelegraph.

Index

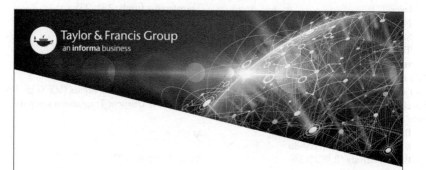

For Product Safety Concerns and Information please contact our
EU representative GPSR@taylorandfrancis.com Taylor & Francis
Verlag GmbH, Kaufingerstraße 24, 80331 München, Germany